1000 QUESTIONS AND ANSWERS

1000 QUESTIONS AND ANSWERS

Edited by Elizabeth Hardy

1000 QUESTIONS AND ANSWERS

octopus

Planned and created by
Berkeley Publishers Limited
20 Wellington Street
London WC2

This edition first published 1978 by
Octopus Books Limited
59 Grosvenor Street
London W1

Under licence from Lynx Press Limited
601 Union House, Hong Kong

© 1974 Lynx Press Limited

ISBN 0 7064 0738 5

Printed in Czechoslovakia

Contents

Natural History

WHERE DOES A SWALLOW BUILD ITS NEST?

A swallow builds its nest inside farm buildings and on ledges in old chimneys. The nest is made of mud, straw and saliva, with feathers and wool to line the inside. It takes a pair of swallows up to several weeks to make the saucer-shaped nest in the rafters of a barn.

Swallows start arriving in Europe at the end of March, a little earlier than their close relatives, the house martins. They spend the winter in South Africa and usually return to the same district—and even the same nest—where they settled before. The female lays four or five eggs, white with reddish-brown speckles. She sits on them for about 15 days before they hatch out. Both parents then feed the nestlings with insects which they catch while flying. Swallows usually lay two sets of eggs.

They leave for their winter quarters in September, gathering in large flocks and often perching on telephone wires, before setting off. The young birds of the first brood leave before their parents and, by an inborn knowledge, know which way to go.

WHAT ARE TEASEL PLANTS USED FOR?

Teasels are used in the making of woollen cloth. The common teasel grows wild in England and Wales and southern parts of Scotland. It is also found in Europe, Asia and North Africa.

The teasel has large prickly flower heads which remain on the dead stems throughout the winter. The actual flowers are tiny deep lilac florets and round the base of the flowerhead there is a ring of spines. The stem and leaves are prickly and the leaves are joined at the stem to collect rainwater.

The teasel belongs to the scabious family and many people collect them in autumn for decoration throughout the winter.

There is also a garden teasel called fuller's teasel, which has little hooks at the end of the spines, or bracts, surrounding the base of the flowerhead. This is the teasel that is used in the making of woollen cloth. The cloth is brushed up with the teasels so that the fibres of wool become separated from each other. This is known as "teasing".

WHY DO DOGS HAVE A GOOD SENSE OF SMELL?

Dogs have a better sense of smell than we do because the physical structure of a dog is better adapted for scenting odours. In dogs this sense has remained keen, while in man it has become comparatively dull. Dogs use scent in feeding, detecting enemies, recognizing mates and offspring and in rivalry.

The chemical sense of smell is called chemoreception and the sense organs chemoreceptors. But there is little in the structure of the nose to provide clues about its mechanism, and relatively little is known about how smell works. There are no accessory structures in the nose, and the receptors and nerve fibres leading to the brain are so fine that they are difficult to study. The chemoreceptors of human beings, dogs and other mammals lie in a cleft in each nostril.

During quiet breathing the main flow of air by-passes the cleft. But when a mammal sniffs, air is drawn into the clefts and over about half a square inch of yellowish tissue in which are embedded several million chemoreceptors. They are long thin cells with hair-like crowns making a web lying on the surface of the tissue which is bathed in mucus. These are connected to a part of the brain called the olfactory bulb, the size of which is a fair indication of the keenness of the sense of smell.

The olfactory bulb of a dog is much larger than that of a man. The moist nose of a dog also aids his sense of smell.

Smells are immensely important to dogs as we see from the way they refuse to by-pass a scent without investigating it and, very often, adding to it. They mark their home range and investigate passers-by. Their keen sense has been used by man as a help in hunting and tracking for many thousands of years.

WHEN DO BIRDS MIGRATE?

Millions of birds of many different varieties migrate at the end of summer. With unfailing regularity they leave the regions where they were born to fly to warmer climates for the winter. The following spring they return to their breeding grounds.

Each year these migratory birds travel as much as 20,000 miles, finding their way back on time with extraordinary precision. Some travel as individuals.

Migration is triggered off by the length of daylight, which apparently affects the birds' nervous systems. When the days get shorter the birds receive the signal to leave for their warmer winter grounds, and, when the daylight increases to a certain level, they receive another signal to return home.

The swallows pictured above are European swallows wintering in Africa.

WHERE WAS THE FIRST ZOO?

The first zoo was formed in China in the 12th Century B.C. But it was not called a zoo. Wen, the ancient Chinese king who started it, wanted to collect different types of animals from all over his empire. He kept them in what he called a "garden of intelligence", near his palace.

Some of the largest zoos are in North America. There are big ones in the Bronx, New York City, and in Washington and San Diego.

WHAT IS REINDEER MOSS?

Reindeer moss is a species of lichen so called because it is the staple winter food of reindeer (and caribou) in Arctic and sub-Arctic regions. The animals reach the plant by scraping away the snow with their feet. But plant growth in those cold northern lands is so slow that the lichen can take more than 30 years to recover after the reindeer have grazed. These domesticated herds therefore have to travel long distances in search of food, and the Laplanders of northern Scandinavia, who depend on the animals for their livelihood, must travel with them.

Fortunately, reindeer moss is especially abundant in Lapland, although it also grows extensively in much of northern Europe, the tundra (or treeless plains) of Siberia and the barren expanses of Arctic America.

During the short summer the reindeer are able to feed on herbage and shoots then accessible in the valleys. These versatile animals provide the Laplanders with meat, milk, cheese and the raw materials for clothing, shoes and tents. They are also a means of transport.

Reindeer moss is sometimes eaten by human beings, after being powdered and mixed with other food. But it leaves a slightly burning sensation on the human palate. This bluish-grey plant grows erect in tufts, and is remarkable for its many branches, which, strangely, resemble a deer's antlers.

WHY DO MANY FLOWERS HAVE A SWEET SCENT?

The sweet scent of flowers is designed to attract insects who seek food in the shape of pollen and the fragrant-smelling nectar. This nectar is a solution of sugars produced in little sacs called nectaries at the base of the flower petal.

The insects have a part in the process of fertilization. Almost all plants perpetuate themselves by means of sexual reproduction, during which a male reproductive cell or sperm fuses with the female reproductive cell or egg.

When bees or other insects visit flowers in search of the sweet-smelling nectar, parts of their hairy bodies become dusted with pollen which contains the male reproductive cells. This rubs off on the flower's carpels which contain the egg or ovule.

Insects seem to be strongly attracted by sweet scents. In fact, some flowers, such as the Meadow Sweet, are so highly scented that insects are attracted to them although they have no nectar to offer. Most insect-pollinated flowers have evolved wonderful devices for guiding the movements of the insect. In this way they ensure that pollen is dusted over the insect's body.

WHEN IS A BUTTERFLY FORMED?

A caterpillar starts to become a butterfly as soon as it enters the chrysalis stage, by wrapping itself in a cocoon. During this phase, known as pupation, the insect gradually develops all the butterfly characteristics, including wings. For some butterflies the transformation may be completed in one or two weeks. But others need many months before they are ready to leave the cocoon and fly away.

From the time it is hatched to the time it starts the pupation stage, a caterpillar or larva does little more than eat, grow larger and moult several times. This larval stage varies according to the species. Small caterpillars will complete their development in a week, but some large varieties will take up to two years or more.

When this period is over the caterpillar spins a cocoon under a leaf or even underground, and enters it to begin the transformation. Many cocoons are of silk.

HOW DO FROGS BREATHE UNDER WATER?

Under water, frogs breathe through their skins. A frog is an amphibian. That is to say it lives both on land and in water. It has lungs, but it has no ribs and therefore cannot expand its chest and suck air into its lungs as do reptiles, birds and mammals. On land air is drawn in and out of the frog's nostrils, which have valves in them, by pulsations of the floor of the mouth. The air is forced in and out of the lungs by contractions of the throat and body muscles. A frog's mouth is always kept tightly closed and the pulsations of the throat vary from 120–140 a minute.

Even on land the skin plays a greater part in breathing than the lungs. However, air can be absorbed only through a moist skin. If the skin becomes too dry, the frog will die. Therefore the skin contains glands which secrete a clear mucus or slime whose function is to keep the skin moist and supple. The skin absorbs water as well as air, for frogs do not drink.

Frogs are cold-blooded. That means they are as warm or as cold as the air or water surrounding them. In winter they hibernate under water, where their body temperature falls, their bodily functions are kept at a minimum and breathing is carried on entirely through the skin.

WHEN DO BEES SWARM?

Bees swarm in late spring in search of a new home. During the winter the queen bee begins to lay her eggs and the colony sets about rearing its young. As the weather becomes warmer and the early flowers appear, the raising of young bees increases rapidly.

By the end of spring the colony has become so overcrowded that a large number of the bees, including the old queen, leave the hive and establish a new colony. In the old colony a new queen emerges who will experience the same swarming instincts the following year. And so the cycle of activity goes on.

WHO FIRST CLASSIFIED BUTTERFLIES AND MOTHS?

Butterflies and moths were first classified by the great Swedish botanist Carl von Linné (1707–78), generally known as Carolus Linnaeus. His method, which applied to plants and all living things, was the binomial system. This meant that each insect was given two scientific and internationally recognized names: the first is a generic name denoting the genus or group to which the subject belongs; the second is a specific epithet indicating the species within the group.

Similarly we all have surnames and forenames. But, in the case of the Linnaean system, Latin or Greek words are used to ensure uniformity regardless of the expert's native language. The first or generic name is spelt with a capital letter, but the second name usually begins with a small one.

Linnaeus published more than 180 scientific works, some of the most important ones after he left Sweden for Holland, where he studied medicine. After visiting England and France he returned to Sweden, where he was given the Chair of Botany at Uppsala University.

WHERE DO BUTTERFLIES GO WHEN IT RAINS?

When it rains butterflies settle on the stems of flowers or stalks of grass. They hang head downwards with their wings folded together over their backs. Most butterflies are difficult to see when their wings are closed, because the undersides have only pale colours and faint patterns.

There are about 10,000 known species of butterfly. They range in size from less than an inch to the swallow-tails which live in north Australia and the Pacific Islands and have a wing span of 10 inches. Most female butterflies have less

A silver-studded blue butterfly

colourful wings than the males of the same species. They lay between 100 and 3,000 eggs, according to the species, placing them on a plant which will provide suitable food for the caterpillars which develop from the eggs.

The caterpillar becomes a chrysalis from which, eventually, the fully grown butterfly emerges. Adult life may last for only a few weeks, but some butterflies hibernate.

Butterflies feed on the nectar of plants and on sweet juices, particularly those of over-ripe or rotting fruit. This food provides them with the energy to fly but is not used for body-building. All growth takes place at the caterpillar stage of a butterfly's life.

HOW CAN YOU TELL A TERRAPIN FROM A TORTOISE?

You can tell a terrapin from a tortoise by its much more streamlined shape, and because, unlike the tortoise, it lives in fresh water as well as on land.

Both tortoises and terrapins belong to an ancient order of reptiles called chelonia.

Their shells are in two sections, the upper domed portion or carapace being made up of a series of horny shields that form a regular pattern. The tortoise's shell normally has a high round dome, while that of a terrapin is flattened and streamlined. Some terrapins have slightly webbed feet. They are also faster on land than tortoises.

In both reptiles the head is covered with scaly skin, and the eyes are exceptionally dark and can be closed behind two eyelids. They also possess a third, almost transparent, skin that can be moved across the eye for protection. They have no teeth but their jaws are sharp, and they have a good sense of smell. They are quite intelligent, learn to recognize their owners, become fairly friendly, and are often kept as pets.

WHY DO FARMERS LIKE THE ICHNEUMON FLY?

The ichneumon fly is known as the farmer's friend because it controls a great many plant pests. Species have even been transported by man to colonize areas where artificial pest controls have not been successful.

Ichneumon flies, of which there are thousands of species spread throughout the world, are parasitic and their larvae feed on caterpillars, pupae and larvae of other insects.

Larva (plural, larvae) is the name given to an insect from the time it leaves the egg till it is transformed into the pupa or grub. The pupa (plural, pupae) is the name given to the chrysalis.

The female fly lays her eggs in or on the larvae of pupae of the host species. When the maggot-like parasitic larvae hatch out, they feed on the body fats and fluids of the host until they are fully grown.

Then the parasitic larvae spin cocoons within which they pupate and from whence the adult fly emerges. In the case of parasitic larvae breeding inside the host, the latter behaves normally until shortly before the uninvited guest larva has fully developed.

There are some ichneumon flies which live on other ichneumon flies and these are called hyper-parasitic. The different species of ichneumon vary greatly in size and the range extends from $\frac{1}{8}''$ up to $1\frac{1}{2}-2''$ in length.

WHO FIRST DOMESTICATED ANIMALS?

Neolithic people were the first to domesticate animals and begin to plant crops. This great step forward towards civilization took place some time between 8,000 and 5,000 B.C. in what is now the Near East, at the eastern end of the Mediterranean.

The first farmers freed themselves and their descendants from complete dependence on hunting, fishing and gathering wild plants and fruit for their food supply. Their animals learned to depend on them for protection and food and had their young in captivity, so ensuring new flocks.

Thus the neolithic (or New Stone Age) people began to form settled communities, for the farmer wanted to stay in the same place to harvest his crops. The first plants to be successfully grown were wheat and barley which were good for food and simple to plant and harvest. The stalks provided fodder for the animals.

The earliest animals to be domesticated were goats, pigs, sheep and cattle and, of course, dogs.

WHAT IS CORAL?

The hard, dry corals seen in stores and museums are made up of the combined skeletons of tiny creatures which once lived joined together as a colony in the sea. The coral animal, or polyp, measures only about a fifteenth of an inch in diameter. It is a primitive type of plant-like creature closely related to the sea anemone. But, unlike the sea anemone, the polyp has a stony skeleton and, once it has made its home, it is unable to move.

Each polyp is like a tiny tube, closed at one end and with a mouth, fringed with tentacles, at the other. The tentacles have a sting and capture minute sea creatures for food.

Coral animals inhabit shallow water in warm seas. In tropical waters colonies form reefs round islands which can be dangerous to ships. Eventually new islands are formed by the accumulated skeletons of billions of dead polyps.

But the romantic coral islands and reefs of the South Seas do not supply the precious material used for beads and brooches. These are made from the red and pink coral found in the Mediterranean off the coasts of Africa and Italy.

WHAT IS THE DIFFERENCE BETWEEN A FRUIT AND A VEGETABLE?

In 1893 the United States Supreme Court tried to clarify the difference between a fruit and a vegetable by saying that vegetables are eaten as part of the main course of a meal, but fruit is eaten as an appetizer or dessert, or for a snack.

But, as with so many words, there is one definition which is correct according to the dictionary and another one which people use in everyday life. Sweet corn, for instance, is eaten as an appetizer, but most people would consider it a vegetable.

In botany, a fruit is the ripened ovary of a plant. (The ovary is the part of the plant where the seeds are kept.) So, strictly speaking, an acorn is as much a fruit as an apple. But, if you went into a store and asked for fruit, the store-owner would not offer you acorns. When we talk about fruit in every-day life, we mean the juicy fruits like apples, grapes, oranges and melons.

"Vegetable" has even more meanings than "fruit". The word covers any kind of plant life, even including trees. But, again, in everyday life vegetables mean food like lettuce, carrots, cabbage and sprouts.

A Sweetcorn (vegetable)
B Tomato (fruit)
C Aubergine or egg-plant (vegetable)
D Avocado (fruit or vegetable)
E Jerusalem artichoke (vegetable)

WHERE DO ELEPHANTS GO TO DIE?

Groups of elephants have been found buried together both in Africa and Asia. The nearness of the animals to each other may be no more than a coincidence. The areas may be no more than sites, since elevated and dried, where elephants have been drowned in bogs or while crossing rivers.

However, many people will argue that old elephants, when their end is near, resort to their legendary "graveyards". The discovery of the remains of a solitary elephant is rare. On the other hand a body in elephant country would usually soon disappear owing to the activities of natural scavengers.

Most experts will accept that there is much truth in the old saying "an elephant never forgets". It does have a retentive memory. Also, when an elephant is dying it is not uncommon for members of the herd to gather round and try to revive it. When all hope is lost they encircle their relation as if in mourning at a funeral.

WHEN DOES A CHAMELEON CHANGE COLOUR?

A chameleon will change colour when it senses danger. This remarkable member of the lizard family can change colour to match its background or, at least, to become almost unrecognizable.

The ranges of colours and patterns of the various species differ widely, but most chameleons can become yellow or cream, green or dark brown. They can also adapt spots either dark or light depending on the colour of the ground.

Apart from its response to danger, the chameleon will change colour according to the light and temperature. This mechanism is controlled from the nervous system and involves the dispersion or concentration of colour pigments in the creature's skin.

WHY DO SOME ELEPHANTS HAVE VERY LARGE EARS?

African elephants have larger ears than Indian, or Asiatic, elephants because they live in hotter conditions and are bigger and more aggressive and active. The huge ears of the African elephant, sometimes three and a half feet wide, enable it to hear more acutely. When the animal charges it fans out its ears, augmenting its terrible appearance and striking fear into the heart of any enemy.

The ears also present a large surface for losing body-heat. African elephants, who are at a disadvantage in the heat because of their large size, wave their ears to keep cool and to chase away flies. The African elephant is the biggest and noblest of land animals, reaching a height of 11 feet and a weight of nearly six tons.

The Asiatic elephant is smaller. It inhabits the forests of South-east Asia from India to Ceylon and Borneo. It does not like heat and seeks the deep shade of the forest.

WHY DO WE HAVE A DAWN CHORUS?

The song of the birds at dawn has given pleasure to millions of people and has been celebrated in poetry and prose for many years. The most usual explanation given in the Middle Ages was that the birds sang each day in praise of God and the beauty with which He had clothed the world. More recently, there was the feeling that the birds sang joyously to welcome the rising of the sun, which meant food, warmth and activity.

However, scientists now think that the dawn chorus is made up of the warning signals of each bird as he re-establishes his territory. The establishment of a territory for courtship, nesting and food getting is the first step in the breeding cycle and the area is defended against competing birds of the same species by a warning song, although seldom by actual fighting. A robin, incidentally, has a particularly strong sense of territory.

WHEN DOES A HERMIT CRAB CHANGE ITS SHELL?

A hermit crab changes its shell when it has grown large enough to need a bigger home. This type of crab has a soft abdomen or "tail", which is folded up under the body, but it is not protected by a shell of its own as are most other crabs. Instead, the hermit uses empty snail shells as portable shelters, often having to fight with another crab for possession of an attractive home. Sometimes the homeseeker pulls out the original occupier, eats it and then takes over the shell.

One of the claws of the hermit is larger than the other. The crab uses this to stop up the entrance after withdrawing into the shell. The last two legs on its abdomen have roughened pads which grip the inside of the shell and hold the body in position. The crab has a spiral-shaped abdomen and moves in and out of its shell with a spiral movement.

One kind of hermit occupies a sponge which conveniently grows at the same pace as the crab. Sometimes sea-anemones enter into partnership with hermit crabs and take up residence on top of the shells. The crab provides the sea-anemone with transport and in return, receives an extra shield against attack.

WHERE DO FLIES GO IN THE WINTER?

During winter flies will hibernate, sometimes in large groups, in any available dry and warm space such as an attic.

The reason there are so few houseflies in winter is that their eggs will hatch only at temperatures between 24° Centigrade and 35° Centigrade (75° Fahrenheit and 95° Fahrenheit). Meanwhile their numbers steadily diminish owing to insecticides and natural causes. This is a good thing since flies often carry diseases.

WHAT IS A SALAMANDER?

A salamander is amphibian—an animal that lives both on land and in the water. It is a lizard-like member of a group of back-boned creatures between fish and reptiles. This class includes frogs and toads. Like fish and reptiles, the salamander is cold-blooded.

It was anciently believed that the first salamander was born out of the heart of a fire and that the so-called fire salamanders were unaffected by heat. In fact, the salamander is active usually only in the cool of the night, when it hunts worms, slugs and insects.

The salamander, which grows up to about 11 inches long, is attacked by few enemies, as its skin glands are poisonous. But the European water snake is not affected by the venom and frequently makes the salamander its prey.

WHY ARE YEWS OFTEN FOUND IN CHURCHYARDS?

Yews have long been associated with religious worship. So it is likely that churches were originally built near the sacred trees rather than the other way round.

These trees live longer than any other species in Europe and can grow to an enormous size. Many are thought to be well over 1,000 years old. Yews were revered by the druids of ancient Britain, France and Ireland and no doubt early Christian missionaries preached in the shelter of the trees before their first churches were built. Hywel Dda—Howell the Good—a Welsh king who reigned in the 10th Century, set a special value on "consecrated yews".

Some yews are even older than the ancient churches beside them, suggesting that the church was built on a spot already devoted to worship. The association continued, and it became traditional for yews to be planted in churchyards.

Also the great age to which yews live caused them to be regarded as a symbol of immortality and, therefore, associated with death, as man only becomes immortal after he dies.

WHERE DOES THE BREADFRUIT TREE GROW?

The breadfruit tree is found in the South Pacific islands and, to a lesser degree, in other parts of the tropics. It is an extremely handsome tree, growing up to 60 feet high. The oval leaves are a pleasant, glossy green and quite large.

There are two distinct forms of breadfruit, one seedless and the other containing many seeds which, when boiled or roasted, taste much like chestnuts.

The breadfruit, which contains a considerable amount of starch, is not really a fruit in the popular sense and is rarely eaten raw. It can be boiled or baked, served with salt, butter or syrup, and even sliced and fried like potatoes.

WHAT IS A LOOFAH?

A loofah is a fibrous, cylinder-shaped vegetable product often used in bathrooms as a kind of rough sponge or gentle brush. It is the dried interior of the fruit of a plant known to botanists as *Luffa aegyptiaca*. Less dignified, though more descriptive, names for this tropical climbing or trailing herb are dishcloth gourd and vegetable gourd.

The luffa belongs to the great gourd family of plants, and its 800 relations include the cucumber, the melon and the pumpkin. In spite of having an unpleasant smell, the luffa is cultivated in Egypt (hence the second part of its Latin name) and in Arabia, India and China. The yellow-flowered climbers can sometimes be seen adorning the trunks of palm trees. Besides being used to make loofahs, the luffa's fruit is eaten in curry.

The development of man-made materials has led to a decline in the loofah's popularity, but many people still use its slightly abrasive qualities to stimulate the skin.

WHERE DOES A LEECH FEED?

Leeches, which are rather slimy worms and vary in length from an inch to several inches, have two suckers, a big one at the rear and a smaller one at the mouth end. They have powerful muscles which enable them to expand and contract their bodies.

This makes them excellent swimmers. They can also use their suckers to crawl on the land. In tropical Asia, the islands of the Pacific and the Indian ocean, there is a particularly vicious and dreaded species of land leech which enters the breathing passages of animals, gorges on the animal's blood and swells so that it cannot escape.

Aquatic or water leeches cling to fishes, turtles and shell fish. Some leeches feed on earthworms and frogs' eggs. Others live on the larvae of insects and even on the microscopic life on the floor of the pond.

Leeches have been used in medicine from early times until quite recently to draw blood from a patient.

WHY DO SOME PLANTS CAPTURE INSECTS?

Some plants capture insects and other tiny animals and use them as food. They do not devour their prey by chewing but decompose them in a mixture of enzymes. The pitcher plant attracts an insect to its large showy leaf by means of sweet-smelling nectar. The leaf has a treacherous lip which precipitates the unwary victim into a deep hollow pitcher full of a digestive "broth", which soon decomposes its body. Other plants, like the Venus's flytrap, snap their leaves shut on their prey as it prowls about the trigger hairs glistening with drops of nectar. The sundews secrete a sticky fluid.

WHEN DO DRONES DIE?

The male bee, or drone, dies when there is no more nectar available from the fields. The reason for this is that, when the worker bees can no longer collect nectar for the hive, the production of honey stops. Deprived of their food the drones rapidly grow weak and are

Workers and drone on honeycomb. The drone has the bigger eyes.

carried from the hive by the workers to die.

The drone takes 24 days to develop from the egg to a fully grown male and may live as an adult for several months. Its only function in the bee's community is as a potential mate for the queen.

WHERE WOULD YOU FIND COWRIE SHELLS?

Cowrie shells are widely distributed and possibly the favourites among shell collectors because of their polished enamel-like surfaces and their beautiful coloured patterns. The cowrie appears in all the warmer seas of the globe. But the great cowries, the tiger cowrie and the orange cowrie are natives of tropical regions. They crawl slowly, browsing on weeds, and are shy creatures remaining hidden during the day in crevices or under rocks.

The best-known and most popular is the tiger cowrie. The shell grows about four inches long and is covered with spots. It was used by 18th Century silversmiths to make shell snuff-boxes and in Italy for burnishing paper and ironing lace. The shells were often distributed in Europe by sailors and gypsies.

Orange cowries at one time sold for large sums on the market. In Fiji and the New Hebrides in the Pacific they are still worn as badges of rank by the chiefs.

The money cowrie is a small oval shell, flat and white underneath with thick yellowish-white edges and a pale lemon upper surface. It is found in enormous quantities in the Pacific, from the Moluccas eastward. Large fortunes were at one time made by European traders who transported shells to the west coast of Africa and exchanged them for ivory, gold and slaves. A slave would be worth anything from 20,000 to 50,000 shells. In 1849 money cowries weighing 240 tons were imported into the English port of Liverpool.

A man at Cuttack in Orissa, India, paid for the erection of his bungalow entirely in cowries. The building cost him £400 which in cowries amounted to 16,000,000 shells. The common method of handling the cowries was by threading them on a string, 40 cowries to one string.

Among the cowries the rarest is *Cypreae leucedon. Only two* known examples of this pale brown, creamy-spotted shell exist. One is in the British Museum, the other in the Harvard University Museum. More than 190 species of cowrie shell are known to collectors. Some species are used as charms against evil spirits.

WHY IS GRASS GREEN?

The green colour in grass–and in most other plants–comes from chloroplast within the cells, each of which contains four different colours or pigments. These are: chlorophyll a, which is the strongest and is blue-green; chlorophyll b, which is yellow-green; xantophyll, which is yellow; and carotene, which is orange and gives carrots their bright colour.

Grass goes from light green in early spring to dark green and brown in summer and autumn because the amount of each pigment changes, like the paint on a palette, to mix new colours.

WHEN DOES A FOREST BECOME PETRIFIED?

A forest becomes petrified or turned to stone under certain conditions, through the action over the centuries of water containing large quantities of minerals.

Tree trunks buried ages ago under mud, sand or volcanic ash have been gradually transformed as water seeped into the empty cells of the decayed wood, filling them with mineral matter and preserving every detail of the original structure.

Petrified forests have been found in many parts of North and South America, dating from different geological periods and containing stone replicas of the trees that grew in those eras. The most famous of these forests is the Petrified Forest National Park in north Arizona, in the United States. There thousands of stone trunks and logs have been exposed to view through the rain washing away the soil in which they were buried. Although now composed of a mineral called silica, the original details of the trees can be studied through a microscope. Some of the trunks are up to 80 feet long and three to four feet in diameter. They are the fossils of cone-bearing trees belonging to Triassic times, the age of the dinosaurs, and are more than 150 million years old.

WHY DON'T TREES GROW ON MOUNTAIN TOPS?

Trees do not grow on mountain tops either because the situation is too exposed, or because the soil is too thin or too frozen to allow their roots to draw nourishment from the ground.

In most mountainous areas there is usually a clearly marked timberline, a boundary above which there is no tree growth. Sometimes the height of the timberline is dictated by local climatic or soil conditions, but as a general rule the boundary gets lower as the distance from the Equator increases. In the far north and south the cold is so intense that it is quite impossible for any trees to grow, and the timberline is therefore at sea level.

A range of mountains on or near the Equator, like the Ruwenzori range in Africa, can be divided into different belts of vegetation according to the types of trees growing at its base and at various heights up its slopes.

Similarly the belts of vegetation change according to the distance from the Equator. The first belt is the tropical or rain-forest region where it is hot and trees grow rapidly. Next comes a hot dry belt where few trees grow because there is so little rain. This is followed by the deciduous or warm and temperate belt, and by the coniferous belt, with very cold winters but fairly warm summers. Then comes the timberline, beyond which trees cannot grow, and finally the regions of permanent ice and snow, where no vegetation at all can live.

WHAT DOES BEE-LINE MEAN?

To make a bee-line is to follow the example of bees in taking the shortest route from one place to another. The expression comes from the belief that bees return to the hive by the shortest possible way after they have gathered their food. And the shortest distance between two points is, of course, a straight line.

But on their return home, the bees sometimes make lines which are far from straight. These are dancing movements in the air to inform other members of the colony about their source of supply. They indicate whether the food is pollen or nectar, the direction and distance from the hive and even the colours of the flowers.

This bee code was discovered by the German naturalist Professor K. von Frisch. He found, for example, that a circular dance says the food source is close to the hive and that a waggle dance indicates longer distances.

WHERE ARE CROCODILES BORN?

A newly-hatched crocodile is about eight inches long and can be found on the mud near the water's edge of marshes, rivers, estuaries and lakes around the tropical regions of the world. For it is here that the female lays her eggs and buries them—30 to 70 at a time— in holes in the warm mud.

Each of the hard-shelled eggs is about the size of a goose's egg. After being covered by vegetation which, as it rots, supplements the warmth of the sun, the batch is guarded by the female until the eggs are about to hatch. Then the crocodile digs down to free them from the mud.

Adult crocodiles vary in size from the three-feet-long dwarf ones of West Africa to those in the estuaries of tropical Asia and Australia which can attain a length of 20 feet.

There salt-water estuary crocodiles, including those that live in the tidal part of the River Nile in North Africa, are occasionally man-eaters and will attack and eat almost any living creature that comes within their reach. They were once thought to weep as they snapped up their victim. That is why in popular speech we often describe a false display of sorrow as "crocodile tears".

WHY DO TREES LOSE LEAVES IN WINTER?

Some trees with broad-bladed leaves lose their leaves in the winter because the tree has a rest period during the cold weather, and the leaves are not needed for the production of food. These trees are called deciduous trees— from the Latin *decidere* which means to fall. They drop their leaves in temperate or cold climates, but remain evergreen in the tropics.

WHEN WAS TEA FIRST GROWN?

We do not know when the tea plant was first cultivated, but the earliest mention of it occurs in a Chinese dictionary, the *Erh Ya*, about the year 350.

The cultivation of tea is believed to have begun in the province of Szechwan in central China. From there its cultivation and use as a beverage spread throughout China and Japan under the patronage of Buddhist priests. Perhaps it was this religious connection which gave rise to the Japanese legend about the discovery of tea. According to this story, tea first grew in China at a spot where the Buddhist saint Bodhidharma, who is said to have spent nine years in meditation before a wall, once fell asleep. He was said to have been so annoyed with himself when he awoke that

he cut off his eyelids and threw them on the ground, where they took root and grew into a tea plant.

Tea was brought to Europe by the Dutch via Java in 1610 and became increasingly fashionable from the middle of the 17th Century. In England tea (pronounced tay) eventually began to oust coffee with the encouragement of the British East India Company who enjoyed a tea trade monopoly. India's tea industry was founded in 1834 after Major Robert Bruce had found the plant growing in the north.

While Britain began to change from coffee to tea, America did the reverse after the Boston Tea Party of 1773 when the East India Company's tea was thrown into the harbour as a protest against British taxation.

Tea is drunk by about half the

Chinese tea cultivation

world's population, but is second to coffee in commercial importance.

HOW DO WORMS DIG THEIR HOLES?

An earthworm digs a hole by pushing into the loose soil with its pointed head end. The front end then thickens, forcing the soil apart. More of the worm's body enters the hole until all of it disappears. An earthworm can stretch itself out to become long and thin or pull itself in to become short and fat. This is because its body has many narrow rings joined together by a softer material that enables it to change shape.

Where the soil is too hard to be pushed aside, the worm eats its way through. The burrows it makes are about as thick as a pencil and lined with particles of soil glued together by sticky substances given off by the worm. Worms have tiny bristles, made of a hard substance called chitin, that help them to move and to cling on to the sides of the burrow.

WHY CAN OWLS SEE WELL AT NIGHT?

The night vision of owls is 100 times as keen as that of human beings, because their eyes are especially adapted for seeing in the dark. But most are almost colour-blind and the pictures they receive are slightly blurred. This is because their eyes contain more rod-shaped receptor cells than cone-shaped ones.

Operating in bright light, cone cells sharpen details and react to colour. Rod cells gather light and owls have 10 times as many of these as do human beings. Each cell contains "visual purple", a substance capable of transforming the slightest glimmer of light into a sight impression.

Owls have exceptionally large eyes and can control the amount of light entering by expanding or contracting the pupil. Each pupil can act independently of the other so that owls can see objects in the shadows and in bright light at the same time. Owls' eyes are so large that they are supported by thin, bony, tubular structures called sclerotic rings. Because of this the eyes are almost immovable and nature has compensated for this by giving owls extremely flexible necks, which enable them to turn their heads through an arc of 270 degrees.

These birds have excellent binocular vision as their eyes are in the front of their heads. This gives them a tremendous advantage in swooping on small lively prey, because distance judgment depends on binocular vision. To add to their advantages at night, the owls have outstanding hearing, keener than that of any other carnivorous bird.

But owls can also see well in the daytime. Although most species hunt by night, others are active at dusk or in full daylight.

WHEN DO SHARKS ATTACK HUMANS?

Some sharks may attack human beings if attracted by underwater noises, erratic swimming, the presence of a large number of bathers, or the glint of jewellery or some other article. But probably the greatest provocation to a shark is the presence of blood, for instance from a speared fish or live bait.

Sharks are most likely to attack during the daytime, the areas of greatest danger being those where the sea temperature is between 16° and 21° Centigrade (60° and 70° Fahrenheit). Most attacks seem to occur about 200 to 300 feet from the shore where the water is shallow—or no more than two or three feet in depth.

Among the kinds of sharks known to attack human beings are the tiger and the blue and grey nurse sharks. The most feared and the largest of all the shark family is the great white shark, a powerful and aggressive creature.

WHAT IS A MANX CAT?

The Manx cat is a tail-less cat found principally upon the Isle of Man, a lozenge-shaped island about 30 miles long and 20 miles wide, which is situated in the Irish Sea, at roughly the same distance from England, Ireland, Scotland and Wales.

The Manx cat is a common household pet on the Isle of Man and is easily recognized by its lack of tail, the pronounced hollow at the end of its backbone, and its very thick, or double, coat. Its back legs are longer than those in front and it therefore runs with a peculiar and very characteristic hopping motion.

A Manx cat may be of any colour and its fur is short. It has the reputation of being an excellent mouser. The only other tailless breed is found in Japan.

WHY ARE BIRDS' EGGS ROUNDED?

The roundness of an egg allows pressure to be applied from the outside which would break it if applied from the inside. Thus a helpless chick is protected until the moment it needs to break out from its shell. It can then do this with the gentlest of tapping.

Eggs are hatched by an adult bird sitting on them, and the best container for round objects is a cup-shaped nest which prevents them rolling about. So the best shape for eggs is for one end to be smaller than the other. The normal position for eggs in a nest is to have the smaller ends pointing inwards. This means the eggs take up the minimum of room and make it easier for the sitting bird to cover them.

Birds with scanty nests, as in the case of most sea birds, have more elongated eggs. If such eggs are caught by the wind while lying on some cliff-face or rocky ledge, they will spin round instead of rolling over the edge.

WHEN DO WORMS TURN?

If the earthworm detects an unfamiliar object next to its skin, the muscles will contract immediately and the body will turn to avoid the object. The worm will also turn in response to heat and, in a lesser degree, to light and sound.

Even the heat given out by an ordinary match some inches away, will cause a worm to retreat. Sound waves will also lead the earthworm to change direction rather than approach what, to human ears, may seem only a slight noise. Light, on the other hand, usually attracts the worm. It turns inquisitively to inspect the brighter patch, even although, of course, earthworms can live underground for long periods.

The phrase "even a worm will turn" is used in the sense that even the humblest of creatures will eventually rebel if goaded or pushed too hard. But the phrase has no real relationship to the activities of worms as such.

WHERE DOES CAVIARE COME FROM?

Caviare is the roe of the female members of the sturgeon family. These fish are found in northern and central Asia, Europe and North America.

The best quality black caviare comes from sturgeon caught during the winter months in the estuaries of rivers which flow into the Baltic Sea. It is regarded as a great delicacy and has been known in western Europe since the sixteenth century. Shakespeare mentions it in his play *Hamlet*. In the Soviet Union and eastern Europe, the coarser quality caviare is a staple food and is traditionally accompanied by gulps of vodka.

When caviare is prepared, the roe is carefully strained to remove fibres and fat. It is then salted and packed into small barrels, jars or tins. Its salty flavour and grainy texture are an acquired taste. But like all expensive foods, it is a taste thought by many people to be worth acquiring. Caviare is usually served as an *hors d'oeuvre* with bread or toast, or on small biscuits with drinks.

As well as the grey and black caviare, there is also a red caviare. This is prepared from the roe of salmon and is considered by experts in these matters to be of inferior quality.

WHY DOES WOOD HAVE A GRAIN?

The grain in a piece of wood is the pattern produced by the annual bands or rings which grow in the trunk of the tree during its lifetime.

The tree's rate of growth varies with the seasons. In the spring soft porous wood is needed to carry sap. In the summer, stronger cells of hard wood develop to support the growing weight of new leaves and branches. The number of these alternate bands of soft and hard wood gives the age of the tree.

WHAT IS A PRAYING MANTIS?

The praying mantis is an insect belonging to the family Mantoidea. The name "mantis" means "a diviner" and the insect has always been surrounded by superstition and legend because of its habit of remaining motionless or swaying gently backwards and forwards with its head raised and front legs outstretched as if in prayer.

In fact it is a ferocious killer and could more aptly be described as a "preying mantis". Most mantids are camouflaged and look very like the vegetation amongst which they live. The front legs are shaped like clasp knives to grasp the mantis's victim in an inexorable grip while it is torn apart by its captor's mandibles. The mantis even devours poisonous insects as well as its own kind. A male mantis may often be eaten by the female after mating.

Most species of mantids are tropical or sub-tropical, but about 20 species occur in Europe.

WHEN DOES THE MALE STICKLEBACK TURN RED?

The male stickleback's belly turns red at the start of the breeding season in spring. Normally the belly of this small fish is silver-coloured, the rest of it varying from brown to green. But when the time comes for him to mate he becomes very active in attracting females with his bright new colour.

In building the home and rearing the family the male stickleback performs many of the functions usually associated with a female fish. He chooses the place for the nest, collects the stems of various aquatic plants and binds them together using a threadlike web secreted from his kidney.

Once the female has been enticed into his nest, she will lay her eggs and depart, leaving him on guard. He watches over the eggs with great care and even looks after the baby fish.

WHY DO BUTTERFLIES AND MOTHS HAVE POWDERY WINGS?

The "powder" on the wings of moths and butterflies is really a layer of tiny, coloured scales which overlap each other almost like the tiles on a roof. If you touch the wing with a finger the "powder" is rubbed off, leaving the wing more or less transparent and colourless.

The scales are generally like the shape of a hand tapered off at the wrist, and the whole surface is often grooved or cross-grooved. They are really hollow bags growing from tiny cup joints formed in the outer skin of the wing membranes.

They are either filled with colouring materials, or so minutely grooved and surfaced that they refract light to give off an irridescent colour, even though they contain no pigment. The brown, red, yellow, white or black scales are pigmented. The blues and greens are irridescent.

Many male butterflies and moths have specially shaped "scent-scales" (androconia). These are long and feather-like or broad and bat-shaped. They contain glands for making scents which attract the females.

WHERE DO SPONGES COME FROM?

The soft, absorbent, natural sponges used in baths are the skeletal remains of a marine animal. Biologists once thought sponges were plants. This seemed natural as sponges have no special shape and attach themselves to one spot on the sea-bed like plants. Also, they have no limbs, mouths or internal organs. Today, however, they are classified as animals.

The familiar commercial sponges are gathered by divers or by dredging ships. They are prised from the sea floor and dried in the sun. After any impurities have been washed out of the sponge, it is ready to be sold in the market.

WHAT IS UNUSUAL ABOUT LEMMINGS?

The strange thing about lemmings is the way they, apparently, commit mass suicide. These grey or reddish-brown rodents look like mice, but are slightly larger. They live in large areas of the northern world, including Alaska, northwest Canada and Scandinavia

But, in fact, only the Scandinavian lemmings stampede in such a suicidal manner. Now and then thousands of them travel miles over land in panic to the sea. Many die on the way, but those that arrive leap immediately over the cliffs into the sea, and swim until they become exhausted and drown.

No one is certain what makes the lemmings behave so strangely. It may be because the weather becomes too warm for them, or because their food supply changes, or simply because they feel they are getting overcrowded.

WHEN CAN YOU SEE A SNAKE DANCE?

There are two occasions when a snake will "dance"–both connected with the mating season. In the first case the dancing partners are both male and their performance appears to be a form of aggression designed to impress the female.

The second occasion is a nuptial dance between male and female. First the snakes pursue each other and coil together. Then the couple raise their necks and heads as if forming the shape of the letter U. During the dance, which may last an hour, the male rubs its chin against the female's neck.

The nuptial dance occurs mainly among European snakes, but the males' dance of aggression is to be seen all over the world especially among rattlesnakes, adders and cobras.

WHY DO RABBITS HAVE LARGE EARS?

Rabbits are timid animals with many enemies and rely on their large ears to warn them of the sound of approaching danger. Their ears act like old-fashioned ear-trumpets. The large area catches a great many sound waves and channels them into the rabbit's inner ear.

Wild rabbits spend most of the day underground, usually coming out to feed between dusk and dawn. They are continually on the alert, their long ears twitching and moving round to pick up the faintest sound from an enemy. They also have a keen sense of smell.

Long back legs give rabbits speed. But they are virtually defenceless and, in fact, often seem to be hypnotized by approaching predators. When this happens, they crouch squealing and make no attempt to run away. Only their extraordinary fertility has enabled them to survive the onslaughts of foxes, badgers, wild cats, martens, stoats, weasels, polecats, dogs, man and disease.

WHEN DO ANIMALS BECOME MUTANTS?

Animals are said to be mutants when they show characteristics different from the rest of their species. Mutations are processes by which the hereditary properties of some of the reproductive cells in animals are altered.

In nature these changes can take place spontaneously and unpredictably. But they are rare, and little is known about this cause, beyond the fact that the longer an animal takes to breed, the less likely it is to give birth to a mutant.

Nowadays, the most common causes of animals producing mutants are chemical substances and radiation. Indeed, radiation is a rapidly increasing hazard.

Animals born from parents who have suffered the effects of more than normal radiation are invariably mutants. Cows have been known to grow a fifth leg. In the Pacific Islands, where nuclear tests have been conducted, there are fish which have forgotten how to swim and have been found on land. Birds have lost the power to fly, and some may have only one wing.

Animal mutants have long intrigued and frightened people. In Greek mythology, mutants such as dogs and horses with two heads were believed to possess magical powers.

Mutant snake with two heads

WHY DO BEAVERS BUILD DAMS?

The beavers of North America build a dam to create an artificial lake in which to construct an island home or lodge. Often the beavers work in colonies. After choosing a narrow place in a shallow stream with a firm bottom, they set to work felling trees by standing on their hind legs and gnawing round the trunks with their large chisel-like teeth. When the tree is down, the beavers lop off the branches and cut the trunk into suitable lengths which they drag into the stream and sink across the current. Sticks, stones and mud are used to keep the dam in position and make it watertight.

In the middle of the lake thus created the beavers use the same materials to build their lodge. When completed this is a dome-shaped, ventilated structure about 8 feet in diameter and rising well clear of the surface of the lake. There are two entrances, both under water. One of these is used for general purposes, the other as an escape route in an emergency or for bringing in food.

The lodge serves as a home, a nursery for the baby beavers and a storehouse for food in winter. The beavers feed chiefly on the bark of trees, of which they keep a plentiful supply at the bottom of the dam, on the bed of the lake and built into the fabric of their home.

In winter, when the lake is frozen over and snow covers the ground, the lodge is virtually an impregnable fortress which the beavers can leave and enter by swimming under the ice. Beavers are experts at keeping the water in the lake at the right level by constructing canals. They work industriously to maintain both dam and lodge—hence the origin of that popular phrase about being "as busy as a beaver".

WHERE IS THE WORLD'S LONGEST SNAKE?

The longest snake in the world—the python—is found in the tropics, in and around the Malay region. It is the reticulated or regal python, which can sometimes be as much as 30 feet long. It kills its prey by coiling itself round the animal and hugging it, so that it cannot breathe. Then it swallows the victim whole.

The python is strong enough to kill an ox, but chooses smaller animals which it can swallow. If a python is disturbed soon after a meal, it is likely to vomit the animal up again, still whole. It rarely attacks man and is not poisonous.

Most pythons live in trees. They also like lying in water where it is cool.

The python lays oval eggs with leathery shells, sometimes as many as 100 at a time. It guards the eggs by coiling itself round them.

The anaconda, which inhabits the rivers and swamps of Brazil, Peru and the Guianas is the largest American snake; it rivals and sometimes exceeds the python in size.

WHERE WOULD YOU FIND PEARLS?

Pearls come from molluscs—a group of animals which includes squids, clams, and oysters.

Under its shell the mollusc has a mantle, or outer-skin. When a particle of dirt, or tiny marine creature gets stuck in this mantle, a hard substance forms around it. This makes the pearl. It is formed of the same material as the mollusc shell—nacre or mother-of-pearl.

Pearls come in many different shapes and colours. The most valuable ones are completely smooth, spherical and usually white. But there is a black pearl from the Gulf of Mexico, which is also extremely valuable.

The people who first discovered how to stimulate the production of pearls were the Chinese. They put the mollusc into a shallow pond, inserted a speck of mud into the mantle, and waited for the pearl to form. After a couple of months they would detach the pearl from the mollusc's mantle—and eat the mollusc.

WHY DO BIRDS PREEN THEMSELVES?

Birds preen themselves to clean and waterproof their feathers, to maintain their general health and to keep them lying smooth and neat. This preening or grooming starts as the nestling's feathers are breaking out of their sheaths. The young bird spends a great deal of time combing the feathers with its bill and freeing them from bits of sheath and other blemishes.

In adult life the bird continues this behaviour and also uses the preen glands or oil glands which are located on the back, just in front of the tail. The birds nibble at the glands and rub their heads against them, spreading the secretion on their feathers. This oil waterproofs the plumage, keeps it supple and maintains its insulating qualities. The oil may also be useful as a source of Vitamin D if swallowed accidentally by the bird.

Many kinds of birds have preen glands. They often combine preening with dust or water bathing. Ducks may be seen dipping their heads under water, flicking their wings and wriggling their bodies while preening. This seems to give them great pleasure and fun.

WHAT IS A TUATARA?

The tuatara is the only survivor of the beak-headed order of reptiles, called Rhynchocephalia, that goes back to the time of the dinosaurs. It hunts by night and its prey are insects. Like the coelacanth, a prehistoric fish that still survives, the tuatara is almost a living fossil.

It can now be found only on some of the small islets off the coast of New Zealand, having been exterminated from the mainland. It basks in the sun during the day and burrows into the soil for safety. It is covered in scales and grows to about 30 ins.

WHEN DID THE AMERICAN BISON NEAR EXTINCTION?

The American bison were near to extinction by 1900, although they numbered more than 60 million when the white man first arrived in their feeding grounds.

Buffalo, as the bison were commonly called, were the prime essential of the Plains Indian's economy. The powerful animal's meat, bones, and hide provided the Indians with food, medicine, clothing and shelter.

At first the white man, too, killed the buffalo for meat and hides. But after 1850, as the American–Indian war neared its climax, United States soldiers began to slaughter the animals indiscriminately to force the Indians to leave their homelands. With the advent of the railroad the killing of the bison became a sport. Travellers would shoot from railroad carriages, leaving the carcases to rot by the tracks. In less than 50 years about 50 million buffalo had been exterminated.

The voices of those who wished to save the animal from extinction were heeded just in time. From the few survivors, new herds were reared. Today buffalo are increasing in numbers, with herds totalling several thousand.

WHY DO PENGUINS HAVE SMALL, STIFF WINGS?

Nearly all birds use their wings for flight, but penguins use theirs as paddles for swimming. They spend most of their lives in the sea and find their food there.

Although many birds can both swim and fly, no other bird can swim as well as the flightless penguins.

Penguins have muscles, bones and organs very much like those of flying birds, so we assume that their ancestors must have been able to fly. Probably they slowly lost the power of flight while learning to swim faster and dive deeper in search of food. This must have happened millions of years ago, for by Miocene times– 25,000,000 years ago–there were penguins very much like those alive today.

The feathers of penguins are short and grow all over their bodies, leaving no bare spots unprotected from cold air and water. The feathers of the paddle-like wing are small and stiff, with broad flat shafts. On the rear edge of the wing are rows of many short feathers with strong shafts.

The bones of the wing are flattened. This allows the whole wing to be thin and streamlined, but yet strong enough to push the bird through the water. Its shape is much like that of the flipper of a seal. Some of the bones have grown together, so that the penguin paddle is stiffer, though thinner, than the wing of a flying bird.

The breast muscles, which work the wings, are as large and powerful as those of any bird, but the muscles in the wings are small.

WHEN DOES A COW START TO GIVE MILK?

A cow starts to give milk between the ages of two and two-and-a half years, after the birth of its first calf. For the first few days the milk is unfit for human consumption and is fed to the calf which is afterwards reared separately. During the milking or lactation period that follows the cow's yield usually reaches a maximum after four to six weeks and continues in decreasing quantities for nine to ten months.

To ensure a steady supply of milk, farmers arrange for their cows to calve every 12 months. Attention to breeding has led to steady improvements in yields. A good cow may produce up to 2,000 gallons during the lactation period.

Cows are normally milked twice a day, morning and evening. Except for the smallest herds, milking in advanced countries is usually done by machines which suck the milk from the cows' udders and transfer it to covered containers. But there are still many countries where milking is largely done by hand, in the traditional way.

WHY DO SOME BIRDS EAT GRIT?

Birds which peck grain and other seeds also peck grit to help them to digest these hard foods. Because birds have no teeth, the work of chewing, which would require muscles and strong jaw bones, is done by the gizzard. This makes it possible for the skull to be delicate in structure and therefore light in weight.

Grit is taken into the gizzard, or ventriculus, which has thick and often very muscular walls and the combined action of the two grinds down the hard food. The ventriculus is the back part of a bird's stomach, the fore part is glandular and secretes digestive juices and is called the proventriculus. Food passes from the ventriculus to be absorbed by the intestines.

WHERE DO TREE FROGS COME FROM?

Tree-frogs are found in Europe, North and South America, New Guinea, North Africa, and warm parts of Asia. They have small sticky discs on the tops of their fingers and toes which help them cling to the branches of trees.

The best-known European tree-frog is less than two inches long. Its Latin name is *Hyla arborea*. Its colour is usually bright green. But tree-frogs can change colour even as you watch them. They can become yellow, brown or black.

In North America there are two main types of tree-frog. One is called the spring peeper. It has a shrill piping voice. The other one is known as *Hyla versicolor*. Versicolor is a Latin word meaning "various colours". This frog can be grey, green or brown. It has a loud croaking voice.

A Larva
B Bean
C Exit.

The larva pushes open this door and emerges to become a moth.

WHAT MAKES JUMPING BEANS JUMP?

Jumping beans are made to jump by the action of little insects inside them. The beans are the long seed of certain Mexican shrubs and contain the larvae or caterpillars of a small species of moth with the large scientific name of *Carpocapsa saltitans*. The second of these two Latin words means jumping.

The larvae are stirred into movement by warmth, and it is this activity that makes the beans jump.

WHY DOES WOOD ROT?

Wood rots or decays because it is an organic substance–that is to say, it is a living thing–made up of tiny box-like units called cells. Like any living things these cells can die. The attacks of insects and the growth of fungi are two of the most common causes of decay.

In leaves or flowers the cells are often square or rounded in outline. But in timber or wood they are mostly long and narrow, for they have to serve as tubes to carry sap from the roots up the tree trunk. Their walls are strong and fibrous because they have to support the weight of the branches and leaves above them. They interlock to form the wonderfully strong and pliable substance which we know as wood.

The cells do not continue to carry sap for the whole lifetime of the tree, because the trunk and boughs grow larger and soon contain more cells than are needed. So the inner part of the trunk and branches ceases to carry sap, and the cells gradually fill up with gums and resins which make them stronger, harder and better able to resist decay and rot.

When wood is cut the cells are full of watery sap. This timber is stacked in the open air for several months, or in a special drying-room, called a kiln, for several days. It is then "seasoned" and ready for use.

WHEN WERE BREAKFAST CEREALS FIRST USED?

Cereals, of course, in the general sense, including wheat, rice, maize (known as corn in Canada and the United States), rye, oats and barley were among the earliest plants grown by man. But packaged or processed cereals are a modern development.

Breakfast cereals owe their origin to the vegetarians of the last century and health fanatics who believed they could save souls by preaching the virtues of a non-meat diet.

Granula, which was the beginning of Grape-Nuts, was launched in 1863 by a man called James C. Jackson, of Danville, New York. Henry D. Perkey brought out Shredded Wheat in 1893 and Puffed Wheat was developed by Alexander Anderson in 1902.

The religious sect, the Seventh Day Adventists, made Battle Creek, Michigan, the cereal headquarters of the world when the sect formed the Western Health Reform Institute at Battle Creek in 1866, later called the Battle Creek Sanatorium. John Harvey Kellogg, who was a doctor and a writer, took over control of the Sanatorium in 1876 and his advocacy of cereals helped to develop what was to become a vast new food industry. His brother, W. K. Kellogg, started a cereal producing company in 1906.

C. W. Post was another cereal pioneer and his Postum Cereal Company formed in 1897 later developed into General Foods Corporation.

The basic idea behind packaged cereals has remained largely unchanged.

WHY DO BATS MAKE HIGH-PITCHED SOUNDS?

Bats use high-pitched sounds to find their way about. They are nocturnal animals. That is they move about by night. So they have developed their hearing to such an extent that they can find their way by a method known as echo-location.

The blind-flying abilities of bats were first studied by Lazzaro Spallanzani (1729–1799). He surgically removed the eyeballs from several bats to prove that they did not need to see to fly.

In the 20th Century, biologists, using electronic instruments, have carried out experiments with bats. They have discovered that bats find out where to go by emitting high-frequency sounds and receiving the echoes as they bounce off objects. Most of the sounds have too high a frequency to be heard by the human ear.

Bats commonly fly together in groups, but apparently they are not confused by the sounds and echoes produced by each other. When hunting in woods and in the rain they are able to discriminate between the faint echoes bouncing off insects and those bouncing off the ground, tree-trunks, branches, twigs and raindrops.

WHERE WOULD YOU FIND LIVE PREHISTORIC FISH?

Numerous fossil remains have been found of coelacanth fish which died over 70 million years ago. In fact the coelacanth is said to have first appeared some 350 million years ago.

But to the amazement of experts the first living coelacanth was found in 1938 off the coast of South Africa. In 1952 a second one was caught on a line by a fisherman from the Comoro Islands, between Mozambique and Madagascar. Since then many more coelacanths have been taken around the Comoros.

Modern coelacanths are bigger than most of the fossil forms. They average about five feet in length and can weigh more than 100 pounds.

Usually they live among reefs, from which they will dart out on their prey. They are strong and powerful flesh eaters. The heart of a coelacanth is an S-shaped tube and is probably the most primitive of its kind in existence today.

WHAT IS A GREENSHANK?

A greenshank is a little bird with a long beak and olive-green legs—a member of a group of birds known as sandpipers.

The greenshank breeds in Scotland, Norway, Sweden and Finland. It builds its nest on the ground, being content usually to settle in a small hollow, lined with heather or dry grass. The eggs are pale buff or stone colour, blotched with purplish-grey and spotted with dark brown.

Worms, insects and tiny fish provide the bird's food. In winter the greenshank migrates, sometimes as far south as Australia or South Africa.

WHY DO MOST FISH HAVE SCALES?

Fish have scales as a protective coating for the skin. In fact, not all fish have them. But we usually think of a fish as a cold-blooded, aquatic animal that swims by means of fins, breathes by means of gills, and is covered with scales. Scales may be of four different kinds—placoid, ganoid, cycloid and ctenoid.

Placoid scales are long, spiny and toothlike, and are made of enamel and dentine. These are found on fishes which have a backbone made of gristle, such as sharks and rays.

Ganoid scales are rather like placoid scales but are mainly bony and covered with a kind of enamel called ganoin. These thick scales are found especially in garfish.

Cycloid scales are thin, large, round or oval scales arranged in an overlapping pattern. They are found in carps and similar fishes.

Ctenoid scales are similar to the cycloid ones, but have spines or comblike teeth along their free edges. These are found in the higher bony fishes, such as perches and sunfishes.

WHERE DOES A BEE KEEP ITS STING?

A bee keeps its sting at the end of its abdomen. At the tip of a bee's abdomen is a shaft where its stinging thorn is to be found. It can sting several times, but once it leaves the thorn in its victim's flesh it will not be able to sting again.

It is not true to say that a bee will automatically die once it loses its thorn. Only female bees can sting. Male bees, or drones, lack this means of protecting themselves.

There is a species of which even the female cannot sting. But these bees which live mainly in Africa and South America are not defenceless. If disturbed, they will fly at the intruder in great numbers, crawl into his eyes, ears and hair and smear him with a sticky substance, causing him to retreat in great discomfort.

WHAT DO BIRDS OF PREY EAT?

Birds of prey are those that feed wholly or mainly on meat taken by hunting. They catch other birds, and small animals, for their food.

There are two chief families, the hawks and the falcons. The hawks include eagles, such as the bald eagle (symbol of the United States) and the golden eagle. The falcons are smaller but share the same general characteristics— hooked beaks, keen vision and outstanding powers of flight. Owls, also, feed on flesh.

Besides being fast flyers, many birds of prey are expert at gliding and hovering. Their principal strategy of attack is the "stoop", when from a great height they sight their prey, close their wings and swoop upon the victim. This manoeuvre calls for a combination of speed and last-second braking unique to this type of bird.

In advanced countries birds of prey have suffered severely from the effects of poisonous agricultural sprays which have polluted their food sources. This has threatened their survival. But the danger has now been recognized, and in many areas their numbers are slowly recovering.

WHEN DID PTERODACTYLS LIVE?

Pterodactyls (or pterosaurs) lived between 150 million and 70 million years ago. These extraordinary reptiles were able to fly. Some had a wing-span of over 25 feet, making them by far the largest flying animals known to man. Their skulls were often longer than four feet.

Unlike the birds, their descendants, pterodactyls must have been unable to perch upright. They probably hung upside down like bats when sleeping or at rest.

Since most remains of pterodactyls have been discovered among marine sediments, it seems likely that these flying dinosaurs found their food in the sea, like seagulls, by diving for fish.

WHY ARE SOME JAPANESE TREES MINUTE?

Many Japanese trees are small because they are dwarfed by the Japanese art of bonsai. This art consists in training and growing dwarf trees as symbols of the Japanese ideal of the immersion of the self in nature. This ideal also finds expression in their poetry, the tea ceremony and flower arranging.

WHERE DID ALL THE DODOS GO?

The dodo was rather a stupid bird. Indeed, it was so stupid that it was named dodo by the Portuguese when they discovered Mauritius– its home–in 1507. The Portuguese word *doudo* means stupid.

Mauritius is an island, 720 square miles in area and lying 500 miles to the east of Madagascar in the Indian Ocean. Until the arrival of man, with his attendant creatures such as the cat and dog, the dodo had been able to live in peace. It had no enemies, which was fortunate because it was big and clumsy and was completely unsuited to fleeing from danger. Its short legs were almost incapable of supporting the weight of the fat, round body (about the size of a swan's) and the ridiculously inadequate, stubby wings were of no use for flying.

Within 180 years of its discovery by the Portuguese, the dodo was extinct. Over the intervening years several were brought to Europe alive, and one was to be seen in London in 1638. By 1680 the dodo had succumbed.

With the help of drawings and by the collection of bones gathered in Mauritius, an almost complete reconstruction has been made of the poor bird. It can be seen at the Natural History Museum in London.

Mauritius is the only place in the world where the bird is known to have existed. A similar bird once lived on the neighbouring island of Rodriguez, but this also has become extinct.

The phrase "as dead as the dodo" is used to mean that something is very dead indeed.

WHY DO FLOWERS HAVE SEPALS?

The sepals of a flower protect it while it is in bud. The flower is really a kind of shoot, in which the leaves have been altered so that they can take on the task of producing seeds.

In a simple flower these leaves are arranged in circles, called whorls. The outermost are five green, leaf-shaped sepals. Inside these are five petals, usually heart-shaped, each with a small flap at its base where nectar is produced to attract bees and other insects.

Both the sepals and the petals are attached at their bases to the "receptacle", the swollen end of the flower-stalk, which looks like a cone in the middle of the flower.

Above the sepals and petals are the parts of the flower used in reproduction. These are the stamens, which contain the yellow pollen, and the carpels, which contain the ovules.

Most flowers are built on this plan but there are wide variations in size, shape and colour, and in the numbers of the different parts of the flowers.

WHERE ARE THE LARGEST ANIMALS FOUND?

Blue whales are the largest living animals. They are cosmopolitan creatures and are found in most of the seas, from the polar caps to the equator. Normally those which inhabit the colder seas will migrate to warmer waters in winter.

Their dimensions are almost beyond belief. Although figures can never be quite accurate, a blue whale can weigh more than 200 tons and many have been found measuring over 100 feet in length. The tongue alone, of a female whale found in Antarctica, weighed well over four tons.

It has been estimated that in the 1930s there were nearly 40,000 blue whales in the world. But by the end of the 1960s there were fewer than 1,000 alive. This was because they became popular victims for the misdirected efforts of over-zealous hunters.

WHAT ARE TERMITES?

Termites are soft-bodied insects belonging to the family Isoptera. They are sometimes called "white ants" but they are like ants only in that both species live in social colonies. They live in the tropics and temperate countries and make various kinds of nests. Some make galleries in decaying tree trunks, some make nests below the ground, but the most spectacular are large structures built above ground called "termitaria". They are built from earth excavated below ground and cemented together by saliva. Some of these nests are 20 feet high and almost too hard to break open even with a pickaxe.

The termite community is divided into four groups, but only two can breed. Each colony is founded by a "royal pair" and the queen's life is devoted to laying eggs.

WHEN DOES A TADPOLE BECOME A FROG?

Frogs' eggs become tadpoles within two weeks of being laid in the water, but tadpoles may take anything from two months to three years to change completely into frogs.

The time taken seems to depend on the environment. Tadpoles will generally develop faster in warmer waters. Also the more advanced species of frog have simplified and shortened the process of transformation.

Tadpoles, like fish, breathe through gills. They develop lungs during the change-over, gain legs and loose their tails. Their diet changes, too—tadpoles live on plants in the pond, but frogs live on very small insects.

WHY DO BIRDS HAVE DIFFERENT BILLS?

The shape of a bird's bill or beak is closely related to the kind of food it eats and the way in which it collects or catches this food.

A crow or jay has a strong all-purpose bill, capable of killing small mammals but fine enough at the tip to pick up small insects. Many songbirds have slender bills for picking up insects from leaves or out of cracks; others have wide flat ones for catching flies or strong thick ones for cracking seeds and nuts.

Birds which dig for worms usually have long bills with sensitive tips while many water birds have broad dredging bills. Divers and grebes have straight spear-like bills and the birds of prey have strong hooked bills for tearing flesh.

Birds which catch insects on the wing (nightjars, swallows etc.) have tiny beaks but an enormous "gape" by comparison.

WHERE WOULD YOU FIND A TRAP-DOOR SPIDER?

Trap-door spiders are to be found just under the surface of the earth. They belong to the class of spiders called *mygalomorphae* which includes the bird-eating spiders of the tropics. All these spiders tend to be rather large. They have four lungs instead of two, and their jaws work vertically instead of sideways.

The trap-door spider has perfected the art of burrowing underground. Its jaws are provided with a special row of teeth with which to dig out its home. It lines its burrow with silk and makes a trap-door consisting of layers of silk and earth. The outside of this door is coated with moss or some other form of camouflage. The spider lies in wait behind its trap-door, darting out to seize its prey.

Trap-door spiders are widespread throughout the hottest regions of the world, with comparatively few in the temperate zones. Specimens of up to four and a half inches have been found. It is estimated that some may live up to 20 years.

WHY DO BIRDS HAVE HOLLOW BONES?

Birds fly so well because they have developed skeletons which are especially light and strong. Most of their bones are hollow, with the interior webbed or honeycombed across by fine girders of bone to give added strength. They are sometimes called "pneumatic" or air-filled bones.

A bird's skull is made of thin bone in remarkable contrast to the solid, heavy skull of the mammal. The bones of its spine are flexibly connected in the neck, strongly

Skeleton of a common bird

Backbone

Leg   Keel

Foot

Bird's bone cut lengthwise

bound together in the front part of the body and united at the rear into a solid, rigid mass. Powerful muscles attached to the breast-bone move the wings.

The bones in the wings have been reduced in number to provide greater strength. Wings can be used also as propellers. They can be shortened or lengthened by flexing, the feathers at the tips can be spread or closed, and the angle of the wings or their parts can be altered. All these adjustments make the aerodynamics of a bird's wings much more complicated than those of an aircraft. Consequently, the flight of a bird is more varied and adaptable.

WHERE DO LICHENS GROW?

Lichens are found throughout the world, often occupying areas where no other plant can become established. They are found in their greatest numbers in the Alpine and Arctic regions, where they are the dominant plants.

Lichens are the products of two distinct groups of plants. Together fungi and algae (seaweed is an algae) combine to produce lichens. Most rocks you will come across have an abundance of these plants. Lichens are almost the only plants able to survive the severe conditions at high altitudes.

In Antarctica, where there are very few flowering plants, more than 400 species of lichens have been found.

WHAT ARE FOSSILS?

Fossils are the remains, moulds, traces or impressions of prehistoric animals and plants found in the ground. The word comes from the Latin *fodere*, meaning "to dig", and originally meant any old, curious object dug out of the earth. But since about the middle of the 16th Century, fossils have been regarded specifically as hard objects showing evidence of earlier forms of life, often many millions of years old.

There are many kinds of fossils. Some are footprints which strange prehistoric animals left behind in mud long since turned to rock. Others are stones which were once soft substances, but still preserve the outlines of extinct plants, or of seashells, or of the bodies of animals. Sometimes even the bones of creatures have survived.

The study of fossils, which is called palaeontology, has enabled scientists to fill many vital gaps in the history of the world and its inhabitants. For example, fossils have shown that rocks in great mountain ranges like the Alps or the Rocky Mountains were once below the surface of the sea. They have indicated that the United States and Europe were once covered by tropical forests. Also, they provide evidence of the common ancestry of animals which today differ widely in appearance.

The subject can be a rewarding hobby for amateurs. Many important contributions to the world's great collections have been made by people who looked for fossils in their spare time or even came across fossils by sheer accident.

WHERE WOULD YOU FIND A RED GIANT?

You would find a Red Giant on the Sierra Nevada mountains of California in North America. It is a huge redwood tree, called a giant sequoia. These trees, members of the conifer family, are the largest in the world and grow to a height of 300 feet. They have a very hard, reddish brown wood and a thick, very rough bark. The giant sequoias were believed to be the oldest living things in the world. The ring marks on the stumps of the oldest trunks have been carefully counted and it is now known that some of the biggest are about 4,000 years old.

Many of these trees were cut down for their timber, which is resistant to attacks by fungus, and termites and other insects. To preserve the remaining groves of these huge redwoods, a reservation called the Sequoia National Park was set up in 1890. The largest tree there is 272 feet high and has a circumference at the base of its trunk of $101\frac{1}{2}$ feet. Its weight has been estimated to be over 6,000 tons.

Some of the other trees are taller but do not have such large trunks. A tunnel has been cut through the base of one of these giant trees which is big enough to drive a car through.

WHY ARE VAMPIRE BATS DANGEROUS?

Vampire bats are dangerous because they carry rabies and other diseases and infect their victims as they suck the blood which is their only food.

Vampire bats (Desmodontidae) are found only in South and Central America. They have extremely sharp teeth and pierce the skin of their prey so gently that the victim does not awaken. Blood is drawn into the mouth by the almost tubular tongue and the vampire bat's whole digestive system is specially adapted for his diet of blood.

WHEN WAS RUBBER DISCOVERED?

Although the remarkable properties of the rubber tree were known to the Aztecs and other South American Indians, for perhaps a thousand years, rubber was unknown in Europe until the discovery of the New World.

Pietro Martyre d'Anghiera, chaplain to the court of Ferdinand of Aragon, Castile and Léon, gave the first written account of the elastic gum in his book *De Orbo Novo*. In it he described a game played by Aztec children using rubber balls. He was particularly amazed by the balls' ability to bounce back into the air after being thrown to the ground.

In 1615, about 100 years later, another Spaniard, Juan de Torquemada, described how the Indians made incisions into rubber trees and collected the milk or sap which oozed out. When dried, this rubber milk was used for making bottles and soles for footwear.

WHAT IS PHOTOSYNTHESIS?

Photosynthesis is the process by which green plants make food for themselves–and, indirectly, for all animals, including human beings.

In photosynthesis plants combine water and salts in the soil, and carbon dioxide in the air to build up organic compounds, such as sugar starch and proteins. To do this they use the energy of sunlight, which is absorbed with the help of the green dye in their leaves called chlorophyll.

This process of manufacturing food from what they absorb through their roots and leaves makes green plants the primary food producers in the world. All animals draw their nourishment from them, either by feeding on plants themselves or by eating other animals that do so. During photosynthesis, which takes place only in daylight, excess oxygen is produced and released into the atmosphere for animals to breathe.

After the Second World War, the American scientist Melvin Calvin wrote a book about how plants capture the carbon dioxide in the atmosphere. In 1961 he received the Nobel Prize in chemistry in recognition of his work.

WHY DO CATS PURR?

Most people think that cats purr to show pleasure or contentment. Purring is a kind of low continous rattling hum, but it is nothing to do with a cat's real voice, for the vibration frequency is far lower than that of the vocal chords. In fact, a mother cat uses purring to call her kittens to feed. At birth kittens cannot see, hear or smell but they can feel the purring of their mother as a vibratory movement and so come towards it to nurse. Once the kittens are feeding, the mother stops purring. So it would seem that purring began as a kind of homing device and your cat may simply be reminding you that he is there so that you will continue to stroke him.

WHEN DOES A TREE HAVE TO BE PRUNED?

Trees have to be pruned to protect their health, improve their appearance or remove danger to people or property. Sometimes it is necessary to remove broken, dead or diseased branches, to restore vigour to an ageing tree by cutting back and to admit more air and light by thinning out the centre.

One of the most obvious reasons for pruning trees is to control their growth within the space available for them to flourish. In this type of pruning, live-pruning as it is called, branches are lopped from the trees to control their size and to maintain a pleasing shape.

Sometimes trees are "topped" by removing some of the upper trunk. Pollard pruning involves cutting the trees back to a point at which strong branches are to be allowed to grow. As shoots grow from these points they are cut back each year. This method makes a very ugly tree shape. The lightest method of pruning is known as drop-crotching, which trims only the upper and outer branches.

Another type of pruning is orchard pruning, for stimulating the production of flowers and fruit on fruit trees. Here the farmer tries to maintain a framework of branches which will best allow the sunlight to penetrate to the middle of the tree's crown.

Most deciduous trees may be pruned at any time of the year. The pruning of evergreen trees with needle-like leaves should normally be limited to the removal of dead wood.

Dead-pruning, or brashing, is the cutting away of dead or dying side branches, most often used with conifers growing in plantations.

The last type of pruning is side-shoot pruning or shrouding, which means the removal of small side branches on such trees as pollards or limes to provide a knot-free bottom length of timber.

Pruning means causing wounds and these may cause disease. Special dressings available at most garden supply stores should be applied to cuts more than an inch in diameter to protect the trees from fungi.

WHEN DOES POLLUTION KILL A RIVER?

A river will die when pollution reaches such a level that all the available oxygen is absorbed.

This can happen if the oxygen is used up by the presence in the water of an excessive number of waste organisms.

Large amounts of nitrogen or phosphorus make a river's oxygen-producing plants grow so rapidly that they become overcrowded and die of exhaustion. Then the fish also die because they are deprived of plant food. Finally various forms of bacteria decay and the water becomes putrefied.

All human industrial waste produces pollution. Excessive quantities of chemicals and minerals deposited in rivers will kill the water by destroying its oxygen content.

Some rivers flowing through industrial areas have been so changed that it is possible to set fire to them. This happened to the Cuyahoga River in Ohio in 1969.

WHAT MAKES A GLOW-WORM GLOW?

The female glow-worm is equipped with one of the most marvellous lighting systems in the world. A wingless beetle, she crawls about at night eating small insects. But on the lower side of her abdomen she possesses a "lantern" which she uses to signal to her winged mate flying above.

This "lantern" has a transparent layer of skin, like the lens of a lamp. Behind this is an oily layer of tissue which produces the light by a chemical process, and a second layer which acts as a reflector.

The glow-worm is able to control this remarkably bright light, using it only at certain times to attract a mate. In fact, the light is a sex-call, and the male has particularly large eyes to enable him to see the signal. An abundant supply of water and oxygen is needed by the glow-worm to maintain the chemical activity producing the light. For a time, even the insect's eggs are luminous.

Glow-worms, which are about half an inch long, are natives of Europe. Other beetles with built-in lighting systems are called fireflies. Both male and female fireflies have wings and use lanterns to signal to each other and to warn off night birds who seem to find them unpalatable. The most famous are the large and brilliant cucujos of tropical America. On special occasions young women fasten them to their dresses where they shine like glowing gems.

WHY DO DOGS MOULT?

Dogs normally moult every year in late spring. As the weather becomes warmer the dog's body temperature is naturally kept down by the process of shedding hair. Dogs in moult should be brushed regularly, so that the old hair does not interfere with new growth.

WHAT IS A CAMEL'S HUMP FOR?

A camel uses its hump as a portable storehouse of fat from which to draw nourishment when food is scarce. A chemical process enables the camel to convert some of this fat into water, an advantage which enables it to survive for up to 17 days in the desert without drinking.

The Arabian camel or dromedary, found in Arab countries of the Mediterranean, has only one hump. But the Bactrian camel of western Asia has two, giving it greater powers of endurance. A camel has a special way of running called "pacing", which looks like a slow run and saves energy. Yet another advantage which enables the camel to survive in regions where food is scarce is its ability to eat twigs and thorny plants which other animals would not touch.

As is the case with all animals, including human beings, the greater part of a camel's body weight consists of water. But, unlike us, this "ship of the desert" can lose up to a quarter of the water through dehydration and live to make another journey.

WHY ARE SOME MOTHS ATTRACTED BY LIGHTS?

Moths are attracted to lights at night because they mistake them for the light of the moon which they use as a means of navigation. These other lights confuse the moths and make them lose their sense of direction.

In trying to keep the artificial light at the same angle as the moon's they circle it and come closer. Collectors use this behaviour to trap moths with a special electric bulb which gives off light rich in ultra-violet rays.

The insects are extremely responsive to these rays. But they cannot see red or yellow. So by using a red light you can watch them feeding at night without disturbing them.

WHEN DO PLANTS BREATHE?

Plants breathe oxygen and carbon dioxide. In daylight they produce their own food at the same time by a process known as photosynthesis. During this process the plants release more oxygen into the atmosphere than they breathe in.

The effect of the plants' feeding and breathing system is that they exhale oxygen during the day and carbon dioxide during the night. This is the reason for the old custom in hospitals of removing plants and flowers from the wards at night and bringing them back in the morning. Without enough plants, the world's atmosphere would not be replenished with sufficient oxygen for the human race to survive.

Generally plants breathe more slowly the colder it becomes. Some plants, including many trees, go into a form of hibernation during the winter, with their breathing reduced to a minimum.

WHERE DO WHELKS LAY THEIR EGGS?

A whelk is a kind of sea-snail. It eats clams, worms, barnacles and smaller snails. The female lays her eggs in hard capsules. These are arranged in clusters of strings and attached to rock, wood, and the shells of other sea creatures.

Fishermen use whelks as bait. They catch the whelks by setting traps and baiting them with crabs.

Whelks are eaten by cod and starfish, the kind of fish that find their food at or near the bottom of the sea bed.

WHEN DOES A TREE STOP GROWING?

A tree never permanently stops growing as long as it lives. But in most countries each year's growth is ended during the cold and dry seasons. The annual period of growth depends on the climate. In moist tropical regions a tree may grow continuously.

Every period of growth is marked by an annual ring. This ring takes the form of a new layer of wood added to the width of the tree.

WHAT ARE CRUSTACEANS?

The word "crustacean" comes from the Latin *crusta* meaning a hard covering shell or crust. Apart from crabs, lobsters and shrimps, there are thousands of different crustaceans. They live in the sea, except for a few species such as the common woodlouse.

Crustaceans differ greatly in size and shape. Many of them pass through remarkable changes of form (metamorphoses) before reaching the adult stage. All of them, however, have bodies and limbs which are divided into segments. All, too, are covered with a tough, hard, lime-impregnated coat, or shell, which is pliable at the joints, so that the creature can move its limbs.

This coat, or cuticle, cannot grow to fit its wearer. As its owner grows, it is split and cast off. A new coat, still soft and pliable, has been forming underneath, and may take several days before it hardens into a truly protective shell. During this time the creature is defenceless and may fall an easy prey to any enemy.

Vast numbers of crustaceans live in the oceans. They provide food for many kinds of fish and also for the largest living mammals, the whales.

WHERE WOULD YOU FIND TRUFFLES?

If you want to sound extremely clever you can confuse your friends by telling them that the real name for truffles is Ascomycetes. That's what the botanists call them. But you're most likely to come across truffles in the very best French pâtés—for example, in the famous pâtés of the Perigord region of France.

These Perigord truffles have a distinct smell, but this is by no means unpleasant. Some truffle hunters can actually smell out the truffle in the woodlands but in France specially trained hounds with a keenly developed sense of smell are used.

Truffles look rather like large spongy walnuts and they grow under the soil. Pigs adore them. In early days pigs were turned loose in the woodlands to root for the truffles buried beneath the soil and leaves. Even today pigs are used to sniff out truffles but they certainly are not allowed to eat them, since truffles fetch high prices as a food delicacy.

The best truffles are considered to be those in the forest regions of the Dordogne area of France, where the climate is warm and moist, and there is plenty of limestone in the earth. This is one reason why Perigord, in the heart of the Dordogne, has achieved such a great reputation for fine pâtés. The most famous pâté of all —the very expensive *pâté de foie gras*—comes from Perigord.

Truffles are also found in the southern counties of France's neighbour, England. The commonest English truffle has the botanical name of *Tuber Aestivam*.

WHAT IS A FLYING FOX?

A flying fox is a kind of bat and is so called because its head somewhat resembles that of the fox. Most bats are small and look like winged mice. But flying foxes can be as big as little dogs and have a wing span of up to six feet.

Their habits are rather similar to those of ordinary bats, except that they are fond of fruit, a peculiarity which makes them great pests in orchards. Flying foxes of different species are found in Malaysia, India and other parts of Asia, and in islands of the Pacific and Indian oceans.

WHY DID THE DINOSAURS DIE OUT?

No one really knows the exact reasons for the extinction of these gigantic reptiles. But many theories have been put forward to account for the dinosaurs' disappearance at the end of what scientists call the Cretaceous Age. This was about 70 million years ago.

Great catastrophes such as floods, earthquakes and volcanic eruptions producing deadly gas and ashfalls have been suggested. But such catastrophes would have had to be almost world wide since dinosaurs were present on all continents.

Food might have been a problem, vegetation underwent great changes during that period of the earth's history. Parasites and diseases might have struck the creatures down. Perhaps the dino-

saurs, which were up to 80 feet in length and bulky in proportion, were unable to adapt themselves to the changing conditions.

The most plausible explanation may be that there was a great cooling of the climate. This would have affected the big dinosaurs much more than birds and mammals who could regulate their body temperatures.

A definite solution of the mystery of the death of the dinosaurs still seems far distant. It may have been due to a combination of some of the theories given here or of others still unknown.

Nevertheless the dinosaurs survived for more than 100 million years. We have been here for only two million years.

WHEN DO SNAKES SHED THEIR SKINS?

Snakes shed their skins when they outgrow them. This happens continually, because snakes keep growing throughout their lives, although more slowly as they get older.

The skins are discarded at regular intervals of one to three months, according to the variety of snake. During this process, which is known as sloughing, the old skin is turned back on itself, beginning at the lips and gradually revealing the new skin underneath. When sloughing has ended, the old skin will have been turned completely inside out and left in one piece.

WHY ARE THERE CLOSED SEASONS FOR GAME?

"Closed" seasons originated to ensure that a plentiful supply of game birds and animals could be guaranteed for the sportsman. The "closed" season is that part of the year when these animals and birds are protected by law and may not be shot or hunted for sport. If indiscriminate hunting was allowed during the breeding season, the survival of the species could be in danger.

The most famous game bird is perhaps the British red grouse. The date when the "open" season for shooting it begins is August 12, or the "Glorious Twelfth". The season closes on December 9. Another game bird, the partridge, is more unfortunate in Britain. Its "open" season lasts from September 1 to February 1. "Closed" seasons apply to many other wild creatures in a number of countries.

WHERE DO SALMON GO TO BREED?

Atlantic salmon, called the "greatest game fish in the world" by sportsmen, spawn in the fresh-water streams of Europe, from Portugal to northern Russia, and in the streams of the eastern seaboard of North America, from Maine up to northern Canada. They are found also in the streams of Greenland and Iceland.

Pacific salmon, of which there are several kinds, spawn in the streams of southern Alaska, British Columbia and the states of Washington and Oregon on the Pacific coast. There is also one kind which breeds in the streams of Russia's east coast.

The females spawn their thousands of eggs and the males fertilize them. Once the Pacific female salmon have spawned they die. The eggs hatch in about 19 weeks. The tiny salmon called an "alevin" hides in the gravelly bed of the stream, living at first on a large yolk-sac under its body. When about a year old it is called a "parr" and looks like a young trout. Six months later when it has a more salmony look it is called a "smolt". On reaching the sea it becomes a "grilse" until it reaches maturity.

The instinct of the salmon to head for the sea after a couple of years in fresh water is one of the great mysteries of nature. So too is its instinct, after ranging the Atlantic and Pacific Oceans and travelling up to 4,000 miles, to return to spawn in the stream where its own life began.

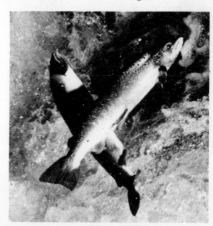

WHEN DOES APPLE SCAB OCCUR?

Apple scab occurs when an apple tree falls victim to a fungus called *Venturia Inaequalis*, a malignant growth which slowly eats away at the leaves and fruit.

It is a widespread and serious disease affecting apple trees all over the world, but is more powerful in warm climates.

Farmers control the fungus by spraying the trees with sulphur. That is one reason why apples should be washed before eating.

WHAT ARE AMPHIBIA?

The word amphibia comes from two Greek words: *amphi* meaning "of both kinds" and *bios* meaning "life". Amphibia are a class of vertebrate (back-boned) animals that can live both in water and on land. They are descended from fishes that lived more than 300 million years ago.

The first amphibia to crawl out of the water were heavily built, and slow and clumsy on land, but more active in water. They had long bodies and tails, and some developed into the highly efficient class of reptiles.

About 160 million years ago many amphibia became extinct. But a few survived to develop into the present-day frogs, toads, newts, salamanders and the worm-like caecilians.

Modern amphibia usually have moist, tough skins. They breathe partly through their skins, although they also have lungs. They usually lay their eggs in water. Here the young live, breathing chiefly through gills, until they change into their adult forms.

They eat insects, snails, worms and similar food, and are eaten by fish, snakes and birds. They are usually small. But the Giant Salamander of the Far East is 5½ feet long and the Giant Frog of west Africa grows to a mature length of almost one foot.

WHERE DO SPIDERS KEEP THEIR WEBS?

A spider does not have a ready-made web. She spins one. If you are lucky, you may be able to watch the female spider doing this.

The material that makes the thread for the spider's web is a liquid which she produces from tiny spinning tubes. These spinning tubes are to be found on small lumps on her body, known as spinnerets. As soon as the liquid comes into the air, it hardens and changes into thread.

When a spider sets out to spin a web she first uses a tough thread to build an outer frame in which she fits spokes, as in a wheel. Next she starts from the hub to weave a spiral crossing the spokes about five times, just to keep them in position. Then she begins again at the outside rim to spin a complete spiral with finer silk, cutting away the "scaffolding" as she nears the centre. Finally she constructs new support-lines for the finished web.

WHY IS THE MACHINEEL TREE DANGEROUS?

The manchineel tree is dangerous because its sap and fruit contain poison. Its other name is *Hippomane*, which comes from the Greek and means "causing horses to run mad".

The tree is a member of the Euphorbiaceae family and grows in tropical America, producing a crop of acrid, bitter apple-like fruits which drop spontaneously and carpet the ground beneath it. The sap is white and highly caustic, so that a drop on the skin produces a burning sensation and raises a blister. It used to be believed by many that to sleep beneath the tree meant certain death. But the great 18th Century naturalist Nicolas von Jacquin "reposed under it for hours at a time without inconvenience".

The wood has often been used for furniture as it is beautifully patterned in brown and white. Before felling the tree by hand, workmen light a fire round the trunk, so that the sap thickens and does not run down the handles of their axes.

WHAT IS A MUDSKIPPER?

Mudskippers are small tropical fish of the eastern Atlantic, the Indian Ocean and the western Pacific from Australia to Japan. They live in estuaries with mudbanks and also in mangrove swamps. Their eyes protrude from their heads and can be moved independently of each other. When the mud is exposed by the ebbing of the tide the mudskippers come out of the water and hunt for crustaceans and other small invertebrates. They crawl and hop about rapidly with the help of their powerful muscular pectoral fins which they use as forelegs. Their gill openings are small and they can live on land for hours at a time, providing the air is humid.

WHY DO LAUREL AND HOLLY TREES HAVE SHINY, WAXY LEAVES?

Laurel and holly trees have developed special kinds of leaves to seal the water inside them during the winter months.

Boths trees are evergreen. Instead of dropping all their leaves in autumn, they shed old ones and grow new ones throughout the year. In winter the soil is too cold for the trees to draw water from it through their roots. Normal leaves would continue to transpire and to give off moisture until the trees died of drought. But the special leaves of the holly and laurel hold the water. Their waxy surface and leathery texture make certain that the water is contained safely within the green tissues.

Some of the holly leaves have a further modification. On the lower branches which are within reach of browsing animals, each leaf has a series of sharp points along its edge. The higher leaves have only a single point.

People and Events

WHO WAS KUBLAI KHAN?

Kublai Khan (1216–94) was the greatest, most intelligent and most cultured of the great Mongol leaders of Asia. He became ruler over more people than had ever before acknowledged allegiance to one man.

Kublai was the grandson of Genghis Khan, the great Mongol conqueror who founded a vast empire as the leader of a horde of fierce nomadic horsemen. As a child, he formed an ambition to complete the conquest of China, started by his ancestors. This he achieved in 1279, establishing himself at Cambaluc (modern Peking), assuming the title of Emperor and founding the Yuan dynasty, which ruled China until 1368.

In his efforts to expand the empire of the Great Khan, Kublai owed much of his success to the great generalship of Bayan, his commander-in-chief. Bayan was described as "the hundred-eyed" because of his ability to see every aspect of a situation before drawing up and executing his military plans. Kublai also hoped to conquer Japan, but the Mongols, though wonderful troops on horseback, were bad sailors and the attempted invasion ended in disaster. Nevertheless, his dominions stretched across Asia from the Arctic Ocean to the Malay Peninsula and from Korea to Asia Minor and the border of Hungary.

Kublai Khan adopted the Chinese way of life and made Buddhism the state religion. Throughout his lands the barriers came down and the highways were opened to the spread of commerce and knowledge between East and West. His fame attracted scholars, merchants, adventurers and envoys from many countries to the Chinese capital. Among them was the Venetian traveller Marco Polo who spent 17 years in the service of the Khan, and whose book describing the splendours of Kublai's court fired the imagination of much later explorers and led eventually to the discovery of America.

*David Bushnell's remarkable
submarine "Turtle".*

I Entry hatch **O** Water ballast **N** Water inlet **P,Q** Water outlets and pumps
E Screw propeller for forward movement **F** Screw propeller for vertical move-
ment **G** Rudder **C,D** Indicator for angle of dive **L** Breathing snorkel **M** Ventilator
S Mine **T** Trigger charge **R** Screw for fixing mine to ship's bottom **A,B** Ballast

WHEN WERE SUBMARINES FIRST USED?

The first submarine which we know to have been used was built by a Dutchman, Cornelius van Drebel, in 1620. It was constructed of greased leather stretched over a wooden frame and was propelled by oars extended through the sides and sealed with tight-fitting leather flaps. Hand vices were employed to contract the sides of the vessel and reduce its volume, thus causing it to submerge. King James I of England is said to have gone for a ride in it, 12 to 15 feet below the surface of the River Thames.

But the first use of a submarine as a weapon occurred during the American War of Independence. In 1776 the Turtle, a one-man wooden submarine with a screw propeller, invented by an American, David Bushnell, tried unsuccessfully to sink a British man-of-war in New York harbour.

Attempts to build an underwater craft were made as far back as the days of ancient Greece. But practical designs had to wait for the invention of the internal combustion engine and the electric motor at the end of the 19th Century. The first truly successful submarine to travel under the sea in rough weather was the Argonaught, a 36-foot, cigar-shaped vessel built by an American, Simon Lake, in 1897.

WHAT IS THE BAYEUX TAPESTRY?

The Bayeux Tapestry, an ancestor of the strip cartoon, is an embroidery showing, on a continuous linen band over 230 feet long, details of the invasion of England by William the Conqueror in 1066.

Its manufacture was probably ordered by William's half-brother Odo, Bishop of Bayeux, who is pictured on it. The tapestry's existence is first recorded in 1476. It was produced once a year as a decoration in Bayeux Cathedral. The first reproduction dates from 1730.

There is general agreement that the tapestry, in worsted wool of eight colours, was made soon after the Conquest. Its description of events tallies well with what is known of the Battle of Hastings.

The tapestry is also noted for its decorative borders, which include figures from Aesop's fables, and farming and hunting scenes.

WHEN WERE DUCKING STOOLS IN USE?

Ducking stools first came into use as a punishment for women at the beginning of the 17th Century and were used in England as late as the beginning of the 19th. A ducking stool was a wooden armchair fastened to the end of a long wooden beam fixed like a seesaw on the edge of a river or pond. Sometimes it was mounted on wheels so that it could be pushed through the streets.

The stool was used to punish nagging wives, witches and prostitutes. An iron band kept the victim from falling out of the chair when it was plunged under the water. It was the duty of magistrates to order the number of duckings a woman should be given.

WHO WAS HEREWARD THE WAKE?

Hereward the Wake, who lived in the latter part of the 11th Century, was the great hero of Saxon resistance to the Norman occupation of England after the conquest of 1066.

Defeat at the Battle of Hastings ended the Saxons' resistance as a kingdom. But from 1067 to 1071 there was constant guerrilla fighting. A group of resistance fighters, headed by Hereward in the fens of East Anglia, harried and taunted the Normans. In 1070 a Danish fleet in the Humber sent detachments of soldiers to the fens, and Hereward led them and his own men to Peterborough. After looting the town the Danes sailed away, but Hereward and his men remained at the Isle of Ely.

William the Conqueror blocked off every outlet on the east of the island and constructed a bridge, two miles long, on the western side. Most of the rebels surrendered, but Hereward escaped through the fens. Tradition has it that the king was merciful to the outlaws, and that later Hereward swore fealty to him of his own free will.

WHERE WAS JOAN OF ARC BURNED TO DEATH?

Joan of Arc, the peasant girl who led the French to victory at Orleans and Charles VII to his coronation at Rheims, was burned to death as a heretic by the English on May 31, 1431, in the Place du Vieux Marché in Rouen. Her great heroism and leadership, which she claimed to be inspired by the voices of three saints, played a decisive part in the revival of France at the crisis of the Hundred Years War against the English invaders.

Joan was born in 1412 at Domrémy, a village between Champagne and Lorraine on the banks of the Meuse. She led cattle to pasture and sang and danced with the other village girls until, at the age of 13, she began to hear voices and see visions. Later these voices urged her to go to Orleans and raise the siege of the city. With the approval of the Church she entered Orleans and defeated the besieging English.

After a famous battle at Patay in June, 1429, in which Joan led the French to a great victory, she persuaded Charles the Dauphin to go to Rheims where he was crowned king. Joan, the Maid of Orleans, stood near the altar during the ceremony, holding her banner aloft.

The Maid was captured by the Burgundians in a skirmish on May 30, 1430, and handed over to the Bishop of Beauvais. After an inquisition by the Church she was delivered to the English. To the very last moment of her ordeal she claimed that her voices were sent to her by God. The executioner later said that her heart would not burn and that he had found it intact in the ashes. This story became part of her legend.

WHEN DID THE VIKINGS REACH AMERICA?

The Vikings discovered America about the year 1000, more than four centuries before Christopher Columbus was born. They were sea adventurers from Scandinavia who left their homes in search of conquest and plunder.

Information about the Viking discoveries comes from two sagas, or narrative ballads, the *Saga of Eric the Red* and the *Saga of the Greenlanders*. These differ considerably, but it seems possible that Bjarni Herjolfsson discovered North America in 986, when driven off course on a voyage from Iceland to Greenland. About 1000, Leif Ericsson sailed west from Greenland and gave the names Helluland, Markland and Vinland to sections of the American coast as he moved south.

The so-called Vinland Map, discovered and published in 1965, dates from 1431–1449 and supports the theory that Herjolfsson originally discovered America. In 1961, a Viking-style settlement was discovered at L'Anse au Meadow, Newfoundland. The Vinland Map itself is now held by some experts to be a clever fake.

WHO KILLED JULIUS CAESAR?

Julius Caesar, generally regarded as the greatest genius of ancient Rome, was murdered on March 15, 44 B.C., by a band of aristocrats who were members of the Senate, or ruling assembly, and were opposed to his one-man system of government.

Caesar, who was 58, had reached a position of dominance in the republic of Rome after a brilliant career as soldier, writer, scholar and administrator. Throughout his life he had seen the state torn by revolution and civil war, and an outworn system of government made powerless by the quarrels of rival claimants to power. In 49 B.C. he embarked on a series of campaigns to gain absolute control, succeeding five years later in being proclaimed dictator for life with the title of Imperator.

More than 50 members of the senatorial party, united by a mixture of selfish and patriotic motives conspired to kill him. Marcus Junius Brutus, who seems to have been a true patriot and had been forgiven by Caesar for fighting against him, was persuaded to lead the conspiracy by the real instigator, Cassius Longinus. Despite a number of attempts to warn him, Caesar took his place in the Senate House on the fateful day of March 15, called by the Romans the Ides of March.

Plutarch, the Greek historian, tells how the conspirators crowded about Caesar, pretending to make a petition. One of them, Metillius Cimber, then gave the signal for the attack and another, Casca, stabbed Caesar in the neck. The others struck at him with their swords, but Caesar continued to struggle until he saw Brutus joining in the attack. Then he fell dying from 23 wounds at the foot of the monument to Pompey, his great military rival whom he had defeated on his way to power.

But the assassins failed to save the republic. Brutus and Cassius committed suicide after being defeated in battle and in 31 B.C. the Roman Empire was founded under Augustus, Julius Caesar's nephew.

WHEN WAS JESUS CHRIST BORN?

Although the Christian calendar is nominally dated from the year of Christ's birth, modern researchers have placed the actual year between 4 and 7 B.C. When the calendar was changed the monk Dionysius Exiguus (500–600) set the date of "the incarnation of the Lord" as the year 753 after the founding of the city of Rome. But his arithmetic was inaccurate.

The Gospels say that Jesus was born while Herod was on the throne, and Herod died about 749, according to the Roman calendar, or about 4 B.C. Also the census mentioned by St Luke as the reason why Joseph and Mary travelled to Bethlehem seems to have been held in the Roman year 747, or 6 B.C.

WHERE ARE THE HEIGHTS OF ABRAHAM?

These cliffs are one of the outstanding natural features of the city of Quebec in Canada and were the scene of a famous battle.

Major-General James Wolfe (1727–59) was only 32 years old when commanded by the British Prime Minister, William Pitt, to capture Quebec from the French during the Seven Years' War (1756–63). The capture of the city lying on the banks of the St Lawrence River in eastern Canada, would open the way for the overthrow of the French forces in North America.

For three months in the summer of 1759, Wolfe attempted to overcome the French by frontal attack from across the river, but the defenders held an almost impregnable position. Wolfe decided to make an attack from the rear. In the early, dark hours of September 13, he led his army across the river above the town and surprised the French soldiers guarding the small cove which now bears his name.

Then came the highly dangerous task of scaling the cliffs–the Heights of Abraham. By sunrise Wolfe and his army of 4,000 had achieved their goal and were on the Plains of Abraham, drawn up in battle array and ready for battle.

Before Wolfe's audacious plan had been carried to its successful conclusion, both Wolfe and the great French commander, Montcalm, lay dying on the battlefield. Knowing that success was his, Wolfe whispered, "I die contented". On the other hand, when told that he was fatally wounded, Montcalm cried out: "Thank God! I shall not live to see the surrender of Quebec."

WHERE WAS KARL MARX BURIED?

Karl Marx was buried in Highgate Cemetery in North London on 17 March, 1883. On his gravestone are carved these sentences from his works:

"The philosophers have only interpreted the world in various ways; the point, however, is to change it."

"Workers of all lands, unite."

Karl Marx had German-Jewish parents. He started work as a journalist, after attending university in Bonn, Berlin and Jena where he studied law, philosophy and history. When he was 25 his newspaper was closed down, and he left Germany in search of freedom. After being expelled from France he went to Brussels where with Frederick Engels he wrote *The Communist Manifesto*.

He eventually settled in England, where he lived with his family in poverty in Soho, London. It was here that he wrote his classic work *Das Kapital*, which describes in an historical setting the working of the capitalist system and what Marx felt would be its ultimate evolution into control of all the means of production and supply by the workers.

WHO WAS "STONEWALL" JACKSON?

Thomas Jonathan Jackson (1824–63), who came to be known as "Stonewall" Jackson, was a general with the Conferate Army in the American Civil War, which lasted from 1861 to 1865.

He graduated from the United States Military Academy in 1846, served as a major during the Mexican War and then became professor of artillery tactics and natural philosophy at the Virginia Military Institute, where he won a reputation for eccentricity. He was also deeply religious and was mockingly called "Deacon" Jackson.

At the outbreak of the Civil War in 1861, he offered his services to the state of Virginia and was commissioned as a brigadier-general. His nickname "Stonewall" was earned at the Battle of Bull Run. A strong Union assault threw some of the Confederate soldiers into confusion, and one of their officers calmed them with the words: "There stands Jackson like a stone wall! Rally behind the Virginians!"

Jackson was made a major-general and took command of the Confederate forces in the Shenandoah valley, where he demonstrated his brilliance as a field tactician. Although outnumbered, he defeated the Union forces at Winchester in 1862, and prevented the main enemy forces uniting.

He became the greatest of the officers under General Robert E. Lee's command and fought in the battles of Antietam and Fredericksburg. After forcing a Union retreat at Chancellorsville in 1863, he was accidentally wounded by one of his own men and died shortly afterwards.

WHAT IS THE MAFIA?

The Mafia, a criminal society, originated in Sicily when the large landowners put their estates into the hands of ruffianly "security men" during the disturbances which followed Napoleon's invasion of Italy. These men terrorized the peasantry, and finally turned on the landowners.

Their principles were never to appeal to the law and never to help in the detection of crime. By faithfully following their savage code, the Mafia soon became powerful not only in the country but in the towns. Successive Italian governments tried in vain to suppress it.

With European emigration to the United States during the last century, an organization similar to the Mafia came into being there, with the familiar set-up of ruling families, infiltration of society, protection rackets, and bloody acts of vendetta and revenge.

Its heyday was probably the Prohibition era. But it is still believed to exert considerable influence in American life.

WHY WAS WHITNEY'S COTTON GIN IMPORTANT?

Whitney's cotton gin was exceedingly important as it more than trebled the amount of cotton which could be picked free of seeds in a day. This stimulated the extension of the cotton plantations and the growth of Negro slavery in the south of the United States. In that way the cotton gin was in-directly responsible for the American Civil War.

Eli Whitney (1765–1825) was born in Westboro, Massachusetts. After graduating from Yale College in 1792, he became aware of the need for a machine which would separate cotton from its seeds. The Industrial Revolution was in full flood and inventions such as John Kay's flying shuttle (1733) and James Hargreaves's spinning jenny (1769) had created a growing demand for raw cotton as the production of finished goods was now so much faster and easier.

Whitney produced, in only a few weeks, a hand-operated machine or gin, and by April 1793 had built a machine that could clean 50 pounds of cotton fibres a day. It consisted of a wooden cylinder encircled by rows of slender spikes, set half an inch apart, which extended between the bars of a grid set so closely together that the seeds could not pass, although the lint was pulled through by the revolving spikes. A revolving brush cleaned the spikes and the seeds fell into another compartment.

The gin was immediately in great demand. Country blacksmiths helped to fulfil the orders when the factory Whitney set up at New Haven, Connecticut, was unable to cope with all the orders. In the South, almost the whole region was given over to cotton growing, increasing the value of slaves and reinforcing the slave system, which had been declining.

HOW DID HOUDINI GET FREE FROM HIS CHAINS?

Harry Houdini (1874–1926), a famous escapologist, had many methods of freeing himself from chains and other forms of restraint. Some of them remain secret even today.

One of his secrets was an ability to expand his muscles to an abnormal degree so that, when he relaxed them, chains that had seemed to be bound tightly round him became comparatively loose. An authority on the mechanism of all kinds of locks, he knew many different ways of opening them. Also, he was amazingly agile, having begun his performing career as a circus acrobat.

Houdini publicly claimed that he could not be injured by a blow to the abdomen. But he died from peritonitis after a blow ruptured his appendix. He was struck unexpectedly by a college student who did not realize that Houdini had first to steel himself to withstand the blow.

WHERE WAS CUSTER'S LAST STAND?

"General" Custer made his famous last stand on the banks of the Little Big Horn river near what is now the interchange for United States Highways 87 and 212, in the State of Montana. Today the Custer Battlefield National Monument marks the scene of the battle.

George Armstrong Custer, born in 1839, was called "General" by the men of the 7th Cavalry Brigade under his command. He had shown his brilliance as a cavalry officer in the American Civil War (1861–65) reaching the rank of major-general.

In 1876 when Sioux and Cheyennes were on the warpath with Chief Sitting Bull as their leader, Custer and his 7th Cavalry Brigade were under the command of General Terry. The brigade of 655 men was ordered by Terry to advance towards the Indians, but not to attack until the rest of the army—composed of three columns under General Crook, Gibbon and Terry—had moved into position.

Custer reached the Little Big Horn to see the large Indian camp on the opposite side of the river. For a reason that will never be known, Custer decided to disobey orders and attack. Dividing his brigade into three, he sent Major Reno and Captain Benteen, each with three companies, to attack the flanks. At the same time he led 264 troopers on a frontal approach across the river.

His force stood no chance when the Indians attacked. The troopers dismounted from their horses to seek cover, but there was none. When the Indians drove off their horses, the troopers' fate was sealed.

Believing that Reno and Benteen would soon come to their aid, they fought bravely, but the flank attacks had been foiled and the cavalry put to flight. Custer and 264 men fought to the last man.

WHY IS AMERICA SO CALLED?

America gets its name from the traditional family name Amerigo belonging to Amerigo Vespucci (1454–1512), who was an Italian navigator and merchant.

The period during which he made his voyages falls between 1497 and 1504. The first took place in 1499–1500 when, it is believed, he discovered the mouth of the Amazon and sailed as far as the Cape of La Consolación or Säo Agostinho (about 6° latitude South). On the way back he reached Trinidad and then made for Haiti, believing all the time that he was sailing along the coast of the extreme easterly peninsula of Asia.

At the end of 1500, under the auspices of the Portuguese government, he reached the coast of Brazil and discovered the Plate river. This voyage was of tremendous importance in that Vespucci became convinced, and convinced others, that the newly discovered lands were not part of Asia, but a New World.

In 1507, a humanist scholar named Waldseemüller suggested that the newly discovered world should be named America, after Amerigo. The extension of the name to North America came later.

Amerigo Vespucci

64

WHEN WERE KINGS THOUGHT TO BE GODS?

Throughout history, kings have often been supposed to enjoy a special relationship with the gods of their people, and in many cases, have been regarded as gods themselves.

In ancient Egypt, the king or pharaoh was believed to be divine and the Hittite kings were deified after their deaths. The Minoan kings of Crete were identified with the bull-headed sun god. In many primitive tribes in Asia and Africa, the king was identified with the sacred and divine animal of his tribe. The Swedes and Prussians of pagan Europe had divine kings, and the rulers of the Aztecs in Mexico and the Incas in Peru were, if not gods themselves, considered to be direct descendants.

Alexander the Great (356–323 B.C.), who had himself declared a god in the last year of his life, was followed by a number of god-kings throughout the Near East. In the Roman Empire the practice of making the emperor a god originated when Julius Caesar was pronounced *divus Julius* after his death. The Byzantine emperors were venerated as God's representative on earth.

The Japanese emperor was thought of as supernatural in some degree, but their term "kami", usually translated as "god", does not have such an all-embracing meaning as in the West. In China kings interceded with the gods for their people.

WHERE DID NOAH'S ARK COME TO REST?

After seven months afloat Noah came to rest, the Bible tells us, "upon the mountains of Ararat". Mount Ararat, an extinct volcanic massif 17,160 feet high consists of two peaks seven miles apart and separated by a saddle 8,800 feet above sea level. It stands in Turkish territory overlooking the point where the frontiers of Turkey, Iran and Soviet Armenia converge, and is about 25 miles in diameter.

The story of the Ark is still a living tradition among the Armenians, who believe themselves to be the first race of men to appear in the world after the Deluge. Local legend maintains that the remains of the Ark were long to be seen on top of the mountain. Near the foot of a mountain chasm stood the village of Aghuri, where, according to tradition, Noah built his altar and made sacrifice after his safe deliverance, and where he planted his vineyard. The village was destroyed by earthquake in 1840. A Persian legend refers to Ararat as the cradle of the human race; the Persian name for it is Koh-i-Nuh, meaning Noah's Mountain.

For centuries the Armenians believed that God forbade anyone to reach the top of Ararat and view the remains of the Ark. However, on September 7, 1829, Johann Hacob von Parrot (1792–1840), a German in the Russian service, made the first successful ascent known. Since then the mountain has been climbed many times.

WHAT IS THE MAGNA CARTA?

Magna Carta is the great charter of English liberty granted by King John in 1215 at Runnymede, near Windsor. It was reissued with some alterations in 1216 and again with further changes in 1217. In 1225 King Henry III reissued it and it is this document that is the Magna Carta of English law and history.

King John had quarrelled with the Church, barons, merchants and eventually the whole nation. Magna Carta, produced by Stephen Langton, Archbishop of Canterbury, insisted that the King should obey that law.

The Charter asserted the right to personal liberty and to property; protested against punishment administered without trial; required that justice should be properly administered and that there should be a right to free trial.

HOW DID SUFFRAGETTES GET THEIR NAME?

The Suffragettes were given that name by a newspaper reporter who wrote that not only did the members of the Women's Social and Political Union *want* female suffrage, or the right to vote, but that they meant to *get* it. The name was accepted immediately, perhaps because words ending in "ette" often denoted something feminine.

The greatest leader of the suffragette movement was Emmeline Pankhurst (1858–1928), who founded the WSPU in 1903. The question of women's right to vote had been raised already by Keir Hardie, Philip Snowden and George Lansbury. In 1905 two suffragettes, Christabel Pankhurst (Emmeline's daughter) and Annie Kenney were roughly handled at a Liberal meeting in Manchester and then arrested as they tried to address the crowd outside. They chose to serve a prison sentence and thereby aroused attention all over the world.

Suffragettes persistently lobbied Members of Parliament, one of whom, Bamford Slack, agreed to introduce a Bill in Parliament. He was prevented from doing so by other MPs prolonging the previous debate. The suffragettes decided on militant action. They were ill-treated, abused, arrested and sent to prison, where they went on hunger strike because they were not treated as political prisoners. They lost some public sympathy by the violence of their demonstrations, which included smashing windows and slashing pictures in public galleries.

Seven suffrage Bills were defeated in Parliament, but gradually public support increased and hundreds of thousands of pounds were given to the movement.

In 1918 Lloyd George's government sponsored the Representation of the People Act, which gave the vote to married women, women householders and women university graduates over 30. Ten years later women voters were given equality with men.

WHY DID THE BRITISH EMPIRE BREAK UP?

It is possible to list at least four basic forces which brought about the dissolution of the British Empire. First, both Britain and her colonies recognized that some kind of self-government was necessary in territories which were separated by thousands of miles from Britain. Administration centred in London was increasingly difficult and expensive.

Secondly, the colonies themselves began to chafe against British rule and to demand to manage their own affairs. A note of aggressive nationalism entered into the appeals for self-government.

In the third place, individual British colonies and other nations began to forge economic, social and political links. Two world wars also greatly reduced Britain's power in the world and made some colonies look elsewhere for leadership.

Finally, many Britons themselves realized that the Empire had become unwieldly and that relationships within it were a handicap rather than a gain.

Nevertheless, there was not a complete break up but the growth of an association of independent nations called the Commonwealth. There were three bonds which united the association. The close economic relationship of trade, labour and capital; the acceptance of many Commonwealth countries of British social, economic, educational, political, military and legal institutions and customs; and the savings that could be made in the member countries by acceptance of British military and diplomatic services.

HOW DID GRANDMA MOSES BECOME FAMOUS?

Grandma Moses (1860–1961) became famous as a painter when she held her first exhibition at the age of 78. She was then "discovered" by a collector, Louis J. Calder, and became internationally known as a modern "primitive", a self-taught naïve painter.

Anna Mary Robertson was born in Greenwich, New York, of Scottish-Irish descent. At the age of 58 she decided to start painting and chose scenes from her childhood, which she presented in bright, uncomplicated colours and peopled with her memories.

In 1940, when she was 80, she had her first solo exhibition in New York and nine years later was received at the White House by President Truman. In 1960 Governor Rockefeller proclaimed her birthday, September 7, as Grandma Moses Day in New York State.

Her works were reproduced on Christmas cards, calendars and birthday cards and became immensely popular because of their simplicity and directness and the faithfulness and love with which they recorded humble scenes now vanished from the American way of life.

First journey

Santa Maria

WHERE DID CHRISTOPHER COLUMBUS LAND?

Christopher Columbus, on his famous voyage of 1492, made landfall after nine weeks at sea on an island he named San Salvador—now also known as Watling Island—in the Bahamas.

Columbus, a Genoese, set sail with three ships, the Santa Maria, the Pinta and the Nina, under the patronage of King Ferdinand and Queen Isabella of Spain. This voyage was the first of his attempts to find a sea route to Asia.

After leaving San Salvador, Columbus discovered the island of Cuba and then Haiti, where he left some members of his crews garrisoning a fort called La Navidad. His flagship had been wrecked and there was not enough room on the remaining two ships to take all the men home.

Believing that he had reached Asia, Columbus returned to Spain where he was given a great reception. He came back with some "Indians" to show at court and evidence of the existence of gold in the New World.

On his last voyage in 1502, Columbus reached Honduras. After much hardship, he returned to Spain in 1504 and died in 1506, an impoverished and broken man.

WHERE WAS THE KLONDIKE?

The Klondike was–and still is–in remote north-western Canada on the borders of Alaska. This area is now part of the Yukon Territory. Dawson, once the capital of the Klondike, lies on the bank of the Yukon river.

For a time Dawson was a bustling town of 10,000 people. Now the population has dwindled to less than 1,000. But there is much less gold than there was at the beginning of the century, and it was only the promise of gold that persuaded people to live so far north in such frozen wastes. For in the streams and creeks of the area the gravel was rich in gold.

At the peak of the Gold Rush in the Klondike more than 30,000 newcomers arrived in four years. In 1900 gold worth more than $22 million was found in the region. Only six years later little more than $5 million in gold was found.

Gold production still continues there. But since the remaining gold is underground and almost all the ground is frozen, mining is today a most expensive and very difficult operation. The glorious days of the Klondike are only a memory.

WHY IS TEXAS CALLED THE LONE STAR STATE?

Texas is called the "Lone Star State" because for almost ten years, from 1836 until its annexation by the United States in 1845, the country was independent.

For three centuries up to 1821, Texas and Mexico had belonged to Spain. In all that time, Spain had shown hardly any interest in this vast territory which is equal in size to the total area of France, Belgium, the Netherlands and Denmark combined. When Mexico gained her independence, Texas was peopled by no more than 7,000 and with only three settlements large enough to be called towns. Beset with her own problems of administration and revolts, Mexico allowed American families to colonize land in Texas.

By 1835 there were around 30,000 Americans settled in Texas, outnumbering the Mexicans by four to one. Too late for her own interests, Mexico tried to discipline the American Texans by abolishing slavery, levying duties and establishing military garrisons. Fighting broke out when martial law was declared by the Mexicans who tried to disarm the Texans. On October 2, 1835, the Texans won the first battle of the Texas revolution at Gonzales. San Antonio was captured in December and the Mexicans withdrew to Mexico.

The Texans were weakened by arguments and lack of unity which allowed the Mexicans to recapture San Antonio on March 2, 1836, but while the Mexicans closed in on the Alamo, Texas declared her independence. The new nation found this independence difficult to manage and was relieved to be annexed in 1845 by a rather unwilling United States of America.

WHO PUT HIS TELESCOPE TO HIS BLIND EYE?

When Admiral Horatio Nelson, Britain's greatest naval hero, was given the signal to retreat at the Battle of Copenhagen in 1801, he put his telescope to his blind eye and remarked: "I really do not see the signal." The battle continued until the Danes were forced to agree to a truce that put an end to Napoleon's hope of overthrowing British naval supremacy.

This event in the Napoleonic War occurred after Tsar Paul I, an ally of Napoleon, had formed an "armed neutrality" against the British with Denmark, Sweden and Prussia. A British fleet under Admiral Sir Hyde Parker, with Nelson as second-in-command, was sent to attack the Danish fleet lying at anchor a mile off Copenhagen in the narrow sound between Denmark and Sweden.

Faced with 40 enemy ships-of-the-line in a strong defensive position protected by shore batteries, Parker agreed that Nelson should open the battle with 12 ships-of-the-line and a number of smaller vessels. While Parker waited at the entrance to the sound, Nelson sailed through the tortuous channels between the sandbanks. The fighting began at 10 am on April 2, and was carried on by both sides with great courage and stubbornness. At 1 pm Parker saw that Nelson's force was in great danger and hoisted signal 39—an order to break off the action.

Nelson's reaction was typical: "Leave off action! No, damn me, if I do!" Turning to his captain he remarked: "You know, Foley, I have only one eye. I have a right to be blind sometimes." After pretending not to see the signal, he remarked: "Damn the signal! Keep mine for closer battle flying. That's the way I answer such signals. Nail mine to the mast." After considerable losses on both sides, the Danes accepted the offer of a truce which effectively ended the threat to Britain of the Northern Alliance.

Some experts believe that there was an understanding between Parker and Nelson, also known to Foley, whereby Nelson would be allowed to use his own judgement even if officially ordered to stop fighting.

WHEN WAS THE FIRST HISTORY BOOK WRITTEN?

Herodotus, a Greek author, known as the "father of history" was born some time in the 5th Century B.C. His book *History*, describing the wars between Greece and Persia, is generally considered to be the first deliberate attempt to see the events of the time against a historical background.

"I am giving," he says in his opening words, "the results of my inquiries (*historiai*) so that the memory of what men have done shall not perish from the world nor their achievements, whether of Greeks or of foreigners, go unsung. They form my theme, and the cause why they went to war."

HOW IS THE ARCHBISHOP OF CANTERBURY CHOSEN?

The Archbishop of Canterbury is appointed by the Crown, that is to say by the sovereign acting upon the advice of the Prime Minister. He is then elected by the chapter of Canterbury Cathedral, who represent the clergy of the diocese. After this election has been confirmed by legal representatives of the diocese, he is consecrated as archbishop, and pays homage to the sovereign for the possessions of his province. Finally the new archbishop is enthroned in the cathedral.

As the Primate of the Church of England, the Archbishop of Canterbury takes precedence over all the nobility, except those of royal blood. It is he who places the crown on the sovereign's head at the coronation.

The province of Canterbury has three dioceses, each administered by a bishop. The amount of authority that the Archbishop has over his bishops is not clearly defined, but experts in church law maintain that he must accept their majority decision.

WHAT IS THE KU-KLUX-KLAN?

This was an underground organization started in the South after the American Civil War to keep down the negro population and resist the expected exploitation by the North.

It sprang from a Tennessee social club, which based its name on the Greek *kyklos*, a circle. The young members used to ride about on horses at night, dressed in flowing white gowns, to frighten the newly-freed slaves and to amuse themselves.

Fanatics turned this amusement into "the invisible Empire of the South", a secret society of terror, indulging in murder and kidnapping. Laws were passed to suppress it, and Klansmen were imprisoned, to be greeted as heroes on their release.

The KKK was revived in 1915 as a general ragbag for all manner of intolerance, but it faded with the Depression of the 1930s, though it is still active today.

WHO WAS THE LORD PROTECTOR?

Lord Protector of the Commonwealth of England, Scotland and Ireland was the title assumed by Oliver Cromwell (1599–1658), the man who, above all others, brought about the downfall and execution of Charles I.

Cromwell was born at Huntingdon, the son of a Protestant family who had acquired lands at the time of the Reformation. When he was 29 he entered the House of Commons. Sir Philip Warwick gave this description of him at that time: "His stature was of a good size; his sword close to his side; his countenance swoln and reddish; his voice sharp and untuneable; and his eloquence full of fervour." He proved an active and determined member, remarkable for his Puritan enthusiasm.

When civil war between Charles and Parliament broke out in 1642, Cromwell returned home and set about raising a well-disciplined cavalry regiment of "God-fearing men" who became famous as the Ironsides and proved their worth in the defeat of Prince Rupert at the Battle of Marston Moor on July 2, 1644. A year later he was second-in-command at the decisive Battle of Naseby when the New Model Army, largely based on the principles of Cromwell's Ironsides, crushed the royalist forces.

After Charles's surrender Cromwell was the man chiefly responsible for the trial, condemnation and execution of the King. By his successful military campaigns against the Scots and the Irish, he forced them to submit to Parliament's authority, but when Parliament quarrelled with the Army Cromwell dismissed it in 1653 and assumed the title of Lord Protector.

After Cromwell's death in 1658, the title passed for a few months to his son Richard, a weak man powerless to resist the tide of reaction then setting in. In 1660 the Stuart dynasty was restored in the person of Charles II. Cromwell's remains were removed from Westminster Abbey, hung up in chains like the body of a common criminal and buried beneath the scaffold at Tyburn.

WHERE DID THE DALAI LAMA LIVE?

The first Dalai Lama, head of an order of Buddhist Monks in Tibet, lived in the Tashilhumpo monastery, which he founded. He died in 1474, and was called Dge-'dun-grub-pa.

Since then, there have been many Dalai Lamas. Most of them have had both political and religious power. The fifth Dalai Lama moved his residence to Lhasa, where he had an enormous palace built, called the Potala. From there Tibet was governed by him and his descendants.

In 1959, the Dalai Lama had to flee to India, because he was thrown out of Tibet by the Chinese Communists.

HOW DID PITT THE YOUNGER BECOME FAMOUS?

Britain's youngest prime minister was William Pitt (1759–1806). He accepted the post on December 19th, 1783, when he was 24, having refused the office when it was offered to him at the age of 23.

William Pitt the Younger–so called to distinguish him from his father, who was also a famous statesman–freed British trade from many restrictions and re-modelled the system of taxation. He introduced Income Tax, for a short time, at two shillings in the pound.

During the Napoleonic Wars which began in 1793 Pitt showed qualities of determination and en-durance which helped to save Britain from imminent invasion and probable defeat. At the same time he controlled industrial unrest.

Pitt resigned in 1801, when George III refused to grant eman-cipation to the Roman Catholics in Ireland. When Britain was again threatened with invasion by Napo-leon in 1804, he was recalled to direct the country's affairs. But the strain at last proved too much for his frail body, and he died at the age of 46, three months after the Battle of Trafalgar.

WHERE DID BUDDHA LIVE?

Buddha's full name was Gautama Buddha, and he lived in north-east India. He was born into a warrior tribe called the Sakyas in the 6th Century B.C. and became the founder of the religion called Buddhism.

Although he was of noble birth, Buddha was not proud and fond of luxury. Even when young, he was serious and thought a great deal. He decided it was better to lead a humble, religious life.

When he was 29, he left his home and became a monk. He found strength in quiet meditation. He saw that the world was full of suffering, and wanted to help people. So he became a wandering teacher.

Buddha gave his first sermon at Benares on the River Ganges. Here, he outlined the beliefs which have guided Buddhists ever since. Buddha said first of all that worldly life cannot give final happiness. You should not be either completely self-indulgent or too strict with yourself. You should try to follow a middle path, maintaining inner peace and dis-cipline. A Buddhist's final spiritual goal is a blissful state called Nirvana, in which he is completely calm and free from any pain or anxiety.

The name Buddha means "The Enlightened One". He died near Benares when he was 80. By then he had organized a community of monks, called the Sangha, to carry on his teachings.

The main countries where Buddhism is practised are Burma, Thailand, Ceylon and Japan. There are about 177,000 Buddhists in North America.

WHEN DID WEST POINT START?

West Point, the United States military academy for the training of regular army officers was established on March 16, 1802 at West Point on the Hudson River about 50 miles north of the city of New York. The place was already famous as the scene, 22 years earlier, of a dramatic incident in the War of Independence, when the traitor Benedict Arnold failed in an attempt to betray the strategically important position to the British.

Three chief reasons for the formation of the academy were: first, the fact that in the War of Independence the United States had been forced to rely on foreign military technicians; second, the belief of army leaders, including George Washington, that military techniques must be studied and not acquired solely through experience; third, the desire of some reformers for a new approach to the education of officers.

In 1812 the academy, which had been training only engineers, was reorganized and given more scope. In 1866 an Act of Congress was passed to allow the selection of an academy superintendent who was not an engineer.

West Point is under the direct control of the army and the four-year course of instruction leads to a science degree and a commission of second lieutenant in the regular army. Studies are balanced between mathematics and engineering sciences (55 per cent) and the humanities and social sciences (45 per cent). The 3,100 cadets must be between 17 and 22 years old and unmarried, with a high school education. Aptitude tests and a medical examination must be passed before admission.

WHERE DID NAPOLEON GO AFTER WATERLOO?

On July 15, 1815, after his defeat at Waterloo, Napoleon surrendered to the British and was exiled to the remote island of St Helena in the South Atlantic, 1,200 miles off the African coast.

The actual surrender was made to Captain Maitland of the British frigate Bellerophon. Napoleon was transferred to the Northumberland and then taken to St Helena.

This island is only $10\frac{1}{2}$ miles long and $6\frac{1}{2}$ miles wide. Napoleon had no force at his disposal, as he did on the Mediterranean island of Elba, where he was given sovereignty during his first exile.

He was to spend six years on the island before his death. He frequently quarrelled with Sir Hudson Lowe, the Governor, who was very conscientious at thwarting all Napoleon's hopes of escape. He never gave up these attempts, but he also found time to write his memoirs.

He died on May 5, 1821. There were rumours that he had been poisoned, but modern historians and doctors believe it is far more likely that he had cancer of the stomach.

74

WHERE DID THE QUEEN OF SHEBA LIVE?

There is a legend in Ethiopia that her emperors are descended from the Queen of Sheba and Solomon, King of Israel, who died about 937 B.C. The story relates that Aksum, the once-splendid city on the high central plateau of Ethiopia, was formerly called Sheba. It is said Queen Makeda of Aksum visited King Solomon at Jerusalem, and that their son, Menelik, became the first Ethiopian emperor.

But Aksum in the time of Solomon was probably not large enough to have a ruler of such wealth and power as the queen of the story. However, there could have been such a Queen of Sheba in the Yemen, the southern part of the Arabian peninsula.

WHAT IS HARA-KIRI?

Ceremonial suicide, or hara-kiri, was undertaken by members of the samurai (warrior) class in old Japan. Voluntary hara-kiri dated back to the 12th Century, and was committed to wipe out the dis-honour of defeat in battle, as a protest at the behaviour of a superior, and for similar reasons.

The word means "belly-cutting". If carried out according to the rules, it was a slow and extremely painful means of suicide, meant to demonstrate the military virtues of great courage and extreme self-control.

Another version of hara-kiri was observed when a samurai was

sentenced to be beheaded for a crime. To escape the shame of the common executioner, he was allowed to stab himself with a short sword. Immediately afterwards the sentenced samurai would be decapitated by a friend or relative waiting behind him.

A recent case of hara-kiri occurred on November 26, 1970, after the well-known Japanese author, Yukio Mishima, failed to incite a regiment of Japanese soldiers to join his "Association of Shields" and stage a coup d'état. Mishima, who was once mentioned as a possible Nobel Prize winner, is shown in full Samurai warrior's uniform.

WHEN WAS KEELHAULING USED FOR PUNISHMENT?

Keelhauling was first referred to as a punishment for offenders in a Dutch naval ordinance of 1560. It was carried out in the British Navy at least as early as the first half of the 17th Century.

The punishment consisted of lowering the victim down one side of the ship and dragging him under the keel to the other side.

It was never "official" in the British Navy but the Dutch retained it until 1853.

WHO SINGED THE KING OF SPAIN'S BEARD?

Sir Francis Drake (c. 1540–96), the most celebrated of the English "sea-dogs" of Queen Elizabeth I, "singed the King of Spain's beard" during a daring raid in 1587. It was Drake's own phrase for the action. He led a force of small ships into Cadiz harbour in southern Spain and burned 33 vessels and a large quantity of stores that were being prepared to take part in an invasion of England. By so doing he delayed the sailing of the Spanish Armada and gave his country an extra year to prepare for the coming attack.

When in 1588 King Philip II's navy of 132 ships did come sailing up the Channel, Drake, as vice-admiral of the English fleet, played a chief part in the running fight that drove the Spaniards to disaster. The story goes that when news of the Armada's approach reached the waiting fleet, Lord Howard of Effingham, the English commander, was playing bowls at Plymouth, Devon, with some of his captains. He was for putting to sea at once, but Drake persuaded him to wait, remarking that there was plenty of time to "finish the game and thrash the Spaniards, too".

The delay lured the Spanish ships into the trap. Next day the English ships poured out of the Channel ports to attack the rear of the Armada as it sailed eastwards in a great half-moon. After a week of harassment with the English "plucking the feathers" of the Armada one by one, the Spanish galleons anchored off Calais. But at night they were forced to put to sea when Drake sent fireships drifting down on them. Still attacked from the rear, the Spaniards decided to try to escape by sailing northwards round the British Isles. Fewer than half their ships reached Spain.

Drake was born at Tavistock in Devon but was brought up in the port of Chatham in Kent where he talked to sailors and nourished his love of the sea. One of his greatest exploits was to sail round the world (1577–80), in the *Golden Hind*, looting Spanish ships and settlements on the way. On his return he was knighted by Queen Elizabeth aboard the *Golden Hind* in the Thames at Deptford. He made many other expeditions against the Spaniards. During one of them he died of dysentery.

WHY DID THE AMERICAN CIVIL WAR START?

The American Civil War (1861–65) arose chiefly over the question of Negro slavery. In the 15th Century the Portuguese found a ready market for Negro slaves, which they captured during their expeditions along the African coasts.

As the American continent developed, these slaves were eagerly sought to labour on the cotton and tobacco plantations, in mines, or in general farm work. Between 1680 and 1786 more than 2,000,000 slaves were transported and it was not until 1833 that the United Kingdom Parliament passed an Act that set free all slaves in its territories.

In the United States the struggle between the slave-owning southern states and those of the North, where there was no slavery, was long and bitter. As the frontier moved westward, new states were seeking admission to the Union. Some had slaves and some did not.

In the north a growing party demanded immediate abolition of slavery, while in the south were some who threatened to leave the Union rather than give up their slaves. In 1860, Abraham Lincoln (1809–65) who favoured the gradual abolition of slavery, was elected President of the United States. Next year seven southern states left the Union and formed the Confederate States, with Jefferson Davis as president. On April 12, the officer in charge of Port Sumter, at Charleston, West Virginia, refused to surrender it to Confederate soldiers, who opened fire and thus began the Civil War.

Although the North had greater numbers, the South had better generals and the war dragged on for four years, with no fewer than 2,260 battles and skirmishes. In 1863, there were great victories for the North at Gettysburg and Vicksburg. It was at Gettysburg that Lincoln delivered his famous address promising freedom for all.

General Lee, commander of the Confederate armies, surrendered on April 9 at Appomatox Court House, Virginia.

WHAT WAS THE GREAT TREK?

The Great Trek is the name given to the mass exodus of Afrikaner settlers from South Africa's Cape Colony between 1835 and 1843.

In those years 12,000 "voortrekkers"–men, women and children–with their cattle, sheep and ox-waggons moved out from the Cape towards the High Veld area around the Vaal River in protest against British rule and what they regarded as the spread of "liberal" ideas.

Originally the Cape was colonized by the Dutch under the control of the Dutch East India Company. By the 1660s there were roughly 2,000 settlers in the Colony, employing more than 1,000 slaves. These settlers were mainly Dutch and German.

By the end of the 18th Century

the white population numbered about 15,000 people, who by that time had developed their own language—Afrikaans, a variety of Dutch—and their own customs. Of this white, Afrikaner, population about half were known as voortrekkers. These people lived a semi-nomadic life. They farmed wherever they could find good grazing and moved from area to area, constantly pushing forward the frontiers of white expansion.

The Cape was conquered by the British in 1795 during the Napoleonic wars. British settlers were introduced to the Colony and soon these settlers began to agitate for a more liberal administration. English became the official language and by 1838 slavery was abolished.

To the Boers this was the final straw. Declaring that the British had "placed their slaves on an equal footing with Christians, contrary to the laws of God", they decided to shake off British influence and commenced their exodus. Thousands of families moved off in their covered waggons, taking their coloured servants with them.

During their journey, the trekkers encountered fierce resistance from the native Zulu warriors. Their waggons were constantly ambushed and their leader, Piet Retief, was killed. The trekkers, however, had the advantages of rifles and superior military techniques and in 1838 defeated the Zulu at the Battle of Blood River.

The trekkers settled in the territory previously occupied by the Zulu and established a new state of their own, the Republic of Natal. But in 1842 the British took over Natal, whereupon the voortrekkers took to their waggons again and moved back north on the Vaal River. The British decided to recognize the independence of the voortrekkers who established a series of republics, including the Orange Free State.

WHERE DO THE STARS AND STRIPES COME FROM?
In the early days of the American War of Independence each state adopted a flag of its own. South Carolina had a flag of red and blue stripes adorned with rattlesnakes. That of Massachusetts bore a pine tree. Even the colours carried by different regiments differed accordingly to the taste of their commanders. This was confusing, especially at sea, where one ship might well end up firing on her own ally!

The Rhodes Island flag was the first to contain any stars. There were 13 stars representing the 13 colonies which later were to become the first members of the United States.

In 1776 Washington's new continental army displayed its flag. This time there were no stars. Still in the top left-hand corner was the British Grand Union flag, with its crosses of St George and St Andrew—a sign, one supposes, that independence was not yet the American's intention. But around the British emblem appeared the stripes: six white horizontal stripes and seven red ones, again giving the total of 13.

It was not until 1777, almost a year after the adoption of the Declaration of Independence, that Congress adopted a design for the national flag. This consisted of 13 stars (in place of the Grand Union flag) and 13 stripes, alternately red and white.

Every time a new state was accepted in the Union a new star and a new stripe would be added to the flag. By 1795 the flag was getting a little cramped; there was no room for any more stripes. So Congress decided that the flag should contain only 13 stripes representing the original states, and that a star for each new state should be added on the July 4 following its admission to the Union.

In 1959 Alaska became the 49th state and in the same year Hawaii became the 50th and most recent.

WHEN DID THE CRUSADES TAKE PLACE?

The Crusades were a series of holy wars authorized by successive Popes and waged by the Christians of western Europe from 1095 to the end of the 13th Century. Their purpose was the recovery of the Holy Sepulchre in Jerusalem and other sacred places from the Mohammedans. The word comes from the Spanish *cruzada*, meaning "marked with a cross".

There were three basic causes for the Crusades: first, the threat to pilgrims journeying to the Holy Sepulchre from the Seljuk Turks who had overrun Anatolia, Syria and Palestine; secondly, a great surge of energy in Christianized western Europe and a desire to expand territory and control trade routes; thirdly, the determination of the Church to make its authority universal.

The First Crusade, summoned by Pope Urban II in 1095, took Jerusalem by storm on July 15, 1099 and set up Christian governments in the city and in the three "Latin states" of Edessa, Antioch and Tripoli. When Edessa was captured by the Mohammedans in 1144, Pope Eugenius III called the Second Crusade (1147–1149), but this was so mismanaged that it accomplished nothing.

The recapture of Jerusalem in 1187 by the wise, brave and chivalrous Mohammedan leader Saladin gave rise to the Third Crusade (1189–1191) led by Philip the Fair of France and Richard the Lion-Hearted of England. In the Holy Land Acre was captured but the two kings quarrelled and first Philip and then Richard abandoned the struggle. The Fourth Crusade (1202–1204) never reached Palestine but instead attacked and captured the Christian city of Constantinople. The Fifth Crusade (1221) was a complete failure but on the Sixth Crusade (1228–1229) Jerusalem was obtained from the Mohammedans by negotiation. The city's capture by the Turks in 1244 brought the Seventh Crusade (1249) in which the leader King Louis IX of France was taken prisoner and ransomed. Louis also led the Eighth Crusade, this time to Tunis where he died of the plague in 1270. The knights held out in Acre until 1291 when they surrendered. Attempts to revive the Holy Wars in the 14th Century failed.

WHERE DID THE LIGHT BRIGADE CHARGE?

The famous Charge of the Light Brigade took place eight miles south of the great port of Sebastopol on the west coast of the Crimean peninsula, near the small harbour of Balaclava. During the Crimean War (1854–56), when the forces of France, Britain and Turkey fought the Russian Army, Balaclava was the Allied base. It was defended by lines of earthworks on the hills around the harbour.

On October 25, 1854, Russian forces attempted to break these lines. Over-running some Turks on the heights and seizing their guns, the Russians then descended to the plains and attacked the British forces. The British Heavy Brigade drove them back over a low ridge of hills crossing the plain.

Then occurred one of the most famous feats in the chronicles of the British Army, the Charge of the Light Brigade. Led by Lord Cardigan, 673 horsemen rode up a valley under heavy Russian fire. They charged a mile and a half up the valley to capture some Russian guns. They achieved their objective, but only 195 men returned. Among them was Lord Cardigan, who behaved as if the charge had been of no special significance. Boarding his yacht, where he was living during the campaign, he bathed, dined and went to bed.

This most gallant action would have never taken place if a mistake had not been made in the giving of orders by the High Command. The 673 men of the Light Brigade had charged straight at the wrong guns!

Alfred, Lord Tennyson, a famous Victorian poet, immortalized the charge of the Brigade in the poem he wrote to celebrate it.

HOW IS THE AMERICAN PRESIDENT ELECTED?

The American constitution, framed at Philadelphia in 1787, provides for the president's election by special electors appointed in each state, the number depending on the size of the population. Every state legislature has now surrendered the right to appoint these electors. They are chosen by popular election on a general "ticket" nominated by each party. Whichever party receives the most votes for its list of candidates wins all the electoral votes for that state.

The presidential electors vote by ballot for president and vice-president. These votes are sent to the president of the Senate and are counted before a joint session of the Senate and the House of Representatives. If no candidate for the presidency receives a majority, the House of Representatives votes on the three leading contenders, each state delegation casting a single vote. For the vice-president, a similar ballot is held in the Senate, with each member casting one vote.

Presidential candidates are nominated by each major party at a national Nominating Convention in the summer before the election, which always takes place in December. Their campaigns are often concentrated on winning the big blocks of electoral votes in highly populated states such as New York and California.

WHO ASSASSINATED PRESIDENT KENNEDY?

President John Fitzgerald Kennedy's assassin in 1963 is generally assumed to have been Lee Harvey Oswald, a 24-year-old self-styled Marxist. The police evidence is that both the bullets that hit the President were fired by Oswald from a sixth-floor window.

The 46-year-old President and his wife Jacqueline had come to Dallas, Texas, on a speaking tour and were on their way in a motorcade to attend an official lunch when the fatal shots were fired at 12.30 pm on November 22. Kennedy's death was announced officially at 1.30 pm, and Vice-President Lyndon B. Johnson was sworn in as the new President before flying back to Washington.

Lee Oswald, who was arrested

shortly after the shooting, was being transferred to Dallas county jail on November 24 when Jack Ruby, a 52-year-old nightclub operator, shot and killed him at close range in full view of a nationwide television audience. So the evidence against Oswald was never allowed to be tested publicly in a court of law. This led to a spate of theories that Oswald was not really the assassin or that he had accomplices, but these have since been largely discounted.

WHERE DID LADY GODIVA RIDE NAKED?

Since 1678 Lady Godiva's legendary ride naked through the streets of Coventry, England, has been reenacted every seven or eight years. But today the lady wears a body stocking. The famous ride, if it took place, happened around the year 1057, according to the chronicler Roger of Wendover (d. 1236). Godiva, her long hair falling loosely round her body, rode through the market place accompanied by two soldiers.

Legend has it that Lady Godiva pleaded with Leofric, Earl of Mercia, to lessen the townspeople's tax burden. Exasperated, the earl declared he would do as she asked, if she rode naked through the town. Lady Godiva did so and the earl cut the townspeople's taxes. Over the years the legend became embellished. The soldiers disappeared and, in the 17th Century, the legend of Peep-

ing Tom crept into the story. Tom is said to have been struck blind because he could not resist peeping at Lady Godiva through a window as she rode by.

The true facts record that Coventry's early fame rested on the foundation of a Benedictine monastery by Leofric and his wife Godgifu (the real name of Godiva) in 1043.

The phrase "to send to Coventry" (to refuse to speak with someone) might well have been the fate of Peeping Tom. But although the origin of the phrase is uncertain it seems more likely to have originated during the Civil War. Captured supporters of King Charles were sent by Cromwell's forces to Coventry for imprisonment.

WHEN DID DRAKE SAIL AROUND THE WORLD?

Francis Drake became the first Englishman to sail round the world in a voyage which lasted from 1577 to 1580. He left Plymouth on December 13 with his flagship the 100-ton Pelican, four other ships and 160 men on an expedition to the Pacific.

After sailing down the coast of South America, Drake passed through the Strait of Magellan. Then he encountered a fierce storm which drove him southward to Tierra del Fuego at the tip of the continent.

Drake's other ships had by now been lost or returned home. But the Pelican, renamed the Golden

Hind, pushed on alone up the coasts of Chile and Peru, attacking towns and plundering Spanish vessels, notably the treasure-ship Cacafuego.

After continuing northwards and claiming the Californian coast in the name of Queen Elizabeth, he decided to avoid the outraged Spaniards by sailing home across the Pacific. On reaching the Moluccas or Spice Islands, he loaded six tons of cloves, but had to throw most of the cargo overboard when the ship struck a reef.

The rest of the voyage across the Indian Ocean and round the Cape of Good Hope was comparatively uneventful, and the Golden Hind returned to Plymouth on September 26, 1580, with treasure worth £500,000. The Queen knighted Drake aboard his ship at Deptford in the Thames.

Sir Francis later became an admiral and helped to defeat the Spanish Armada in 1588. He died at sea on January 27, 1596.

WHO WHERE THE MEDICI?

The Medici of Florence were the greatest of the many brilliant families who contributed to the cultural splendour and magnificence, as well as the political history, of the Renaissance in Italy. Their first successes were gained as merchants, but the real founder of their wealth and power was Giovanni de Medici (1360–1429) who amassed a great fortune and turned banker and patron of the arts. His sons Cosimo and Lorenzo founded the two main branches of the family.

Cosimo (1389–1464) became the virtual ruler of Florence through his skill in securing the election of friends to positions of power in the city government. He greatly added to the family's riches by developing a large banking and commercial business with branches in London, Rome, Venice, Geneva, Bruges and other centres. He gave generous patronage to artists, writers and scholars, founded libraries and erected splendid buildings.

His most famous descendant was his grandson Lorenzo the Magnificent (1449–92), who was the patron of Michelangelo and the painter Botticelli and himself a man of learning. He escaped the fate of his younger brother Giuliano, who was stabbed to death in a conspiracy by Florentine rivals, and proved himself an able administrator. His influence among church leaders in Rome secured the election as Cardinal of his 14-year-old son Giovanni, who was later elected Pope Leo X. A nephew of Lorenzo became Pope Clement VII.

In 1560 the two chief branches of the family were united under Cosimo the Great (1519–74), who took the title of Grand Duke of Tuscany. During the next 200 years members of the Medici married into various royal houses of Europe. The most famous of these was Catherine de Medici (1519–89), great-grand-daughter of Lorenzo the Magnificent, who married one French king, Henri II, and became the mother of three others, Francis II, Charles IX and Henri III. She was held chiefly responsible for the massacre of Protestants on St Bartholomew's Eve, August 24, 1572. The ruling branch of the Medici died out in 1737, but descendants of other branches still live in Italy today.

WHEN WERE THE LAST CONVICTS SENT TO AUSTRALIA?

The last convicts were sent to Australia in 1849. They arrived in a ship called the Hashemy, the first convicts to arrive in the colony since 1840. The Hashemy docked in Melbourne, but public protests against the landing of the prisoners caused the authorities to move the ship on to Sydney. There the public outcry was even greater and the Hashemy sailed to Brisbane, where the convicts were put ashore.

The protests arose because many Australians, especially tradespeople and wage earners, were bitterly opposed to the continued flow of free labour to the colony. But transportation (the sending of convicts) was still favoured by sheep owners and farmers, who wanted the labour,

HOBART TOWN CHAIN GANG.

and by the British Government, who found it a cheap way of getting rid of unwanted citizens.

After the convicts from the Hashemy had finally disembarked, anti-transportation leagues were formed and attracted so much public support that it was decided to send no more convicts to any part of the colony.

WHY WAS LOUIS XIV CALLED THE SUN KING?

Louis XIV was the King of France from 1643 to 1715 and was known as the Sun King because of the general style and magnificence of his reign. Although he became king when he was four, he did not assume his full powers until 1661, after the death of the famous Cardinal Mazarin. Louis then became his own "first minister" and embarked upon years of personalized government.

Louis thoroughly enjoyed being king. He desired to shine in his role and a prime aim of his government was to foster any project that added to the king's glory.

He became a great patron of the arts and gave personal encouragement to writers who were to become some of the greatest names in French literature, including Molière and Racine.

Architecture, of course, was one of the most obvious ways of adding to the grandeur of his reign. The Palace of Versailles also took shape under his direction. He constantly changed his mind and frequently altered the plans for the palace. In 1685 Versailles, by then one of Europe's most beautiful palaces, became the Sun King's permanent seat of government. Louis entertained on an appropriately lavish scale and the grace, elegance and excesses of his Court became a by-word throughout the civilized world. But he did have excellent taste. The delightful château of Marly-le-Roi is another example of this. Life at Court was governed by careful and meticulous rules, although the Sun King's love affairs were greatly resented by the nobility since his various mistresses were given high rank and exercised a considerable influence on policy. But despite Louis' very dubious private life he revelled in the title of "most Christian king" and did his best to protect the Catholic religion This resulted in him making life for his Protestant subjects thoroughly uncomfortable. Indeed, in 1685 he issued an edict under which Protestantism was no longer tolerated in France. It is easy to smile at some of the Sun King's escesses but even Voltaire, the great French satirist, extolled his reign for the glory it added to the fame of France and French civilization.

Louis encouraged good administration, promoted industry and attended diligently to his duties as "first minister" and steered France through the long war of the Spanish Succession.

HOW IS A NEW POPE ELECTED?

The Pope is elected by ballot, the votes being cast by the cardinals of the Roman Catholic Church in conclave at the Vatican in Rome.

After the death of a pope, nine days of mourning, the Novendialia, are observed in the Basilica of St Peter's. Eighteen days after the Novendialia the cardinals, who have come to the Vatican from all over the world, enter a part of the palace that is closed to outsiders. The doors giving access to it are walled up and messages are passed in by rotas, or turning boxes, set in the walls.

Each morning and afternoon the cardinals vote in the Sistine Chapel. The votes are immediately counted by three scrutineers, who are changed at each session. If no candidate receives the necessary majority of two-thirds plus one, the votes are burned in a stove in the corner of the chapel with wet straw so that black smoke is produced. When a cardinal is chosen, dry straw is used and the resulting white smoke signals the election to the crowd on the piazza of St Peter's.

WHO WAS LE DOUANIER ROUSSEAU?

Le Douanier Rousseau (1844–1910) was a self-taught French painter who had an important influence on art at the end of the 19th Century and became the acknowledged master of a style known as naïve or primitive painting. His real name was Henri Rousseau. He was patronizingly called "Le Douanier" (French for customs-house officer) because he worked for some years in a Paris toll-house, and the nickname stuck because it helped to distinguish him from Theodore Rousseau (1812–67), leader of a group of landscape painters.

After a spell in the army, the younger Rousseau spent about a quarter of a century as a minor civil servant. About 1880 he began to paint in his spare time. In 1886 he exhibited for the first time at the Salon des Indépendants in Paris, but the naïvety of his work aroused derision and he did not decide to paint professionally until his retirement in 1893. Gradually the strength and originality of his pictures gained recognition. He was introduced to Paul Signac, a neo-Impressionist painter, and through him met the artists Gauguin, Pissarro and Seurat. Among the painters who most admired his style were Renoir and Toulouse-Lautrec. The young Picasso, who used to visit him in his rooms, gave a banquet in his honour in 1908.

Le Douanier continued to exhibit at the Salon des Indépendants until the year of his death. He longed to be able to paint in the academic way, but brought a splendid quality of directness, simplicity and sensibility to his work. Among the most remarkable of his paintings are jungle scenes.

WHO BECAME KNOWN AS CLIVE OF INDIA?

Robert Clive (1725-74) was the founder of Britain's Indian Empire. Yet at school he was idle, unruly and turbulent and became the ringleader of a gang of youths who terrorized his native town of Market Drayton, Shropshire.

Both Market Drayton and the Clive family must have been relieved when, at the age of 18, he left England to become a clerk with the British East India Company in Madras. At first he was so depressed by his new environment that he twice tried to shoot himself, but his opportunity for greatness came with the outbreak of war between the French and the British for supremacy in India. In 1751, when the tide was running against the British, Clive led a few hundred English and Indian troops to seize the great fort at Arcot the capital of one of France's Indian allies. For 53 days his small force held the fort against repeated assaults until the besiegers were forced to retreat, leaving the district to be ruled by an Indian who favoured the British. Clive followed up this success with further victories which led to a settlement in south India in Britain's favour in 1752.

He returned to England in 1753 with a large fortune, but soon spent it and went back to India as Governor of Fort David. He was sent north to re-establish British power and defeated the Nawab of Bengal, Siraj-ud-Daula, at the great Battle of Plassey in 1757, replacing him with Mir Jaffir, who was sympathetic to the British. Clive accepted a gift of £200,000 from the new ruler and when Mir Jaffir died was left lands with an annual revenue of £30,000.

He sailed for England in 1760 but five years later returned as Governor of Bengal and tried to curb the corruption which was rife in India and to which he himself had contributed in earlier days. In 1767 he left India for the last time.

At home he was cross-examined about his great wealth by a strongly critical parliamentary committee which found him guilty of fraud and greed. Because of his services, he was not prosecuted. But the bitter attacks on him, together with the strain of his life in India, so affected his mind and health that he committed suicide in 1774.

WHERE WAS HORATIO NELSON BORN?

The great British naval hero, Horatio Nelson, who defeated the French at Trafalgar in 1805 in one of the most memorable of all sea battles, was born at Burnham Thorpe in Norfolk, England. His father was rector of that parish. Horatio's mother (née Suckling) was related to Sir Robert Walpole the British statesman and Prime Minister.

Nelson's uncle, Captain Maurice Suckling, who later became Comptroller of the Navy, gave Horatio his first taste of the sea. Horatio, who was educated in his home county of Norfolk by the North Sea, was entered in the ship Raisonnable by Captain Suckling in 1770 when there was an alarm of war with Spain. But the dispute with Spain was quickly settled, and Nelson was packed off in a merchant vessel to the West Indies to gain experience.

This was the beginning of a hard

apprenticeship during which time Nelson visited such remote areas as the Arctic and the East Indies.

Five years after his first appointment at sea Nelson fell ill and was invalided home. It was not until two years later, having just passed his examination as lieutenant, that his remarkable career began in earnest.

WHEN WAS THE UNITED KINGDOM FORMED?

The United Kingdom was formed in 1801 when an Act of Union brought Ireland under the same parliament with England, Scotland and Wales. The official name of the country was changed to the United Kingdom of Great Britain and Ireland. But 26 Irish counties left the Union in 1922 and formed the Irish Free State, now the Republic of Ireland. Five years later the Royal and Parliamentary Titles Act named the union as the United Kingdom of Great Britain and Northern Ireland.

Wales was the first to unite with England, having been subdued by King Edward I in 1282. The heir to the English throne has been known as the Prince of Wales ever since Edward gave the title to his baby son in 1301. But it was not until 1536 when Henry VIII, a Tudor monarch of Welsh descent, was on the throne, that an Act of Union peacefully incorporated the Principality into the kingdom.

The name Great Britain came into use after James VI of Scotland succeeded to the English throne in 1603 as James I and united the two crowns, though not the nations. Another Act of Union brought England and Scotland under one government in 1707.

The Union flag of the present kingdom is composed of the flag of England (white with an upright red cross), the flag of Scotland (blue with a diagonal white cross) and the red diagonal cross of Ireland.

On May 29, 1953, under the Royal Titles Act, a proclamation was issued which gave the Queen the title: Elizabeth the Second, by the Grace of God, of the United Kingdom of Great Britain and Northern Ireland and of her other Realms and Territories Queen, Head of the Commonwealth, Defender of the Faith.

WHY IS PAUL REVERE FAMOUS?

Paul Revere (1735–1818) is famous for his ride on horseback during the American Revolution to warn Massachusetts colonists of the approach of British troops.

Paul Revere's father, a Huguenot refugee, who had settled in Boston, Massachusetts, taught his son the art of silversmithing. Revere became a great artist in silver but, in his need to support his family he also sold spectacles, replaced missing teeth and made surgical instruments.

He was a fervent patriot, cut

many copper plates for anti-British propaganda and was a leader of the Boston Tea Party in 1773, when a group of citizens disguised as Indians threw a cargo of tea into the sea as a protest against the British tax on it.

In 1775, when the American Revolution broke out, Revere constructed a powder mill to supply the colonial troops. He enlisted in the army and in 1776 was a lieutenant-colonel, in command of Castle William, at Boston.

But his most famous exploit took place the year before when, as principal express rider for Boston's Committee of Safety, he warned Middlesex County, on April 18, that British troops were leaving Boston to seize military stores at Lexington and Concord. His exploit has been immortalized in the poem *Paul Revere's Ride* by Henry Wadsworth Longfellow (1807–1882).

After the colonists' victory, Revere set up a rolling mill for the manufacture of sheet copper in Massachusetts, and became rich.

WHERE IS POMPEII?

For nearly 1,700 years Pompeii in southern Italy was a dead and buried city, forgotten by all except historians. But for more than 600 years before disaster overtook it, Pompeii was a proud city and port of the Roman Empire in the shadow of Mount Vesuvius on the Bay of Naples.

On the morning of August 24, in the year A.D. 79 an event occurred that was to preserve for us the story of Roman everyday life. Sixteen years previously an earthquake had damaged Pompeii, a city where wealthy Romans had their country villas, and the damage had been repaired. Now, Vesuvius once again erupted violently. For three days the sky was darkened, and a deadly hail of volcanic ash and pumice rained down upon the doomed city.

By the time the eruption settled down, Pompeii lay under a blanket of pumice eight to ten feet thick. The outlines of the land had been so altered that the sea was now nearly two miles away. Two thousand of the city's 20,000 inhabitants died in the disaster, suffocated by the sulphurous fumes or crushed by falling roofs. Pompeii, it seemed, had been wiped off the face of the earth.

So it was until, in 1748, a peasant digging in his vineyard unearthed some statues. This led to a remarkable record of a Roman city in its heyday being brought to light.

Excavation has revealed rows of shops and houses, the forum or market-place, with temples adjoining business houses, an open air theatre, and public baths. In the museum at Naples are many thousands of objects recovered from Pompeii—statues and paintings, pens and ink-bottles, coins, looking-glasses and even charred food served on the day of the eruption nearly 1,900 years ago.

WHEN DID AKBAR BUILD HIS EMPIRE?

Jalal-ud-Din Mohammed Akbar (1542–1605), the greatest of the Mogul emperors of India, was a ruler only in name when he came to the throne in 1556. His Mongolian grandfather, Baber, had established a Mohammedan empire in northern India through a combination of daring, luck and military skill. But his father had been driven from the capital, Delhi, by a usurper.

With able generalship, Akbar overthrew all his rivals and embarked upon a career of conquest which, by 1562, gave him domain over the Punjab and Multan, the basin of the Ganges and Jumna Rivers, Gwalior to the south and Kabul in Afghanistan in the northwest. Subsequently he crossed the Narbada River into the Deccan and extended his dominion southward. By 1605, his empire contained 15 provinces, or *subahs*, and stretched from the Hindu Kush mountains to the Godocari River and from Bengal to Gujarat.

He was not only a great general, but also a great statesman. He established an excellent administrative system and came to be on friendly terms with the former Hindu rulers, respecting their religion and marrying two of their princesses. Under his rule, art and literature flourished, while scholars from all over the world were invited to court and encouraged to discuss with Akbar all aspects of philosophy and religion.

After 1582 he formed a religious sect with himself as spiritual leader, but did not force his subjects to become members. He died at Agra on October 16, 1605, and is remembered as a wise, sincere and generous leader.

WHO WAS BENEDICT ARNOLD?

Benedict Arnold (1741–1801) was an American officer in the Revolutionary War who betrayed military secrets to the British and plotted to surrender an army base to the enemy. He changed sides partly for money, partly in revenge for being reprimanded and partly, perhaps, because of the influence of his second wife, who had no sympathy for the rebellion.

Before war broke out between the Americans and the British, Arnold had served in the French and Indian wars and become a druggist and bookseller as well as being active in the West Indian trade. He was an early hero of the Revolution, taking part as a captain in the Connecticut militia in Ethan Allen's successful attack on Fort Ticonderoga, New York State, in 1775. The following year he was wounded at Quebec and promoted to brigadier-general in recognition of his brave leadership. After other acts of valour, which resulted in his being crippled, he was appointed military commander of Philadelphia in 1778.

He enjoyed the city's social life but his extravagance and association with Loyalist members of the community disgusted the patriots and aroused their suspicions. He was accused of misusing public property and authority for personal profit and was awaiting court martial when he married Margaret Shippen, 18-year-old daughter of a Loyalist. Even before the court martial was held Arnold offered his services to the British forces as an informer. When in December, 1779, he was found guilty of two minor offences and reprimanded gently by George Washington, he again entered with his wife into treasonable correspondence with Sir Henry Clinton, the British commander-in-chief. He sent news of the proposed invasion of Canada and later offered—for £20,000—to surrender the strategic military base at West Point on the Hudson River where he expected to be appointed commander.

Clinton agreed and sent his aide, Major John André, to meet him under a flag of truce on the night of September 21, 1780. Returning overland in disguise, André was captured and incriminating papers were found in his boot. Arnold escaped along the Hudson to the British Army, but André was hanged as a spy.

Arnold received £6,315 for his treason and was made a brigadier-general of provincial troops on the side of the British. After carrying out raids in Virginia and Connecticut, he sailed in 1781 for England where he was treated with scorn and distrust, and ostracized by society. He died an embittered man in London in 1801. His wife survived him by only three years.

HOW DID HITLER COME TO POWER?

Adolf Hitler was able to seize power in Germany because the economic slump of 1929 gave him the opportunity to gain the support of the magnates of business and industry, and also of the lower middle class and of the unemployed. To the business men he promised a strong right-wing government; to the lower classes he gave faith and hope, proclaiming that Germany would triumph over her suffering and reassert her natural greatness.

Hitler was born at Braunau, Austria in 1889, but he resented the Austro-Hungarian government and fought for Germany in the First World War. In 1920 he joined and soon became leader of a new party, the National Socialist German Workingmen's Party (Nationalsozialistische Deutsche Arbeiterpartei) later to be abbreviated to "Nazi". In 1923 he was sent to prison as a revolutionary and wrote *Mein Kampf* (My Fight). He believed that inequality between races was inevitable and that the Aryan race must dominate. He determined that Germany should rule the world and expressed his fanatical hatred of all Jews.

On leaving prison in 1924 Hitler skilfully built up the Nazi strength. At the 1930 election it became the second largest party in the country with more than 6,000,000 votes. By 1933 so many Nazis had been elected to Parliament that the President of the German Republic, Field Marshal Hindenburg, was persuaded that the country could no longer be governed without their leader's help. Hitler was invited to join the government and soon became Chancellor. Once in power he proceeded to establish an absolute dictatorship. In March 1933 a Bill giving him full powers was passed in the Reichstag by the combined votes of Nazi, Nationalist and Centre Party deputies.

Hitler took control of the police and established special Nazi forces, the SA and the SS. When Hindenburg died on August 2, 1934, the offices of Chancellor and President were merged, and Hitler became an undisputed dictator.

WHY WERE SLAVES TAKEN TO THE WEST INDIES?

Negro slaves were taken to the West Indies because the original population had almost become extinct.

While Christopher Columbus explored all parts of the West Indies, his successors colonized only those islands which were peopled by the Ciboney and Arawak Indians. They avoided the Carib Islands of the Lesser Antilles because they had no gold and the Carib Indians were fierce and difficult to subdue. As the Spaniards conquered each island, they rounded up its Indians and put them to work in mines or on plantations.

Many were worked to death, some starved, others died from diseases introduced from Europe and still others were killed when they tried to rebel. By 1550, the Ciboney were extinct and only a few Arawak remained.

In the 16th Century, the Spaniards introduced Negro slaves to replace the dwindling supply of labour. They did not bring in many, for their mines were exhausted, and they owned cattle ranches which did not require much labour. The main shipments of Negro slaves came in the 18th Century, when sugar plantations were developed by the French in Haiti and the Lesser Antilles.

After the French Revolution, the slaves in Haiti revolted and set up an independent Negro republic. The French went to neighbouring British and Spanish islands, established new plantations and imported more slaves.

When slavery was abolished in the first half of the 19th Century the British imported Chinese and Indians from Asia who rapidly increased in numbers until, by the middle of the 20th Century, they comprised more than one third of the population of Trinidad. Throughout the Antilles the Negroes and Asians have assumed more and more prominence, so that they now dominate the area except in countries like Cuba and Puerto Rico.

clothes, ornamented coffins, chariots, and the mummified body of the young king himself, wearing a gold mask.

When the Egyptians buried a pharaoh, they took trouble to surround him with beautiful and useful things. They did not believe he was really dead. They thought he would go on living if he were provided with enough things to protect him in his journey through the underworlds, and afterwards.

Most of the kings' tombs were robbed, frequently by local people, of their jewels and gold.

There are several chambers in the tomb–the Antechamber, the Burial Chamber, the Treasury, and the Store Room. In the Antechamber was a beautiful alabaster wishing-cup and a painted wooden casket with brilliant designs. At the doorway of the Treasury was a figure of a God called Anubis, a sort of jackal-like dog, who was supposed to keep watch over the dead. Round his neck he wore a scarf decorated with lotus and cornflowers.

WHERE IS THE TOMB OF TUTANKHAMUN?

Tutankhamun's tomb is in Egypt, in a place called the Valley of the Kings. Tutankhamun was a pharaoh, who died in 1352 B.C. His name was familiar only to scholars until his tomb was discovered in 1922 by Howard Carter. The tomb was filled with precious jewels, ornaments, vases, furniture,

WHEN WAS AMERICA'S LAST WAR WITH ENGLAND?

America and England were last at war with each other from June 1812 to December 1814. War broke out for two reasons: first, America's expanding trade was threatened because the British were maintaining a blockade to prevent supplies reaching the French, with whom they were at war; secondly, there was a growing sense of nationalism in America, a feeling that she must fight to preserve her independence, sovereignty and honour.

When war was declared by President Madison, the Americans immediately invaded Canada, but were driven back. In 1813, after talk of an armistice came to nothing, more skirmishes broke out on the Canadian border and British sailors began to raid the American coast. By October 1814 it became clear that the Americans could not successfully invade Canada, while the British Navy could do no more than harry the coasts of America.

The chief sufferers were the merchants of New England. Also the financial state of the American government was so bad that it had no money to pay its bills abroad. Governor Strong of Massachusetts openly spoke against the war, and was suspected of planning to take his state over to the British.

However, no one in Britain wanted to fight the War of Independence all over again. The desire was to trade with and not to fight against the United States. On December 24, 1814 the Treaty of Ghent was signed and the war was over. Neither side gained.

HOW DID THE GREAT FIRE OF LONDON START?

The Great Fire of London began by accident in the house of King Charles II's baker at Pudding Lane,

near London Bridge, on September 2, 1666.

Although it was the worst fire in London's history, it performed a great service, for it cleansed the city after the Great Plague, which had rampaged through the country since 1664. During the Plague more than 75,000 Londoners died and many thousands more fled the city, leaving parts of it deserted.

The fire raged for four days and burned the whole city except for the north-eastern and extreme western parts. The Royal Exchange, St Paul's Cathedral, nearly all civic buildings, 87 churches and about 13,000 houses were destroyed. Schemes were put forward for reconstruction, notably one by the great architect Sir Christopher Wren; but there was not enough money to replan the city entirely.

However, many improvements were made. Streets were widened, many houses were built of brick, markets were enlarged or resited, and Sir Christopher Wren's genius created the beauty of a more splendid St Paul's and 49 new churches.

WHY IS SOUTH AMERICA LARGELY CATHOLIC?

South America is largely Roman Catholic because the continent was first discovered and opened up by explorers from the strongly Roman Catholic countries of Spain and Portugal.

Venezuela was the first of the

South American countries to be colonized by the Spaniards. Christopher Columbus discovered it on his third voyage in 1498, and settlers soon followed in the early 16th Century. Uruguay, discovered by the Spanish explorer, Juan Diaz de Solis, in 1515, was claimed over the years–until its independence in 1830–by both the Portuguese in Brazil and the Spanish in Argentina. Brazil, although first discovered by a Spaniard in 1500, was declared a possession of the Portuguese crown in the same year by Pedro Alvares Cabral.

In the early 16th Century, Colombia and Ecuador were also conquered by the Spanish. In 1532, Francisco Pizarro added to the Spanish dominions by the conquest of Peru and its Inca empire, which at that time included much of what is now Bolivia, Chile, Columbia and Ecuador.

Paraguay was claimed for Spain by Sebastian Cabot in 1526. The

Conquistadores landing in South America

Spanish captain, Pedro de Mendoza, established a settlement on the site of what is now Buenos Aires in 1536. Although this was soon burnt down by Indians, Juan de Garay and other Spanish settlers reestablished the settlement in 1580 and gave it the name Santos Trinidad y Puerto de Santa Maria de Buenos Aires. This long name which means Holy Trinity and Harbour of Our Lady of Kind Winds, was soon shortened to Buenos Aires.

This history of the Spanish and Portuguese control in South America is one of oppression and exploitation. In the early 19th Century, the colonies revolted and established republics. One of the strongest forces remaining from the centuries of colonial domination is the vital Roman Catholic faith of the conquistadores–the conquerors.

WHERE DID PRESTER JOHN LIVE?

Nobody knows for certain and, indeed, nobody has ever succeeded in proving that Prester John ever lived. The legend of Prester John or John the Priest–Prester is a shortened form of Presbyter–dates from the Middle Ages. According to these early legends Prester John was a mighty Christian potentate, a sort of King Priest of the Indies, of fabulous wealth and power.

In the year 1165, the story goes, a letter was sent by Prester John, King of the Indies, to various European rulers, in which he claimed to be a "lord of lords" and hinted that he enjoyed a divine authority.

The land of John was apparently an earthly paradise flowing with milk and honey. Justice and peace ruled supreme. Envy, flattery, greed, theft–none of these evils existed in John's kingdom. Poverty, too, did not exist. So many people enjoyed high-sounding titles at John's court, the letter claimed, that John himself used the plain title of Presbyter or Priest. Apparently John's butler, in this fabled kingdom, was an archbishop and even his cook was a king.

The idea behind this alleged letter to the European princes was that they should feel humbled that one as mighty as John should use such a modest title. Really the letter was an ingenious forgery and a satire on the princes of Europe.

But the fable of a great Christian ruler lingered on. The crusaders loved the idea of this powerful Christian monarch ruling in the mysterious East. So the territories of Prester John were duly shown on medieval maps, although the boundaries were always vague.

In later centuries it was suggested that the land of John really lay in Ethiopia, and gradually this became the accepted version of the legend. Robert Louis Stevenson makes use of the story in his adventure novel, *Prester John*.

WHO WAS MAHATMA GANDHI?

Mohandas Karamchand Gandhi (1869–1948) was a great Indian political leader who played a major part in his country's struggle to win independence from Britain. The title Mahatma, or Great Soul, was given to him by the Indian poet Rabindranath Tagore in 1915.

In 1893 Gandhi went to South Africa as a lawyer and championed the cause of the Indian community there against discrimination. It was while he was in South Africa that he was converted to a strict personal regime of self-denial, called *brahmacharya*, which was closely interwoven with his creed of non-violent resistance, which he named *satyagraha*, or truth force.

Gandhi returned to India in 1914 and soon became the recognized leader of the Indian National Congress in its struggle to establish an independent republic. Although he attacked the British Government, Gandhi asserted that he respected the British people. In their turn most Britons admired Gandhi even when they did not understand him.

He adopted the loincloth as his dress and toured the country promoting the spinning wheel as a means of freeing India from dependence on Lancashire cotton mills. In 1922 he was imprisoned for two years for sedition as the leader of a mass campaign of civil disobedience.

Gandhi published newspapers and pamphlets, identified himself with the Untouchables (low-caste Hindus), whom he called Children of God, and introduced a system of hygiene and first aid in remote villages. Millions of followers of all classes called him Bapu, meaning Father. But his efforts to bring Muslims and Hindus together did not meet with great success.

Finding progress towards self-government too slow, Gandhi increased his harassment of the British authorities. He was frequently sent to prison, for the last time in 1942 when he declared that the Allies could expect support only from a "free India".

After the Second World War, Gandhi agreed to the formation of the separate Muslim state of Pakistan as a condition of independence. When riots broke out between Hindus and Muslims, Gandhi entered on his fourteenth fast, which he swore he would maintain until death or the end of the bloodshed. For a time he was successful in halting the fighting. But on January 30, 1948, shortly after the end of his fast, he was shot dead by a Hindu fanatic on his way to conduct a prayer meeting.

WHEN WAS THE AMERICAN DEPRESSION?

The American Depression began in September 1929 with a great collapse of the stock market in Wall Street, New York. During the money-making mania which accompanied the great prosperity of the 1920s, "paper" fortunes were made and the prices of shares soared to record high levels.

President Herbert Hoover tried unsuccessfully to abate the fever. On September 7 a reaction set in and on October 24 came the great Wall Street crash. On that Black Thursday, 13,000 million shares of stock were sold and prices plunged faster than ever before.

Huge fortunes were lost by many businessmen, and the savings of millions of small investors vanished. Factories were closed, the number of unemployed rocketed, foreign trade fell, banks failed, mortgages were foreclosed and, all the time, the prices of wheat, cotton, copper, oil and other commodities kept sinking. The buying power of the United States was paralysed.

These were the days of "Buddy, can you spare a dime?". All over the country people lined up at emergency "soup kitchens". Young men rode freight trains looking for work and old people died of starvation. By February 1932 a full third of the American workforce was idle. The rest of the world, too, was affected and international trade dwindled to a third of its 1928 volume.

In 1933 a new president, Franklin D. Roosevelt (1933–1945) was elected. He launched the New Deal and set up a vast system of public works paid for by the state. Contractors' orders for these schemes revived heavy industry, and workers' wages restored prosperity to the towns. Trade unions were encouraged, tariffs lowered and many laws passed which helped to save the economy.

HOW OLD IS THE OLDEST ROYAL FAMILY?

Hirohito, Emperor of Japan, is the 24th in line from the first emperor, Jimmu Tenno or Zinmu. The dates of the first emperor's reign are traditionally given as 660–581 B.C. and would give Japan the distinction of being the oldest ruling house. But today it is thought that the reign may have been from about 40 B.C. to 10 B.C.

If this is so, the Shah of Iran belongs to the oldest royal family. He claims descent from Cyrus the Great who reigned from about 559–529 B.C. Little is known about Jimmu Tenno. He might be better described as a clan chief than an emperor. But Cyrus the Great was an outstanding soldier and statesman who founded a Persian Empire stretching from the river Indus to the Aegean Sea and the borders of Egypt. He left behind him a reputation for justice and mercy.

WHERE DID THE WORLD'S FIRST IRON BATTLESHIPS FIGHT?

The first battle involving "ironclads" was between the Monitor and the Merrimack in March, 1862.

The Monitor was built by the Federals in the North during the

The Monitor, with its round turret, is in the foreground.

Civil War. She had a displacement of only 987 tons. Meanwhile, the Confederates in the South also built an ironclad, the C.S.S. Virginia, better known by her former name Merrimack. She had been a wooden frigate, but was burned down to the waterline by enemy action and rebuilt as an ironclad, sheathed in two inches of metal. Her displacement was 4,636 tons.

In 1862 the ships of the North were maintaining a blockade to prevent supplies reaching the South and the opposing vessels met in battle at Hampton Roads off the south-east coast of Virginia. Thousands of people lined the

shores to watch the fight as the ships passed on opposite courses, turned and passed again.

Both crews lacked training and their shooting was ineffective. The Merrimack had more guns, but was heavy and slow. The Monitor was lightly armed, but much faster. The battle was indecisive–the Monitor sheered off and the Merrimack returned to the navy yard.

On the previous day the Merrimack had achieved spectacular success by ramming and sinking the sailing sloop Cumberland and then destroying the Federal sailing frigate Congress by gunfire. Her prowess convinced the public that the day of the wooden man-of-war was ended.

The first ironclad, or armoured warship, had been completed in France in 1858. Next year the British Admiralty ordered two iron-clads, the Warrior and the Black Prince. Completed in October 1861 and September 1862 respectively, they each displaced 9,210 tons, could attain a speed of 14 knots and had a complement of 707 officers and men. These two ships, with the French Gloire and Couronne, were the first battle-ships, although the name was not then applied to them.

WHO WAS ROMMEL?

Erwin Rommel (1891–1944) was an outstanding German general of the Second World War, winning a great reputation as a brilliant tactician during the desert fighting in North Africa.

He was born at Heidenheim, near Ulm, in the state of Baden-Württemberg and educated at Tübingen. Entering the army as a cadet in 1910, he distinguished himself in the First World War and afterwards became an instructor at Dresden Military Academy.

An early Nazi sympathizer, he was attached to Adolf Hitler's bodyguard in 1933 and com-manded his headquarters guard during the German occupations of Austria, the Sudetenland and Czechoslovakia, and throughout the campaign in Poland. During the invasion of France in 1940, he led a Panzer division and displayed such drive and initiative that he was promoted to command the Afrika Korps in Libya, North Africa, with the task of driving the British out of Egypt.

Rommel pushed the British Eighth Army back to El Alamein in Egypt, recaptured Tobruk in 1942 and was raised to the rank of field marshal. His brilliance in the field gained him the title of "the Desert Fox", and the admira-tion and respect of both his own soldiers and his opponents. He was a great opportunist and had a talent for improvization. Perhaps his chief fault was a tendency to desert his headquarters and move "up forward", thus putting himself in danger of losing control of the battle. His troops were defeated at El Alamein in November, 1942 by the strongly reinforced Eighth Army and forced out of Egypt, Libya and Tripolitania. He was re-called from Africa at the prompting of Mussolini who claimed that the Italian generals could do better.

The final phase of Rommel's career began with the Allied in-vasion of France where he com-manded an army corps. In July, 1944 he was wounded in an air raid and sent home to recover. Rommel had become increasingly disillusioned with Hitler's conduct of the war and by the atrocities that were being committed. He acquiesced in a plot to kill Hitler and would have been proclaimed Head of State if the conspiracy had succeeded. However, the plan was discovered and Rommel was given a choice of death before a firing squad or suicide. He chose the latter to save his family from disgrace and on October 14, 1944 was taken from his home by car and handed some poison to swallow. He was given a State funeral with full military honours.

WHY WAS THE TAJ MAHAL BUILT?

The Taj Mahal was built by the Mogul emperor Shah Jehan (1614–66) as a tomb for his favourite wife, Mumtaz Mahal. It is situated at Agra in northern India and is one of the most beautiful buildings in the world. When the Moguls arrived in India early in the 16th Century, they brought Persian civilization with them. The tomb is a perfect example of the Persian style of architecture.

The name of the tomb means "Crown of the Palace", one of the titles given to the Empress Mumtaz. It is built of white marble, inlaid with precious stones, and is eight sided, 130 feet across at its widest points and nearly 200 feet high to the top of the huge dome. It is flanked on each side by two slender minarets and stands on a vast marble terrace overlooking the River Jumma and surrounded by Persian gardens.

Inside, under the dome, are the marble cenotaphs or monuments of Shah Jehan and his empress, on which the sun flickers through marble screens as delicate and intricate as lace. The walls are covered in floral designs and inscriptions from the Koran, picked out in onyx, jasper, cornelian and other semi-precious stones. The tombs which hold the royal bodies are in a vaulted chamber below and, in contrast to the chamber itself, are quite plain.

According to a legend the marvellous building appeared to Mumtaz in a dream and the Shah searched the whole of India for an architect. The plans were said to have been drawn up only after the architect had been given a drug which enabled him to see a vision of the monument in all its splendour and glory.

WHEN WAS THE ILIAD WRITTEN?

According to ancient Greek tradition the Iliad was written by the poet Homer (8th–7th Century B.C.). He was said to have been the author of many epic or heroic poems, of which only the Iliad, the story of the siege of Troy, and the Odyssey, the story of Odysseus' wanderings, survive.

The "Homeric question", the attempt which has gone on ever since to find out whether Homer really existed, and, if he did, whether he wrote the poetry, began towards the end of the 6th Century B.C. the first to inquire into the matter was Theagenes of Rhegium. Two writers in the early 7th Century B.C. mention Homer as a poet, but the first person to name his poems was the historian Herodotus in the 5th Century B.C.

What little information is available about Homer suggests that he was born in Smyrna about 740 B.C., trained as a bard (a singer-poet) and travelled about the Greek world until he went blind. Then he settled on the island of Chios and gathered pupils about him. He is believed to have composed the Iliad and perhaps the Odyssey towards the end of his life and to have died about 670 B.C. while on a visit to the island of Ios.

The works credited to him were admired so much by later Greeks that they often referred to him simply as "the poet". The Iliad and the Odyssey are among the greatest works of world literature.

WHERE DID THE AMERICAN WAR OF INDEPENDENCE START?

The American War of Independence started at Lexington, near Boston, Massachusetts, in 1775. The military governor of Massachusetts had sent troops from Boston to Concord to seize a store of illegal weapons. On the way back, at Lexington, the troops were attacked by angry farmers and 273 of the 800 soldiers were killed. When the news of this battle reached Britain, war was declared on the rebellious colonists.

Although this was the first open conflict, the colonists' resentment against Britain had been growing for several years. This was mainly caused by the taxes imposed by the British government on certain goods imported into America. The taxes were intended to help pay for the Seven Years' War which Britain had fought against France to defend the American states. The Americans considered these taxes to be unjust and refused to pay them. Eventually all these taxes were abolished, except for the tax on imported tea.

When war was declared, the Americans had no regular army. But one was soon formed under the command of a Virginian, George Washington. This army was badly equipped and lacked training. But it was fighting over vast territories against a British army 3,000 miles from home. Many times in the following six years the American army was nearly defeated by the superior training and numbers of the British troops, but gradually the tide turned. As the war continued, France and Spain sent help, declaring war on Britain.

On July 4, 1776, Congress, the American parliament, drew up the formal Declaration of Independence in Philadelphia. This stated that America would no longer obey the British government and that the United States would be an independent republic.

In 1781 at Yorktown in Virginia, the British forces were forced to surrender to a combined American and French army, and it became clear that the United States had won. For a time George III and the British government refused to accept defeat. But at the Treaty of Versailles in 1783 the independence of the colonies was recognized and peace was made between Britain, America, France and Spain. The war was over and the United States had gained her independence.

WHEN WAS THE BATTLE OF HASTINGS?

The Battle of Hastings was fought on October 14, 1066, on a ridge 10 miles north-west of Hastings in Sussex, England.

The events which led to the battle began when William, Duke of Normandy, in France, extracted a promise from Harold, chief minister of the Saxon king Edward the Confessor, that he would support the Norman's succession to the English throne. When Edward died on January 5, 1066, and Harold was chosen king by an assembly of nobles and citizens, William decided to seize what he claimed was his by right.

William the Conqueror.

In September, while the Normans were still waiting for the wind to change to carry them across the English Channel, Harold had to march northwards into Yorkshire to repulse an invasion led by Harald Hardrada, the seven-foot king of Norway.

The Saxons crushed the invaders in a desperate battle at Stamford Bridge, but Harold was still in York when he received the news that William's army had landed near Hastings. He instantly hurried south, mobilized a new, largely untrained, army of about 7,000 men and led them against the Normans 5,000 strong.

During the battle Harold defended a piece of high ground protected by a barricade. At first the two-handed Saxon battle axes beat back the Norman attacks. But William triumphed with cunning generalship, luring the Saxons from their strong positions by pretended retreats and ordering his archers to aim high in the air so that their arrows fell on heads unprotected by the wall of shields. A chance arrow killed Harold and, as darkness fell, the English survivors scattered.

On December 25 William the Conqueror was crowned king of England in London.

HOW DID POCAHONTAS BECOME A LEGENDARY FIGURE?

Pocahontas became a legendary figure by saving the life of Captain John Smith, leader of the American settlers of Jamestown, Virginia. Smith was captured by a Red Indian tribe and condemned to death. But as he was stretched out on the sacrificial stone, Pocahontas, the little daughter of Chief Powhatan, threw herself on his body and pleaded successfully for his life.

In April 1613, when she was still only about 18, Pocahontas was kidnapped by a settler called Samuel Argall, became a Christian and was baptized with the name of Rebecca. She helped to bring about peace between the settlers and the Indians and married one of the colonists, John Rolfe. In 1616 the governor of the colony, Sir Thomas Dale, took Pocahontas and her husband to London to advertise the London Company of Virginia. She was much admired, invited to many balls and parties, and was presented at court.

Pocahontas died during the return journey and was buried at Gravesend. She had a son, Thomas, who later settled in Virginia.

WHERE IS GOLGOTHA?

Golgotha is just outside the walls of the old city of Jerusalem in Israel. It is named in the New Testament as the place where Jesus was crucified.

Jesus was brought before the Roman governor of the province, Pontius Pilate, and accused of blasphemy. Pilate could find nothing to support the charge and offered to release Jesus. But the chief priests and elders persuaded the people to demand his death. Jesus was beaten by the Roman soldiers, dressed in a scarlet cloak and crowned with thorns to mock him as "King of the Jews". Afterwards he was forced to carry his own cross through the streets of Jerusalem to Golgotha.

The name Golgotha, meaning the place of a skull, is derived from the Aramaic language spoken in that part of Palestine. The word Calvary comes from "calvaria", which is the Latin translation of Golgotha. No one knows why Golgotha was so called, but a very ancient story says that Adam's skull was buried there.

WHY DID THE ROMAN CIVILIZATION FALL?

Rome's conquest of the Near East, mainly in the last century B.C. probably sowed the seeds of decay which led to the fall of one of the mightiest empires ever known.

Beginning as a tiny settlement on the Palatine Hill, about 17 miles from the mouth of the Tiber in central Italy, Rome had become the conqueror and leader of the western world.

But then the ancient and sturdy simplicity of the Roman character gave way to Oriental luxury and bitter hostility developed between the wealthy aristocracy and the poverty stricken majority.

The death of Tiberius Gracchus in 133 B.C. marked the beginning of a century of revolution and civil war which ended in the downfall of the republic and the establishment of an empire. Julius Caesar (102–44 B.C.), the great warrior-statesman, welded the tottering structure together and two centuries of peace followed. They included periods of great splendour, such as the wise rule of Hadrian (A.D. 117–138), when the empire reached its greatest extent.

The Christian religion spread until, in the reign of Constantine (280–337), it became the official faith of the Roman Empire. Rome was prosperous and her influence in art and letters reigned throughout the known world, but prosperity brought corruption and self-indulgence completed the ruin.

Diocletian (284–305) took the first step which led to the division of the empire, entrusting an associate with the government of the west, while he ruled the east. Then Constantine the Great in 330 moved the capital to the Greek city of Byzantium, renaming it Constantinople.

The story of the Byzantine Empire is long and glorious but that of the western empire is one of weakness and decline. Northern barbarians invaded Italy and in 410 the Visigoth King Alaric conquered Rome. The western empire from that time became the prey of successive waves of fierce barbarians.

In 476 Romulus Augustus, the last of the imperial line in the west, was deposed by the barbarian leader Odoacer, and the Roman Empire was formally brought to an end.

However, in reading the history of France, Italy and Spain, you will see that the end of the Roman Empire was in a way only its beginning. These new kingdoms governed themselves mainly by Roman law, spoke forms of Latin and professed the Christian religion. Thus even though a great empire decayed and fell, Rome had won a dominion which persists to this day.

WHEN WAS CHARLEMAGNE CROWNED HOLY ROMAN EMPEROR?

Charlemagne (Charles the Great) was crowned Holy Roman Emperor at St Peter's Basilica in Rome on Christmas Day in the year 800.

It is one of the most important dates in the Middle Ages, the beginning of a new era in European history. The man thus charged with the task of restoring order and unity out of the chaos which had followed the downfall of Christian Rome was already an emperor in fact, though not in name.

When his ally Pope Leo III placed the crown on Charles's head—unexpectedly, it was said, while he knelt in prayer—this heir to the Caesars already ruled lands stretching from Denmark to Rome and from the Atlantic to the Danube.

Charlemagne was born in 742, the grandson of Charles Martel who, 10 years before, had saved Christendom from the Saracens at the Battle of Tours in France. At the age of 26 he inherited the kingdom of the Franks and set out to bring order to western Europe and Christianity to heathen tribes. At the time of his death in 814 he had extended his rule from the Baltic Sea to the Pyrenees and from the coast of Brittany eastwards across Germany and Italy to the lower valley of the Danube.

Although he never learned to write, Charlemagne did much to encourage education and the arts. After his death the Frankish empire broke into pieces. About 130 years later the Holy Roman Empire was again revived and lasted with dwindling power until its extinction in 1806. But the fragmentation of western Europe persisted through the centuries with continual outbreaks of warfare up to the end of the Second World War.

WHY DO SOME COUNTRIES HAVE COLONIES?

Some countries still have colonies and dependencies because these are usually small territories, often with few inhabitants, which do not have the capacity to carry out all those aspects of administration and government necessary to an independent state.

Nowadays, the possession of colonies is an embarrassment rather than an advantage to the country having them, and few are retained against the wishes of their people. Before the great decolonizing years which followed the Second World War, having colonies seemed a natural part of being a great power.

France had many overseas territories such as Algeria, French Morocco and those of French West Africa, but all of these are now self-governing republics. Italy had Eritrea, now federated with Ethiopia, and Italian Somaliland, now the Somali Democratic Republic. Holland's old Dutch East Indies is mostly the present-day Republic of Indonesia.

As in the case of the British Empire the breaking up of these empires left many small territories who were not big enough for independence or who preferred to wait. These saw advantages in remaining under the protective umbrella of a greater power.

Such protection means that defence, external affairs, internal security, and the safeguarding of the terms and conditions of public officers is the responsibility of the colonizing power through its appointed governor.

In some cases the governor is also responsible for the financial and economic stability of the territory. But internal affairs are normally in the hands of the locals.

WHERE DID MONTEZUMA DIE?

Montezuma was an emperor of the 16th Century ruling over the Aztec empire from one of the greatest capitals in the world at that time–Tenochtitlan in what is now Mexico.

"It was like an enchantment . . . on account of the great towers and temples rising from the water . . . things never heard of, nor seen, nor even dreamed." So wrote the Spanish chronicler Bernal Diaz of the city of some 200,000 people. Montezuma's capital was on an island in Lake Texcoco which had been enlarged by a system of drainage canals, and was joined to the shore by causeways.

Across these causeways Hernán Cortés in 1519 led a force of 400 Spaniards, to be greeted by Montezuma as a god. The Spaniards were shown over the shrine-topped pyramids where human sacrifices were made to the Aztecs' stern war god, Huitzilopochtli.

"The figure . . . had a very broad face and monstrous and terrible eyes, and the whole of his body was covered with precious stones, and gold and pearls . . . There were some braziers and in them were burning the hearts of three Indians they had sacrificed that day." Diaz wrote, describing the scene he witnessed with Cortés. The Aztecs held the Spaniards in awe, but suspicion took over and they realized that Cortés was no god. In this atmosphere, Cortés took Montezuma as a hostage. Hostilities flared, and Montezuma was injured and died.

In the Noche Triste or Night of Sadness which followed, the Spaniards were all but annihilated by the Aztecs. Cortés and some of his men escaped. A year later they captured Tenochtitlan and razed it to the ground. The Spaniards built a town upon the ruins. It is still the capital of a nation–Mexico City.

WHEN WAS THE COLOSSEUM BUILT?

The great Flavian Amphitheatre, or Colosseum, was built between A.D. 69 and 81 by the Emperors Vespasian and Titus on the site of an artificial lake in the grounds of Nero's palace, the Golden House. The name Colosseum was bestowed on it, because of its colossal size, some time after the 8th Century.

In its full magnificence the Colosseum must have been one of the most imposing buildings in the Roman Empire, a gigantic oval measuring 620 feet by 513 feet with a height of 160 feet. Round the actual arena–287 feet by 180 feet–tiers of marble seats provided accommodation for 50,000 spectators.

The building was constructed to house gigantic spectacles organized by the authorities for the entertainment–and distraction–of the public. It became a scene of much bloodshed. Here were staged gladiatorial combats (fights to the death between men) and contests between wild beasts or between men and animals. And here, too, many of the early Christians met martyrdom with a courage that helped greatly to spread their faith.

The highest tiers of seats and the fourth storey were rebuilt in the 3rd Century, and the building was seriously damaged by lightning and earthquakes during Roman times and the Middle Ages. For hundreds of years this symbol of Roman power was used as a quarry. But even today its ruins form one of the most famous buildings in the world.

HOW WAS JEAN PAUL MARAT ASSASSINATED?

Jean Paul Marat (1743–93) was assassinated by being stabbed to death in his bath.

Marat was a political journalist whose writings were directed towards inflaming the French people to revolution. He was forced into hiding but, when the insurrection began on August 10, 1792, he joined the Paris Committee of Police and Surveillance and approved the September massacres.

He was elected as a deputy to the Convention and accepted the republic decreed on September 22. He voted for the execution of Louis XVI and helped to establish the Revolutionary Tribunal and the Committee of Public Safety which eventually brought about the Terror, as the mass-guillotining of the French Revolution was called.

The Girondins, a political group opposed to Marat, accused him of preaching pillage and murder and attempting to destroy the sovereignty of the people. Marat was acquitted by the Tribunal and turned the tables by having the Girondin leaders arrested. Thirty-one Girondins were given a so-called trial and all of them were guillotined.

By this time, Marat was suffering from a disease of the skin and lungs, and found relief only in warm baths.

On July 13, 1793, Charlotte Corday (1768–93), a young follower of the Girondins from Normandy, gained admittance to his house on the pretext of giving him information. She found him in his bath, drew a knife from under her dress and stabbed him through the heart. She was arrested on the spot and executed on July 17.

WHO WERE THE TOLPUDDLE MARTYRS?

The Tolpuddle Martyrs were a group of farm labourers in Dorset, England, who were punished by transportation to Australia because they formed a trade union. Their trial in 1834 is an important chapter in the history of the trade union movement.

In the second quarter of the 19th Century poverty was widespread in England and the distress of farm workers was so great that many were driven into open rebellion. Violent demonstrations, such as the burning of hayricks and the destruction of machinery, were met with violent reprisals. Nine men were hanged, nearly 500 deported and others imprisoned. For a time the labourers were silenced but, learning of the trade unions in the towns, they began to organize their own. At first they were successful and wages were raised from seven to ten shillings a week.

At the village of Tolpuddle, near Dorchester, George Loveless with his brother James and four others, James Brine, Thomas Stanfield, his son John, and James Hammett, formed the Friendly Society of Agricultural Labourers. Loveless was a good organizer and the progress of his society alarmed employers, who, however, felt unable to act against the members because trade unions were legal.

Eventually an excuse was found in the oath of secrecy which the men had sworn for reasons of security on joining the society. The six leaders were arrested in February 1834 under an Act of 1797 that said certain types of oath were criminal. Although law-abiding men, they were sentenced to be transported to Australia for seven years.

There was a public outcry, but the sentences were not remitted until March 1836. The labourers subsequently returned to England, but later Geroge Loveless and others emigrated to Canada. Despite this setback to the trade unions, the public sympathy aroused by the case proved an inspiration and a help to their later progress. The martyrdom of the Tolpuddle pioneers had not been in vain.

WHEN WAS SLAVERY ABOLISHED?

The first big step to rid the world of slavery was taken in 1811 when Britain abolished slave-trading. In 1833 an Act of Parliament was passed emancipating all slaves in the British colonies, thus setting an example which was followed by other European countries.

In the United States a number of conflicting interests led in 1861 to a civil war between the Northern states who wished to abolish slavery and the seceded Southern states who wanted to retain it on the plantations. In 1863 President Lincoln issued his famous Emancipation Proclamation, and two years later the victory of the North led to a constitutional amendment which prohibited slavery in the United States for ever.

In South America, a kind of agricultural slavery of the Indians continued under the name of peonage, and laws prohibiting the system did not succeed immediately in stamping it out. Even today conditions of slavery, sometimes disguised as forced labour in payment of debt, exist in some countries.

Until people's consciences began to be stirred by the efforts of humanitarians like William Wilberforce (1759–1833), slavery had generally been regarded as an inevitable part of the natural order of things. From earliest times men had forced their captured enemies to work for them. Slaves were a vital part of most ancient civilizations, providing food and services for their masters and the labour to build such man-made marvels as the pyramids. In Greece and Rome many slaves became skilled workers and held responsible positions.

After the discovery of the New World large fortunes were made by the transport of Negroes from Africa and their exploitation in the Americas.

WHERE DID CAESAR LAND IN BRITAIN?

Julius Caesar landed in Britain on a low, shelving beach somewhere between the modern towns of Deal and Walmer in Kent.

Caesar decided to invade Britain when he was Proconsul in Gaul. Only vague ideas prevailed about the British islands, but they were known to be rich in tin. So, late in

August 55 B.C., Caesar sailed across the channel with 80 transports and two legions. After a short, ferocious fight amid the waves, his men reached the shore and put the Britons to flight.

But Caesar's troubles had only just begun. His cavalry, in 18 transports, was caught in a sudden gale and driven back to Gaul, while the high tide battered the ships that lay at anchor. The Britons again attacked, were once more driven back and finally submitted. Caesar made no attempt to penetrate further inland and never even pretended that his expedition had been a success.

The following year he returned with five legions and some cavalry in 800 ships. He spent 10 days having all his ships hauled ashore. Then he crossed the River Thames near Brentford. The British had found a leader, Cassivelaunus, who harassed the Roman troops severely. Caesar was glad to negotiate with the British chieftain, to accept some hostages and tribute and then to quit the island.

For nearly 100 years no invading army landed again in Britain.

Julius Caesar (102–44 B.C.) was a member of a noble family but also became a favourite with the people of Rome. As Overseer of the Public Games in 65 B.C., he organized magnificent spectacles to win popularity, for he felt himself to be the man who would save Rome from decay. In 59 B.C. he was elected Consul and a year later was sent as Proconsul to Transalpine Gaul (now France).

WHAT ARE MERCENARIES?

Mercenaries are soldiers who give their services, and, if necessary, their lives, to anyone who will pay them enough to do so. They were common even in ancient times.

Sometimes they were slaves, as were the Nubians who served the first Pharaohs, or freebooters, such as the Philistines who were found in armies throughout the ancient Near East.

In mediaeval armies, professional soldiers often went to war instead of vassals who owed allegiance to a king or noble. The vassal had to furnish a certain number of armed men to fight in his lord's service for 40 days a year, but an alternative levy of gold was permitted which was used to hire mercenaries.

Mercenaries dominated the turbulent period from the Black Death of the mid-14th Century to the end of the wars of religion three centuries later. The bands which devastated France in the Hundred Years' War (1337–1453) were like those which ruined Germany in the Thirty Years' War (1618–48). The wealthy cities of Renaissance Italy gave them long-term contracts for they were tough, skilful men who could cope with any kind of disturbance.

There are still men whose love of adventure and action leads them to enlist with any army who will pay them enough. Many governments, especially those in developing nations, are anxious to pay for their daring and expertise.

Through the ages mercenaries have become heroes, murderers, and the inevitable face of war.

WHEN DID HAMLET LIVE?

Hamlet, the hero of Shakespeare's great tragedy, seems to correspond to a figure called Amleth, who appears in a history of Denmark, written by Saxo Grammaticus late in the 12th Century.

However, it is impossible to say whether he did in fact exist. The figure of the young man whose father was murdered by a brother who later married his victim's widow appears in many legends. In all of them the son pretends to be mad in order to revenge his father's death. Such stories are found as far back as the Icelandic saga of Amlöoi, mentioned by the 10th Century poet, Snaebjörn.

The story of Hamlet is told in the fifth volume of *Histoires Tragiques* (1570) by François de Belleforest and an English version of this, *The Hystorie of Hamblet* was published in London in 1608. Shakespeare's tragedy was written about 1601, but a play about Hamlet believed to have been written by Thomas Kyd was performed in about 1509.

As he often did, Shakespeare borrowed the plot from others and transformed it by his genius into a great work of art.

HOW ARE THE CELTS DISPERSED?

If there are any true Celts today, they are probably living in Ireland, the Highlands of Scotland, Wales, Brittany or the Isle of Man. Only in these most western parts of Europe did the once powerful Celts manage to maintain their language and racial characteristics in the centuries of Roman expansion and the later invasion of Germanic tribes that swept westward across Europe from beyond the river Elbe.

It is mainly in those regions that any distinctive Celtic traces have survived—the Erse, Gaelic, Welsh, Manx and Breton languages, and Celtic traits, folklore and traditions. Elsewhere the individuality of the tribes has been merged with that of their conquerors. Yet even there Celtic traces remain in earthworks, stones and fortifications, in the names of many places that were once their homes and in some of the words in modern European languages.

The Celtic tribes grew from a mixture of prehistoric peoples who settled in western and central Europe, having migrated, perhaps, from beyond the Caspian Sea. By about 400 B.C. they had developed into a warlike race holding vast territories all the way from Ireland to Asia Minor.

It was the advance of the Roman legionaries that sapped their strength and hastened their decline. With the collapse of the Roman Empire they fell a prey to the waves of invaders from the west until even across the sea the Celtic Britons had been enslaved or driven into the remoter parts by the Anglo-Saxons. With them disappeared the mysterious religion of the Druids, who held the mistletoe sacred and performed strange ceremonies in the oak forests.

In a sense the Celtic race has been dispersed throughout a large part of the world because they were among the chief ancestors of most Europeans and therefore of North and South Americans, Australians, New Zealanders, South Africans and many others.

WHY WAS THE GREAT WALL OF CHINA BUILT?

The Great Wall of China was built in the Third Century B.C. to keep out the raiding Tartars of Mongolia. It is 20 to 30 feet high and 15 to 25 feet wide at the top, with towers 60 feet high every few hundred yards.

The Wall stretches from Shanhaikwan on the Yellow Sea to the borders of Kansu and Sinkiang in the west, crossing high mountains and deep valleys. Probably over 500,000 workers were employed to build it. Even today, the Wall is in a wonderful state of preservation.

This marvellous structure is constructed of brick and stone. The sides have battlements—parapets with openings or embrasures through which weapons could be discharged.

All large cities of China were provided with similar walls, and the gates were closed at night to give the citizens protection against surprise attack. For China has been envied by her neighbours throughout history. Many times these neighbours have invaded the country, seized the capital and begun a new dynasty.

WHO LIVED AT 221B BAKER STREET LONDON?

At 221B Baker Street, London, lived Sherlock Holmes, the greatest of all fictional detectives. He was the creation of Sir Arthur Conan Doyle (1859–1930), who published 60 stories about him, including three full-length novels. The character was in part suggested by that of Dr Joseph Bell, an eminent Edinburgh surgeon, under whom Conan Doyle studied medicine. The author's experience as a doctor also gave him the necessary background for the creation of Dr Watson, the supposed narrator of the Holmes stories, who served as a foil for the great detective and became almost as famous as his companion.

Sherlock Holmes arrived at his solutions by acute observation and brilliant reasoning. His first case was *A Study in Scarlet* (1887), a full-length novel. But it was not until short stories began to appear regularly in the *Strand Magazine* that he and his creator became famous. After the stories had been collected in two books, Conan Doyle became tired of his hero and arranged a suitably heroic death for him in a struggle with his great enemy Moriarty. However, the public refused to accept that Holmes's life really ended in that struggle, so the detective was resurrected, and Conan Doyle continued to write about him until his own death.

Apart from Holmes, Conan Doyle wrote other fine stories, including *The Lost World, The White Company* and *The Poison Belt*. He was also the author of a *History of Spiritualism*, and histories of the South African War and the British campaigns on the Western Front in the First World War.

WHEN DID THE INCAS RISE TO POWER?

The Incas, a race of South American Indians, are believed to have started their rise to power in Peru about five hundred years before the arrival of the Spanish conquerors in the 16th Century. They are said to have climbed into the Andes mountains from the eastern forests calling themselves "children of the Sun".

According to their favourite legend. Manco Capac, the founder of the race, came out of Lake Titicaca in Peru with his sister who was also his wife. The sun god was said to have given him a staff and told him to build a city at a spot where it sank into the ground—in other words, where the ground was fertile. This city was given the name Cuzco, meaning navel, because the Incas regarded it as the centre of the earth.

It was not long before the Incas began to conquer or absorb the neighbouring tribes. By 1460 their empire extended from the Amazon forests to the Pacific Ocean, from the borders of what is now Ecuador, deep into Chile. This 2,000-mile territory was governed by a mild form of despotism. The

Inca mask

term Inca properly applied only to the upper caste of the nobility and those of royal blood.

Property was held in common, money was not used and the products of labour were divided in three equal portions between the church, the governing classes and the people. Inca skills included the spinning of woollen clothes, mining, engineering with tin and copper tools, the fashioning of gold and silver ornaments, irrigation and the use of fertilizers. They used a system of writing by means of knots tied in lengths of string.

The doom of this thriving and industrious civilization was sealed when the Spanish adventurer Francisco Pizarro sailed from the Isthmus of Panama with fewer than 200 men in 1531 to conquer and loot the country. Pizarro seized the Inca ruler Atahualpa and had him put to death after accepting a vast gold and silver ransom for his life. With their leader executed and their chiefs slain, the people were forced into submission. Slaughter, plunder and oppression followed. But today the remains of massive stone temples and palaces survive as reminders of the high state of Inca culture.

WHERE IS WILLIAM PENN BURIED?

William Penn (1644-1718), who gave his name to the state of Pennsylvania in the United States, is buried in the graveyard of an early Quaker meeting house in Jordans, in the English county of Buckinghamshire.

He was the son of Admiral Sir William Penn (1621-70) and became a convert to Quakerism in 1661. These peaceful people were persecuted and despised. William Penn was expelled from Oxford University because he joined the sect, and was later imprisoned in the Tower of London.

In 1681 Charles II granted Penn a domain of some 50,000 square miles of English Crown land in America in payment of a debt owed by the Crown to his father. Persecuted in England, the Quakers were not allowed to enter any of the established American colonies. To found a haven for people of all religions, and in the hope of converting the warlike Red Indians, Penn sent out the first settlers to his newly-acquired colony which he named Pennsylvania (Penn's forestland). He, too, went out a year later.

He gave the settlers democratic government and made friends with the Delaware Indians who agreed to "live in love with William Penn and his children as long as the sun and moon gave light". Penn lived at Philadelphia, the capital of his colony, but after two years was called back to England on business and was absent for 15 years.

After a period of trouble he revisited Pennsylvania in 1899 and granted a charter to its 20,000 inhabitants which remained in force for 75 years until the American War of Independence.

In 1701 Penn returned to England to find that his unscrupulous steward had robbed him of his fortune. He was imprisoned for debt and the conditions of the jail affected his health. His friends secured his release, and he lived quietly until his death on May 30, 1718. The fine old building in whose graveyard he is buried has been preserved and is open to the public.

WHY ARE ASSASSINS SO-CALLED?

Some murderers are called assassins because this name was given in the 11th Century to a sect of Shi'ite Muslim fanatics who pledged themselves to murder those who did not believe in their religion.

The word assassin comes from the Arab *hashishi* or hashish eater, supposedly because the killers were alleged to take hashish to give ecstatic visions of paradise before setting out on a mission which might well end in their own deaths. We use the word now for one who kills a public figure.

The history of the Shi'ite Muslim sect began in 1090 in Persia, where it was founded by Hassan ibn al-Sabbah and where its endeavours were chiefly directed against the regime of the Seljuks, a Turkish family who had invaded western Asia and founded a powerful empire.

In the 12th Century the assassins extended their activities to Syria, where the expansion of Seljuk rule and the arrival of the Christian crusaders gave them ample scope. They seized a group of castles and waged a war of terror against rulers and crusaders. At one time, they made a pact with Saladin (1138–1193) and murdered Conrad de Montferrat, a crusader who had been made King of Jerusalem. The successive assassin chiefs in Syria were known as the "Old Man of the Mountain". The chief of the sect in Persia proclaimed himself as ruler or Imam.

The end of the power of the assassins came in the 13th Century. The last of their castles fell in 1272. There are still followers of the sect to be found in Syria, Iran and Pakistan, where they are known as Khojas.

Today they owe allegiance to the Aga Khan, as the spiritual leader of the Nizari Isma'ili sect of the Shi'ite Mohammedans.

WHAT WAS THE AUTO-DA-FÉ?

The auto-da-fé (act of faith) was the name of the public ceremony which followed the secret trials of the Spanish Inquisition established in 1478 during the reign of King Ferdinand of Aragon and Queen Isabella of Castile.

These two Christian monarchs, having united most of Spain by their marriage, were about to complete the age-old battle to free the country from "the infidels" by the conquest of Granada from the Moors. The time was ripe for them to seek to encourage national unity and strengthen the authority both of themselves and of the Church.

So it was a mixture of motives that led Ferdinand and Isabella to persuade Pope Sixtus IV to set up the Spanish Inquisition, with the declared purpose of disciplining the flourishing and influential Jewish community, whose wealth aroused envy and whose presence seemed to offer the greatest obstacle to unity. Soon the powers of the Inquisition (from the Latin *inquiro*, to inquire into) were directed not only against Jews but also against Moors, Christian Protestants and even Catholics whose behaviour was deemed to threaten the solidarity of the Church on which the royal authority also rested.

After secret interrogations, sometimes aided by torture, the auto-da-fé was celebrated. First came a procession of priests, officials and accused persons who had confessed their guilt and declared themselves penitent. This was followed by a solemn mass, an oath of obedience to the Inquisition and the reading of sentences whether of punishment or acquittal. Those condemned to death were handed over to the civil power to emphasize the fact that the Church did not itself shed blood.

But the severity of the first Grand Inquisitor, Tomás de Torquemada (1420–1498) is thought

Torture during the Spanish Inquisition.

to have led to 2,000 burnings at the stake and unsuccessful attempts at mediation by the Pope.

After the reigns of Ferdinand's successors, Charles I (1516–56) and Philip II (1556–98), the Inquisition gradually dwindled in influence and was finally suppressed in 1834.

HOW DID BOTANY BAY BECOME FAMOUS?

Botany Bay became famous as the place in Australia to which English convicts were transported after Captain James Cook had taken possession of the continent for Britain in 1770.

Cook sailed up to Botany Bay, near the site of the present city of Sydney, and named the continent New South Wales, because he thought its coastline resembled that of South Wales. Botany Bay was so called by Joseph Banks, a botanist in Cook's expedition, because of the bay's rich plant life.

Until then Britain had transported most of her convicts to work on the American plantations. But when the North American colonies gained their independence in 1782, it was decided to send the convicts to Australia, chiefly because of the great distance.

In January 1788, a fleet of nine transports carrying 828 convicts, of whom 300 were women, and escorted by two warships, arrived in Botany Bay. Captain Arthur Philip (1738–1814) who was in charge of the expedition and was appointed governor, established a settlement which he called Sidney, after Lord Sidney (1733–1800) who was British Colonial Secretary.

The colony became a dumping ground for the rejects of Britain but many of those transported were guilty only of small offences. Some free men also settled there, and the convicts worked as unpaid servants to the officials and free settlers. Even when they had served their sentences, most preferred to remain in Australia, where they were given grants of land, and helped to build a colony.

WHY IS DEMOCRACY CONSIDERED GOOD?

Democracy is considered good because it recognizes the rights of the individual and strives to maintain and protect those rights, for instance freedom of speech and religion.

The word democracy comes from the Greek "demokration", from "demos", the people, and "kratos", rule. The concept of rule by the people for the people undoubtedly goes back to prehistoric times but, in western political tradition, we associate it with the city-states of ancient Greece.

There it was a form of government known as direct democracy. Decisions were made by the whole body of citizens, acting under the procedure of majority rule. However, we must remember that not

120

everyone was a citizen. Women were not allowed to vote and there were many slaves who had no rights at all.

It is easy to see how difficult this system would be to organize in a large country and indeed there was a gap of about 2,000 years before the idea of representative democracy arose. This is a form of government where the citizens exercise the same rights as in direct democracy, but through representatives chosen by and responsible to them.

Nowadays, most countries in the world are democracies, in name at least. That is, they claim a form of government, elected by the people, whose powers are limited by a constitution. Theoretically this means that although the majority are in power, they are bound by law to guarantee individual and collective rights to those who are in the minority. But in many countries theory does not always conform with practice.

We also use the word democratic to describe any political or social system which is attempting to bring about equality among the people, especially in the distribution of private property.

WHEN WAS THE GUNPOWDER PLOT?

"Remember, remember the fifth of November, gunpowder, treason and plot" – so goes the old English chant associated with the yearly burning on thousands of village greens and in millions of private gardens throughout England every fifth of November of the effigy of Guy Fawkes. For November 5th celebrates the discovery of the famous plot to blow up the English House of Lords.

Guy Fawkes was a Catholic gentleman who played a major role in Robert Catesby's plot to blow up King James I and his Parliament for failing to honour James's pledge to extend more toleration to the Catholics.

Catesby apparently had vague ideas of a Catholic take-over of the country.

There were five main conspirators, including Fawkes. In May 1604 they rented a house near the Parliament building and started to dig a passage which was designed to reach a point just below the House of Lords. But in 1605 the conspirators were able to rent a neighbouring cellar which was directly beneath the Palace of Westminster. They linked their passageway to this cellar and Fawkes was allotted the task of preparing the explosion. He gathered together at least twenty barrels of gunpowder in the cellar and covered them up with wood and coal.

All seemed set for the great day, which was the November opening of Parliament. By this time the number of conspirators had risen to thirteen, one of whom, Francis Tresham, had a brother, Lord Monteagle, in the House of Lords. Tresham sent a secret letter warning his brother that a "terrible blow" was to be delivered against Parliament and adding "yet they shall not see who hurts them".

Monteagle took the letter to the King's ministers. On November 4th they had the cellars at Westminster searched and Guy Fawkes was discovered there with his gunpowder.

WHERE IS DUNKIRK?

Dunkirk is a seaport of Northern France lying between Calais and the Belgian coast, but for millions of people all over the world Dunkirk is one of the most evocative names of the Second World War. For it was from Dunkirk and its 10-mile stretch of beaches that the British evacuated some 338,200 soldiers after the collapse of Belgium and immediately before the collapse of France. Today, Dunkirk has become another name for the supreme heroism that can snatch a victory from defeat.

The troop evacuation took place between May 26 and June 4, 1940. The men were under constant German bombardment both from the land and from the air. At home in England, the British organized an immortal flotilla of small boats. Thames pleasure boats, cabin-cruisers, fishing smacks, even rowing boats were pressed into service –all, of course, on a volunteer basis. The "little ships" ferried the troops from the beaches to the waiting Navy ships.

Evacuation first began from the damaged harbour at Dunkirk, but by May 28 heavy German bombing had severely restricted the harbour's usefulness. By the end of June 1 the greater part of the British Expeditionary Force had been removed, although rescue operations continued until June 4.

The toll of ships was considerable. Out of 41 destroyers used by the British, 6 were sunk and 19 damaged. Most of the expeditionary force's supplies and materials were lost. The British were reduced to their weakest point. But Dunkirk was the great turning point in the war. Hitler's Germany had, it seemed, reached its greatest point of menace, and was never to seem so threatening again.

WHAT WAS THE BLACK DEATH?

The Black Death was a plague that raged through Europe from 1347–1350. It was caused by fleas living on rats which were carried to Europe from Asia by Genoese trading ships. It is suggested that the Black Death was probably bubonic plague, that is to say the sufferers developed "buboes" or inflamed swellings.

About one in three Europeans died of the disease. The sudden decrease in population brought serious social problems. An acute labour shortage led to higher wages and there was a short-lived slump in trade. Many people became obsessed with the idea of death, for there were many recurrences of the plague, notably during the years 1361-3, 1369-71, 1374-5, 1390 and 1400.

On the other hand, the plague speeded changes that had already begun, changes which had their roots in growing trade and the increasing use of money. It became profitable to export wool and wheat. So land gained a new importance, and many nobles, who had lost labourers and were forced to pay much higher wages to those remaining, chose to sell their estates' land to rich merchants. Thus arose a new class of landowners where wealth counted as much as birth.

The population of western Europe did not regain its pre-1348 level until the beginning of the 16th Century.

WHO WAS KNOWN AS RASPUTIN?

Grigori Efimovich, called Rasputin, (1872?-1916) was a Russian peasant and mystic who became a powerful and notorious favourite at the court of Tsar Nicholas II. He received virtually no education, but had an extraordinary magnetic personality. Assuming the role of a holy pilgrim, he left his family in Pokrovskoe, Western Siberia, and in 1903 arrived in the Russian capital, St Petersburg (now Leningrad). There he was befriended by high churchmen, and his hypnotic powers made him the centre of a circle of admirers, particularly women. His claim to have a divinely inspired power of healing by physical contact gave him an excuse for sexual excesses.

In 1905 he was presented to Tsar Nicholas and Tsarina Alexandra. Their son, the young Crown Prince Alexis, suffered from haemophilia, a physical weakness that leads to severe bleeding. Rasputin's powers of suggestion seemed to have a remarkable healing influence on the boy, and he came to be regarded by Alexandra as a saint sent by God to save the royal family and the country. But his arrogance, debauchery and interference with the government made him many enemies. Parliament denounced him in 1912 as "a mysterious tragi-comic figure, an apparition of the Dark Ages" and he was sent into exile.

Two years later, however, he was allowed to return to St Petersburg. In 1915 when the Tsar assumed supreme control of his armies on the battlefields against Germany, Rasputin, who was against the war, exploited his influence over the Tsarina to control affairs in the capital. A group of aristocrats, jealous of his power, disgusted with his scandalous behaviour and suspecting him of treachery, determined to kill him. On the night of December 29-30, 1916, he was trapped in a house to which he had been invited, poisoned, shot, and finally, it is told, bound and dropped through a hole in the ice on the Neva river where he eventually froze to death.

WHY DID THE MAYFLOWER SAIL TO AMERICA?

The Mayflower sailed to America to transport the Pilgrim Fathers from England to Plymouth, Massachusetts, where they established the first permanent colony in New England in 1620.

The Mayflower was a square-rigged sailing ship which had formerly carried wine and was armed with 12 cannon. Among the leaders on board were John Carver, William Bradford and Captain Miles Standish, who had been hired for his military knowledge.

The ship sailed from Southampton, England, on August 15, 1620 with 102 passengers and soon ran into fierce storms which necessitated some repairs. The voyage lasted 66 days. One child–a boy–was born to Elizabeth Hopkins at sea. Another was born on board to Susanna White as the ship lay at anchor off Cape Cod.

At Cape Cod the Pilgrims drew up a covenant, now known as the Mayflower Compact, which bound them to obey the government which should be set up. Within 10 years the colony was prosperous and expanding, and was able to dissolve the financial partnership it had made with merchants back in England. The first settlers did not become known as the Pilgrim Fathers until two centuries after their arrival when Daniel Webster made a speech beginning: "We have come to record here our homage to our Pilgrim Fathers..."

A reconstruction of The Mayflower set sail for America in 1957.

WHAT HAPPENED TO THE ABORIGINES?

The original inhabitants of Australia, the Aborigines, met the usual fate of widely-scattered native peoples when the white settlers began to arrive and multiply. Their numbers fell drastically.

This was not due to any policy of cruelty or repression. From the start intentions towards them were good. But the vision of the white administrators was not equal to bridging the gulf between the intensely religious and ceremonial native culture, and the materialistic aims of the settlers.

By a natural process–perhaps the result of apathy or despair– the number of Aborigines fell from 350,000 in the 18th Century to some 40,000 in the 1930s. But since then, with more sympathy and understanding, their numbers have started to rise again.

The main effort is now being directed to stop them becoming a permanently underprivileged minority.

WHY ARE SOME DICTATORS CALLED BENEVOLENT?

We call a dictator "benevolent" if he uses his powers for the good of the people, not simply for his own. The word "benevolent" is derived from the Latin and means "well-wishing", but though many dictators have promised to defend the rights of the populace, most of them have failed to do so.

A dictator is a ruler who, usually because of some emergency, is given extraordinary powers of government. The office was first instituted in ancient Rome in 501 B.C. to deal with serious military, civil or criminal disturbances. The dictator was described as the "administrative dictator" (*rei gerundae causa*) and held office for six months.

Modern dictators, like the ancient ones, have taken over the reins of government in times of crisis, but they have used their powers to establish a permanent and often tyrannical rule. Both Benito Mussolini and Adolph Hitler eventually became heads of government formally, in accordance with the constitution. Other famous dictatorships include the long-established figure of Spain's General Franco and more recently Uganda's President Amin.

Perhaps the best example of a benevolent dictator is Napoleon Bonaparte (1769–1821), Napoleon I of France from 1804 to 1814 and again for the "Hundred Days" in 1815. He seized absolute power in France, but his ambitions were for his country and his people rather than for himself. Under his rule industry expanded and the universities flourished, while he left enduring legacies in the shape of the Code Napoleon (the codification of French civil law), the reorganization of the judicial system, the Bank of France and the establishment of the military academies such as St. Cyr.

WHERE DID ROBIN HOOD LIVE?

Robin Hood lived in Sherwood Forest, near Nottingham in the centre of England. In those 12th Century days a vast region of open tracts, woodland glades and great oaks used to stretch for many miles from the city northwards. This region was called Sherwood Forest.

Until the time of the Normans the forest was used for hunting by the people of that region, or shire, and thereby acquired its earlier name of Shire Wood. The common people's right to hunt ceased when the Norman kings took over the forest for their own use. Strict laws were passed and special courts were set up to preserve them.

Whether Robin Hood and his merry band of followers, which included Little John, Friar Tuck, Will Scarlet and Maid Marian, ever existed is difficult to establish. Certainly by the end of the 12th Century, with control of royal Sherwood in the hands of feudal barons, the common people deeply resented the harsh and oppressive rule under which they lived. The time was ripe for stories about a man who robbed the rich to feed the poor.

The character of Robin Hood represented the ideals of the common people of the late Middle Ages. Ballads about his exploits have been preserved and may date from the 14th and 15th Centuries. In 1795 Joseph Ritson first published a collection of these in book form.

Over the years stories of the carefree folk-hero and his band of happy followers, living an idyllic life in the woodland glades of Sherwood during the days of the Plantagenet kings, have become the subject of many books.

WHEN IS WAR SAID TO ESCALATE?

War is said to escalate when it increases rapidly in scale or intensity. The word was added to the military vocabulary by the Americans during the Vietnam War to denote the increasing degrees of United States involvement in the fighting. It has also been used by military writers to describe the development of a possible war between two powers through successive stages from the use of conventional weapons to the localized employment of atomic weapons and, finally, an all-out exchange of annihilating nuclear missiles.

It is a far cry from the use of the word escalator by the American Jesse W. Reno to describe the moving staircase he invented in 1891. Both words come from the Spanish *escalada*, meaning the scaling of the walls of a fortress by means of ladders. A staircase moving inevitably upwards provides a more fitting image than a scaling ladder of the horrifying expansion of which war today is capable.

Medicine and the Body

WHERE DO DREAMS GO WHEN YOU WAKE UP?

The simple answer is either they are stored in your memory or you forget them. But this question makes us ask a great number of other questions. What is the difference between day-dreaming and the dreams we have when we are asleep? Can dreams fortell the future? How long do they really last? Do we have dreams in colour or only black and white? Why do we forget some dreams and remember others? Are dreams good for us, or bad? Why do some dreams wake us up at once and others not?

Some experts say that to be healthy in mind, we have to dream every night, whether we remember them or not. There is a book called *An Experiment with Time* by J. W. Dunne, which tells us that the author used to note down in the morning the dreams he had in the night, and that sometimes his dreams foretold what was going to happen in the future.

He suggests that when we are wide awake our sense of time is vertical, so that we are aware only of the present moment, but that when we are asleep, time becomes for us horizontal, so that we can travel into the past and the future. Other experts say that we dream of doing the things which for various reasons, we cannot do in our waking hours. So we try to realize in our sleep wishes that cannot be realized by day.

WHEN WAS BLOOD-LETTING COMMON?

Blood-letting was a common form of medical treatment from before the time of Hippocrates (400 B.C.), the Greek "father of medicine" and was still much in fashion for various ailments a century ago. A bleeding-glass formed part of the symbol of the physician in ancient Egypt.

The old ideas about blood-letting, or phlebotomy, arose from a theory that certain body fluids, known as "humours", controlled a person's illnesses and decided his character. Today we call a person "sanguine" if he is optimistic or cheerful, but to a doctor in the Middle Ages a sanguine man was one in whom hot blood predominated over his other humours. A "phlegmatic" or stolid man was one who suffered from too much cold, wet phlegm.

For many illnesses it was considered that the best cure was to restore the balance of humours by relieving the body of diseased blood. Bleeding became almost a panacea, a cure-all. Monks were bled regularly to keep their minds from worldly thoughts. Madame de Maintenon (1635–1719) was said to have been bled to stop her from blushing.

Blood-letting was prescribed by doctors, but performed by barbers. The barbers took over as surgeons in 1163, when a papal decree forbade the clergy to shed blood, and they continued the profession for six centuries. On a barber's pole the red stripes represent the blood and the white ones the bandages, while the gilt knob at the end is the symbol of the basin in which the barber-surgeon caught the blood–or the lather.

In the 19th Century many people still had themselves bled regularly as a treatment for various illnesses, especially those due to over indulgence in food and drink. Frequently people died not from the disease but from the supposed cure. Blood-sucking worms called leeches were often used, being regarded as an essential part of a doctor's equipment.

Even today the withdrawal of blood is said to help certain conditions, and leeches are still used in some countries, particularly in the East.

WHY DO WE TURN WHITE WHEN FRIGHTENED?

We turn white when we are frightened because the blood in our cheeks is diverted to do a more urgent job. At the same time our hearts begin to beat much faster, and we breathe more quickly.

When we sit still, our hearts beat at about 70 or 80 times a minute, pumping the blood through our bodies. The blood carries nourishment from food, and oxygen from the air we breathe, both of which are vitally necessary for the body to function.

If we take violent exercise, our muscles need to work much harder and faster than when we are sitting or walking. They therefore need extra nourishment and oxygen. The nerves carry the message to that part of the brain called the hypothalamus, the centre of an automatic nervous system in control of internal bodily functions such as the pumping of the heart, breathing and digestion.

Impulses from the hypothalamus travel down the spinal cord and excite other nerve cells– "sympathetic" neurons–which end in the centre or medulla of the adrenal glands just above the kidneys. These glands release the hormone adrenalin into the bloodstream which causes the heart to beat faster and more efficiently, dilates air passages in the lungs and the blood vessels that supply the muscles, and increases the concentration of energy-giving glucose in the blood.

In fact, when we are frightened, exactly the same physical changes take place and our bodies are immediately and efficiently prepared for the violent exercise of flight or fight without any voluntary effort on our part.

WHAT HAPPENS WHEN WE BLUSH?

When we blush we go red in the face, particularly in the cheeks and neck. This is because a sudden emotion, such as embarrassment, a sense of shame or pleasure, causes the very small blood vessels just below the surface of the skin to become larger. As these blood vessels, called capillaries, are full of blood, the skin looks red.

When people blush they usually feel hot and uncomfortable, and imagine that their red faces are very noticeable. This is not always so, because some people's blushes do not show. It depends very much on the colour of the skin. Blushing is most noticeable on a fair-haired, pale-skinned person. Young people, particularly girls in their teens, are supposed to blush more easily than older people. This is true of many girls. As they grow older, they usually blush less easily, because they are embarrassed less often, and learn to cope with sudden emotions.

HOW DOES THE HEART WORK?

The heart, which is a muscular pump, beats about 72 times a minute through a continuous and automatic process of muscular contraction and relaxation. It is about the size of a fist, weighs about 9–11 ounces and is placed snugly between the lungs, a little more to the left than to the right. A partition runs down the centre of the heart, dividing it into left and right sections which work at the same time but deal with two different types of blood. Each section is again divided into upper and lower parts, the auricles and ventricles. The blood is pumped through all four chambers in turn in the course of being circulated through all parts of the body.

The heart's first purpose is to supply a steady flow of oxygen to all the body cells and to return carbon dioxide to the lungs. On its journey the blood distributes dissolved foods and carries away wastes.

Two large veins pour the dark, used blood into the first chamber, the right auricle, which passes it into the chamber below, the right ventricle. The muscle surrounding this part contracts in a beat that pushes the blood into the lungs where the carbon dioxide is removed and replaced with vital oxygen. Meanwhile fresh scarlet blood from the lungs enters the left auricle to be transferred to the left ventricle. From there it is forced by the contracting muscle through a valve into the aorta, the body's largest artery which distributes it all over the body.

The heart beats about 100,000 times every 24 hours and pushes several quarts of blood through miles of arteries, veins and capillaries. A healthy heart keeps this up for a lifetime without faltering.

WHERE ARE THE SWEAT GLANDS?

Sweat glands, of which everybody has approximately two million, are distributed all over the body on the skin surface. They are not, however, distributed evenly. The palms of our hands and the soles of our feet may have as many as 2,500 sweat glands per square inch, whereas on our backs there may be as few as 500 per square inch.

Each gland breaks the skin surface in the form of a sweat pore. These pores are too small to be visible to the naked eye, except on the palms and soles, where there are so many that they just become visible.

In some diseases nerve function is lost in certain areas of the body, and these areas also lose the power to sweat. Sweat is a solution of about 99 per cent water with a little sodium chloride (common salt). The body can produce from zero to 2,000 grammes of this substance every hour and even more in strenuous activities.

WHEN DOES THE BODY PRODUCE ADRENALIN?

A person's body produces adrenalin when he is angry, frightened or challenged, or when he needs to be functioning at maximum efficiency to meet some sort of stress.

Adrenalin is a hormone, a substance which acts upon tissues and organs. It is secreted in the adrenal glands, which lie like a pair of pyramid-shaped caps, one on top of each kidney. Each gland has two parts, the outer shell, or cortex, and the inner core, or medulla. The adrenal hormones come from the medulla and are released into the bloodstream. They stimulate the liver both to release its sugar and to speed up its manufacture for muscular action. They also contract blood vessels, diverting blood from the skin and raising the pressure at which it is pumped through the brain and lungs and muscles. The heart and pulse quicken, the breathing speeds up, the body heat rises and muscular fatigue is postponed. At the same time the ability of the blood to coagulate in the event of the person being wounded is increased.

This series of defence reactions occurs almost immediately. Adrenalin released by the glands is reinforced by more hormones produced at the sympathetic nerve ends. A hormone produced in the brain, called serotonin, stimulates the transmission of nerve impulses.

WHY DO WE HAVE TWO EYES?

We have two eyes placed in the front of our heads because we need to be able to judge distances and to see in depth. The change in the position of the eyes from the side of the head in our remote ancestors probably came about because they needed to be able to judge distances accurately as they swung from branch to branch in the trees.

With both eyes in front, their separate fields of vision overlap. We see two images superimposed one upon the other but, because of the space between our eyes, the image from each goes a little way

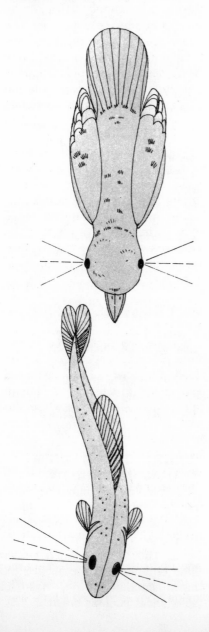

around its own side of the object. This is called stereoscopic vision, or vision in depth, which we share with apes and monkeys. Many other animals and fish do not have this advantage. To them the world appears flat. One exception is the owl, who sees better than any of us, and has not only stereoscopic vision, but telescopic vision, too.

Our judgement of distances depends, with near objects, upon our stereoscopic vision. As the distance increases, there is less difference between the left-eyed and the right-eyed view. So we depend upon other factors as well.

Experience tells us that the farther away an object is, the smaller it looks. Its colour also changes, its details disappear, its outline softens. Nearer objects give us a measure against which to judge the distance of farther ones. Then there is perspective, the familiar illusion that parallel lines converge towards the horizon.

WHO DEVELOPED INSULIN?

Insulin extracts, which save the lives of many thousands of people, were developed by the combined efforts of three physiologists, Sir Frederick Banting from Ontario, Canada, Charles H. Best from Maine, United States, and John James Rickard Macleod from Perth, Scotland. In 1921 they became the first to obtain the hormone in a form consistently effective in the treatment of diabetes.

Normally, insulin is manufactured in the human pancreas, which lies behind the stomach. It enables the liver to store surplus sugar and the brain and muscles to be nourished by this essential food. When the insulin supply fails, the body can no longer use this fuel and an excess of sugar may spill through the kidneys into the urine. Diabetes, as this condition is called, previously meant almost certain death. The achievements of Banting, Best and Macleod at the University of Toronto, Canada, gave sufferers the prospect of a long and healthy life.

The three men were following up the work of two German physicians, Joseph von Mering (1849–1908) and Oskar Minkowski (1858–1931), who in 1889 showed that the removal of the pancreas in dogs caused diabetes. With this link established, scientists set out to discover what contribution the pancreas made in preventing the disease. In 1909 one of them, J. de Meyer, suggested the name insulin for this supposed internal secretion. Finally the three Toronto researchers discovered how to obtain the insulin from the pancreas of an ox and inject it into human beings. In January, 1922, Banting administered crude insulin to a patient for the first time.

Banting and Macleod won the Nobel Prize for Medicine in 1923, and Banting insisted on sharing his award with Best. Banting, who was knighted in 1934, was killed in a plane crash on February 21, 1941, while on a war mission connected with aviation medicine. Best succeeded him as head of the Banting and Best Department of Medical Research at Toronto University. Since their discovery, the extract has been refined, and many patients control their diabetes by administering their own insulin injections.

WHAT HAPPENS WHEN THINGS GO MOULDY?

The moulds we find on bread, cheese and other foods are fungi, like the mushroomy substances that grow on the ground and on trees. They appear when certain little organisms in the air find the moist conditions they need in substances such as bread.

Fungi are very important on account of the great good or harm the different kinds can do. One particular green mould has proved of tremendous benefit in medical treatment because Sir Alexander Fleming discovered in 1928 that it stops the growth of certain bacteria. Doctors have used this mould, which is called penicillin, and others like it as "antibiotics" to destroy more serious bacteria which cause disease. Such moulds have been cultivated on a gigantic scale to produce substances of unequalled curative power.

Moulds have many other uses. Some fungi produce the fermentation needed to brew beer or turn grape juice into wine. Others are used in making bread or delicious cheeses. Fungi also perform the important action of turning dead leaves and animal bodies into useful components of the soil.

WHERE ARE THE ISLETS OF LANGERHANS?

These islets are not to be found in an atlas but are located in the human pancreas, which manufactures juices to aid the digestion of fats and continues the work of the saliva and gastric juices.

Langerhans was a German anatomist (1847–88) who gave his name to two other parts of the body. He discovered cells in the epidermis called Langerhans Cells and also the Langerhans Layer which is a layer of the skin.

There are many groups of cells without ducts distributed through the pancreas. But the importance of the Islets of Langerhans is that their beta cells are a source of insulin. It is damage to or removal of the Islets of Langerhans that leads to pancreatic diabetes. Insulin, which is a protein, is synthesized by the beta cells.

WHY DO WE BRUISE?

We bruise because the body has received a heavy blow which injures the bodily tissues without rupturing or tearing the outer covering of skin.

A bruise is a wound, and a wound may be defined as a breach in the continuity of any body tissue. Often the skin is cut or torn. But closed wounds, such as the rupturing of internal organs, may leave no visible external sign.

A bruise, or contusion of the skin, is caused by the rupture of the blood vessels in the deeper layers of the tissues under the skin. The blood escapes from the damaged vessels into the surrounding tissues and brings about discoloration of the skin, which at first goes red, and then "black and blue". As the blood pigments break down, the bruise changes to yellow and green, and eventually fades away. Usually bruises show in the area where the blow has fallen. But there are times when the blood will track along muscles and the planes of connective tissue, causing the bruise to appear some way away from the injury.

WHEN WAS THE SIGN LANGUAGE FOR DEAF-MUTES INVENTED?

Sign language for people who could not hear or speak was developed in the 18th Century. The Abbé Charles Michel Epée (1712–1789) studied the sign language which had grown up among such people over the centuries and organized it into a systematic language which could be used in education and communication. His work was developed by the Abbé Sicard (1742–1822). A code of manual gestures evolved, some representing letters of the alphabet and others symbolizing whole words or phrases.

The Abbé Epée concentrated on gestures in his school for deaf-mutes, but other teachers believed that the deaf should be taught to lip-read and, if possible, to communicate by sounds. One of the greatest teachers of the latter method was the German Moritz Hill (1805–1874). Today many educators use a combination of both methods. The example of Helen Keller (1880–1968), a blind deaf-mute, who was taught to speak by a devoted teacher, Anne Sullivan, made millions of people realize that deaf-mutes failed to develop speech only because they are unable to hear other people speaking.

In the 20th Century tremendous advances have been made in the early recognition of impaired hearing and in the training of teachers and other specialists.

F

R

A

N

C

E

WHAT IS HYPNOTISM?

Hypnotism is the art of putting a person's brain into a trance-like state which the hypnotist can then control. It is a way of exploring the deeper areas of the mind and, by so doing, releasing a patient from unconscious worries and strains.

For hypnotism to succeed, the patient must trust the hypnotist and cooperate with him. Once the patient is in a trance, his mind returns to a more simple, childlike state. He often remembers incidents that happened to him when he was young, incidents which may have affected him deeply and which have made him the sort of person he is. The hypnotist, who in these circumstances should also be a trained doctor, will help him to understand his fears.

The first doctor who used hypnotism as medical treatment was called Franz Mesmer. He was Viennese. His technique of hypnotism was known as Mesmerism.

WHERE DOES THE BODY STORE ITS ENERGY?

Certain cells of the body store surplus food in the form of fat or animal starch. This is released from storage when there is not enough food in the blood to supply the energy demands of the body.

Few of the things we eat can be used directly by the body cells. They must be changed chemically before they can supply the energy required. This is called digestion and is carried out in the stomach and in the small intestine, from where this digested food must be transported to the cells.

Now the food, in the form of digested sugars, proteins, and starches dissolved in water, passes into the blood system where, as blood, it can circulate through the body in less than one minute. Once the food is in the blood stream it is soon delivered to all the cells of the body by means of the red corpuscles in the blood.

It is when this supply falls low that the energy stores come into action.

WHY DO WE HAVE KIDNEYS?

Our kidneys perform four functions, of which the most obvious is the ejection of waste materials containing nitrogen from the body. They also keep the acid-base balance of the blood constant, and regulate the volume of circulating blood and the fluid content of the body as a whole. Finally they regulate pressure relationships between the blood and the tissues.

The kidneys, bean-shaped and about four inches long, lie on the back wall of the abdomen just above the waist, one on each side of the spinal column.

Blood enters the kidney by the renal artery. Some of its plasma is filtered off and, after other processes, ends as urine. The rest leaves the kidney by the renal vein to return to the heart. The urine collects in the central cavity (pelvis) of the kidney, passes down to the bladder via a tube (ureter) and is finally expelled.

A human being can survive without kidneys for only two or three weeks. Nearly one-fifth of the blood pumped out of the heart goes through the kidneys. The kidneys thus regulate the body fluid–a fluid which Claude Bernard (1813–1878), the great French physiologist, called our "internal environment".

HOW DID THE DOCTORS' HIPPOCRATIC OATH ORIGINATE?

The Hippocratic oath binding physicians to observe the medical code of ethics is named after Hippocrates (about 460–377 B.C.), an ancient Greek physician called the "father of medicine". It was first drawn up in the 4th or 5th century B.C., possibly by Hippocrates himself. Hippocrates belonged to a medical family. He was trained by his father and spent long years practising medicine as he travelled through Greece in its golden age–the time of Plato, Socrates, Sophocles and Euripides.

He was such a brilliant physician that many people hailed him as the direct descendant of the god of medicine, Aesculapius. He was the first to separate medicine from superstition and magic and to base his treatment on actual observation and experience. He and his pupils made careful records of their cases, and some of their observations are considered to be true even today.

Hippocrates himself was the "ideal doctor"–wise, kindly and humane with a deep respect for his patient and his calling. He left many writings, including perhaps the Hippocratic oath. This is still the basis of medical conduct, and generally included in a doctor's inaugural ceremony. Here is part of it, that expresses one of the central themes of the medical code.

"I will follow that system of regimen which according to my ability and judgment I consider for the benefit of my patients, and abstain from whatever is deleterious and mischievous. I will give no deadly medicine to anyone if asked, nor suggest any such counsel . . . Whatever, in connection with my professional practice or not in connection with it, I see or hear in the life of men which ought not to be spoken of abroad, I will not divulge. . ."

WHEN DOES THE BRAIN BEGIN TO DECLINE?

The brain begins to show signs of decline after a certain proportion of the nerve cells or neurons of which it is formed have died.

A grown man has no more nerve cells than he did when he was born. These cells do not multiply as the body grows, as bone and skin cells do. Indeed, as a person grows older he has fewer and fewer nerve cells, because those destroyed are not replaced.

At the age of 70 or 80, as many

as a quarter of the nerve cells may have died. That is the reason some old people cannot hear well or have poor memories. Yet others manage to retain their faculties and abilities until they are very old. Recent techniques have made it easier for scientists to study how our brains function, but there is still a great deal to discover.

WHAT MAKES WRINKLES?

Just as clothes hang in folds when they are old and have been stretched and washed a lot, so does the skin. The skin ages in five different ways. Some of these begin when you are a child, others at puberty and others after middle age.

The five symptoms of skin ageing are: loss of elasticity; changes in nerve endings which take place from early childhood; a tendency for the apocrine sweat glands which developed at puberty to disappear (old people sweat less); changes in the colouring matter in the skin, causing blotchy patches on the backs of old people's hands and darker freckles; and changes in the skin of the scalp. (This is quite thick when the person is a child, gets thicker and then goes relatively thin with age.)

WHERE ARE THE NERVES?

Your nerves are spread all over your body. The organs of the body are composed of tissues. These in turn consist of microscopic units called cells, specialized to perform particular functions such as secretion (glands), contraction (muscles) or conduction (nerves). Likewise the tissues that make up our nervous system are composed of billions of individual cells located all over the human body. No part of our body is completely insensitive to pain or some other sensation, because nerves are to be found in every part of the human anatomy.

The nervous system is usually considered to have two parts, the peripheral or outside system, which is in direct contact with the things that cause pain or pleasure, and the central system, consisting of the brain and the spinal cord. It is in our central nervous system that all our sensations and reactions are finally registered.

WHY ARE YOUNG BABIES FED ON MILK?

Young babies are fed on milk because it is their natural food. The females of all backboned animals whose young are nourished with milk, store this fluid in their breasts, or mammae. The milk of each species of mammal is a complete food for its own young after birth.

Although the same ingredients are present in the milk of all mammals, the proportions differ a great deal. The ingredients are water, protein, fat and milk sugar. Milk protein contains all the essential amino-acids. The fat globules remain enclosed in a soft curd which milk forms in the stomachs of the young, so that digestion can proceed smoothly without the disturbance that fatty foods often cause.

Human babies, if not fed by their mothers, may be fed with pasteurized cow's milk, diluted and sweetened, or a liquid reconstituted from laboratory-prepared dried milk. In various countries babies have been fed on milk from the ass, goat, water-buffalo, reindeer, caribou, sheep, camel, llama, bitch and mare.

Other foods have been tried. In the 17th Century babies were fed on pap (bread cooked in water) or, as a French doctor advised, bread cooked in beer! After about four or five months human babies are gradually weaned from an exclusive diet of milk and given other forms of nourishment.

WHAT IS PUS?

The pus we see oozing out from a septic cut is made up of the dead bodies of white blood cells which have fought against the infection.

These white cells, or corpuscles, live in the blood and float around the body ready to fight infection. There are at least five kinds of white cells. The ones which fight the kind of infection that happens when a spot or a cut goes bad are called leucocytes. A speck of blood, the size of a pinhead, normally contains about 5,000 leucocytes. But it may have 30,000 in a really bad septic wound. This is because the leucocytes gather at a point of infection and multiply.

Antibodies in the blood help to fight bacteria. When these have killed the bacteria, the white cells move into destroy them. If a doctor suspects that the blood may not contain enough antibodies to counteract the infection, he prescribes extra antibiotics, like penicillin, which do the same job.

Often the infection is defeated even without help from injections and pills, but not before many of the white cells have been killed, and discarded as pus.

HOW THICK IS THE AVERAGE SKULL?

The thickness of the average skull, or that part of the skull called the cranium that encloses the brain, is a quarter of an inch. The skull is made up of two thin layers of bone sandwiching a thin layer of bone marrow. It is most thin around the temples, where the thickness may be only an eighth of an inch.

In the case of Paget's disease, which is indicated by the thickening of bones, the skull has been known to be as much as one inch thick in parts.

WHEN WAS THE IRON LUNG INVENTED?

The iron lung was invented by Philip Drinker of Harvard, United States in 1929. This machine enables people whose lungs are paralysed by disease or accident to breathe. It does so by alternately reducing and increasing the air pressure round the patient's body. When the pressure is reduced, the chest expands and air streams into the lungs through the normal air passages in the head which is outside the machine. When the pressure is increased, the chest contracts and air is automatically expelled from the lungs.

This life-preserving apparatus is a tube on wheels in which the patient lies on a foam rubber bed with adjustable head and foot rests. It is operated by electricity, but has a safety device which gives a warning signal in the event of a power cut. The machine can then be operated by hand.

The cover on top of the iron lung can be opened to give access to the patient. When this is done, the patient's head is usually enclosed in a plastic dome in which the air pressure is alternately raised and lowered to enable breathing to continue.

WHERE ARE THE METATARSALS?

The metatarsal bones are found in your feet. The foot is made up of the tarsus, or ankle, which consists of seven bones; the metatarsus, which consists of five bones, or metatarsals; and the five free digits or toes.

Metatarsals are short and irregularly cube-like in shape. Their surfaces are rough for the attachment of ligaments. In number and general form they are like the similarly positioned bones of the hand, which are known as the metacarpals.

Although the bones of the feet and hand move in a generally similar sort of way there are, of course, important differences. One of the most obvious differences is that in the bones of the hand the thumb has a far greater play of movement than the big toe in the foot. A joint at the base of the thumb allows many more movements than in the case of the big toe.

This "opposable finger and thumb" is one of the physical attributes that has enabled man to reach the peak of the animal "league" table. It is one of the keys to human development.

WHY DO WE SOMETIMES NEED TO SCRATCH?

One of the commonest causes of an itchy skin is an allergy. The word was coined in 1906 by Professor Clemens von Puquet of Vienna to describe a special state of exceptional sensitivity of the body to certain substances brought into contact with it. Such substances are called allergens, and include furs, feathers, foods, dust, pollens and drugs.

Most people have experienced allergy in some degree at some time, and about 10 per cent of the population show more or less permanent symptoms of allergic illnesses.

An allergic reaction is always the same, no matter what has caused it. The reason is thought to be that a process similar to the antibody reaction is set off, not in the bloodstream but on the surface of the body cells.

This allergen-antibody damages

the cell walls and sets free a substance called histamine which produces two responses. It allows fluid to escape from the blood vessels into the surrounding tissues and it brings about an involuntary contraction or spasm of certain muscles.

When contact with an allergen is external we develop an itch which may be caused by light, heat, cold, hair or fur. It can also be caused by eating foods such as shellfish, mushrooms and strawberries or by an allergy to some drugs and medicines. If the allergen is inhaled there may be, as in hay fever, an excessive secretion of mucous, or, as in asthma, a severe spasm of the lung's air passages.

A true allergen is always a protein, a complex substance which forms an essential part of animal and plant tissues, but the abnormal reaction is produced only by a particular substance or group of substances.

WHAT ARE OUR EYES MADE OF?

The outer shell of the eyeball is made up of three coats: the fibrous tunic, the uveal tunic and the retina. The fibrous tunic is tough and elastic. It is opaque at the back, where it is called the sclera, and transparent at the front where it is known as the cornea. The uveal tunic is so called because of its similarity to a grape (Latin: *uva*). It contains the cho-

roid membrane which supplies blood to the eye. The retina, or innermost coat, is an extremely delicate tissue and is only a fraction of a millimetre thick. Its inner layers carry blood from the central artery to the central vein.

At the centre of the eye is a circular opening, the pupil, and immediately behind it is the crystalline lens, which consists of a great many transparent fibres arranged in sheets like the layers of an onion and enclosed in a clear, elastic membrane, the capsule. The perfectly smooth surface of the lens is curved and it is suspended by a number of delicate threads.

WHEN DO BONES BREAK?

Bones break under varying degrees of pressure according to age, health and other circumstances. They are made of hard, strong connective tissue and normally resist considerable force before breaking or fracturing. But when a bone has been softened by disease or grown fragile with age, fractures may follow very minor accidents or even occur spontaneously (pathological fractures).

The bones of children are not fully mature and are still relatively flexible. In childhood a severe blow or fall often results in a "greenstick" fracture, in which the bone appears to bend but does not completely break into two separate pieces.

An impacted fracture occurs when the broken ends of the bone appear to be jammed together by the force of the injury. A comminuted fracture is one in which the ends are shattered into many pieces. A fracture is called simple (closed) when the overlaying skin is not broken, or compound (open) when the bone is exposed.

All fractures attempt to heal themselves by producing new tissues to join the broken pieces together. At first this tissue is like putty and easily injured. So, generally a fractured limb should be straightened, immobilized and protected by a plaster cast while the healing takes place. In time the new tissue, or fracture callus, changes into mature bone.

WHO WAS ANTON VAN LEEUWENHOEK?

Anton van Leeuwenhoek (1632–1723) was a Dutch scientist whose experiments with microscopes led to his becoming the first person to make observations of bacteria and other microbes. He had no formal education as a scientist, but first worked as a clerk in a textile business in Amsterdam. Later he opened his own business in his native town of Delft, where he spent much time experimenting with magnifying glasses. He ground more than 400 lenses and produced one-lens microscopes of high quality.

Through his microscope Leeuwenhoek discovered a new world of "tiny animals", hundreds of thousands of which, he estimated,

would scarcely equal the bulk of a large grain of sand. "How be it", he wrote, "that I clean my mouth with salt every day, yet all the people living in the United Netherlands are not as many as the living animals I carry in my mouth?" He sent the results of a series of microscopic observations, begun in 1673, to the Royal Society in London.

Leeuwenhoek made a particular study of small forms of animal life. He was able to show that weevils, lice and fleas were not, as was thought, produced spontaneously or bred from dirt. He studied ants and proved that what had been thought to be their eggs were really chrysalises containing the perfect insects. He also demonstrated that mussels were not generated from sand and that eels were not the product of the dew, as had once been thought.

However, his work had little immediate effect on medical thinking. For many more years people went on thinking that tiny creatures were "spontaneously generated" and scientists were still reluctant to believe that far smaller creatures, germs, were capable of self-reproduction.

WHY DO WE GROW OLD?

Scientists have evolved three main theories to explain why we grow old. The first concerns the loss of cells or of irreplaceable parts. Brain cells undoubtedly die off in their hundreds of thousands and

This is a detail from Dürer's picture of his ageing mother.

cannot be manufactured again after a very infantile stage in human life.

However, this cannot be the complete explanation because people who suffer heavy damage to brain and body do not necessarily show the effects of ageing. Moreover, animals have totally different ageing rates, but suffer cell destruction at similar speeds.

A second theory concerns mutations or alterations. A dividing cell does not always divide correctly. All kinds of errors may creep in, aided by natural radiation. Sometimes the mutated cells may be harmful or put out of commission, with powerful effects on other cells, such as the endocrine glands or constituents of the blood. In the 1960s this theory was supported by the discovery that 10 per cent of the cells of very old women had lost an X chromosome.

A third explanation, which is not now so widely believed, is concerned with the accumulation of unwanted chemicals. It is suggested that some vital substances can only be replaced at cell division and that a general decline in the rate of cell division could lead either to a lack of needed substances or an excess of unwanted ones.

WHERE IS THE CERVIX?

The cervix is the name doctors give to the neck of the womb. It is a small opening surrounded by folds of mucous membrane containing mucous-secreting glands. It is supported by two folds of tissue that attach to the backbone.

The first stage of a child's birth occurs when the cervix starts to expand under the influence of rhythmical muscular contractions, until the head can pass through.

The cervix is recognized as a possible cancer site. There is now a service that tests women at regular intervals – three years is usual – for signs of this disease, so that effective early treatment may be started. Scarring or infection following a difficult childbirth may make the cervix more vulnerable.

WHEN WAS ASPIRIN FIRST USED?

Aspirin was first introduced into medicine in 1899 by H. Dreser of Germany. The word aspirin is actually the trade name for a preparation of acetylsalicylic acid.

During the last century many preparations of this acid were introduced for medical purposes, but Dreser was the first person to produce one which was considered satisfactory.

The main ingredients of aspirin occur naturally in the flowers, fruits, leaves and roots of many plants. South American Indians were familiar with the beneficial effects obtained from the bark of sweet birch and the leaves of the wintergreen shrub, which produce a medicine very similar to aspirin.

Aspirin is widely used for the treatment of headaches, sickness, colds and influenza. But too many aspirin tablets, instead of relieving the patient, may cause dizziness, headaches and sickness, and so they should be used carefully.

WHAT IS SKIN?

Apart from protecting our body, skin is a vital element in our physical make-up and well-being. It helps to regularize our body temperature and enables us to sweat. Thanks to the thousands of different nerve endings in our skin we can sense touch, pain, cold, heat and many other kinds of sensations. In a minor way we can also get rid of certain waste substances through our skin.

In man the skin varies considerably in thickness according to the area of the body covered. For example, the skin of our eyelids is approximately one-twenty-fifth of an inch or 1 mm, whereas on our palms and on the soles of our feet it reaches a thickness of about an eighth of an inch or 3 mm. Human skin has five layers –the basal cell layer, the stratum spinosum (which is several cells thick), the stratum granulosum, the stratum lucidum and, finally, the surface layer which is called the stratum corneum. This can consist of as many as 20 layers of cells but the cells nearest the surface tend to flake off.

Skin is practically waterproof and this quality allows the fluid "body" to live and function in dry air. There are many varieties of skin diseases and the skin also reflects in the form of rashes diseases that attack the body– chicken pox, measles and scarlet fever are examples.

One of the most obvious attributes of skin is its capacity to support hair growth but in man hair on the skin has little practical function or purpose. Hair is continually shed and replaced. The average life-span of the soft, downy hairs is only a few months while the long tougher hairs on the scalp can have a life of several years. Most of the human body's skin is actually covered by hair although for the most part the hair is so fine that we cannot see it without a magnifying glass. However, human beings do not grow hair on the soles of their feet or on the palms of their hands.

In one sense we can be said to register emotions through our skins, since any emotional stimulation can produce perspiration of the skin on the hands, feet and under the armpits.

One of the main functions of skin is to act as an early warning system to the rest of the body about outside conditions.

Skin remains taut and supple during most of our lives, but in old age, when the muscles begin to slacken, it loses this elasticity.

WHY DO MEDICINES COME IN DIFFERENT FORMS?

Medicine is given in different forms because of the necessity for convenience or for speed. It can be given by mouth (orally) in the form of tablets, capsules or draughts. It can be inhaled in the form of gases, fine aerosols or, very rarely, exceedingly fine powder. Injections of medicine are given subcutaneously (beneath the skin), intramuscularly or intravenously. Sometimes solid implants in the form of tablets may be placed subcutaneously. Injections may also be given in the spine or brain. Medicines can be given through the rectum as solids (suppositories) or enemas, or through the vagina as pessaries or douches. Finally, there are solutions, powders, creams and ointments which are placed locally on the skin.

Convenient medicines are those which can be taken or administered easily by the patient himself. Oral medicine and inhalations are convenient and a great deal of research is carried out to make these more palatable.

Manufacturers prefer oral preparations because they can be attractively coloured and flavoured and made impressively mysterious in size and shape. They can also be code-stamped or named for identification. Injections have to be sterile and kept in appropriate containers and are therefore relatively expensive.

WHERE IS THE AORTA?

The aorta is the great artery rising from the left side of the heart, through which the blood passes on its way to all parts of the body except the lungs, which are supplied by another system.

After rising from the heart, the aorta forms an arch, descending down the left side of the body. It passes through the diaphragm into the abdomen, where it divides into two lesser arteries. One of these terminates under the end of the backbone, where man has the

vestige of a tail. In animals it continues into the tail as the caudal artery.

The aorta is one of the elastic- or conducting-arteries, which take the blood to the muscular-or distributing-ones, which connect with the veins and smaller blood vessels.

Three valves at the exit of the aorta protect the heart from any back pressure that might develop in the artery and force the blood in the wrong direction.

Inflammation caused by an illness such as rheumatic fever may sometimes cause these valves to leak. This is a serious condition requiring considerable medical care and attention. But in normal cases your aorta will continue to function reliably throughout your life.

WHAT MEDICAL INSTRUMENTS DID THE ROMANS USE?

Some 200 surgical instruments of various kinds have been discovered in the ruins of Pompeii but, in general, the contribution of Rome

Tweezers

Scalpel

to medicine was not very marked.

"The Romans", said Pliny, in the 1st Century A.D., "got along without doctors for 600 years". In fact, if it had not been for the Greeks they might well have never had any. In the early days the Romans relied on herbs and salts as well as some horrible potions like gladiators' blood and human fat. The first Greek doctor to win fame was Asclepiades in about 91 B.C. and he insisted upon regular diet and exercise, fresh air and cleanliness. Galen (c.A.D. 130–200), the most famous of all, emphasized the need to study anatomy.

Drills, scalpels, tweezers, forceps and even a four-jawed clamp were used as surgery, through trial and error, became more skilful. Fractures and dislocations were treated effectively and artificial legs were not unknown. However, there were no anaesthetics and antiseptics and many operations, such as appendectomy, were beyond the surgeon's skill.

WHEN DO GALL STONES OCCUR MOST OFTEN?

Gall stones occur most often in women who are overweight and have had children, for in the late stages of pregnancy cholesterol, which makes up a large proportion of gall stones, is deposited in

Scalpel

Forceps

Shears

Forceps

Roman surgical instruments.

the liver in such quantities that the organ may not be able to take it all in. The liver also stores sugar, but overweight people usually take more sugar than they need. So once again the liver may not be able to cope.

Lying on the underside of the liver, the gall bladder drains the bile, stores it and then conveys it to the intestines. However, if the stones block the tube called the bile duct, or the gall bladder itself, severe pain will result. This is felt under the ribs on the right radiating up to the right shoulder, and lasts until the stone causing it passes out of the bile duct. If the stone is wedged, cholangitis or infection of the gall bladder may occur.

The treatment of cholelithiasis, or gall stones, usually necessitates an operation, for there is no known drug that can dissolve the stones. Drugs can be given to ease the pain and to relax and smooth muscles of the ducts. Often small stones cause more trouble than large ones, which stay in the gall bladder without emerging to block the bile ducts.

WHY DO WE SMILE?

We smile to show our pleasure or amusement in something or with someone. In fact, smiling seems to be an expression with which we are born, for most babies smile during the first weeks of life.

Charles Darwin (1809–1882), the great English naturalist who established the theory of organic evolution in his work, *Origin of Species*, also published, in 1872, a book, *Expressions of the Emotions in Man and Animals*, in which he studied the facial expressions of men and animals. Most of the experiments connected with facial expression have been based on this book.

It has been suggested that a baby begins to realize within its first year of life that a smile is a "good" expression because it is greeted with pleasure by mother or nurse. The smile develops, some time after the twentieth week of life, into laughter but there are great differences between the frequency of laughter and smiles in individuals.

As the child grows up, the action of smiling becomes bound up with a growing awareness of what is socially acceptable in certain situations. In an adult it is often difficult to be certain whether the response is truly emotional or not. Recently different kinds of smiles have been more closely observed. It is notable that the pattern of the smile alters, according to the situation, from a wide spontaneous grin akin to laughter to a tight, nervous grimace which is nearer to a reaction of fear.

WHERE IS YOUR FUNNY BONE?

Your funny bone is in your arm. It is the long, almost straight bone which extends from your shoulder to your elbow. At the top end it is attached to your scapula, or shoulder blade. At the elbow it is attached to the two bones in your lower arm which are called the radius and the ulna, which in turn are attached to your wrist and hand.

The funny bone carries the very strong biceps muscles – the ones which bulge up on the top of your arm when you bend your elbow and bring your hand up to your shoulder. The bone is grooved to carry the nerves to your hand. These nerves convey messages to and from your brain so that you can control your hand and use it to feel things.

Some people think your funny bone is so called because, when you knock a particular part of your elbow, you get a funny, tingling sensation. The real reason is because the medical name for this bone is the humerus – and since it is pronounced "humorous", the description of "funny bone" has now passed into universal use.

WHO DISCOVERED THE BODY'S REFLEX ACTIONS?

The theory explaining the body's reflex, or involuntary, actions was formulated by Marshall Hall (1790–1857), an English physician. Hall studied in Edinburgh, Paris, Gottingen (Germany) and Berlin. Finally he settled in London and there carried out a seven-year study of the reflex action of the spinal system which culminated in 1837 in the publication of his most important paper, "On the Reflex Function of the Medulla Oblongata and the Medulla Spinalis". The medulla spinalis is the spinal cord and the medulla oblongata is its continuation, forming the hindmost segment of the brain.

A reflex movement is one of the simplest forms of activity performed by the nervous system. A good example is the immediate jerking away of the hand if it touches a hot stove. The involuntary action is caused by a nerve cell being stimulated by the heat of the stove to send an immediate impulse down the nerve. This causes the muscle to contract. Another reflex is the sudden narrowing of the eyes against bright light. Doctors make use of reflexes to check the health of the nervous system. A tap below the knee with a mallet, for example, should elicit a jerk of the leg.

Marshall Hall's scientific explanation of these movements was at first greeted with criticism and ridicule, and the Royal Society refused to publish his paper. But his ideas met with a more sympathetic response by some European scientists whose studies confirmed the validity of his principles.

WHAT IS A SQUINT?

A squint, or *strabismus*, is the name given to a condition in which both eyes do not point in the same direction. The movements of each eyeball depend upon the action of six muscles, four of which are straight and two slanting. Defects in these may produce a squint.

Long-sightedness in children often produces an inward squint, especially if the child is looking at something close at hand. Short-sightedness may produce an outward squint. Paralysis is the usual cause of a squint which appears after the years of childhood. This is caused by some disease affecting the brain or the nerves of the eye muscles.

If one eye has better vision than the other the good eye may be used much more than the other, which may begin to function less and less well. Treatment for squinting must begin as early as possible with the wearing of glasses, which may have one dark lens over the good eye to stop it being used. This prevents the bad eye from becoming worse. Special exercises, called orthoptic exercises, which help to strengthen the eye muscles, are given and, in some cases, an operation is necessary to strengthen a weak eye-muscle or to weaken an over-strong one.

Early stethoscopes.

Dr Cammann's binaural stethoscope of 1855.

Dr Laënnec's stethoscope of 1816.

WHEN WAS THE STETHOSCOPE INVENTED?

The stethoscope was invented by a French doctor, René Théophile Hyacinthe Laënnec, in 1816. His stethoscope was a perforated wooden cylinder one foot long, and he got the idea for it from the sight of children scratching one end of a wooden beam with a pin and listening to the transmitted sound at the other end.

He put one end of the tube to his patient's chest and listened to noises made by the heart and

Modern stethoscope with bell-shaped and flat chestpieces.

pieces. In listening it is often necessary to use both a bell-shaped, open-ended chestpiece for low-pitched sounds, and a flat chestpiece covered with a semi-rigid disc or diaphragm for high-pitched sounds. Many modern stethoscopes have both kinds of chestpieces, readily interchanged by turning a valve.

lungs. He gathered evidence of what these sounds meant by comparing the various noises heard in living patients with the type of disease seen after they died. In 1819 he published his findings in one of the great books of medicine *De l'Auscultation Médiate*, and the stethoscope soon came into general use.

Auscultation (listening to sounds within the body) is most commonly used in diagnosing diseases of the heart and lungs. Nowadays a stethoscope is generally binaural (for both ears) and has two flexible rubber tubes attaching the chestpiece to spring-connected metal tubes with ear-

WHY DO WE VACCINATE AGAINST SMALLPOX?

We vaccinate against smallpox to allow the body to develop antibodies which will make it more or less immune to attack from the disease. In fact, by vaccination or inoculation we mean that a person is injected with the organism that causes the disease or its toxin (poison). This organism is modified physically or chemically, so that, without doing any damage, it triggers the body's immunizing defences. We call these modified cultures vaccines.

Vaccination against smallpox was first carried out in the East. Poisonous material taken from the blisters of a mild case of smallpox was inserted into the arm of the person to be protected. This produced a mild case of smallpox and enabled the body to manufacture the antibodies.

Vaccination was introduced into England in 1721 by Lady Mary Wortley Montagu, wife of the British ambassador to Turkey, who had her own children inoculated at Constantinople. However, this method could result in a severe or fatal attack of the disease.

Dr Edward Jenner took the next step in 1796 when he inoculated a boy named James Phipps with poisonous matter from the arm of Sarah Nelmes, a dairymaid suffering from cowpox (a mild disease closely allied to smallpox). Some weeks later he inoculated James Phipps with smallpox, but the boy did not contract the disease.

In 1798 Jenner published a book on his experiments, and the practice of vaccination spread throughout the world. The principle has been applied to many diseases. Babies and young children are particularly susceptible to complications from whooping cough and diphtheria, so they are immunized soon after birth. Poliomyelitis (infantile paralysis), cholera, yellow fever, and typhoid are all dangerous diseases which inoculation has been able to control.

WHAT MAKES EYES DIFFERENT COLOURS?

What a baby is going to look like depends on the 46 genes in his body cells. Half of these genes he inherits from his mother, and half from his father. Some of these genes determine his eye colour.

All eyes contain blue cells, but some people have other coloured cells as well so that their eyes look green or grey or brown or hazel. Babies all have blue eyes because the other cells, if there are any, do not grow until the baby is about two. Sometimes people have eyes which are partly blue and partly brown or green. This is because half of their eye has only the usual blue colour, while the other half has some other colour as well.

When two blue-eyed people have a baby only blue cell-genes are being passed on, so all their babies will have blue eyes. But when one parent has brown eyes, a mixture of blue and brown eyes is being inherited, and the colour of the babies' eyes will depend on whether there are enough brown genes to dominate the blue ones. Even two brown-eyed parents may not have enough brown genes between them to have a brown-eyed baby.

WHEN WAS ACUPUNCTURE FIRST USED?

Acupuncture originated in China as a form of medical treatment about 2,500 years ago. It has been practised by the Chinese ever since.

The treatment involves the insertion of small metal needles into one or many of 365 spots on the human body. Each of these spots, designated by ancient Chinese doctors, represents a particular function or organ of the human body. Accordingly a heart or liver line can be traced by linking the appropriate spots which relate to the particular organ. If a patient has eye trouble the needles will be

inserted into his eye line, which may not necessarily come anywhere near the eye. The needles do not go deep, and are not painful. A single treatment may last only 10 minutes.

It is not clear why acupuncture works, but some scientists have suggested that the needles may relieve the nerves affecting a disease.

Since the beginning of this century the treatment has been introduced in the West. At first there was much scepticism, but recently acupuncture has been widely accepted and has been found to be not only a cure but also a valuable form of anaesthetic.

WHY CAN YOU NOT BREATHE WHEN YOU SWALLOW?
You are not able to breathe when you swallow because your respiratory (breathing) system is closely linked to your alimentary (nourishing) system. In fact, both the air you breathe and the food you eat travel down the pharynx, a wide muscular tube situated behind the nose and mouth.

The air must reach the larynx or "voice box" on its way to the trachea (principal air passage) and the lungs, while the food has to go by way of the oesophagus (gullet) and stomach. Obviously, some kind of device must be used to prevent the two from becoming mixed up.

Swallowing temporarily inter-rupts breathing by closing the air passages while food is propelled from the mouth to the gullet and stomach. If a particle of food goes the wrong way the lungs respond immediately by trying to expel the food with a cough. Also some air does find its way to the stomach and can, if excessive, cause flatulence or "wind".

WHO DISCOVERED THE CURE FOR SCURVY?
James Lind (1716–94) discovered the cure for scurvy–a disease caused by a deficiency in diet–through his experiences as a British naval surgeon and his studies while a physician at the Haslar Hospital for men of the Royal Navy at Gosport, Hampshire.

Lind, who was born at Gosport, observed thousands of cases of scurvy and the conditions on board ship, particularly the sailors' restricted diet, that cause it. In 1753 he published A Treatise of the Scurvy, in which he advocated the use of lemon and lime juice and fresh vegetables. At that time more British sailors were dying of scurvy than were killed in battle.

The book was read by William Monkhouse and William Perry, the surgeons on board the Endeavour, which was under the command of the famous British explorer Captain James Cook and was about to sail for New Zealand. They followed Lind's principles and throughout the voyage, which lasted nearly three years, only one man died from scurvy. About 150 years earlier, Dutch sailors had benefited from taking the juice of oranges, lemons and other citrus fruits. But it was not until Lind's book was published that the relationship between scurvy, dietary deficiences and treatment was scientifically established.

The introduction of citrus fruit in sailors' diet brought about the swift eradication of scurvy, which is a disease caused by a lack of vitamin C, resulting in weakness, spongy gums, bleeding and profound exhaustion. The practice of prescribing lime juice in British ships led Americans to coin the word "limey" to mean a British sailor. Later the word came to be applied to British people generally.

WHAT ARE TEARS?

Tears are made of salt water, as you will know if you have ever licked a finger after wiping them away. They happen when the gland which provides moisture to keep the eyeball rotating properly produces more water than usual. The eye cannot drain all this water as it does normally, so a flood occurs.

The gland which makes tears is called the lachrymal gland (*Lacryma* is the Latin word for tear). It is about the size of an almond nut and is situated above the eye. It opens on to the surface of the eyeball by six or more little ducts. Every time we blink the water is spread over the eye. Any extra water is collected in two little canals at the inner corner of the eye where the upper and lower eyelids join, and carried away to the lachrymal sac near the nose.

The tear gland makes more water than usual when stimulated by a really pungent smell, like onions, or household ammonia, or by a situation of great emotional stress, whether happy, sad or frightening. The lachrymal sac then becomes too full and water enters the nose. The canals overflow and this overflow manifests itself as a stream of liquid.

WHERE DO TEETH COME FROM?

Teeth are formed from specialized cells which produce the three parts of the tooth – root, neck, and crown. The outer coating of the crown is made of hard enamel. This covers the dentine which forms most of the bony framework of the teeth. Channels in the dentine contain blood vessels and nerves which make up the innermost part of the tooth, the dental pulp.

Most of the higher animals, including man, are born without teeth. They develop two sets, called the milk teeth and the permanent teeth.

A human mouth contains 32 teeth. Their function is to cut, tear, and grind food, and they are specialized for this. So in each jaw there are four incisors (for biting), two canines (for holding or tearing), four bicuspids (chew-

Crown

Enamel

Dentine

Pulp
chamber

Root canal

Root

swellings that appear after joint injuries belong to the first group, which includes bruises, black eyes, sprains, fractures and infectious swellings such as boils and abscesses. Swollen joints can be eased by the application of cold compresses, or pads, and ice packs. Firm bandages are used to give support.

True tumours or swellings are composed of masses of tissue developed from body cells which already exist. They have a tendency to keep growing. Some of these tumours have normal cells and are said to be benign or harmless. In others the cells are slightly different from their parents and the tumours are generally malignant.

ing teeth with a cutting edge), and six molars (for grinding).

"Wisdom" teeth, the largest of all, are situated at the back of the jaw, and may not arrive until we are grown up.

WHY DO INJURED JOINTS SWELL UP?

The swelling of an injured joint, like a knee or an ankle, is caused by the multiplication of normal cells to cushion the affected part. This sudden increase is called hyperplasia. There is also a certain amount of internal bleeding as a result of injury.

Swellings are divided into two main groups, false tumours and true tumours. The inflammatory

WHEN DOES THE MENOPAUSE BEGIN?

The menopause, climacteric or "change of life" may begin for women at any time from the late 30s to early 50s, but usually occurs at around the age of 45. The menopause is the sign that the reproductive period of a woman's life is coming to a close. The female ovaries no longer produce eggs or hormones and, therefore, menstruation ceases.

From the time a woman begins to have a regular menstrual or monthly period, a single egg ripens in the ovary each month. This egg is shed from the ovary and passes down the oviduct to the womb or uterus. If the egg is not fertilized, it dies and the lining of the womb, together with some blood, is shed and passed out through the vagina. Afterwards a new lining grows, ready for the next egg.

Some women feel depressed and unwell at the time of the menopause as their bodies adjust themselves for the next phase of life. But these symptoms usually disappear with time. The length of the menopause varies.

Men also pass through a menopause when there is a marked decline in the production of sperms. But the outward symptoms are not usually very marked, and the change usually takes place later in life, between 55 and 60.

HOW DO CERTAIN DRUGS PUT US TO SLEEP?

Some drugs, called hypnotics, put us to sleep by producing a depressive or slowing-down effect on our central nervous system. They act upon an area of the brain that controls the wake-sleep cycle. The drugs differ greatly in the medicinal dosage required, the duration of their action and the margin of safety between a helpful dose and a dangerous one.

Long-acting barbiturates, such as phenobarbitone or Luminal, are effective for six to ten hours and prolonged use may make the user drowsy next day. Intermediate acting drugs, like butobarbitone or Soneryl, and amylobarbitone or Amytal, last for about five to six hours. Short-acting ones like pentobarbitone or Nembutal last from

two to three hours and ultra-short acting drugs like thiopentone or Pentothal are used mainly as forerunners to anaesthetics. Barbiturates can have injurious effects and should be taken only under strict medical supervision.

WHEN WAS THE FIRST HUMAN HEART TRANSPLANT CARRIED OUT?

The first human heart transplant took place on December 3, 1967 at Groote Schuur Hospital, Cape Town, South Africa. A team of 20 surgeons, headed by Dr Christiaan Barnard, operated on Louis Washkansky, aged 55, using the heart of a 24-year-old donor, Denise Ann Darvall, who had been killed in a road accident.

Both the donor and the recipient were of the same blood group and the heart was kept in cooled oxygenated blood for more than three hours before transplantation. The operation took five hours and the new heart was only half the size of Washkansky's. The operation itself was a success, and within a few days Washkansky was sitting up, eating and talking happily. The doctors were anxious about transplant rejection by the body and also post-operative infection which, in fact, did kill Washkansky within a month of the transplant.

In January 1968 a second transplant was carried out on Philip Blaiberg, a 58-year-old dentist, who subsequently overcame a severe liver infection and lung condition, thought to be the result of his body trying to reject the new heart. By the end of 1968 more than 100 transplants had been carried out in the United States, Britain, France, India, South America, Canada, Czechoslovakia and Israel. More than 40 patients survived. Blaiberg remained alive until August 17, 1969 and other patients survived for up to two and a half years, but the number of operations declined. From December 1970 to May 1971 only six operations were performed. Caution took the place of optimism.

WHY DO WE GET INDIGESTION?

Indigestion is most often brought about by interference with a marvellous piece of engineering contained in 30 to 32 feet of continuous hollow tubing called the alimentary canal.

In this system the food is broken down, churned, diluted, dissolved and chemically split into simpler compounds which can be absorbed into the blood.

The alimentary canal is formed of membrane which has to resist a chemistry that dissolves bone, gristle, animal and vegetable matter far tougher than the membrane itself. The stomach's gastric juice, one of the chief agents in digestion, has a high concentration of hydrochloric acid. This can dissolve a hard boiled egg in a few minutes. Why does it not dissolve the stomach? One reason seems to be that the stomach secretes not only acid but also ammonia, an equally powerful alkali which acts as a neutralizing agent.

This powerful gastric juice can be hindered by many causes, with the result that we may get the pains we know as indigestion.

The alimentary canal makes its preparations for a meal well in advance. The sight and smell and even the thought of food set the salivary and gastric juices flowing, while the stomach blushes in anticipation as the glands begin working and the capillaries widen to bring in an extra blood supply for the activity of digestion.

But the prospect of an unappetizing meal or disagreeable company, and the emotions of worry, irritation, anger and fear may stop these preparations. They may even cause the stomach to turn pale. Indigestion is the result.

We may also get indigestion if we eat too quickly without chewing our food or eat too many foods which are difficult to digest, thus overloading and disrupting the system.

WHAT IS PLASMA?

Plasma is the liquid part of the blood, in which the red and white blood cells float. It is the red oxygen carrying cells that give the blood its red colour. The plasma itself is straw-coloured. You may have seen some oozing out round a burn. Plasma is 90 per cent water, with various proteins, including the blood-clotting one, and salts dissolved in it.

Along with the red cells, the plasma helps to carry oxygen from the lungs to the body tissues which need it to break down their food. When the tissues have finished with the oxygen, the blood carries the carbon dioxide waste back to the lungs in order for it to be breathed out.

It also carries food, at various stages of absorption, round the body to the tissues, and takes the waste away to the kidneys from where it is passed out of the body as water.

Plasma is also a vehicle for toxins and antitoxins, special substances designed to fight infection. These substances with the white blood cells which destroy bacteria are in charge of defending the body against infection. So, despite the unassuring appearance of plasma, clearly it is extremely important to our bodies.

WHO FOUNDED THE MAYO CLINIC?

The Mayo Clinic in Rochester, Minnesota, United States, was founded by William James Mayo (1861–1939) and his brother, Charles Horace Mayo (1865–1939). Both brilliant surgeons, they worked with their father, also a surgeon, at the small and recently established St Mary's Hospital in Rochester, each specializing in a different branch of surgery. William operated on the stomach and Charles concentrated on goitre, a swelling in the front of the neck.

News of their success in working together and pooling the benefits of their experience spread throughout the medical world. The group partnership developed into an internationally famous institution that combined hospital treatment with teaching and research.

The Mayo brothers were intensely hard-working and set themselves the highest standards. They were quick to use the advantages of discoveries in antisepsis and anaesthesia, and for 40 years had a profound influence on American and world medicine. The brothers both died in 1939, leaving the famous clinic to carry on as a monument to their memory.

WHAT IS THE CAUSE OF FLAT FEET?

When you make wet footprints on the bathroom floor, you will see that there are blank patches in the middle between the toe marks and the heel marks. This is because the middle parts of the feet are raised off the ground by two sets of muscles, called the tibial and the peronal muscles which make the arches of the feet. If these muscles weaken, the feet spread out and the arches sink to the ground. The footprints are flat, with no gaps in the middle. This is called having flat feet, or fallen arches.

Sometimes people get flat feet because their jobs keep them

standing around too much. Policemen, waitresses and nurses often suffer from flat feet.

The cure is exercise which tightens up the muscles again. Supports to be put inside shoes are worse than useless. They make the muscles slacken, weaker instead of stronger.

WHEN WERE ANTISEPTICS FIRST USED?

Antiseptics were first used in 1865

by a surgeon called Joseph Lister, in London. He was helped by his knowledge of the work of Louis Pasteur, a French doctor, who had discovered that putrefaction (rotting), was caused by live bacteria and not by a chemical process.

Lister, shown below, thought that bacteria could be destroyed before they entered a wound and poisoned it. He first tried the treatment on a compound fracture. Carbolic acid was applied to the wound in the hope that this would

Joseph Lister.

provide a barrier against the germs in the atmosphere. The experiment was successful and led to a great advance in surgery. Various kinds of antiseptics came into general use to combat bacteria.

HOW DOES A KIDNEY MACHINE WORK?

A kidney machine filters the poisons from the blood of a person whose kidneys are not operating properly. A human being's two kidneys are fist-sized, bean-shaped organs, placed beneath the small of the back. Each kidney acts like a tiny chemical factory and contains more than 100 miles of tiny tubes through which the blood circulates. In the kidneys, the blood gives up its poisons which are expelled in the form of urine.

Until the 1940s nothing could be done for patients whose kidneys failed. Poisons built up in the bloodstream, fever and pain increased steadily and death followed. But in German-occupied Holland in 1940 a young doctor named Willem Kolff found a long-forgotten medical paper on haemodialysis (blood-washing). The main problems were to find a good material for a filter and a substance to keep the blood from clotting.

After the war, Kolff went to live in America. There he constructed a device which was the engineering prototype of nearly every subsequent artificial kidney. Blood circulated through cellophane tubing and an acid, heparin, was used to

prevent clotting. Small clots were trapped in a filter. Around the spiral tubing circulated the dialysis solution. Poisons in the blood filtered through the cellophane into the solution which could be changed frequently.

Artificial kidneys can be used to tide a patient over a critical period or, in chronic cases, to keep people alive for undetermined periods. At regular intervals, usually twice a week, the patient is attached to the machine by tubes inserted into his bloodstream. His blood is then passed through the machine to be purified before returning to his body.

At present, artificial kidneys have to be large machines because the filters used are much less efficient than real kidneys and much larger areas of membrane are required. Medical engineers are at work on a portable kidney, perhaps worn on a belt, that could be part of the patient's circulatory system. Beyond even this, lies the ultimate hope of an implantable artificial kidney.

WHY DO ANIMALS NEED OXYGEN?

We must have oxygen to live. Every living animal cell needs oxygen for its vital metabolic activities (the process of converting fuel to energy), and every cell must also get rid of its carbon dioxide, the gaseous waste of its metabolism.

In the simple animal forms each

cell gets oxygen for itself out of the surrounding invironment and gives off carbon dioxide in the same way.

In the more highly developed organisms a special mechanism makes the exchange of oxygen and carbon dioxide on behalf of the entire body, and a carrier fetches the oxygen and carries away the waste for all the cells. The carrier is the blood in its circulatory system, and the special exchange mechanism is the respiratory system with the lungs as the key organs.

We have developed from water-dwelling creatures and still spend the first nine months from our conception lying in a bath of warm fluid, called the amnion, receiving the oxygen necessary for the cells to do their work from our mothers.

In fact, we are still essentially water-dwellers, carrying our watery environment around within us, inside our skins. Because we have evolved lungs instead of gills we are able to live on land, but the air must be sufficiently rich in oxygen – about 20 per cent. Above 8,000 feet breathing begins to become difficult and the symptoms of mountain sickness, headache, nausea and vomiting may appear.

If we did nothing but rest, needing only a minimum supply of air, we would still need 300 quarts of oxygen every day. In a single minute of ordinary activity half a pint of oxygen has to be transferred from the air to the blood. For this half pint the lungs must process about five quarts of air every minute. An athlete running a race at sea level breathes as much as 120 quarts of air a minute to get the oxygen he needs to keep him going, which shows the importance of healthy lungs.

WHAT IS THE UVULA?

The uvula is a small mass of muscle covered by mucous membrane that hangs down from the middle of the soft palate at the back of the mouth. The soft palate is a movable fold of tissue and, with the hard palate, forms the roof of the mouth.

The word uvula comes from the Latin word "uva" or grape and the word describes its shape very well. Occasionally, if the throat is infected or relaxed, the uvula may become elongated, but it is never cut, since it recovers its proper size as the condition of the throat improves.

In certain animals, to whom the sense of smell is very important indeed, the uvula is joined to the epiglottis, a leaf-like piece of cartilage which stands upright between the tongue and the entrance to the larynx. This means that the animal is forced always to breathe through its nose. In man there is a gap between the two and consequently food may sometimes accidentally pass into the larynx and windpipe, causing great discomfort. Choking like this can even cause death.

WHY DOES SKIN COLOUR VARY?

People vary in the colour of their skin because of a network of pigment-forming cells called melancoytes. This network is interspersed between, and lies underneath, the cells of the deepest layer of the epidermis, or outer skin, which is called the stratum basale.

The melanocytes have slender, branchlike extensions which touch one another and also extend upwards between the cells of the deeper portions of the epidermis. There are about 1,000 to 3,000 melanocytes in each square millimetre of skin, and each one produces the dark pigment melanin formed as a result of oxidation.

This oxidation is catalysed by a copper-containing enzyme called tyrosinase, which gives the reddish spectrum of colour changes. Various stages of formation produce pale yellow, tawny, orange, reddish, brown and, finally, intense black.

Human skin contains greater or lesser amounts of melanin. In fair-skinned races the deep skin layer of melanocytes contains very little pigment. In the darker races, the deposits are heavy, and other melanocytes are to be found in the upper layers of the epidermis.

Melanin is a natural protection from harmful sunrays and, on exposure to sunlight, man's skin normally undergoes gradual tanning. This increase of melanin pigment, helps to safeguard underlying tissues. In blondes and redheads the pigment cells respond only slightly and rather unevenly. The consequence of this may be a "freckling" effect rather than a sun-tanned look.

WHAT IS THE COCCYX?

The coccyx is the lower end of the spinal column of man and consists of four nodules of bone, like tiny vertebrae, corresponding to the tail, which is found in lower animals. The bones are deeply buried in muscle tissues, but occasionally they jut backwards and are surrounded by a fold of skin, so as to form an actual tail.

The name coccyx was given by the Greek physician Galen (c.A.D. 130–200) and comes from the Greek word for "cuckoo", as the bone rather resembles a cuckoo's bill.

WHEN WAS PENICILLIN DISCOVERED?

Penicillin was discovered in 1929 by Sir Alexander Fleming, then a professor and lecturer at the Royal College of Surgeons in London. He wanted to find a substance which would kill bacteria but would not also poison the tissues of the patient's body.

Fleming discovered penicillin by accident while he was researching into influenza. He was examining a staphylococcus, a kind of germ, when he noticed that it had created a bacteria-free circle of mould around itself. When he experimented further, he discovered that this liquid mould, which he named penicillin, prevented further growth of the staphylococcus germ even when diluted and made 80 times weaker. Also. penicillin had no poisonous effect on the human cells.

Sir Alexander Fleming published his results in the *Journal of Experimental Pathology* in 1929.

For some time it was thought

that there was only one penicillin, but later it was discovered that the mould could produce four penicillins. They were distinguished by the letters F, G, X and K. The best known is penicillin G, which came into widespread use after the Second World War.

HOW TALL WAS THE WORLD'S TALLEST MAN?

Many claims have been made, but the tallest man about whom we have clear, recorded evidence was Robert Pershing Wadlow, who was born on February 22, 1918 in Alton, Illinois, in the United States of America.

Dr C. M. Charles, the Associate Professor of Anatomy at Washington University's School of Medicine in St Louis, Missouri, measured Wadlow on June 27, 1940. At that time, Wadlow was 8 feet 11.1 inches.

Wadlow began growing at an abnormal rate early in life. At the age of five he was 5 feet 4 inches. Nine years later he was 7 feet 5 inches. He was still growing at the age of 22, when he died on July 15, 1940.

The cause of death was cellulitis (severe inflammation) of the feet, which was brought about by a badly fitting brace which he wore as a support.

At the time of his death, Wadlow weighed 439 pounds, his shoes were $18\frac{1}{2}$ inches long and his hands measured $12\frac{1}{4}$ inches from wrist to tip of middle finger.

WHY ARE SOME PEOPLE COLOUR BLIND?

Scientists think that some people are colour blind because they have an abnormality of the three pigments in the cones in the retina of the eye which, it is supposed, are necessary for colour vision.

The theory of colour vision depends on the fact that any colour in the spectrum can be matched by a mixture of three pure spectral colours of variable intensity but fixed wavelength. In colour blind persons, all three pigments are usually present, but are of an intensity different from normal.

They can see all the colours, but have difficulty in distinguishing between red, green and yellow, or between blue, green and yellow. Absence of one or more pigments is rare but does exist, while the complete absence of colour vision resulting from lack of cones in the retina sometimes occurs.

Most colour blind people are ignorant of their abnormality until it is demonstrated to them by means of a special test. Usually it is not a great handicap. But there are situations, and jobs, such as an air pilot, in which it may be important to distinguish colours quickly.

WHAT IS THE PITUITARY GLAND?

The pituitary gland is a small structure about the size of a pea which is attached to the base of the brain. It consists of four parts and is the most important gland in the body for it controls the hormone output of all the other ductless glands, including the thyroid and sex glands.

The pituitary hangs by a little stalk just behind the nasal passage and was named after the Latin word for "nasal secretion" by the Belgian Andreas Vesalius (1514–1564), known as the "father of anatomy", who mistakenly believed that it discharged mucus into the nose.

If the pituitary is not functioning properly, gigantism or dwarfism may result. Premature old age, extreme thinness, extreme fatness and disturbances in sexual development are other disorders which may occur.

WHEN DO PEOPLE STOP GROWING?

People stop growing when their bones do, and that is usually between 15 and 25 years of age.

Bones are made up of living tissue, composed of special cells which secrete round themselves material rich in calcium salts and as hard as marble. The formation of bone (ossification) is a complex process which usually begins in cartilage (gristle).

In a child the bone begins to form in the middle of the cartilage and spreads towards both ends, turning it all to bone with the exception of the tips. From these points the bone grows in length and so does the child. When the growing period is over the tips of the bones close by joining the main shaft of the bone.

Bones vary greatly in shape and size. Long ones act as levers. Flat ones are centres for muscle action. But each has a cavity containing bone marrow. Around this the bony substance is spongy in texture, becoming hard nearer the surface where the calcium is densest. On the surface of the bone is a special layer of fibrous tissue (the periosteum) which is rich in bone-building cells.

WHO WAS VESALIUS?

Andreas Vesalius (1514–64) was the founder of modern anatomy. He was born in Brussels of a medical family and at the age of 23 became Professor of Anatomy at Padua, Italy, one of the greatest medical centres in Europe.

At the outset of his career he was greatly influenced by the writings of the ancient Greek physician, Galen. His six anatomical tables, published in 1538, attempted to standardize the form and meaning of anatomical terms in the light of Galen's teachings. Later he began to doubt some of Galen's theories.

In 1543 Vesalius published his most important work on the structure of the human body, *De Humani Corporis Fabrica*. This great work, which heralded the advent of biology as a science, contained drawings of muscle dissections by Jan Stephen van

Calcar, a pupil of Titian. The book was based on actual dissection and observation of human bodies and, in many cases, contradicted the traditional views that had been handed down over the centuries.

Vesalius had been court physician to Emperor Charles V and his son King Philip II of Spain. But his fame did not save him from being condemned to death by the Inquisition for body-snatching and human dissections. However, the sentence was cancelled on condition he undertook a pilgrimage to Jerusalem. On the return journey he died.

WHY SHOULD WE WASH OUR HANDS BEFORE MEALS?

We should wash our hands before meals as a protection against infections. We live in a world full of germs (micro-organisms or microbes) and those which are dangerous to us prefer to live and multiply in organic material. So it is wise to remove as many as possible before coming into contact with food.

Most of what are commonly called germs are harmless and some are even beneficial. Others, which are called pathogenic (disease producing), invade the body and live by feeding off body tissues.

Bacteria, which are tiny single-celled organisms, cause diseases such as diphtheria, cholera, leprosy, whooping-cough, typhoid fever, tetanus and scarlet fever, etc.

Viruses are so small that scientists can see them only under immensely powerful electron microscopes. Yet they are responsible for an enormous range of human diseases, from colds to rabies.

In hospitals, antisepsis and asepsis are used to maintain standards of hygiene. Antisepsis aims to destroy germs already present in a wound by applying chemicals. Asepsis keeps the germs away from wounds through the sterilization of the surgeon's hands, instruments, dressings and every other possible source of any infection.

The antiseptic system was introduced into surgery by Lord Lister (1827–1912), who worked on the discoveries of the French scientist Louis Pasteur (1822–95). At first he used pure carbolic acid, which was too strong and often damaged human tissue. Then better disinfectants were discovered.

The method of asepsis began with the sterilization of instruments by superheated steam. Penicillin and other new drugs have made the control of germs much less difficult.

WHAT MAKES PEOPLE FAINT?

The most urgent need of the body –more important even than food or drink–is oxygen, which is found in the air we breathe. When we breathe in, the oxygen is absorbed through our lungs into the blood which is carried round the body by the veins and arteries with the heart working as a pump. The most important place for the blood and oxygen to reach is the brain which controls the rest of the body through the nervous system. If the brain does not receive enough blood and oxygen, it can no longer control the limbs, and the person's legs give way under him in a faint.

There are all sorts of ways this could happen. It might be due to something blocking the blood

Guardsman fainting on parade.

flow, a tight collar or some more serious cause. But fainting is mostly due to stuffy atmospheres, lacking in oxygen.

If a person with you faints, get the victim into the fresh air, loosen the clothes and put the head between the knees, so that the weak blood supply does not have to climb upwards into the head, but can run downwards. Usually the circulation will get going again quickly and the person will soon come round, with no damage done.

HOW DO OUR TASTE BUDS WORK?

Our taste buds are contained in the mucous membrane of the epiglottis at the base of the tongue, of the tip, sides and root of the tongue and of the soft palate in the roof of the mouth. They are shaped rather like barrels with an outer covering of flattened cells. These enclose a bundle of spindle-shaped cells which end in thin, hair-like threads and are joined at the base with the nerves of taste. The taste buds transmit taste to the nerves which in turn send the message to the brain.

Tastes can be divided into four groups: sour, salt, bitter and sweet. To these classifications are sometimes added metallic and alkaline tastes. In most cases, the flavour depends upon smell almost as much as taste.

The taste buds seem to be in special groups designed to recognize different tastes; for the tastes are not equally easy to arouse in all parts of the mouth. Sweet things are tasted better at the tip of the tongue, and bitter things at the back.

WHY DO WE HAVE BONES?

We have bones to give us shape and support the body, to protect and contain the body's delicate vital organs, and to help us move about.

Bones are made from living tissue, composed of special cells which secrete around themselves hard material rich in calcium salts. In a child the bones are soft and cartilaginous (cartilage is gristle, the elastic substance of the ear or nose). Bone-making, or ossification, is a gradual process. A baby has as many as 270 bones, but an adult only 206, for some bones grow together as they get older.

All bones have a middle cavity filled with a yellow or red fatty substance called bone marrow, the blood-making factory of the body, which also keeps bones light without reducing their strength.

The basic part of the skeleton is the spine, which has 33 bones or vertebrae. The spine carries the weight of the body, is extremely flexible and contains and protects the delicate spinal cord. The skull shelters the brain while the ribs protect the heart and lungs.

Bones fit together at the joints and are held firm by ligaments, which are made of tough tissue like cords or straps. Inside each joint is a thin membraneous bag which secretes a lubricant to make the joint move smoothly.

Some glide on one another, as the lower jaw slides on the upper. Some, such as the elbow and the knee, hinge on each other and others, like the hip, make a ball and socket joint. Bones are sometimes fused together and immovable, as in the five large, lower vertebrae called the sacrum.

WHO DISCOVERED TYPHOID VACCINE?

Typhoid vaccine, which gives immunity against typhoid fever, was discovered by Sir Almroth Wright (1861–1947), a British scientist specializing in the study of bacilli, the tiny organisms that cause disease. He was following up the work of Louis Pasteur (1822–95), the great French chemist. Pasteur built up people's resistance to diseases by the injection into their blood of vaccines, or collections of weakened germs, thus encouraging the production in the body of the germs' natural enemies.

Wright discovered that dead bacilli could also be used for vaccines, so eliminating the risk of the inoculation producing the disease in a virulent form. As Professor of Experimental Pathology in the University of London, he was especially interested in the problems of typhoid fever, a contagious disease caused by contaminated food or water. In the Crimean War more deaths had been caused among British troops by this disease than by enemy action.

After trying out his vaccines on himself and fellow surgeons, Wright in 1896 initiated antityphoid inoculation by injection with a vaccine composed of killed cultures of the typhoid germ, *Bacillus typhosus*. At the start of the South African War (1899–1902) Wright wanted all British troops to be inoculated. But bitter opposition from influential persons prevented more than 4 per cent being treated. As a result there were 50,000 typhoid cases, 9,000 of them fatal.

An Anti-Typhoid Commission was set up, and its report in 1913 led to the official adoption of antityphoid inoculation by the British Army. Later came the introduction of a vaccine known as T.A.B., which gave combined immunity against typhoid and the related strains of paratyphoid A and paratyphoid B.

WHAT IS A STITCH?

A stitch is simply a sharp pain in one's side. What happens is that when we use muscles that are normally almost inactive, they contract and tighten, squeezing our nerves and causing pain.

This acute, internal pain is often experienced by runners, but it soon passes off, and is not serious.

There is a hedgerow plant called stitchwort which people once thought could cure stitch.

170

WHY DO WE HAVE BRAINS?

The brain directs and coordinates movements and reflexes, registers sensations and is the supreme nervous organ by which man acquires knowledge and the power to use and adapt it. It shapes our personalities, and without it we would be more helpless than the tiniest human baby.

There are three main parts of the brain: the forebrain (or cerebrum), the midbrain and the hindbrain. They have the consistency of soft jelly and are protected by three membranes (meninges), a tough outer envelope called the dura and a watery fluid (cerebrospinal fluid) which acts as a support and a cushion. The brain is connected to the spinal cord, and its surface is highly convoluted.

The cerebrum which forms nearly nine-tenths of the brain, is divided into two halves (hemispheres). Generally the left half of the cerebrum controls the right half of the body, and the right half of the cerebrum controls the left half of the body. Some areas are connected with the special senses of man, but there are so-called "silent areas" which scientists believe are connected with memory and the association of ideas. The thalamus, a mass of grey matter which is buried in the cerebrum, is the source of instinctive feeling and emotion.

The midbrain is concerned with eye-movements, while the hindbrain contains the nerve cells responsible for breathing, heart action, digestive juices and so on. The

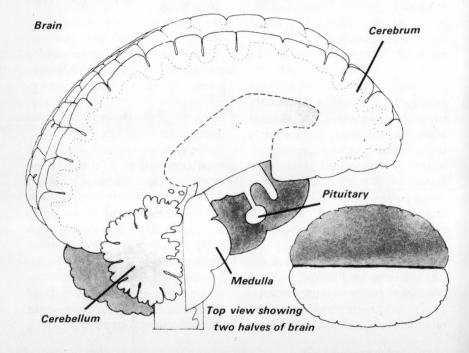

Brain

Cerebrum

Pituitary

Medulla

Cerebellum

Top view showing two halves of brain

cerebellum, a part of the hindbrain, plays an important role in the execution of the more highly skilled movements.

WHEN DO DOCTORS GIVE ELECTRIC SHOCKS?

Electric shock treatment, or electroconvulsive therapy, is sometimes used with people suffering from mental illnesses in which severe depression is the main symptom.

It was first used in 1938 by U. Cerletti and L. Bini in Rome, and was recommended for the treatment of manic-depression and schizophrenia (literally, "splitting of the mind").

WHAT DOES AN X-RAY SHOW?

X-rays are electromagnetic rays of very short wavelength which can penetrate matter through which light rays cannot pass. We call this opaque matter. An X-ray photograph shows a picture of the internal structure of the body allowing doctors to diagnose broken bones and examine the organs of the body. In order to show the position and shape of the stomach and intestine a harmless liquid containing barium is swallowed, and other opaque substances may be injected to show the outlines of other organs. Oxygen can also be injected into the brain to make its outline sharper.

The discovery of X-rays was recorded in January 1896 by Professor Röntgen, Professor of Physics at Würzburg. Chest X-rays led to the early diagnosis of pulmonary tuberculosis and from these beginnings the science of radiography and radiotherapy developed until now countless X-ray installations are in daily use throughout the world. X-rays are used both to diagnose and to treat deep-seated diseases like cancer. Scientific laboratories use them in experiments while industry uses them in work of investigation. By using high-tension apparatus giving up to 300,000 volts, steel can be examined for faults and hidden weaknesses can be discovered in aeroplane construction.

WHY DO WE BECOME SEA-SICK?

We become sea-sick because our balancing organs, the labyrinthine portions of the inner ear, are disturbed by out-of-level movements, by sudden turning movements, or by sudden changes in movements in a straight line, either horizontal or vertical.

The ear has three semicircular canals, filled with fluid and set on different planes in the ear. When sudden movements occur, each canal is affected differently. As a result, nerves in the canals send conflicting information to the brain, so giddiness is likely to occur.

Nowadays, seasickness comes under the general heading of motion sickness, a name invented by Sir Frederick Banting in 1939, which includes the discomfort people feel while travelling in all kinds of vehicles.

Sea-sickness may vary with individuals from slight uneasiness to complete prostration. The symptoms are pallor, cold sweating, nausea and vomiting. People who have lost their ear labrinths because of disease do not become seasick. Others become resistant to it. We say they develop their "sea-legs", but it would appear to be an adjustment of the central nervous system rather than the organs of balance. Some people find it helpful to keep their gaze firmly fixed on a steady object.

WHEN DOES BLOOD CONGEAL?

Blood congeals when a part of the body is wounded. If it failed to congeal the injured person would die from loss of blood.

The congealing, or coagulation, of the blood, is the first step towards healing a wound. It closes the wound and builds a scaffold for new tissue by means of a chemical process in the plasma, the fluid part of the blood. In this process the platelets (small cellular bodies in the blood) produce thromboplastin. This changes fibronigin, a protein in the blood, into fibrin. Finally a spongy network of fibrin connects the edges of the wound and prevents the loss of any more blood cells. Often, a scab is formed over the wound as a protection.

WHO FIRST USED A POWERED DENTAL DRILL?

The first powered dentist's drill was made by George Washington's dentist, John Greenwood, who adapted his mother's spinning wheel with its foot treadle to rotate his instrument.

Earlier dentists had operated their drills by means of bowstrings, a method which must have required skill, determination and physical stamina on the part of the dentist, as well as a great deal of courage from the patient. Later drills were operated by turning a handle at the side.

In 1829 James Nasmyth, the Scottish inventor of the steam hammer, used rotary power to improve the efficiency of the drill. A hand-operated drill with a flexible cable was patented by Charles Merry, an American dentist in 1858; and George Harrington, an Englishman, invented in 1864 a drill driven by a clockwork motor.

WHAT MAKES YOU FEEL DIZZY?

Dizziness most commonly occurs when a person who has been moving around with speed stops suddenly. The sensitive liquid in the inner ear, which mainly controls balance, continues to move around for a time after the body has stopped. So the surroundings appear to be still in motion. However, it takes only a few seconds, for the fluid, and balance, to settle.

This sensation, which is also

called vertigo, may also occur to someone looking down from a height or on board ship. Here the cause is probably not so much physical as a nervous reaction which affects the fluid in the inner ear.

WHY DO DOCTORS TAKE YOUR TEMPERATURE?

The body temperature of a human being is an indication of his physical condition, so that an abnormally high or low temperature is generally a sign that something is wrong.

The normal temperature is usually given as 36·9°C. (98·4°F.), but as the body temperature varies throughout the day, anything between approximately 36·7°C. (or 98·1°F.) and 37·2°C. (or 99·0°F.) may be taken as normal.

For instance, the temperature rises after a large meal, during hot weather and after violent exercise. Your temperature is at its lowest at night when you are asleep.

Control of body temperature is exercised by a centre in the brain which ensures that a balance exists between heat production and heat loss. A raised temperature is often the sign of bacterial or virus infection. It may be due to heatstroke, to certain types of brain injury or disease or to shock.

A very high temperature, or fever, may begin with a "rigor" (an attack of shivering and cold), in which the whole body may tremble uncontrollably and the teeth chatter. Although at this stage the skin feels cold and clammy, the temperature within the body is raised. Soon the skin becomes hot and dry, pulse and breathing rate are speeded up and there is a feeling of exhaustion, aching muscles, headache, thirst and perhaps delirium and loss of the sense of time. Finally this stage is succeeded by profuse sweating and a gradual relief of the symptoms.

WHEN WAS THE THERMOMETER INVENTED?

The first practical thermometer or instrument for measuring temperature was invented shortly before the end of the 16th Century by the famous Italian astronomer Galileo. It was an air thermometer giving only a rough indication of the degrees of heat and cold, and later he increased its efficiency by using alcohol instead of air.

The principle on which most thermometers work is that a liquid or gas used for measuring expands or contracts with changes in temperature more rapidly than the glass containing it. Thus when a coloured liquid is confined in a thin glass tube the difference in expansion, as shown by the level of the liquid against a graduated scale, indicates the temperature.

About 1714 the German scientist Gabriel Daniel Fahrenheit designed a thermometer which, for the first time, used mercury as the

174

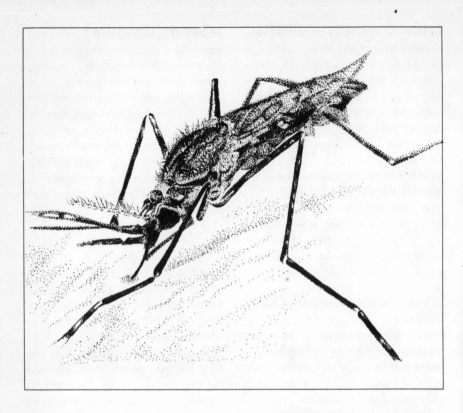

The malaria-carrying mosquito.

measuring agent. He also introduced the scale named after him
in which 32° is the freezing point
of water and 212° the boiling
point. Mercury is still used in most
thermometers because it has a
high boiling point (674°) and a
low freezing point (−38°).

An alcohol thermometer, still in
use in some countries, was made
by René de Réaumur, a French
naturalist, about 1731. About 11
years later Anders Celsius, a
Swedish astronomer, used the
centigrade scale for the first time,
with freezing point 0° and
boiling point at 100°.

WHERE WOULD YOU CATCH MALARIA?

The most likely places to catch
malaria would be in tropical and
sub-tropical countries, especially
in the forested parts of Central and
South America, central Africa,
Asia, and southern Europe. This is
because the female anopheles
mosquito, whose bite transmits
the disease, breeds in the warm,
stagnant, marshy pools found in
those parts.

Malaria is said to derive its
name from the Italian for "evil
air". It causes chills, fever and
anaemia, and is sometimes fatal.

In India a million people are likely to die from it every year.

The first effective remedy for it, quinine, was used in the 16th Century. It is an infusion from the bark of the cinchona tree. Modern drugs, too, have greatly reduced the threat of malaria. In particular the use of sprays on the mosquitoes' breeding places has been highly effective.

In 1955 the World Health Organization started a mosquito-eradication programme of benefit to nearly 1,200 million people.

WHAT IS THE UMBILICAL CORD?

Inside the womb of a pregnant woman or animal a placenta is formed, through which the unborn baby is nourished. The baby is connected to the placenta by the umbilical cord, which is joined to the unborn child at the navel.

The umbilical cord is the baby's lifeline. Everything the child needs to survive will pass through it— air, blood and nourishment. At most it is no more than an inch wide and, perhaps, only a foot long.

Once the baby is born the placenta, which serves a purpose only during the pregnancy, will be discarded.

The umbilical cord will be cut with scissors a few inches away from the newborn baby's stomach. This is quite painless because the umbilical cord has no nerves. The baby will now breathe on its own.

HOW DO WE GRIP?

We take a grip on things by using our muscles to exploit the development of the human thumb. The importance of this thumb is that it can be moved across the palm of the hand to touch the index finger. In contrast the digits of a monkey's hand are more rigid. This difference explains why a human being can handle an instrument with such precision.

The mechanism of the hand is operated by way of the wrist, a hinge joint composed of eight small bones (carpals) packed firmly together to give elastic stability. Below the wrist project five small, long bones (metacarpals) which give the palm firmness. Four of the bones have hinge joints and are connected to the fingers. But the joint connected to the thumb allows it to move round and meet the fingers and palm, thus providing a firm grip.

Possession of such a hand has enabled man to form a society and culture based on the use of tools. It is thought the hand developed from the five-rayed forepaw of an early vertebrate. However, occasionally a child is born with an extra tiny thumb or little finger and some people believe that the forepaw was originally seven-rayed.

The human thumb has lengthened with evolution and is much longer in proportion than that of an ape. About 92 per cent of human beings are right-handed, but apes tend to use both hands with equal ease.

WHEN WERE CONTACT LENSES INVENTED?

The first contact lenses were made by A. E. Fick in 1887, but were not successful. During the early part of this century opticians tried to produce extremely thin shell-like lenses to fit closely over the eye. An impression was taken of the eye and a glass shell made which, with a suitable fluid under it, covered most of the eye. After 1938, plastic was used instead of glass, and in about 1950, smaller lenses were introduced which covered only the cornea and floated on a layer of tears. These lenses, only 7 to 11 mm in diameter and 0·1 to 1 mm thick can usually be worn all day without being removed.

Besides being invisible, contact lenses provide a much wider field of vision than spectacles. They are more practical for use in active sports because they are not easily lost or broken, and they can be tinted for use as sunglasses. But contact lenses are not effective in all cases of eye trouble. They are also expensive, and some people find difficulty in learning to wear them.

As research continues, even smaller and more flexible lenses are being developed.

WHY DO WE SLEEP?

Some scientists consider that sleep is an instinct, a basic need for the body and mind to relax and to escape from the responses needed while awake. We become tired in body and mind if we do not sleep, and scientists have proved that when we do sleep the electrical activity of the brain slows down, although it may be stimulated when we dream.

One chemical theory is that a substance needed to maintain the waking state becomes exhausted and may be replenished in sleep. A contrary suggestion is that some poisonous substances built up in wakefulness may be destroyed when we go to sleep.

Other theories connect the need for increased wakefulness with the development of the more sophisticated areas of the brain. This could explain why new-born babies whose powers of reasoning have not yet developed, spend most of their lives asleep. It has been demonstrated that a particular part of the brain, the reticular formation, if severed, causes continuous sleep.

Although we are not sure why we sleep, there is no doubt that we need to do so and so do most other animals. The pattern of sleep and wakefulness is closely connected with our habits and senses. Animals which depend upon sight for food, shelter and defence, like man, are diurnal. That means they are for the most part active during the day and asleep at night.

The amount of sleep needed by a person to remain in full health varies considerably with age, with different individuals, and even, perhaps, with race. Pre-school children generally need ten to twelve hours sleep, schoolchildren nine to eleven hours and adults seven to nine hours. Adults seem to need progressively less sleep as they grow older, and exceptional cases are known of elderly people who have remained healthy on two to three hours a night. It has been said that the Japanese, both children and adults, sleep less than Europeans, but that may be due to habit rather than to race.

WHAT IS MUSCLE?

Muscle is the body tissue which, because it has the power of contraction, enables the higher animals to move their bodies. Muscles are divided into two great groups, voluntary and involuntary, the former being controlled by the will, while the latter act independently.

Most voluntary muscles are attached to the skeleton and range in size and shape to suit the particular jobs they perform. They can get into action within a few hundredths of a second, exert an enormous pull on the bone to which they are attached and, if necessary, support 1,000 times their own weight. Involuntary muscles include heart muscle and the muscles of the digestive system, and the fibres of which they are composed are very much smaller than those of voluntary muscle.

Because of its exceptionally rich blood supply, muscle is the most infection-free of the body's basic tissues. If it is over-taxed it tires and will stop contracting altogether, but if used normally will give little trouble.

WHO USES A CARDIAC PACEMAKER?

Cardiac pacemakers are used by sufferers from "heart-block". They do the work normally performed by the body's natural pacemaker in controlling the rate and rhythm of the heart beats. This natural pacemaker is a small collection of specialized nervous tissue situated at the base of the heart. It forms the starting point for the impulses that initiate the heartbeats.

"Heart-block" is a serious condition in which the conducting mechanism between the cavities of the heart (atrium and ventricle) is impaired or destroyed. When this happens, the atrium and ventricle beat at different rates independently of each other because the impulse from the pacemaker is not reaching all parts of the heart. Fainting, convulsive attacks or complete stoppage of the heart may follow, but the condition can be overcome by the use of an artificial pacemaker.

This acts as a battery to stimulate the heart, allowing it to beat regularly at normal speed, about 70–80 impulses a minute. The pacemaker is either fixed to the outside of the chest or implanted in the armpit and connected to an electrode tube, which is passed through the main vein in the neck into the heart.

Geography and the Earth

WHEN WAS THE OCEAN FLOOR FIRST MAPPED ACCURATELY?

The shape of the ocean floor was not accurately determined until the 1920s. Until the end of the last century mapping had depended on the accounts by sailors of rock formations and deep troughs in the ocean bed.

Recent scientific developments, and new instruments and techniques have enabled maps to be drawn with greater accuracy and detail. By transmitting sound waves from ships to the sea bed, and back, it is possible to make a record of the changes in depth.

Mechanical, acoustical and electronic instruments have pictured the ocean floor not as a vast plain but as a series of mountain ranges, valleys, peaks and canyons. Some of the mountains are far higher than most of those on land and the deepest part of the ocean is much farther below sea level than the highest land mountain is above it.

WHERE IS THE MOHO, OR MOHOROVICIC DISCONTINUITY?

The Mohorovicic discontinuity is to be found between the earth's crust and the earth's mantle. Mohorovicic was a famous Croatian scientist, a seismologist. He specialized in the composition of the earth, and particularly in earthquakes and in faults in the structure of the earth, which are a cause of earthquakes.

Mohorovicic made a most important discovery. Scientists knew that the earth is made up of a series of layers, rather like an onion. There are many of these layers, all of different materials and all in a different state of development. The main layers are called the crust, the mantle, the liquid core and the solid core.

The great pressure inside the earth force the weaker areas of the rocky layers out of alignment and this pushing, twisting movement is experienced as an earthquake on the surface. These great forces set

Crust

Mantle

Moho

Inner core

Outer core

up a series of waves throughout the various layers of the earth, known as seismic waves.

Mohorovicic discovered a curious fact about the behaviour of these earth waves or tremors. He noticed that the shock waves travel comparatively slowly through the actual crust of the earth. But when they reach the

lowest level of the crust—the layer called basaltic rock which rests on the next layer called the mantle—the waves increase dramatically in speed. Sometimes they also change direction.

This curious fact was proved by Mohorovicic's experiments. The importance of his discovery was that it proved the earth's crust is different from the mantle beneath.

So the "Mohorovicic discontinuity" is the scientific term used to describe this strange behaviour of the earth's shock waves.

Usually this level of the earth's composition is called the Moho, since even scientists found Mohorovicic's name difficult to pronounce! By plotting these earth waves on sensitive shock recording machines known as seismographs we have found that most of the outer crust of the earth is between 20 and 25 miles thick in continental areas, but only three miles thick under some oceans.

WHAT IS THE TUNDRA?

The tundra is a desolate, flat region of land lying to the north of the coniferous forests along the shores of the Arctic Ocean, as in Russia. Winters are long and cold and summers short and cool. Snow covers the ground and ice covers the rivers and lakes for eight or nine months of the year.

Even in the summer only the surface of the soil thaws out and little grows but mosses, lichens and dwarf trees, shrubs and sparse brushwood. In some grassy spaces brilliant polar flowers flourish for a short time, in others, grey rocks and clay-like soil form a dismal landscape.

In the tundra there are many birds, rodents and carnivores, while reindeer roam the region in great herds. Until recently the inhabitants of the tundra led a precarious nomadic existence, based on hunting, fishing and reindeer breeding. Now coal, petroleum, mineral ores and some rare metals have been discovered and vigorous industries are growing in the tundra.

WHY IS MERCATOR'S PROJECTION IMPORTANT?

Gerardus Mercator's (1512–94) projection is important to geographers because, unlike other projections, a straight line drawn on it gives a true compass bearing.

A projection is simply a means of transferring a round section of the world on to a flat sheet of paper. This is more easily said than done, for, no matter how hard you try, you cannot do it without altering the shapes or sizes of countries or the distances between them.

You can try this for yourself. Draw a rough map of the world on an orange with a felt tip pen, then cut the orange into sections. When you have eaten the orange, try to arrange the curved pieces of peel into a flat map. You can see that if the lands by the Equator, or the widest parts of the orange peel, are touching, there are large gaps to the north and south. To make a map in which there are no gaps, it is necessary to stretch these lands in the north and south—and this is just what Mercator did.

The history of projections goes back to the Greeks who realized as long ago as 500 B.C. that the world was round. Eratosthenes, a Greek who lived at Alexandria in the 2nd Century B.C. even calculated the circumference of the world to be 25,000 miles. His estimate was only a little more than the correct distance which is 24,901·8 miles at the Equator.

Mercator's projection increases the distances between the lines of latitude (the lines parallel to the Equator) as one moves further north or south. While this makes the map useful for navigation, it also gives people many wrong ideas about the world. It makes some countries, such as Greenland, appear too large. The areas of land at the Equator on Mercator's projection are correct. But those at 45° North or South are doubled, and those at 75° are nearly 16 times too large.

WHERE IS THE WORLD'S HIGHEST WATERFALL?

The world's highest waterfall is in Venezuela, South America. It is known as the Angel Falls and lies on the River Carrao. This magnificent waterfall tumbles 3,212 feet down to the river.

The Venezuelans did not even know about Angel Falls or the surrounding country until the 1930s, because steep rocks made overland travel to the region impossible. It was not until aircraft started penetrating the region that the falls were discovered.

The falls get their name from the United States adventurer and explorer James Angel who crashed near them in an aeroplane in 1935.

HOW MANY OCEAN CURRENTS ARE THERE?

There are about 25 great ocean currents or drifts. They are caused by three main forces: the prevailing winds, the earth's rotation and differences in the sea's density.

Winds exert drag or friction on the waves and cause surface currents. This is particularly noticeable in the belts of the westerlies and the trade winds. The rotation of the earth gives these currents circular movements.

There is also a circular movement from the deeper layers of water to the surface where currents meet or diverge. Water rich in nutrient salts comes welling up from the depths of the ocean and stimulates the growth of plant life in the surface layers. This abundance of plant food attracts fish, and many great fishing grounds are situated along the paths of the ocean currents.

One of the most interesting currents is the warm Gulf Stream of the Atlantic that gives western Europe and parts of eastern North America a temperate climate. It begins in the westward-drifting waters travelling across the Gulf of Mexico, passes through the straits of Florida and flows north-east across the Atlantic. Although it is always comparatively warm, the temperature does vary a few degrees from year to year.

Currents caused by differences in the density of sea water are usually under the surface and slow-moving. They are responsible for the general circulation of the deep layers of the ocean and are formed from the large volumes of ice-cold water pouring into the oceans from the polar regions. These plentiful supplies keep the temperature of the ocean low.

Warm currents increase the rainfall of the countries near which they flow. The warm air over the currents becomes heavily charged with moisture and condenses over the land as rain or snow.

WHERE IS ALICE SPRINGS?

Alice Springs is a town situated in the heart of the continent of Australia, centred in the lower third of the Northern Territory.

The surrounding countryside, "the Centre" as Australians call it, is parched. The lakes and rivers are dry for most of the time and the cattlemen on the few homesteads depend on water pumped from bores hundreds of feet deep.

The town of Alice Springs was founded in the middle of the 19th Century after the discovery of a sheltered, watered plain among the MacDonnell Ranges, a series of hills which ripple for 250 miles across the land. By 1872 a telegraph station had been built at a water hole beneath a rocky hill. It was called Alice Springs after the wife of Charles Todd, superintendent of telegraphs in Adelaide, but it is always known as Alice to Australians.

Next came prospectors looking for gold. They left a ghost town at Arltunga not far from Alice. Once, back in 1880, they thought they had found rubies by the million, but the gems proved to be cheap garnets, not worth transporting. Cattlemen soon followed, for much of "the Centre" is marginal land that provides good feed when it rains. They knew the rains did not come often, but felt one good season could carry five bad seasons. Often it has had to carry seven or eight bad ones.

The growth of Alice Springs in recent years has astonished everybody. The railroad linked it to Adelaide in 1939 when its population was less than 100. By the Second World War 1,000 people lived there. It was used as a military base after the Japanese bombed Darwin. Stuart Highway – still called simply "the bitumen" – was completed from Darwin to Alice, a distance of 954 miles.

Today, Alice Springs is a prosperous town of 6,000 people. It attracts crowds of tourists especially during the fine winter weather from June to September. They come for the spectacular scenery, the famous aboriginal artists, and to visit surrounding cattle stations.

Attractions include the tremendous monolith of Ayers Rock which towers 1,143 feet above the plain and is six miles around – the biggest "pebble" in the world, surrounded by a flat desert.

Since the 1950s the area has been suffering from the worst drought people can remember. It is feared that "the Centre" may turn into a huge dustbowl. So it looks as if the future of Alice Springs lies in its tourist trade and the mineral wealth which experts believe lies under the rugged landscape.

HOW DOES THE SEVERN BORE OCCUR?

A bore in this sense is a tidal wave of great height and speed caused by the meeting of two tides or the rush of a tide up a narrowing estuary. Conditions particularly favourable for the creation of such a wave occur in the Severn, Britain's longest river. The Severn ends its 200-mile journey from Plynlimon in Wales as a long estuary which widens to 10 miles where it enters the sea near Bristol.

The Severn Bore occurs every month just before and soon after a spring tide. It is most impressive at the time of the spring tides nearest the vernal equinox (March 21) and the autumnal equinox (September 23).

As the tide moves up river it meets a residue of slack or ebbing water and causes a tidal wave that reaches a height of about 33 feet. The bore starts near Sheerness. At Fretherne, where the river narrows, the bore rears up like a wall, to be followed by two more waves and finally the tide itself, seething and roaring.

Daniel Defoe (1661–1731), the author of *Robinson Crusoe*, described the bore "rolling forward in a mighty wave: so that the stern of a vessel shall in a sudden be lifted up". Above Gloucester the bore normally subsides. But an exceptionally large one has been known to ruffle the tideless water of the Severn at Worcester.

WHY DOES A COMPASS POINT NORTH-SOUTH?

When the magnetic needle of a compass is allowed to move freely it will automatically place itself in line with the earth's magnetic field, one end pointing to the magnetic North Pole while the other indicates the South.

Natural magnets, such as loadstone or pieces of iron which have been touched by a loadstone, are

Earth's magnetic field

Geographic North

Magnetic North

to be found the world over. It was the discovery that loadstone would always place itself so as to lie in a magnetic north-to-south position that led to the invention of the magnet.

During the 15th Century it was realized that the magnetic North Pole and the Geographic North Pole were not exactly in the same place. The small angle between the two is known by seamen as "the variation". Some experts have claimed, however, that the Chinese were already aware of the existence of variation as early as the 11th Century. Again, in the 15th Century, it became apparent that the earth itself was a great magnet.

WHEN WAS THE PANAMA CANAL BUILT?

The Panama Canal was finally opened on August 15, 1914. It had taken ten years to build. At first much delay was caused by uncertainty over the type of canal that should be built. Some experts contemplated a high-level canal with locks at either end, while others suggested a canal at sea level. After two years the high-level plan was adopted. It was decided that the alternative system would threaten the land on either side of the canal with flooding and also put ships at risk in stormy weather.

The building of the Panama Canal, one of the great engineering feats in the world, was masterminded by John F. Stevens. The canal zone was formally acquired by the United States from Panama in 1904 for 10 million dollars plus an annual payment of 250,000 dollars. The United States was to be responsible for the construction of the canal and for its perpetual maintenance, sanitation, operation and defence. Since that date the treaty has been amended several times.

Since 1904 the canal, which is just over 40 miles long, has cost the United States well over 6,000 million dollars. But it has shortened the distance for ships travelling between that country's Atlantic and Pacific coasts by 8,000 miles. Ships going from Europe to Australia make a saving of nearly 2,000 miles.

Among the canal's many engineering marvels, its great locks attract particular attention. They are deep enough to take vessels drawing forty feet of water and have a length of 1,000 feet. Some of the "leaves" of the lock weigh as much as 730 tons and are more than 80 feet high.

WHAT ARE THE NORTHERN LIGHTS?

The Northern Lights are long, waving streamers of light, often seen in the night sky in the Northern Hemisphere during both warm and cold weather. These marvellous, wavering illuminations are also called the Aurora Borealis, from the Latin words meaning a "northern dawn". They are most frequently seen between 65° and 80° northern latitude, but the area of visibility extends further south in North America than in Europe. The aurora of the southern hemisphere is called the Aurora Australis, from the Latin for "southern dawn".

The bands of light in the aurora seem to radiate from an arc and send their rays far across the heavens. They are most often white, but are sometimes green, red or yellowish. The luminous streamers may be almost straight, or they may wind backwards and forwards like glimmering snakes in the sky. Sometimes the rays look like a fan, or form a crown round a dark centre. At other times the long beams of light may seem to fall downwards like the folds of a gigantic, shimmering curtain. Their apparent movement is often so rapid that they have been called the "Merry Dancers".

Scientific studies of auroras began in 1716 with a spectacular display that was visible over the whole of Europe. The English astronomer Edmund Halley (1656–1742) proved a connection between them and the earth's magnetism. But the exact cause of the auroras is still not completely understood. The most likely theory is that they have their origin in streams of electrically charged particles from the sun, which are turned aside to the north and south magnetic poles on reaching the upper layers of the earth's atmosphere.

Auroras are most pronounced during magnetic storms, that is during the time that the earth's magnetic field is most disturbed. They also tend to occur when there have been signs of unusual activity in the sun.

WHERE IS THE HELLESPONT?

The Hellespont is the ancient name given to the strait of the Dardanelles which joins the Eastern Mediterranean to the Sea of Marmara. The Sea of Marmara is almost landlocked – except for the Hellespont and the Bosporus which flows into the Black Sea between the Soviet Union and Turkey.

The shores of the Hellespont are formed by the peninsula of Gallipoli in Europe on the north bank and by Asia Minor on the south. The Hellespont is only 38 miles long and between three-quarters of a mile and four miles wide.

Many famous castles overlook the strait including the Old Castle of Anatolia and the Old Castle of Rumelia. The strait has long been prominent in history. The army of the Persian king Xerxes crossed it by a bridge of boats. This expedition against the Greeks probably explains the origin of the name Hellespont: "Helles" comes from "Hellenic" or "of the Greeks" and "pont" means "bridge".

During the First World War, the Hellespont was the scene of much fierce fighting.

An elaborately decorated map of the Middle East.

WHY WERE EARLY MAPS DECORATED?

Many early maps were decorated because the map-makers or cartographers had little real idea of geography and presented the world in symbolical terms. One map of Roman times showed the world as a T within an O. The O represented the ocean boundaries of the earth and the T the known world, with the Mediterranean as the upright and the horizontal bar as the meridian from the Nile to the River Don. Jerusalem was at the centre and elaborate decorations often included Paradise and the Last Judgment.

As the shapes of more coastlines were discovered, the unexplored land masses behind them were often filled in by map-makers with decorative portrayals of imagined animals and vegetation. The seas contained monsters and pictures of ships.

Even when maps became more accurate, decorations survived because cartographers saw their craft as a mixture of science and art.

Some maps were specially commissioned to be given as gifts to noble patrons or sovereigns. Unlike ordinary maps for use at sea, these special productions were magnificently decorated, with the seas and lands full of fabulous animals and the winds portrayed as human. The houses and ships shown were usually accurate pictures of those in use at the time the maps were made.

WHEN DOES PEAT FORM?
Peat bogs are formed in mild and humid climates when the land drainage is so bad that pools of water submerge masses of partially decomposed vegetable matter and prevent complete decay.

After being dug out of the bog, the peat is left to dry in the open air. When the water has evaporated it will burn readily. Vast quantities

of peat exist in many parts of Europe, North America and northern Asia, but it is normally used as a fuel only in countries or regions where there is little coal. Large quantities are used for fires and ovens in Ireland, Scandinavia and the Soviet Union.

WHO WERE HUMBOLDT AND RITTER?
Friedrich Heinrich Alexander, Baron von Humboldt (1769–1859), and Karl Ritter (1779–1859) were two Germans whose combined travels and researches changed the whole concept of geography.

Humboldt, who was born in Berlin, travelled widely, exploring South America between 1799 and 1804 and Central Asia in 1829. As a scientist he was especially interested in the relationship of living things with their surroundings. He had a passion for correct, careful field observation. His two great books were an account of his American travels and *Kosmos*, a description of the physical geography of the earth.

Ritter, who was born at Quedlinburg, regarded himself as Humboldt's disciple. He also was a great observer, but confined his travels to Europe. He was the founder of scientific comparative geography, and his most important work was *Die Erkunde*, which stressed the relationship between man and his natural surroundings. He also wrote papers giving geographical interpretations of history.

WHAT MAKES THE WIND?

Wind is the movement of air across the surface of the earth, caused by warm air rising and being replaced by cooler air.

Except for the monsoons, the chief global winds are constant in direction. The strength with which they blow is affected by seasonal changes in air pressure and temperature. The winds are named after the direction from which they come. For instance, a south wind travels towards the north and a wind from the sea is called a sea-breeze.

Instruments called the anemometer and the wind vane are used to measure the force and direction of the wind. To obtain accurate measurements, they must be in a position where there are no obstructions. The wind vane shows the direction of the wind, and the anemometer its force.

WHERE IS THE NORTH-WEST PASSAGE?

The North-West Passage is a sea route along the north coast of North America between the Atlantic and Pacific oceans. It was first sailed by the Norwegian explorer Roald Amundsen in 1903–1906 in the 47-ton Gjöa.

The search for the Passage started in the 15th Century, when Bristol merchants commissioned the Genoese mariner John Cabot to find a direct sea route between Britain and the Indies by sailing west. He failed, but discovered the mainland of America on his voyage.

Over the next 350 years, others were to seek the route and many died in the attempt. These brave pioneers included famous characters such as Henry Hudson and Sir Humphrey Gilbert.

In 1845, Sir John Franklin made his ill-fated voyage. With 129 officers and men in two ships, the Frebus and Terror, Franklin's expedition became icebound in the Victoria Strait. Franklin died and the crew abandoned their vessels and eventually perished.

It was ironic that out of the Royal Navy's efforts to find Franklin came the first successful completion of the North-West Passage, although much of the journey was made on foot. That was in 1854.

The many succeeding voyages included those of the United States nuclear powered submarine Seadragon, which made the first underwater trip in 1960, and of the 1,005 foot S.S. Manhattan, which in 1969 made a voyage from New York to Alaska and back in a little over two months.

But the North-West Passage has never become the great sea route to the East which men dreamed about for so many centuries. Today the Panama Canal provides the only transcontinental sea-link from the West to the East.

WHY DO CLOUDS HAVE DIFFERENT SHAPES?

Clouds vary in shape according to their height and temperature, and they contain minute drops of water or ice particles or a combination of both. And, of course, their formation is greatly affected by wind changes.

There are basically three groups of clouds: high clouds between 17,000 and 45,000 feet (cirrus, cirro-cumulus and cirro-stratus); middle clouds between 7,000 and 23,000 feet (alto-cumulus, alto-stratus and nimbo-stratus); and low clouds up to 7,000 feet (strato-cumulus, stratus, cumulus and cumulo-nimbus. Their height and temperature decide how much pressure is exerted on them by the atmosphere.

Finally, the shapes of clouds differ according to the time of day. Towards evening clouds tend to thin out, rise a little and flatten out.

WHEN DOES SHEET LIGHTNING OCCUR?

Sheet lightning usually occurs during a storm as the result of a discharge of excess electricity within a single thundercloud. The outline is obscured and the result is a diffused light spread over a large area of the sky in contrast to the vivid spiral or ribbon-like flashes of chain, forked or zig-zag lightning. The most favourable conditions for sheet lightning are provided when the electric field is equal throughout the area. Unlike other forms of lightning it does not reach the ground and the channel cannot be distinguished.

What is often referred to as sheet lightning is merely the lighting up of the sky by flashes occurring beyond the horizon.

All lightning is the natural discharge of large accumulations of electric charges in the atmosphere. It may take place between neighbouring clouds or between cloud and earth. Just before the discharge the cloud's electric potential is often built up by the action of falling raindrops or other natural processes.

HOW DID CONSTANTINOPLE GET ITS NAME?

Constantinople, now the Turkish city of Istanbul, was called after the Roman emperor Constantine the Great. The name means city of Constantine. He was born at Nish in what is now Yugoslavia about A.D. 280 and was educated at the court of Galerius, the ruler of the Eastern Roman Empire. In A.D. 306 he was proclaimed Caesar.

At this time the Roman Empire was governed by four rulers. But the system did not work well, and Constantine decided there should be only one ruler–himself. He became a Christian as the result of visions he had seen promising him victory over his rivals if he embraced the new faith. Rome fell to his troops and in A.D. 323 the last of the independent rulers was defeated, leaving Constantine in command of the whole empire.

He changed the capital from Rome to the ancient city of

Byzantium, on the shores of the Bosporus. He enlarged the city, renamed it Constantinople and enriched it with many churches and palaces.

WHAT IS THE DATE LINE?

The Date Line (usually called the International Date Line), is a north-south line through the Pacific Ocean where, according to international agreement, the date changes. East of the line it is one day earlier than it is to the west.

The line is necessary because the earth is divided, longitudinally, into 24 one-hour time zones (15° longitude each) which make one full day on the earth. Since the earth rotates eastwards, the time on the clock progresses westward round the world. Thus, 12 o'clock noon arrives in London (0° longitude) five hours before it does in Washington, D.C. (75° west of London) and eight hours before it does at San Francisco (120° west of London). When it is noon in London it is midnight 180° to the west.

On either side of the 180th meridian the time is the same. But you would lose a day if you crossed it from the east and gain one if you travelled across it from the west.

The Date Line has some variations from the 180th meridian to allow for land areas or islands. The line bulges eastwards through Bering Strait to take in eastern Siberia and then westward to include the Aleutian Islands with Alaska. South of the equator it bulges east again to allow various island groups to have the same day as New Zealand.

WHERE DO ICEBERGS GO?

Icebergs are huge masses of ice which have broken away from glaciers in the Arctic and Antarctic regions. They gradually melt away as the upper part is warmed by the sun and the lower part by the warmer waters into which they drift.

An iceberg may be as much as 250 feet high, although only one-ninth is above the surface of the sea. It can be a hazard to shipping.

The worst disaster was to a British passenger liner, the Titanic. This fine ship was thought to be unsinkable, because she had a double skin and 15 watertight compartments. In April, 1912, the liner struck an iceberg in the North Atlantic. Despite her double skin and watertight compartments she was holed and quickly sank. Of the 2,207 people on board, more than 1,500 were drowned.

WHEN WAS COFFEE FIRST GROWN?

A legend says the coffee plant first grew in Kaffa, a province in south Ethiopia, where it was discovered by a goatherd called Kaldi about the year 850. Kaldi's goats were

Right: *coffee beans drying in the sun in a small Guinea village.*

reported to have skipped and pranced in a strange manner after feeding on an evergreen plant. The goatherd, so the story goes, tried some of the berries himself and excitedly dashed to the nearest town to tell of his find, which was called coffee after the name of the province.

Another theory is that the word coffee is probably derived from the Arabic *qahwah*. Certainly coffee was introduced into Europe from Arabia during the 16th and 17th Centuries. The first licence to sell coffee in the United States was issued to Dorothy Jones of Boston in 1670. The coffee houses of this time became famous meeting places for discussion.

As the drinking of coffee became more popular, its production spread to Java, Haiti, Dutch Guiana, Brazil, Cuba, Jamaica, Puerto Rico, Costa Rica, Venezuela, Mexico, Colombia, the Hawaiian Islands and, in this century, Africa.

WHERE IS SURTSEY?

Surtsey is a volcanic island a few miles south-west of the Westman Islands which are situated off the south coast of Iceland. The island appeared as a result of a volcanic activity on November 15, 1963. The Icelanders took the infant island into their care because it appeared in their territorial waters.

They called the volcanic vent Surtur, and the island Surtsey (island of Surtur): In old Icelandic mythology Surtur was a giant who brought destructive fire from the south as a weapon in his fight with Frey, the god of fertility.

During its early life there was doubt about the island's chance of survival, and many thought it might disappear. A similar one did vanish in 1783 after erupting from the sea 65 miles south-west of Reykjavik, the Icelandic capital. Survival and long life were assured when repeated outpourings of thin flowing lava followed the first violent eruptions. The lava capped the volcano with a gently sloping regular dome which acted as a protective shield.

The arrival of Surtsey was no real surprise. For the 10,000-mile Mid-Atlantic Ridge, of which Iceland forms the largest above-sea land mass, had been active along its length for some years up to 1963, although since then things seem to have settled down, although further activity is always possible. The neighbouring Westman Islands were produced by volcanic activity 8,000 years ago.

WHAT IS TWILIGHT?

Twilight is the faint light which appears a little before sunrise and again after sunset before it gets really dark.

On the moon there is no twilight. Darkness comes suddenly as soon as direct sunlight ceases to reach the moon's surface. This does not happen on earth because of the halo of air, called the atmosphere, which surrounds it. When the sun goes below the horizon, its light leaves the earth but is reflected downward from the upper atmosphere.

Poets and writers have written of the evening twilight–or "the gloaming", as it is called in Scotland–as an enchanted time. Perhaps one reason is that familiar objects become distorted in the half-light and we imagine we are seeing things that are not really there.

WHY DO RIVER DELTAS FORM?

A river winding its way down to the sea, from its mountain source, will inevitably choose the lowest land through which to flow. By the time the river approaches the sea the speed at which it is travelling will have decreased considerably, thus allowing the water to drop its load of sediment and other solids.

These solid particles (alluvium), therefore, form the land pockets which are characteristic of the various branches of a river delta. Owing to the slow pace of a river at this stage, it will wind its way round any elevated land points rather than go over them.

Deltas are most likely to form where the sea, into which the river flows, is particularly calm for most of the year. Notable deltas in the world include the Mississippi (the largest) the Ganges, and the Nile. A delta is so called because it is the name of the fourth letter of the Greek alphabet whose shape it resembles.

WHEN DOES A GEYSER OCCUR?

A geyser occurs when a hot spring erupts, hurling a column of water and steam high into the air. These springs are situated in regions which were formerly volcanic and which have retained considerable heat near the surface.

They usually have craters with well-like shafts penetrating into the earth. The water which gathers deep down in these shafts becomes heated until the lower part is changed into steam. The pressure of the steam steadily mounts to a point when it suddenly hurls the water above it into the air, sometimes to a height of over 100 feet.

The chief geyser districts are in Iceland (home of the Great Geyser), in the Yellowstone National Park, Wyoming, United States, and in New Zealand. For four years Waimangu in New Zealand, the greatest of all geysers, was capable of spouting jets up to 1,500 feet.

WHERE ARE THE EVERGLADES?

The Everglades are in Southern Florida in the United States. The peninsula of Florida, low lying and with a climate ranging from warm temperate to subtropical, stretches out from the American mainland towards Cuba. In the south of Florida lies the state's biggest stretch of inland water, Lake Okeechobee. Spreading south from this is the huge wet prairie called the Everglades which, after 100 miles, gives way to the mangrove forests fringing the peninsula's broad tip.

The Everglades have a slope to the south of only two inches to the mile and, along the eastern side of the great prairie, there is a river with an almost imperceptible flow. This river, which is only a few inches deep and 50 miles wide, moves slowly towards the south. Along the west side tall cypresses, hundreds of years old, stand in the Big Cypress Swamp. The whole area is waterlogged, for beneath the peat beds there is a porous rock which soaks up water like a sponge. All this freshwater-soaked land keeps back the salt water of the Atlantic Ocean, and the excess of water flows into the sea.

Grasses grow in the shallow, slow-moving river. Tall cypress trees flourish in the swamps. The area is rich in vegetation and wild life. A primitive world, thousands of years old, continues into the present and the Americans sought to preserve this by creating the

Everglades National Park. But in spite of these efforts, civilization is destroying this primitive world. Agricultural land is being reclaimed by draining the swamps. Water is being taken from Lake Okeechobee and diverted from the river to quench the thirst of the Atlantic seaboard cities of Palm Beach and Miami. On the surface, the peaty soil dries out and becomes easily ignited tinder. Carelessly thrown cigarette ends create hundreds of fires.

As the swamps dry out and become barren, Nature's balance is destroyed and the wild life is threatened with extinction. The Everglades may well be doomed.

HOW CAN SCIENTISTS CONTROL THE WEATHER?

Since the 1940s scientists have discovered techniques by which several weather conditions can be controlled. For example, it is possible to prevent lightning by using an electrical earth to diffuse the electrical content of a cloud. The American scientist V. J. Schaefer has shown that it is feasible to produce greater concentrations of ice in clouds than occur under normal conditions.

Weather experts already are taking advantage of these discoveries to increase snowfall on mountains for winter sports, to prevent damaging hailstones and to moderate, or even prevent, the development of dangerous storms. Scientists are now able, in some cases, to make a cloud burst to produce rainfall over parched areas.

These local efforts may lead the way to large-scale weather control. But before then scientists may have to learn to cope with the damaging effect of air pollution on weather conditions.

WHAT IS GRANITE?

Granite is a very hard kind of rock made up of small pieces of mica, quartz and felspar and sometimes other rocks as well. There are many kinds of granite and they may be pink, grey or white. But the most striking thing about granite is that the pieces of rock from which it is made are all crystalline and shine like a wall of snowflakes.

One city in Scotland, called Aberdeen, is known as the silver city, because of the way the granite from which it is built shines in the sun.

This rock is widely used for building, and is especially useful for large engineering jobs such as the making of breakwaters. Not only does it stand up well to the weather but, unlike many other rocks, it can be quarried in huge slabs. It is also used as an ornamental stone after being polished to a smooth surface.

Granite is found all over the world and forms part of most of the world's mountain ranges. There is a city in the State of Illinois called Granite City, while the mountain State of New Hampshire on the eastern side of the United States

Granite quarry.

is sometimes called the Granite State on account of the granite quarries there.

You may have heard the expression "granite features" used to describe persons. This means that they have cold, hard faces, like a granite rock.

WHY DOES INDIA HAVE MONSOONS?

The seasonal winds of south-west Asia known as monsoons are associated particularly with India because of the tremendous effects they have on the lives of the inhabitants. The winds are drawn to India by changes in the temperature of the great land mass. A good monsoon season with plenty of rain means a comparatively good supply of food. A bad monsoon with little rain means a bad rice crop and, perhaps, starvation for many millions.

Monsoon comes from the Arabic *mausim*, meaning season. The summer season monsoon is a great inrush of moisture-laden air from the ocean. The winter monsoon blows from the land to the sea.

In India there are three seasons: the hot dry season from March to June; the hot wet season from June to November; and the cool dry season from December to March. During the hot dry season the great plains of northern India becomes like a furnace and a region of low pressure develops.

By mid-June, the pressure is low all the way to the Equator and draws the south-east trade winds to India, filled with water-vapour as they cross the Indian Ocean. When they meet the hot dry air over India, violent thunderstorms result, followed by steady rain in July. By November India has received three-quarters of its annual rainfall.

Then the land mass cools and the lower pressure to the south attracts the north east trade winds. These bring no rain to India except to the Coromandel Coast and Ceylon, where the rainfall in late September is heavy, because the winds have picked up water vapour as they cross the Bay of Bengal.

WHERE IS THE WORLD'S HIGHEST MOUNTAIN?

The world's highest mountain is Mount Everest, on the Nepal–Tibet frontier in the eastern Himalayas. Mount Everest was named after Sir George Everest who discovered it in 1856, when he was surveyor-general of India. At that time its height was estimated by trigonometry as 29,002 feet, but more recently it has been established as 29,028 feet.

Everest is not only the highest mountain in the world, but also the most magnificent and inaccessible. It is swept by icy winds and gripped in a coldness that often drops far below zero. There are great glaciers and crevasses, ice-falls and sheer rock faces, and the rarified atmosphere as its greatest heights has defied generations of climbers.

It was not until 1920 that the Dalai Lama of Tibet was persuaded to permit a British climbing party into his territory. Until then both Nepal and Tibet had forbidden any such intrusion.

Several unsuccessful British expeditions were made to conquer the mountain and 16 men were lost in the attempts. In 1951 Eric Shipton made an approach from the south through Nepal. Before then all the expeditions had made their approach from the north. Shipton had no intention of attempting an assault on the summit. His object was to gather information for future expeditions.

With the help of this information a British expedition, using light-weight oxygen-breathing apparatus and other weight-saving equipment, reached the summit in 1953. It was led by Colonel H. C. J. Hunt, later Lord Hunt.

Nine camps were made during the climb, and on the morning of May 29 a New Zealander, Edmund Hillary, and Sherpa Tensing Norgay made the final assault. At 11.30 a.m., after a hard climb, they reached the summit.

WHAT IS LOAM SOIL?

Loam soil is half way between clay and sandy soils. It is the best soil for horticultural and agricultural use, containing enough clay and humus for the retention of water and for the provision of food for plants. It also has sufficient sand to allow the passage of air and the drainage of water, which prevents waterlogging, and enough lime to prevent acidity.

River basins are often covered with a powdery, yellowish-grey loam called loess. This loam has been brought downstream by the river and is derived from glacial deposits of very fine silty, unconsolidated material. Some of the best farming land in the Rhine and Danube basins is composed of this soil. Other loess deposits have no connection with glacial action and are accumulations of fine material picked up by the wind in the world's arid regions. When water is introduced into these loess areas by means of irrigation they make unusually fertile soil.

There are loess deposits in the plains of south Russia, the Argentine pampas and China, and in Iowa and Illinois in the United States. These are among the richest agricultural regions in the world.

WHEN ARE CONTOUR LINES USED ON MAPS?

Contour lines are used when maps are designed to show the physical nature of the land. They do this by linking all points which are the same height above sea level. The width between the contour lines indicates the steepness of gradients or slopes in the area. The closer the lines are together, the steeper is the slope.

On physical maps giving the

height of mountains, rivers, lakes and principal towns all areas between certain heights are generally shown in the same colour. This is known as layer colouring.

Other methods for indicating heights include relief maps moulded in plastic to the physical feature raised as on a model. Spot heights may be shown, but these merely give the heights above sea level of certain points of the map and it does not follow that the ground rises evenly from one point to another.

Very old maps have mountains drawn on them. Later ones have lines called hachures radiating from a central point, with longer lines to show gentler slopes. Another system is to show the form of the land by hill shading. But none of these methods is so effective as the use of contour lines.

WHY DOES HOLLAND HAVE SO MANY WINDMILLS?

The large number of windmills in Holland, or The Netherlands, is due to the fact that they were needed to pump water into the canals off the rich, low-lying land reclaimed from the sea. Windmills are still used for this purpose today, but pumps worked by electricity are more usual.

There is an old Dutch saying, "God made the world, but the Dutch made Holland". They certainly did make a great part of their land by dragging it from the sea, and the battle to hold it never ceases. The name Netherlands (from the Dutch *nederland*) means low land, and more than one-third of Holland's land area of 12,530 square miles lies below sea level.

Along the coast are dunes of sand – nature's dykes – thrown up by normal tides. The Dutch plant them with marram grass, which holds the sand together with its long, strong, creeping roots. Behind the dunes the Dutch built three dykes of close-packed stone, clay and earth on wooden and concrete piles. The dyke nearest the sea is called a "waker". Behind it lies a "dreamer" and behind that again a "sleeper". Some of the dykes are 200–300 feet high and many have a road or, some, a railway running along the top.

In 1170 the North Sea swept into the country and formed the bay called the Zuyder Zee (South Sea). In 1421, another high tide flowed in to form the Hollandse Diep (Dutch Deep). The great spring tide of 1953 (two feet higher than any previously recorded) smashed the waker dykes, overflowed the dreamers and drowned about 1,900 people. About 50,000 were forced to flee from their homes.

A famous Dutch story tells of a brave boy who stood for hours with his hand thrust into a hole in a dyke and so prevented the sea from rushing in and widening the breach in the wall.

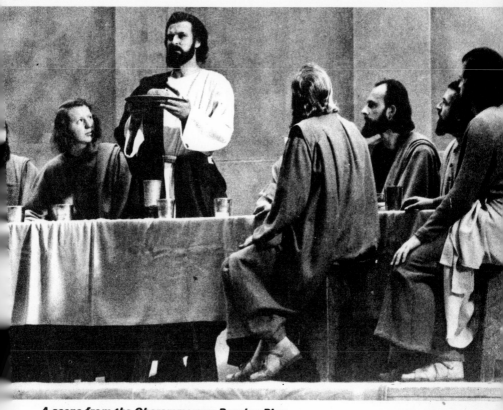

A scene from the Oberammergau Passion Play.

WHERE IS THE VILLAGE OF OBERAMMERGAU?

Oberammergau is a small village in the Bavarian Alps near Germany's border with Austria.

In the winter of 1632 the village was struck by the Black Plague, which spread devastation through Europe. By the following summer one-eighth of Oberammergau's population of 1,000 people had died.

The village elders called all those who could walk to the church and everyone made a vow: "A solemn promise to devote one year in 10 to the preparation and presentation of the tragedy of our Lord's Passion to keep the Christian principle of the redemption of the world before men for all time."

There were no more deaths from the plague, and the villagers believed God had heard their vow.

Apart from an occasional lapse, due in the main to wars, the village people of Oberammergau have presented their Passion Play every 10 years. The first performance was held in the church in 1634. Nowadays a huge theatre, looking rather like a great aircraft hangar, is used. It seats 6,000 people and has room on the stage for crowd scenes with 500 actors. Only native-born villagers may be considered for the 600 parts in the play. Selection for the principal parts is made by ballot more than 12 months before the performance. Rehearsals begin in May for the first performance in May of the following year.

The Passion Play has given Oberammergau worldwide renown and visitors travel long distances to see the eight-hour play.

The play is divided into episodes. These episodes are introduced by the Passion chorus, which consists of fifty singers.

The whole community becomes involved in the production in a completely medieval way.

WHAT IS COAL?

Coal comes from the remains of trees, shrubs, and plants that grew millions of years ago, at a time when the weather was mild and moist.

The coal beds of today were once vast swamps. When the plants and trees died, they fell into boggy water. They did not rot away completely. They changed into a slimy material called peat. Then the sea washed over the peat, bringing up sand and stones, and changing the soil around it. Over millions of years, water, weather and the continual movement of the soil compressed and dried this original peat into good coal.

WHEN DOES COAL BECOME A PRECIOUS STONE?

Coal is basically a compound consisting largely of carbon. When a piece of carbon deep underground is subjected to great heat and pressure, it may gradually be transformed into a diamond. The heat turns the carbon into a liquid and the pressure causes it to crystallize.

Thus the carbon loses its black unattractive appearance and becomes the most precious of stones.

It has been calculated that this extraordinary process takes place at least 75 miles beneath the earth's surface, the diamonds being afterwards transported upwards by natural forces.

Some iron meteorites full of carbon have been found to contain diamonds deep inside. Here the heat and pressure conditions would once have been much the same as those formed underground.

Much the same conditions are created in the laboratory to make synthetic diamonds for industrial purposes, such as cutting hard materials. Only industrial diamonds are man-made. The diamonds that are considered the most precious stones in the world took thousands of years to form.

WHERE IS TRISTAN DA CUNHA?

Tristan da Cunha is one of five small and remote islands in the South Atlantic midway between Buenos Aires in Argentina and the

Cape of Good Hope, South Africa. Tristan is the only one of the five to be inhabited.

The island is 37 square miles in extent and was named after the Portuguese admiral who discovered it in 1506. Tristan da Cunha was created in prehistoric times when a volcanic eruption raised it 18,000 feet from the sea-bed. Cultivation is possible only on one part of the rocky outcrop, on a small plateau squeezed between the sea on one side and 2,000 foot cliffs on the other.

In 1816 Britain landed a small force of men on the island and took possession. The garrison stayed for a year. When it departed, one of its members, Corporal William Glass, was allowed to remain on Tristan with his family. With the arrival of shipwrecked sailors and of five women from St Helena, the population grew to 260 by 1961.

For 150 years the islanders' way of life changed little. But in 1961 the volcano erupted and forced their departure to England. This evacuation seemed to be the end of life on Tristan but, weary of contact with modern civilization and longing for their island ways, the people began to return two years later.

The Tristan da Cunha Development Company now provides the island's sole industry. By 1967 Tristan had a small harbour for the first time in its history. After that a road, a new hospital and a sewage system were built, and electricity was introduced. The island now has something approaching the best of both worlds, isolation and "away from it all" atmosphere but some modern amenities, too.

WHO OPENED UP THE KIMBERLEY DIAMOND MINES?

Cecil Rhodes, son of an English vicar, and Barney Barnato, son of a London Jew, both made fortunes by opening up the Kimberley diamond fields. The great diamond rush began in 1866 after a Boer farmer's son discovered a glittering stone on the Orange river near Hopetoun, South Africa.

As the number of mines increased, the walls began to cave in, and water flooded the deeper pits. Rhodes bought a large steam pump and hired it out. With the money he acquired more pumps and then began to buy claims, gaining control of the vast De Beers mine. Meanwhile Barnato had secured a large amount of stock in the Kimberley mine. A struggle for the control of both mines ended in Barnato turning over his Kimberley stock to Rhodes in return for shares in De Beers. The result was the formation in 1888 of the De Beers Consolidated Mines Company.

The Kimberley diamond deposits are believed to have come from 150 miles beneath the earth's surface, having been formed from carbon subjected to great heat and pressure. The volcanic rock bearing the diamonds is called "kimberlite". As the miners dug, they came across a strange heavy rock in the shape of pipes, which were filled with kimberlite. These pipes were the throats of ancient volcanoes, up which the kimberlite is thought to have been squeezed at least 70 million years ago.

WHY WOULD YOU GO TO DEATH VALLEY?

You would go to Death Valley, as do half a million visitors each year, to look at its magnificently varied scenery and to recapture the flavour of those days of privation and hardship which gave the valley its name.

Death Valley National Monument is in the state of California in the U.S.A. In its 3,000 square miles can be found sheer-walled canyons, desert springs and sands, an extinct volcano, snow-topped mountain ranges, desolate wastes of salt crystals and gardens of fragile wild flowers.

There is a 200 square mile salt pan that contains the Western Hemisphere's lowest point—282 feet below sea level—and is the driest spot in the U.S.A.

Death Valley also contains long-abandoned mines, silent witnesses to the gold seekers of 1849 who lived and died in its inhospitable terrain. Coffin Canyon, Deadman Pass, Hells Gate, Starvation Canyon and Suicide Pass are names which perpetuate the despair and suffering of these pioneers.

HOW DO COUNTRIES GET THEIR NAMES?

Countries do not all have universally accepted names. Holland is officially The Netherlands. Finland is called Suomi by its own people. The names of countries often spring from the discoverer and sometimes from a native tribe or even a conquering people. America is named after Amerigo Vespucci, the explorer, France after the Frankish invaders, and England after the Angles.

Iceland's name derivation is self-explanatory—yet the island is also famous for its natural hot geysers!

The Greeks and Romans called England "Albion" – which is probably derived from *albus* meaning white and is a reference to her white cliffs – the first things the Romans would have seen on their arrival. Spain in Spanish is España and in Latin, Hispania. An amusing story of the origin of Quebec in Canada is that it was so called because the French sailors who first saw the rocky promontory cried: "Quel bec!" or "What a beak!"

WHERE ARE PRECIOUS STONES FOUND?

Precious stones, or gems, are minerals used for adornment, and they are found in rocks. Rocks are divided into three groups. The igneous (fire-formed) rocks may be fine-grained or coarse-grained; a very coarse-grained type, called pegmatite, is an important source of gem minerals such as diamonds. Gems are also found in the cavities of the igneous rocks granite and obsidian.

Sedimentary rocks are layered rocks and, except for turquoise and opal, are the source of very few gems. However, when the original rock contained heavy minerals – and gem minerals are heavy – lumps of them tended to be deposited as pebbles in a river bed and such deposits form the gem gravels of Upper Burma, the "byon", and those of Ceylon, the "illam".

Metamorphic rocks – rocks which have been altered by pressure – are a fruitful source of gem minerals, for instance the rubies found in Burma.

There are also precious materials of animal origin – pearls from oysters, ivory from elephants and coral from the tiny sea creatures which give their name to it. There are also amber and jet, whose origin is vegetable. Amber is the fossilized resin of a coniferous tree which grew in the Eocene period. Jet is a variety of fossil wood.

Gems are found throughout the world and are prized for their rarity and beauty. Their charm may depend on transparency and depth of colour as in the ruby and emerald, on colour only as in the turquoise, on purity and "fire" as in the diamond, and on "play of colour" as in the opal.

WHAT IS CHINA CLAY?

China clay is a type of clay first used by the Chinese for making chinaware and porcelain. From the hill, Kao-ling, close to the famous pottery-producing centre of China, comes the clay's other name of kaolin.

Kaolin is produced by the disintegration of muscovite-biotite-granite rock which is easily decomposed by atmospheric agents into its present form. It is composed of 46 per cent silica, 40 per cent alumina and 14 per cent water.

One of the most famous and largest of china clay deposits is to be found in the far west of England, in Cornwall and West Devon. This clay has been produced by ascending hydrothermal solutions from the inside of the earth's crust, such as superheated steam, boron and florine compounds, or carbon dioxide, as opposed to descending atmospheric solutions.

The uses of china clay are varied. By far the largest amount goes into the manufacture of paper. It is used also in the production of pottery, some chemicals and cosmetics, and in pharmacy. Kaolin also makes a good poultice, as it retains heat.

WHEN WAS THE GREEN REVOLUTION?

The increase in agricultural production throughout the world since 1945 has been so great it has come to be known as the Green Revolution.

World agricultural production in 1964 was one and a half times that of 1948. Much of this increase was due to the redistribution of land and to the grouping of small holdings into larger units.

Scientists have contributed new varieties of grass that provide better cover and strength, thus holding the soil in place. Advances have been made in the development of new kinds of plants capable of withstanding drought and maturing fast enough to avoid frost damage. Research has led to better production methods, fertilizers and pesticides.

WHY ARE THERE MANY KINDS OF SOIL?

The basic material of the surface of the earth is solid rock, and the surface of the landscape we see is nearly always the result of weathering, the action of sun, wind, frost, rain, ice or snow. Therefore, there are many kinds of soil depending upon the climate and the type of parent rock. There is also a third factor which influences the kind of soil formed. This is the vegetation.

The first step in weathering is the breaking down of the rock. Water plays an important part at this stage, either by freezing and shattering the rock as it expands or by washing away some of the minerals of which the rock is composed, thereby loosening its particles.

The climate is also important for most rocks contain much quartz as well as silicates. In a cold climate, the crystals of the silicates are dissolved more quickly than the quartz. In a hot moist climate however, the quartz is washed away and the silicates left behind. Every intermediate stage can be found between these two extreme types of soil.

Vegetation also plays its part by splitting rocks with its roots. Also dead branches and leaves fall on to the ground, decay and add a layer of humus to the soil, rich in nutrients which enable larger plants to grow. These larger plants support animals, some of which help to mix the soil still further.

There are other types of soil

such as those formed from the silt deposited by rivers – alluvial soils – or where bogs and marshes occur. But one thing is common to all soils. They are very unstable if the vegetation which covers them and aids in their formation is removed. Then they are easily washed away and the result of centuries of slow development is lost.

WHAT ARE MOUNTAINS OF THE MOON?

The Mountains of the Moon, or the Ruwenzori mountain range, forms an eighty-mile long backbone on the frontier of Zaïre and Uganda in East Africa, and extends northwards to within 70 miles of Lake Albert. Springing from the bottom of a rift valley, it reaches a height of 16,794 feet with Margaret Peak.

The name "Mountains of the Moon" is a very ancient one, for Herodotus, Aristotle and Ptolemy all had vague ideas that the source of the great River Nile lay in some far distant mountains, the fabled "Mountains of the Moon", the silver peaks whose glistening snows fed the lake sources of the Nile.

However, it was not until 1888 that the Ruwenzori Range was first discovered for the Western world by the great American explorer Henry Morton Stanley, and climbed for the first time in 1906 by the Duke of Abruzzi.

Several earlier explorers had camped within the area, but had been defeated by heavy rainfall.

WHERE IS THE WORLD'S LARGEST REEF?

The largest reef in the world is the Great Barrier Reef off the northeast corner of Australia. From Anchor Cay (or island) above the northern tip of Queensland, the reef runs parallel to the mainland at a distance of about 60 miles, to Lady Elliot Island, 1,250 miles away to the south.

This reef, which is 80,000 square miles in area, was discovered in 1770 by Captain Cook. He called one of the many navigable passages Providential Channel after he had edged his ship through it to the coast. He named Endeavour Reef, where he ran aground, after the ship itself.

The fantastic coral forms give shelter to a collection of other living creatures, such as fish, crustaceans, worms, molluscs and starfish, of greater variety than can be found anywhere else. Ninety per cent of the reef is under water and the remainder is composed of some 200 islands dotted along its length. A few of these islands remain permanently dry and swarm with bird life. They are used also by turtles who come ashore to lay their eggs.

The Great Barrier Reef is a delicately balanced system suffering, from time to time, an upset in its regular routine. Such an upset began in the 1960s with the invasion of the large poison-spined starfish, which is still going on. Appropriately called "crown-of-thorns", this starfish has infested some parts of the reef and by feeding on the polyps has ravaged vast areas of living coral. Even so, the reef remains one of the most colourful regions of the world.

WHY DOES THE SAHARA CHANGE SHAPE?

The Sahara, the world's greatest dry hot desert, stretches right across the north of Africa where there is almost no rainfall and, consequently, little or no vegetation to anchor the soil. The sand is blown constantly by the wind, much of it into a landscape of great shifting dunes which constantly change shape, while the edges of the desert eternally encroach upon the land around.

The Sahara extends over three and a half million square miles of land, where the average rainfall is generally much less than 10 inches a year. The prevailing winds come from the heart of Asia and carry little moisture.

The temperature during the day exceeds 100°F in the summer, and even in the winter averages 60°–70°F. The surface of the sand is sometimes as hot as 170°F. The sun beats down from a clear sky all day, but at night the same cloudless sky allows the land to cool quickly, and there is often frost at dawn in winter.

The wind acts as a great sand-blasting machine, constantly wearing down rocks and carrying sand and small pebbles along. The few desert plants survive because they have long roots or thick fleshy leaves, and stems that reduce water loss and may even store moisture.

A desert oasis is simply a place where there is water. The greatest oasis of all is Egypt, where for thousands of years life has depended on the careful use of the waters of the River Nile.

WHO NAMED MARTHA'S VINEYARD?

Martha's Vineyard got its name from its discoverer, Bartholomew Gosnold, who gave it the name of his wife Martha and also commemorated the abundant growth of wild vines on the land.

The twin islands of Martha's Vineyard and Nantucket lie South of Cape Cod off the south-eastern coast of Massachusetts, United States. Both are triangular in shape, but Martha's Vineyard is larger and more rugged. It is nearly 20 miles long and ranges from 2–10 miles in width. There are wide, hard beaches on the southern side with safe sheltered shores within the deep bays. The north is hilly, but in the south and eastern parts there are wide stretches of moorland covered with heather and wild flowers.

Both islands were discovered early in the 17th Century and granted to Thomas Mayhew in 1642. The Indians were quiet and friendly, and the first settlers fished for a living, making large fortunes from whaling. With the decline of

The movement of the great glaciers is too slow to be measured by eye.

whaling and sailing ships, the islands were almost forgotten until about 60 years ago when their value as summer resorts was realized. Families bought the old mansions of the whaling captains and the shanties of the fishermen, renovated them and now return to the beautiful and secluded islands year after year for their summer vacations.

WHEN DOES A GLACIER MOVE?

A glacier moves because the huge pressure of the ice and snow lowers the freezing point of its lower layers, causing them to melt. Consequently, the river of ice tends to flow like tar, although very slowly. The glacier must be quite old before enough material accumulates to exert the pressure needed to move it–usually when it is about 60 feet thick.

The movement of glaciers is too slow to be noticed by the eye, but measurements have shown they may travel as much as 150 feet a day. The bodies of mountaineers buried by avalanches have been carried several miles in a few years.

Glaciers cover 10 per cent of the earth's land surface.

WHERE IS THE BIGGEST LAKE IN THE WORLD?

The world's biggest lake is Lake Superior, between America and Canada. It covers an area of nearly 32,000 square miles. But Superior is not the lake with the most water. Lake Baikal in southern Siberia has far more water, because although little over 12,000 square miles in area, it is nearly 6,000 feet deep.

Lake Superior is nearly as big as Austria. It is nearly 400 miles long and receives the drainage of about 200 rivers.

There is virtually no tide. But during autumn and winter storms, waves can reach extremely dangerous heights. These waves are gradually eroding the shore, so the lake is slowly getting even bigger year by year.

Owing to the lake's great industrial advantages and transport facilities the water has become seriously polluted. Since 1965, however, the United States Government has made efforts to purify the great lake.

WHAT IS SHALE?

Shale is a fine-grained, earthy, sedimentary rock rather like clay, but, unlike clay, it is formed in thin layers. It is usually harder than clay and does not so easily dissolve in water. It is normally coloured grey, yellow, green or red.

Shales are made up of sediments that collected hundreds and thousands of years ago on the beds of lakes and oceans. Some of them contain other ingredients than clay minerals and may be called sandy shale, limy shale and so on. They are used a great deal in the making of bricks, tiles and portland cement.

The Rocky Mountains are an example of shale rock which contains a great amount of oil. But the cost of extracting it is high.

WHEN WERE THE ICE AGES?

The Ice Ages ended about 10,000 years ago after lasting about two million years. At its greatest extent the ice covered nearly 30 per cent of the land surface of the world, compared with about 10 per cent today. The great glaciers reached as far south in America as present-day Nebraska and Kansas and extended over the whole of northern Europe down to a line linking London and Berlin.

But there were a number of intervals when temperatures rose and the ice retreated temporarily to its present limits. During these warm periods, which totalled several hundred years, the liberated areas were repopulated. The climate is believed to have been warmer at times than it is today.

HOW IS IT POSSIBLE TO ESTIMATE THE AGE OF FOSSILS?

It is possible to estimate the relative age of fossils, that is whether they came before or after a particular period, because most fossils are found in sedimentary rocks. These are rocks made of sediment which has been compressed or cemented together in layers.

Older rock layers, or strata, are usually at the bottom. So each layer is younger than the layer below it and older than the one above. Fossils may be present in igneous rock (hardened volcanic lavas) and metamorphic rocks (formed by pressure and heat within the earth) but they are usually destroyed.

Telling the age of fossils in terms of years, or absolute time, is a much bigger problem. But scientists use several methods. The tree ring method, counting annual growth rings, can give a scientist a reasonably accurate date back to about 3,000 years ago.

The varve method, based on counting the annual layers of sand and clay deposited in a lake, bay or river by melting glaciers, can be used for deposits less than about 15,000 years old. Similar calculations based on the rate of sedimentation, erosion, salt accumulation etc. have been successfully applied to very much older rocks.

The third method is concerned with radioactive decomposition and is based on actual changes in some of the rock elements or in the fossils themselves. Radioactive uranium gradually changes to uranium lead, radiocarbon to nitrogen and so on. From the proportion of uranium lead to uranium in the rock we can date the oldest rocks and fossils, nearly 3,000 million years old.

WHY DOES VENICE HAVE SO MANY CANALS?

Unlike most canals, those in Venice are not man-made. If anything, man has made the land around the canals.

In the 7th Century this North Italian town was no more than a series of tiny islands and mud flats. After the fall of the Roman Empire, political exiles sought refuge in the Venetian lagoons. Gradually a town emerged with many of its buildings having been constructed directly over the water, supported by massive foundations on the sea bed.

The canals between the groups of houses were left, and consequently, the only form of transport in Venice today is by boat.

The vibrations of motor vehicles would soon shatter the foundations of this beautiful city, which in some cases are precariously poised on nothing firmer than sand. In the days of the gondola all seemed well, but the wash produced by motor boats has greatly weakened Venice's structure.

To add to this historic city's problems, much of the main island is slowly sinking into the sea, largely because of the dredging and water pumping activities of a nearby industrial area.

The Italian government has now embarked on the difficult project of trying to keep this marvel of medieval and renaissance archi- tecture and engineering afloat.

HOW ARE MOUNTAINS FORMED?

The first mountains and valleys were the crust formed as a result of the cooling of the molten mass of the earth. As the planet con- tracted the crust twisted and cracked, forming new mountains.

Mountains are still being formed by volcanic eruption. A crack in the earth's crust allows molten rock and ash to be forced out, forming a cone-shaped mountain growing as it continues to erupt.

Fault-mountains are formed when the earth's crust cracks, or faults, under pressure from inside, and one side of the break is pushed up against the other to form a cliff.

The highest mountains are in the Himalayas where some are over 25,000 feet. Only in the Rocky Mountains and in the Andes are any others over 20,000 feet.

WHERE IS THE OLDEST REPUBLIC?

The tiny country of San Marino, a few miles from Rimini on the Adriatic coast and surrounded by Italy, set up its own government in the 10th Century. This makes San Marino the oldest surviving republic in the world.

According to legend it was founded in the 4th Century by Marinus, a stone cutter from Dal- matia (now part of Yugoslavia). He fled to a mountain retreat, Monte Titano, to escape persecu- tion by the Roman Emperor Diocletian.

Marinus bequeathed this retreat to his followers to remain evermore as an island of liberty in a tyranni- cal world. The republic's capital, San Marino, is built around the three craggy tops of Monte Titano, which rises to a height of 2,425 feet almost in the centre of the country's 24 square miles.

Over the centuries the republic has been invaded several times but has always regained its in- dependence. In 1861, the people of San Marino, considerate of others, wrote to Abraham Lincoln expressing their concern over the troubles in America. An apprecia- tive Lincoln wrote back: "Although your dominion is small, your state is nevertheless one of the most honoured in history."

Napoleon had offered this "model of a republic" additional territory in 1797, but San Marino declined to accept it.

The inhabitants are of Italian

origin but they have one big problem. Over the centuries the families of the republic became so inter-related that the citizens found it impossible to provide a completely impartial system of law enforcement. Because of this they decided to "import" their judges and police forces from Italy. In this way the San Marino families have avoided feuds and family charges of favouritism.

WHAT IS A DEPRESSION?

A depression is an area of low pressure, usually bringing unsettled weather. A deepening depression has a lowering of pressure at its centre.

The profile of a depression would read as follows: "A warm front bringing a wide belt of layered clouds with steady rain. It will be followed by a cold front bringing first showers then brighter, more settled weather. In the warm sector between the two fronts we can expect quiet, dull weather broken by storms."

Official weather observers make their observations of the atmospheric conditions at the end of each six-hour period during the day. Daily reports from many different observers on land and at sea are collected together to make up a weather-map summary.

The weather-map consists of patterns of lines, very similar to the contours on a geographical map, along with various other signs and symbols.

WHY DO DESERTS FORM?

Deserts in hot climates owe their origin to lack of water resulting from the capacity of warm air above the land area to retain most of the available moisture. This, combined with the high evaporation rate, turn the land into desert.

Another factor in the formation of deserts is a high mountain range, such as the Andes. These enormous mountains lie across the path of the rain clouds and moist winds, thus forming a shield. So most of the rain clouds burst over the mountains before they ever reach the plains. Other deserts, such as the Gobi in Central China, are so deep within the continent that the moisture-laden winds hardly ever reach them.

WHEN DOES A RIVER FLOW UNDERGROUND?

An underground river is formed when the top soil of the land makes it extremely easy for water to pass through to a more solid soil structure. Another kind of underground river is created when a powerful spring in a mountain has to find a channel to the surface owing to the solidity and compactness of the rocks.

Finally, an underground river may form as an effluent to a larger river above ground, if there are faults in the surrounding land.

Some rivers travel underground only for a part of the journey, such as the Rhône in France.

WHERE IS THE GULF STREAM?

The Gulf Stream is in the Atlantic. It is a warm ocean current which flows steadily from the Gulf of Mexico north-eastwards. One branch reaches the Canary Islands, turns southwards and moves back across the South Atlantic. The other branch flows past the western coasts of northern Europe.

This current, which is like a river in the sea, is 50 miles wide at its narrowest and nearly 2,000 feet deep. It sweeps along with it many forms of warm water life from the tropics, but these die before they reach the European coasts where the warm water mixes with cold water moving down from the Arctic.

The Gulf Stream has a great effect on the weather of Britain and Norway. The prevailing south-westerly winds are warmed by it and collect moisture which turns into rain. In winter the warm water keeps open the cold northern ports, such as Hammerfest, in Norway, and Murmansk, in the Soviet Union, while harbours in the Baltic, many miles farther south, are blocked with ice. In summer it causes bright flowers to bloom on the west coast of Spitzbergen 500 miles north of Norway. In contrast, the east coast, cooled by Arctic water, is bleak and colourless.

In 1912 the United States Congress was asked for money to build a jetty which, it was thought, would divert the Gulf Stream and make it flow up the east coast of the United States. Although this scheme was unlikely to be successful, it was just as well for Britain and Norway that it was never tried. Without the Gulf Stream, Britain's winters would be very much longer and colder, and Norway's harbours, which are vital to the country, would be frozen over for many months.

WHO FIRST TRAVELLED THE LENGTH OF THE AMAZON?

A party of Spanish explorers led by Francisco de Orellana became in 1541 the first Europeans to travel the length of the Amazon river. The journey followed a meeting in Peru between Orellana and Gonzalo Pizarro, half-brother of Francisco Pizarro, the Spanish conqueror. Gonzalo Pizarro, who was governor of Quito, was about to lead an expedition into the unexplored eastern region. Orellano was appointed his lieutenant and sent ahead of the main party by boat with 50 men to search for food. When he reached the junction of the Napo and Maranon rivers, his desire to explore on his own account led him to desert Pizarro's expedition. He pressed on with his party and followed the huge river system down to the Atlantic Ocean, which he reached on August 26, 1542.

It is said that he named the river after a tribe of fighting women whom he encountered near the mouth of the tributary Trombetas and who reminded him of the battling Amazons of Greek mythology.

The Amazon is the greatest river in South America, flowing from its source in the glacier-fed lakes of central Peru for 4,000 miles across Peru and Brazil to enter the Atlantic at the equator.

WHAT MAKES A RIVER BEND?

A river always takes the easiest course through channels and soft ground to the sea, flowing swiftly down mountain sides but much more slowly on the level plains.

On the plain the river takes advantage of every difference in gradient. This winding course is accentuated by the process of silting and erosion. As a river flows round a curve, the water on the outer bend moves more swiftly to cover the greater distance in the same time as the water flowing past the inner bend.

The more rapidly moving water will tend to wear away the banks of the channel, while the slower movement of the water on the inside wall will allow silting to take place. When the curve becomes more pronounced it is known as a "meander". Notable examples of meanders are to be found in the Wye in England, and the Meuse in France.

Sometimes the river erodes the bank so fiercely that a new channel is formed, leaving an island of earth in the middle of the stream.

WHEN IS PUMICE STONE FORMED?

Pumice stone is formed when molten volcanic glass, ejected from beneath the earth's crust, cools so rapidly that there is no time for it to crystalize.

After the pumice has solidified, the gases inside are suddenly released and the stone swells up into its characteristic light and airy form. If the substance had cooled under greater pressure it would have turned into solid glass.

The stones have long been used for cleaning and polishing. Since the Second World War it has been employed widely in railroad building, masonry and insulation. Good pumice is found in Iceland, the Canaries, New Zealand, Greece, the Pacific coast of the United States and many other areas with a volcanic background.

WHERE IS THE WORLD'S SMALLEST COUNTRY?

The smallest country in the world is the Vatican City. The Vatican is an independent and sovereign state within the boundaries of Rome in Italy.

Although the Vatican has always been the spiritual and administrative centre of the Roman Catholic Church, it did not become an independent state until 1929.

The city state has a daily newspaper, a railway station, and its own bank. It has an area of 0·17 square miles and a population of about 1,000.

The imposing facade of St. Peter's in the Vatican.

There are no frontier formalities for those entering Vatican City where millions yearly visit St Peter's and the exhibition galleries.

The chief treasures to be seen are the Michelangelo frescoes in the Sistine Chapel, paintings by Raphael, Fra Angelico and Caravaggio, the frescoes of Pinturicchio and the Codex Vaticanus of the Greek Bible.

WHY IS THERE MORE SEA THAN LAND ON THE EARTH'S SURFACE?

The answer to this question lies in the composition of the rocks which make up the outer portion of the earth's crust. Over large areas of the earth's surface, these rocks are lightish in colour, relatively light in weight and are called granitic rocks, because granite is the most common type. Over still larger areas of the earth the rocks are darker, heavier and are called basaltic rocks, since among them basalt is the chief type.

We know that the earth at a depth of a few hundred miles below the surface is molten and that the surface or crustal rocks, which are about 50 miles thick, are really floating on this liquid core.

The granitic rocks stand higher than the basaltic, just as a cork floats higher than wood, and therefore the granitic areas are the continents, and the basaltic, the ocean basins. If all crustal rocks were of the same composition, the earth's surface would be one vast ocean, more than a mile deep.

But why is there water in the sea? There are three reasons. First, the elements hydrogen and oxygen were present in the mass of material from which the earth was formed. These later formed water in vapour and liquid forms. Secondly, the earth's gravity stops the vapour from escaping into space, just as it also retains the atmosphere we breathe. Thirdly, the pressure-temperature relationships on earth are such that the water is mainly in liquid form.

The water in the sea is salty because of the 2,000 million-year-old disintegration of the earth's crust. The soluble materials or salts remained in the ocean. The insoluble materials have formed sedimentary rocks and the ocean sediments.

WHERE IS THE SARGASSO SEA?

The Sargasso Sea is in the Atlantic Ocean south of the Bermudas and several hundred miles east of the American mainland. It is famous for its seaweed and as a spawning ground for eels.

When these eels are eight or more years old and spawning time is due, they leave the pond or stream where they have been living and make their way, over land if necessary, to the sea.

When they reach the area known as the Sargasso, the females lay their millions of eggs at a depth of 1,500 feet and the males fertilize them. The baby eels hatch out after a few days and float to the surface. Vast masses of seaweed lie on the surface of the Sargasso.

Carried along by winds and ocean currents from the Gulf of Mexico and Caribbean Sea, this floating seaweed is concentrated into an area many thousands of square miles in extent. There it gives refuge to myriads of sea creatures, such as fish, sea-worms, molluscs, crabs and jellyfish. Sea birds find it useful as a resting place.

This floating "island" may have given rise to the famous legend in ancient times of the lost land of Atlantis. Christopher Columbus recorded taking two weeks to sail through it in 1492.

But what happens to the baby eels? Drifting at first, they eventually make their way to the ponds and streams of their parents. The American eels go to America and the European eels to Europe. The old eels do not return but die after spawning.

The Sargasso Sea is the subject of many legends. Ships are said to have vanished in it, but there is no truth in the legend that associates it with the lost land of Atlantis.

WHAT IS AN ANTICYCLONE?

The name anticyclone was first introduced by Sir Francis Galton, the English meteorologist, in 1861 to describe weather conditions opposite to those of a cyclone. Anticyclones are characterized by fine weather and weak winds.

In weather maps and climatic charts, anticyclones appear as a region in which the pressure is higher than in its surroundings. So when the weather forecaster starts to talk about anticyclones you can be prepared for the weather to remain stable for some time, usually sunny and with occasional light rain.

In a cyclone or low-pressure area the winds circulate anticlockwise in the northern hemisphere and clockwise in the southern hemisphere. Cyclones are usually areas of strong, violent winds and indicate bad weather.

WHY WERE THE TEMPLES OF ABU SIMBEL MOVED?

When construction began on the High Dam at Aswan, in southern Egypt, it was realized that the temples of Abu Simbel would be completely submerged as the waters of the Nile rose behind the dam to create a much needed reservoir.

In 1959 Egypt, and its southern neighbour Sudan appealed for help to the United Nations Educational, Scientific and Cultural Organization. The first archaeological surveys began in 1960 and U.N.E.S.C.O's response grew into what was to become the biggest archaeological rescue operation in history.

Abu Simbel consists of three temples of Rameses II built more than 3,000 years ago. The most important and impressive temple included four gigantic seated statues of the king, each 65 feet high. By 1968 these four enormous

monuments to Rameses had been cut out of the rock and reconstructed, exactly as they were, high up on a cliff.

Six more great statues of Rameses and his queen (about 30 feet high) were also excavated and moved to a dry sanctuary above the old river bed, along with everything else that could be salvaged.

WHEN DID THE RIFT VALLEYS FORM?

The great rift valleys of the earth took shape during the pleistocene age, about two million years ago. They were caused mainly by volcanic eruptions powerful enough to split a mountain range, thus creating a rift between the two sides of the volcano.

Rift valleys are to be found in all parts of the world where volcanic action has been common. The most impressive example is the Great Rift Valley which extends from Jordan in south-west Asia to Mozambique in southern Africa. Many big lakes are situated within the valley's boundaries.

Extremely steep edges are characteristic of these valleys. In Africa their edges rise to heights of 10,000 feet on either side.

WHERE IS THE DUST BOWL?

The name Dust Bowl was given to the man-made desert in the central United States in the 1930s. There

218

dust storms blew which were as severe as any on record. One storm in 1933 was traced for 1,300 miles to northern New York.

For the origin of the Dust Bowl we must go back to the late 1800s when homesteaders were advancing relentlessly towards the west and planting their crops in the short-grass country, land known previously as the American desert. The farmers brought with them strains of hard winter wheat that were resistant to drought, disease and insects. They ploughed into the thin grassland and sowed the seeds both of wheat and tragedy.

The states involved were western Texas, Oklahoma, Kansas, Nebraska and North and South Dakota to the Pacific coast. Wheat was the principal crop. Dry farming techniques were developed. These enabled farmers to conserve the meagre moisture in the soil by a process of dust mulching and by permitting the land to lie fallow to build up moisture for the following crop year. However, the farmers did not know how to conserve their soil and prevent the erosion of semi-arid earth which had been anchored only by the cover-crop of thin grass.

The great drought of 1932–7 led to the Dust Bowl and caused the abandonment of vast areas of land. Many people left their farms for California, where they joined other migratory workers in search of jobs as fruit and vegetable pickers.

Meanwhile the American government, with Franklin D. Roosevelt as president, took action to aid the ravaged area. Starving cattle were moved to better ranges, or bought and slaughtered. Loans were extended to the distressed farmers. Mortgage foreclosures were stopped in 1933 by the extension of government credit. Soil erosion was attacked by encouraging farmers to use more effective methods of keeping their land in condition, and a great irrigation programme was begun.

WHEN WAS THE SEXTANT INVENTED?
The sextant was invented in England in 1731 by John Hadley. Hadley's instrument is used mainly at sea to determine a ship's latitude, or distance from the Equator.

Its invention laid the foundation of modern navigation with the aid of the sun and stars.

The instrument is so called because it is equipped with an arc which is usually one-sixth of a circle, or 60°. It measures the angle of the sun's or a star's altitude above the horizon. As this angle varies with the distance from the Equator, the information obtained helps the navigator to calculate his position. All he needs in addition is the time, the date and the longitude which can be found by comparing local time with the time at Greenwich.

To operate the sextant, the navigator looks through its small telescope straight at the horizon. At the same time, an image of the sun is reflected by mirrors into the user's field of vision. When the sun is made to appear exactly on the horizon, the arm which moves the mirrors gives the required measurements to calculate the ship's position.

The handling of a sextant is generally referred to as "shooting the sun".

WHAT ARE ARTESIAN WELLS?

Artesian wells are those from which water flows freely. These wells are man-made and are created by boring into the rock to a channel that is lower than the water source.

The resulting artesian well has the advantage over vertical wells of not requiring a pump. The water will pour out naturally without the aid of any mechanism until the well runs dry. For this reason artesian wells, although often several hundred feet deep, may be only a few inches wide. This prevents undue loss of water.

The term "artesian well" is derived from Artesium, the ancient name for Artois in Northern France, where a famous free-flowing well was excavated early in the 12th Century.

WHY ARE THERE LOCKS ON SOME CANALS AND RIVERS?

Locks are watertight chambers which enable boats to ascend or descend to different levels in a canal or river.

The lock is usually rectangular in shape with gates at either end. If a boat has to go to a higher level it enters through the bottom or downstream gates of the lock, which are then closed. The water level in the lock is raised to that of the higher part of the canal by filling from the upper level and the upstream gates are opened to let the boat out. The opposite procedure takes place when a boat needs to descend.

Locks used to be made of timber, brick or stone, but now concrete and steel piling are more usual. Originally the chamber was filled or emptied by sluices in the gates. Nowadays, as locks become bigger, these are often replaced by conduits or pipes running the whole length of the structure, with offshoot pipes running into the lock to give an even discharge of water. Old locks may be manually operated but new ones are worked by hydraulic power.

Locks vary tremendously in size from about 126 by 17 feet (38 by 5 metres) on small canals to the giant locks on the Mississippi River in America, which are 1,200 by 110 feet (366 by 33·5 metres).

WHERE DO EARTHQUAKES OCCUR?

Earthquakes occur mainly in the regions of the earth where mountains are being formed, and where the earth's crust is under strain.

Some mountains are formed of great thicknesses of folded sedimentary rock laid down beneath the sea. Heat currents deep within the earth are thought to suck down sections of the undersea crust and so produce great trenches thousands of feet deep. When the heat currents die away the material forming the bottom of the trench begins to rise because it is lighter in weight. Eventually it is thrust up as a mountain range.

This is never a smooth process but is accompanied by great friction and heat, as well as by rending and shearing and tearing. The tearing and shearing of deep underground rocks connected with mountain formation cause earthquakes. Even small underground movements may produce violent

surface shocks. The great Tokyo earthquake of 1923 which is believed to have killed 25 million people was caused by the twisting of a section of the earth's crust in Sagami Bay.

As might be expected, ocean trenches are the seat of a great many earthquakes, for there the earth's crust is in an unstable state. Indeed all the deep earthquakes—those taking place more than 160 miles below the surface—originate around the Pacific trenches. About 90 per cent of the intermediate earthquakes (30 to 160 miles deep) also originate there, as do 40 per cent of the shallow earthquakes (less than 30 miles deep).

Some shallow and intermediate earthquakes are caused by volcanoes or by a slight shifting of layers of rock at a weak place or "fault" on the earth's surface. One of the most famous and widely publicized of these is the San Andreas fault on which San Francisco is built.

WHAT IS THE HELIGOLAND BIGHT?

The Heligoland Bight is an arm of the North Sea extending south and east of the red sandstone island of Heligoland. Heligoland is a small remote island of the German North Frisian group lying in the North Sea between the coast of Schleswig-Holstein and the estuaries of the Jade, Weser and Elbe. It is 5,249 feet long and 1,640 feet wide at its broadest point.

In 1807 Heligoland was a Danish possession but it was seized by the English in 1814 and given to Germany in 1890. Before 1914 Germany developed it as a great naval base with an extensive harbour in the south-east. There was a network of underground fortifications and coastal batteries and it was known as the "Gibraltar of the North Sea". The Heligoland Bight became famous as the scene of a naval battle between the British and the Germans on August 28th, 1914.

Heligoland became a stronghold again under the Nazis and the capital town of Heligoland was destroyed by Allied bombers. In 1947 the whole character of the island was changed by the destruction of the fortifications.

WHY DID THE CONTINENTS DRIFT APART?

One of the most convincing explanations of why the continents drifted apart is that the earth expanded considerably after its creation. This theory can be illustrated by imagining the earth as a balloon and the continents as pieces of paper stuck on the outside. As the balloon is blown up the pieces of paper will grow farther apart.

Other theories suggest that the continents only appeared to drift apart because masses of land were drowned under volcanic waters. But it has been demonstrated that land masses are, in fact, made to drift, by the heat generated from the earth's interior and from earthquakes.

Probably a combination of various theories may be necessary to provide a complete explanation.

WHO FIRST EXPLORED THE MISSISSIPPI?

A Spanish explorer, Fernando de Soto (1496–1542) was the first European to encounter the wide and muddy waters of the Mississippi river. A veteran of Pizarro's conquest of Peru, he was governor of Cuba when in May 1539 he set out with 600 men on an expedition in search of gold. By 1541 his wanderings had led him to the Mississippi but a year later he died of fever on its banks and was buried in the river at night to conceal his death from the Indians.

The next white explorers were two Frenchmen, Father Jacques Marquette, a Jesuit missionary, and Louis Jolliet, a trader, who in 1673 descended the Mississippi as far south as the Arkansas river.

Their trip inspired another Frenchman, René Robert Cavelier, Sieur de La Salle, to complete the exploration. He obtained permission for the expedition from King Louis XIV of France and in 1682 travelled down first the Ohio and then the Mississippi to its mouth in the Gulf of Mexico. He named the new territory he had explored Louisiana in honour of his sovereign, but was assassinated while trying to establish a colony.

222

WHEN DOES AN ATOLL START TO FORM?

An atoll or coral reef begins to form when tiny marine animals called coral polyps attach themselves to rocks on the sea bed. The reef, which eventually takes the shape of a ring or horseshoe enclosing a lagoon, is made up of the lime-based skeletons of innumerable polyps.

After building skeletons round themselves, coral polyps produce new polyps, which in turn surround themselves with skeletons. The young polyps remain attached to the parents so that succeeding generations combine to produce a great mass of coral.

Atolls occur only in shallow water where the temperature is over 65°F (18·3°C). They are found in the West Indies, the Indian Ocean, along the coast of Brazil and, notably, in the Pacific. North-east of Australia huge reefs have formed and some atolls may stretch 40 miles in diameter and more than a thousand feet in depth.

WHAT IS A NATIONAL PARK?

A National Park is an area where natural scenery and wildlife is protected by law to preserve them for future generations. It is only recently that man has realized that he must make a positive effort if many species of wildlife and areas of great beauty are not to disappear for ever.

There are many kinds of areas of conservation and their central priorities may differ slightly. In the U.S.A., a national park such as Yellowstone safeguards natural features and wildlife in a way that will contribute to public enjoyment. In Africa generally, as in the Amboseli Game Reserve, the chief purpose is the preservation of the remnants of the great herds of animals which once roamed the country.

National Parks depend on tourists for revenue but the animals must remain unmolested. To solve the problem many parks restrict visitors' movements by setting aside areas for hotels, restaurants and parking places and providing a limited number of roads through the park. National Parks may be small or large, privately or government owned.

WHERE ARE THE PILLARS OF HERCULES?

The Pillars of Hercules are on either side of the Strait of Gibraltar. The legendary Greek hero Hercules was said to have erected the Pillars on a journey to capture the Oxen of Geryon, a monster with three bodies who lived on an Atlantic island. Passing out of the Mediterranean he threw up the rocks on either side of the Strait of Gibraltar. They were the Rock of Gibraltar and the headland on the Moroccan side.

Hercules' journey was one of the 12 labours that the son of Zeus had been set by Eurystheus, King of Tiryns, whose servant he had become. One of the most famous of these labours was the cleansing of the Augean stables. So innumerable were the herds of cattle that used these stables that, as they returned from pasture, they seemed to reach endlessly across the plain. Their stables were heaped high with manure and had not been cleaned for years. Hercules diverted the Rivers Alpheus and Pereus through them, and completed the task in one day.

For his last labour he braved the Underworld to capture Cerberus, its three-headed watchdog. .

WHY ARE BEACH PEBBLES ROUND?

The pebbles that are to be found on a beach are invariably round and smooth owing to the constant battering they have received from the sea.

Originally pebbles were part of much larger rocks, but various natural phenomena, such as earthquakes and volcanoes, have gradually broken them down. Caught in the movement of the sea, and constantly rubbed against other hard materials, the pebbles finally lose their irregularities and present a smooth round surface.

Many of the rocks of today will be pebbles in thousands of years' time, and many of today's pebbles will eventually be turned into sand by the constant, wearing action of the sea.

WHERE ARE STALACTITES FORMED?

Stalactites are the stony deposits hanging like icicles from the roofs of caves. Stalagmites are similar deposits rising in columns and cones from the caves' floors.

Caves occur chiefly in limestone and chalk formations, because water dissolves these rocks. The River Lesse, for example, in its passage through the caves of Han, in Belgium, has been estimated to dissolve some five tons of limestone in a day. It is redeposited as carbonate which builds up the stalactites and stalagmites.

The seepage of water down the cave walls and through the roof produces constant dripping and evaporation. Stone icicles form on the cave roof, slowly growing with the addition of successive layers of calcium carbonate. The word "stalactite" comes from the Greek and means "drop by drop". There is, too, a general term "dripstone" which is used to cover all formations.

Stalactites are at first hollow, for the depositing of the carbonate is fastest at the outer ring of the water drop. As the evaporating water deposits its mineral matter, the cavity slowly fills up and the stalactite becomes solid. When water trickles out of a narrow cleft in the roof, instead of a small hole, a hanging curtain of stone will form in place of a conical stalactite.

If the water flows so quickly that it splashes on the floor of the cave, it deposits its calcium carbonate there and small cones and domes of stone called stalagmites begin to rise. These may grow up to join the stalactites above and form single columns. Some cave floors are covered with stalagmites. They may grow so high that they block the cave entrance.

The tallest known stalagmite, measuring about 98 feet high, is located at Lozère, France, in the Aren Armand cave.

WHAT IS FLINT?

Flint is one of the various forms of silica, which is among the common materials making up the largest part of rocks. Some other forms of silica are quartz, opal, chalcedony, agate, jasper and onyx. Flint (essentially, silica with some water, a little lime, oxide of iron and, occasionally, carbon) can be grey, greyish-white, smoke-brown, brownish-black, red or yellow. It occurs as layers in other sedimentary rocks.

Because it flakes and can easily be chipped into a sharp cutting edge, flint was used by prehistoric man to make axe heads, arrow heads, knives and other such sharp-edged implements.

The study of implements from the Paleolithic, or Old Stone Age, and the Neolithic, or New Stone Age, has helped us understand how people lived then.

WHEN DOES FROST FORM?

Frost comes from the atmosphere when the temperature falls below freezing, and invisible water vapour in the air turns into white ice crystals, without first becoming a liquid. It usually occurs when the skies are clear, when there is no wind and when a mass of cold air descends on the land.

This often happens during the night in the spring and autumn of areas with temperate climates. In the morning the fields and roofs are white with what would be dew if the temperature had been above freezing point. It is the most common type of frost and is often called hoar frost.

Sometimes only the leaves of plants are fringed with white rime. This is formed when very small droplets of the moisture from fog have frozen on coming into contact with a cold object.

There is also black frost. This occurs when water vapour turns first into liquid and then freezes into a thin layer of ice instead of white crystals. As it is invisible, it is particularly dangerous when it forms on roads.

The beautiful patterns, looking like trees, ferns or feathers, which are sometimes seen on windows, are made when the water vapour in a cold room condenses.

WHY ARE RAIN FORESTS SO-CALLED?

Rain forests are so-called because they grow in the wet lowlands of the tropics where the annual rainfall is more than 80 inches (2,000 mm) and the average temperature is between 20° and 30°C (68° and 86°F).

They consist of evergreen trees which never completely loose their luxurious leaves and grow over 100 feet high. Although it is possible to find as many as 100 different kinds of trees in a small area, most of them are similar.

Contrary to popular belief the rain forest is not a jungle. In most cases there is little vegetation apart from the trees and few flowers. This is because the tops of the trees are so dense that little sunlight reaches the ground.

Those plants that do grow beneath the tree line are mostly climbers winding their way up the barks of trees and such flowers as are found are usually the most exotic varieties on earth.

HOW IS CLAY FORMED?

Clay is formed from earth and various minerals as a result of weather conditions such as heat and rain. Occasionally clay is produced by processes dependant on hot underground springs.

Wet clay has much the same consistency as a soft plastic and is capable of containing water. When dry, clay becomes hard and

A potter forming a bowl from a spinning mass of clay.

thus takes on a permanent shape.

No other material on earth can be used in so many different ways. Clay provides the mechanical and chemical environment for almost all plant life and, therefore, can be said to support all the life on earth.

Once extracted from the soil, clays are used in a wide variety of industries, including engineering, paper making, brick making, cement and chemicals. The use of clay in pottery predates recorded history, and it has largely been due to pottery finds that archaeologists have been able to analyse and record past civilizations.

WHAT ARE THE ANTIPODES?

The antipodes are places on the opposite side of the world to each other, such as New Zealand in the South Pacific, and Iceland near the Arctic Circle. Iceland might refer to New Zealand as "the antipodes".

"Antipodes" comes from a Greek word *antipous*, meaning "having the feet opposite". If you look at a globe, you will see why.

WHERE IS EASTER ISLAND?

Easter Island, one of the most mysterious islands in the world, is in the South Pacific, 2,000 miles west of Caldera in Chile and 1,000 miles east of Pitcairn, its nearest inhabited neighbour. It was annexed by Chile in 1888. The island which is volcanic in origin, was discovered by the Dutch admiral Jacob Roggeveen on Easter Sunday, 1722. It is 11 miles long and 15 miles wide.

Easter Island is noted for its mysterious statues of remote and unknown origin. These statues, consisting of giant heads facing inland, fringe the island's coastline. They stand on huge ramparts or platforms which slope landwards, in some cases to a width of 250 feet. At the end of this sloping rampart there is a paved area.

There are some 260 of these platforms on the island and each one was designed to support between one and 15 of the strange giant heads, carved from compressed volcanic earth. The heads have upturned faces tilted towards the sky, and long ears. They vary in height from 12 to 20 feet. At one time they were topped by huge hats or crowns between six and eight feet in diameter. These hats are made from a red volcanic material different from the material used for the heads themselves.

The island is full of ancient curiosities including long, narrow boat-shaped houses flanked by stone chicken huts. The inhabitants are descendants of Polynesian people who migrated across the Pacific.

There is a legend of a war between the "long-eared" people and their "short-eared" attackers. The long-eared defenders of the islands were said to have been burned in a vast earth oven, but the latest scientific evidence suggests that the "earth oven" was in fact a vast defensive ditch. Ashes in this ditch date from the 17th Century, only a short time before the island's discovery.

But the real truth about Easter Island and its mysterious statues will probably never be known until someone finds out how to read the curious sign language inscribed round the platforms. These signs, which are geometrical in form, are really symbols such as birds, plants and fishes. They may be like the "memory aids" of the ancient Aztecs, but experts believe they are an elementary form of writing.

WHEN DOES AN AVALANCHE OCCUR?

An avalanche occurs when a mass of snow which has built up on a mountain side begins to slip and finally to fall. There can also be avalanches of earth, stones, rock and ice, but usually the word is used to describe a rapid fall of snow.

Snow builds up to great thickness on steep slopes, especially if the surface is not smooth. Even a very small disturbance may set it in motion. The vibration of a passing vehicle, the movement of a man or animal, the fall of a tree branch or even a sound can cause thousands of tons of snow to crash down a mountainside.

The speed of an avalanche varies enormously, but some have been estimated to move at about 200 miles an hour. A big avalanche hurtles down the side of the mountain with a thunderous roar, crushing or sweeping away anything in its path.

The swiftly moving mass of snow pushes the air in front of it with such violence that it fans out sideways as well as driving directly ahead. This wind sometimes reaches a force almost equal to that of a tornado. This great wind is often a more powerful force of destruction than the avalanche itself.

WHAT IS BRINE?

Brine is salt water. So the sea, which is the main source of salt water, is sometimes known as "the briny".

Salt water has various special properties and the fish that live in the sea and in salt lakes are usually not the same kinds that live in fresh water rivers.

Salt water cannot be drunk for refreshment, as it makes the drinker thirstier, or even sick. But it is possible by using expensive desalinization plants to remove the salt and make the water drinkable.

The sea contains many valuable minerals and salts. In some parts of the world, such as coastal Brittany, in France, the sea is allowed to flood the marshes to a shallow depth when the tide comes in. The sun evaporates the water and leaves the salts to be collected.

HOW ARE ROCKS FORMED?

Sedimentary rocks are formed from the sediment, or broken pieces of the earth's rock structure worn down by weather and erosion. The fragmented pieces become compacted and in time much of it is cemented in to form rock.

Igneous rocks originate either from volcanic action as molten lava, which hardens, or from the slow cooling of molten masses beneath the earth's surface, which are exposed after a volcanic eruption or after much erosion.

Many important minerals, notably uranium, have been found enveloped in igneous rocks. The chief sedimentary rocks are sandstone, shale, dolomite and limestone.

WHERE ARE THE VICTORIA FALLS?

These famous falls, among the most spectacular in the world, are on the boundary between Rhodesia and Zambia in southern Africa. The falls form the most remarkable feature of the Zambezi River. They are midway up the Zambezi near the town of Livingstone, which is named after David Livingstone, the Scottish missionary and explorer, who discovered the falls in 1855.

For some distance before the Victoria Falls the Zambezi flows over a level sheet of basalt—a hard, blue volcanic rock—in a valley between sandstone hills. Curiously, the Zambezi does not increase its speed of flow as it nears the mighty falls. The water pours over an almost vertical precipice, nearly a mile wide, at a rate of between four million and 75 million gallons a minute, depending on the season. The minimum flow is between November and December and the maximum between April and May.

The Victoria Falls are wider than Niagara Falls and more than twice their height. At the highest point the water plunges 355 feet.

The only outlet for this vast force of water is a narrow channel cut in the opposing barrier wall near its western end. The river is forced through this narrow, 100-foot gorge for nearly 400 feet. This part of the Falls is aptly known as the Boiling Pot.

From the Boiling Pot the water emerges into an enormous zig-zag which forms the beginning of the Batoka Gorge, about 60 miles long.

At one time it was thought that these fantastic falls were the result of a volcanic fault in the earth. Now it is believed they are caused by the check on the natural erosion of the river bed provided by the hard basaltic rock sheets.

WHAT IS THE MISTRAL?

This is the name given to a wind which blows in the Rhône Valley in France. The wind is caused by an exchange of air between the cold hinterland of France's Central Plateau and the warm Gulf of the Lion in the Mediterranean Sea.

High mountain ranges near flat

country produce unpleasant winds, especially where the mountains descend to a warm sea. Atmospheric pressure is high above the cold mountains, but low above the sea. Air, therefore, flows towards the sea and is not warmed because it has not crossed enough land.

The north-westerly mistral, funnelling down the construction of the Rhône Valley, blows at a speed of 30 to 60 m.p.h. on at least 50 days each year. It bursts out on to the Mediterranean coast, filling holidaymakers' caravans with sand and capsizing yachts caught unaware at sea.

HOW DID THE RED SEA GET ITS NAME?

The Red Sea got its name because its surface sometimes has a reddish tinge. This colour comes from a free-floating type of alga, or water plant, called *Trichodesmium erythraeum*. The algae are normally blue-green in colour but have an additional red pigment that sometimes becomes dominant and dyes the sea red.

This sea is a narrow strip of water about 1,200 miles long. It varies in width from about 250 miles in the south to 130 miles in the north, where it divides into two parts, the Gulf of Suez and the Gulf of Aqaba. Extending south-south-east from Suez to the Gulf of Aden, the Red Sea separates Saudi Arabia and the Yemen from Egypt, Sudan and Ethiopia.

WHERE IS THE MAGYAR LANGUAGE SPOKEN?

The Magyar language is the official language of Hungary (or, in the Magyar language, the country of Magyarorszaq). In 1967 the population was 10,197,000 with another two million Magyar-speaking people living outside Hungary—mainly in Czechoslovakia, Rumania and Yugoslavia. Nearly half a million Magyars live in the United States of America.

Magyar belongs to the Arabic language family. Apart from Finland, where the language is closely related to Hungarian, the only part of the world where you are likely to hear anything similar is in western Siberia.

Because several suffixes, or smaller words, are often added, the Magyars can produce words of considerable length. For instance, "the very biggest" would be "legeslegnagyobb" in Magyar.

The first written example of Magyar, a short funeral oration, dates from about 1200.

WHEN IS MARBLE FORMED?

Marble is formed when granular limestone or dolomite rocks crystallize twice under the influence of heat, pressure, liquids and chemical action. These rocks undergo what is known as metamorphism, a complete change from one state to another.

Most of the marble existing today was formed many millions

A quarry of Carrara marble in North-West Tuscany, Italy

of years ago and is usually quarried from deep under the earth. It is used for buildings and monuments, sculpture and table tops. The chief discoveries of marble have been made in Italy (Carrara marble), Mexico, the United States (onyx), Norway and Greece.

HOW DEEP IS THE DEEPEST OCEAN?

The deepest part of the ocean is the Marianas Trench off the Philippine Islands in the South Pacific. There the sea floor lies 36,198 feet below the waves. So the distance to the surface is more than a mile greater than the height of Mount Everest.

Jacques Piccard and Lt. Donald Walsh descended to the bottom of the Marianas Trench on January 23, 1960 in the United States Navy bathyscaphe Trieste. It took four and a half hours to make the trip to the bottom, where the water pressures was eight tons to the square inch. This is the nearest men have come to making a journey to the centre of the earth.

The average depth of water in the world's oceans is 12,000 feet. But, apart from the Marianas Trench, there are other trenches in the seabed more than six miles deep.

The floor of the ocean is, of course, as well defined with canyons and "mountain" peaks as the dry land of the earth, something we do not normally consider when we look at the ocean surface.

WHERE IS THE KREMLIN?

The Kremlin was the palace of the Russian Tsars in Moscow until Peter the Great (1672–1725) moved the whole imperial court to the newly-founded city of St Petersburg (now Leningrad) early in the 18th Century.

In 1922 Moscow was chosen as the capital of the Union of Soviet Socialist Republics. Once again the Kremlin became the headquarters of government.

Encircled by great battlements erected in the 15th Century, the citadel covers an area of 65 acres and is almost a city itself. Around the walls are 19 towers and five gates, the finest of them being Spasskaya (Saviour's) Tower and Gate which houses the Kremlin chimes. Men used to doff their hats as they passed by this gate in Red Square.

Within the walls are churches, four cathedrals and many palaces. In 1955 the Kremlin was opened to the public and the palaces now exhibit the riches of Tsarist days.

Outside the walls is Red Square, 900 yards long by 175 yards wide, where the great military parades are held annually to commemorate the revolution of 1917. The embalmed body of Lenin (1870–1924), leader of the revolution, lies in its mausoleum in front of the Kremlin's wall.

The defensive fortresses at the centre of many medieval Russian cities were also called Kremlin, which is where the word comes from.

WHAT IS THE GOLDEN GATE?

The Golden Gate is the name given to the break in the long chain of mountains running down the Pacific Ocean coastline of California. This gate, or gap, forms the sea entrance to San Francisco Bay.

The gap was mapped in 1846 by John C. Frémont, an American Army officer and explorer, who named it CHRYSOPYLAE – which is Greek for Golden Gate.

The bay itself had been discovered by accident in 1769, when a Spanish explorer, Gaspar de Portola, intending to establish a mission-cum-garrison at Monterey Bay, overshot his objective by several miles.

A small settlement was gradually established until, in 1848, San Francisco became the base for the gold strike in the famous Sacramento Valley. Within a year the population increased from 2,000 to 25,000. In the latter half of the 19th Century wharves and warehouses sprang up on the bay. Houses and offices, restaurants and bars spread rapidly over the steep slopes of its hills.

Rudyard Kipling, the English author, visited San Francisco in the 1880s and found it to be "a mad city inhabited for the most part by perfectly insane people whose women are of a remarkable beauty".

The great earthquake and fire of 1906 destroyed almost a third of the city. Apart from killing 450 people, it left over 100,000 homeless and did millions of dollars worth of damage.

Even so San Francisco continued to be an increasingly important maritime centre. Now about 12,000 ships use it annually. Whether liner, small cargo boat or yacht, every vessel must sail through the Golden Gate to reach the open sea.

Landlocked San Francisco Bay extends over an area of 422 square miles, but the Gate is only two miles across at its widest point. It has a tidal flow half as big again as the water flow of the River Amazon.

In 1937 work was completed on the Golden Gate Bridge to speed traffic along the coast from San Francisco. It is one of the world's man-made marvels with a central span 4,200 feet long.

WHY DOES DEW FALL OVERNIGHT?

Dew is the result of condensation on the surface of the earth. At night the earth sometimes becomes colder than the air, and when water vapour in the air touches leaves and other objects on the earth's cold surface in the early hours of the morning, it condenses to form "dewfall". If the earth is very cold the vapour freezes and hoar frost, instead of dew, is formed.

If, on the other hand, water vapour rising from the earth meets a leaf colder than itself, it will condense to form a different kind of dewfall.

Science and Technology

WHAT IS A SOLARIUM?

A solarium may be a sundial. It may also be a terrace, a balcony or a room exposed to the rays of the sun, especially one used for the treatment of illness by sunbathing.

A sundial tells the time by means of the shadow cast by the sun's rays. The earliest known sundial still preserved is an Egyptian shadow clock dating from at least the 8th Century B.C.

The Greeks and Romans constructed very complex sundials, and the Renaissance produced many beautiful designs. By the 19th Century, clocks and watches were so accurate that the sundial was used only as an ornament in gardens. But some specially designed for scientific purposes were made as late as the beginning of the 20th Century.

The fact that the sun's rays may be beneficial to man was not scientifically proved until fairly recently. Vitamin D is now known to be activated by the ultra-violet rays in sunlight. Nevertheless, in the late 19th Century, it was observed that many people found "sunshine baths" of great help when recovering from an illness. Many hospitals and large private houses had solariums or sun rooms.

The rays of the sun not only induced a feeling of well-being, but helped to clear up some skin diseases and imparted a glowing colour to the body. Before this time, a light, delicate complexion had been a mark of wealth, an indication that one had no need to toil in all weathers to earn a living.

WHEN WAS THE FIRST WRISTWATCH MADE?

The exact time the first wristwatch appeared is not known. But soon after the beginning of the 20th Century women's small pocket watches began to be fitted into specially made leather or gold adaptors to be worn on the wrist. They were immediately successful, and their popularity rapidly increased in the First World War because they could be consulted without undoing a coat or uniform jacket.

The first self-winding wrist-watch was invented by John Harwood, an Englishman who patented it in 1924. Today the largest watchmaking industry in the world is concentrated in the Jura Mountains and the valley of the Aar in Switzerland.

HOW IS MILK PASTEURIZED?

Milk is pasteurized by heating it to a temperature of about 62°C (about 143°F) and then maintaining that temperature for about half an hour.

The treatment kills most of the bacteria which cause milk to go

The French scientist Louis Pasteur at work in his laboratory.

sour quickly or may produce disease in human beings.

This temperature is chosen because it is the lowest temperature that will kill the microbacterium tuberculosis, the carrier of tuberculosis which used to kill people of all ages in their millions. At the same time it is low enough not to alter the taste too much.

Pasteurized milk is therefore much safer than untreated milk, especially for babies, and in many countries is the only milk allowed to be sold. The process is named after the French scientist Louis Pasteur (1822–1895) whose discoveries revolutionized knowledge about the effects of bacteria.

WHY DO OIL AND WATER NOT MIX?

Oil and water do not mix because the molecules (tiny particles) of which they are composed are so different. The molecules in oil are much bigger and contain many more atoms than those of water.

When different liquids mix, it is because they have similar types of molecules which readily link up with each other, like milk and water. In the case of oil and water the groups of molecules prefer to stay apart.

The patches of oil floating on top of the water are usually circular because of another characteristic of molecules, which produces what scientists term surface tension. This is a cohesive force caused by the attraction of the molecules to each other. They cling so tightly that they produce a surface layer which acts like an elastic skin or the rubber envelope of a balloon. The molecules are trying to pull the liquid into as small a space as possible. As well as producing a circular shape, this tension makes the surface area of each oil patch as small as possible.

WHAT WAS AN ALCHEMIST?

An alchemist was an early student of the science of chemistry. According to one theory the word "alchemy" is derived from "Khem", the ancient name for Egypt. That country was the source of a great deal of the pioneer work in the various sciences.

Much of the early work of the alchemists is frowned on by today's scientists because it was bound up with experiments to find "the elixir of life" and "the philosopher's stone" which would turn all base metals into gold. The alchemists also studied magic and astrology.

However, we have to thank the alchemists for such words as "hermetically sealed", alcohol and alkali, and for the discoveries of sulphuric, nitric and hydrochloric acids, and of metals such as antimony, bismuth and arsenic.

The "hermetic art" is another name for alchemy. Hermes Trismegistus was the name given by the Greeks to the Egyptian god of alchemy. Thus hermetic sealing is derived from the method of air-tight sealing used by alchemists in their experiments.

The alchemists also associated the planets with certain metals and used the astrological symbol as a shorthand sign for the metal. The sun stood for gold, the moon for silver, Venus for copper, Mars for iron, Jupiter for tin and Saturn for lead.

WHEN DOES COLOUR FADE?

An article's colour fades when subjected to a chemical reaction in which oxygen is released. This oxygen combines with the natural colouring matter or with the dye to produce a colourless compound. Thus the colour of the article becomes paler and is finally taken out altogether, or bleached.

The most famous bleaching agent is the sun, and the process by which it makes colour fade is called photo-chemistry. The old-fashioned method of bleaching textiles by laying them out flat in the sunlight is still used in places.

Chemical bleaching is much quicker, but needs to be controlled with great care. In about 1790 it was discovered that chlorine gas and its compounds were good bleaching agents and chloride of lime (calcium hypochlorite), made by the action of chlorine on slaked lime came into use. This "bleaching powder", as it was called, was dissolved in water. It was removed when the bleaching was complete by washing the article or immers-ing it in neutralizing solutions. More modern bleaching agents are sodium hypochlorite, hydrogen peroxide and sulphur dioxide.

WHERE IS COBALT USED?

Can you think of any connection between a delicate Ming vase and a nuclear explosion? Difficult, isn't it? And yet there is a connection in the sense that different types of one particular substance–cobalt–have been used in the production of both.

In ancient China the beautiful blues used in the finest porcelains came from a cobalt ore. Until the early years of this century most of the world's production of cobalt went to provide colour for the porcelain and glass industries.

Today, cobalt, which in its natural state is a hard silvery-white metallic substance, serves many purposes. A "cobalt bomb" can be a terrible weapon capable of distributing lethal radioactive cobalt-60 through a nuclear explosion. It can also be the means of treating certain illnesses by deep X-rays.

About a quarter of the output of cobalt goes into the making of magnets, since the metal has a high magnetic quality. It has many engineering uses. It can be employed to take away the slightly yellow tint of the iron in plate-glass windows. There is a call for it in dentistry and bone surgery.

In Australia and New Zealand ranchers were puzzled by the poor condition of sheep and cattle grazing on apparently good pasture land. Eventually it was discovered that the land did not have enough cobalt. Today small quantities of a cobalt-based compound are added either to the water supplies serving the cattle or to the land itself in the form of fertilizers.

Cobalt is also an essential food ingredient for human beings. Liver, cabbage, spinach, lettuce and watercress all contain comparatively high levels of it. About 20,000 tons of cobalt are produced every year.

WHY ARE FERTILIZERS USED ON FARMS?

Fertilizers are used on farms to increase crop yields by ensuring that soils contain the chemical elements required by growing plants. These chemical elements include oxygen, carbon, hydrogen, nitrogen, phosphorus, potassium, sulphur, calcium, magnesium, and iron. If soils are lacking in any of these, the deficiency can be made good by the right fertilizer.

Until the 19th Century, farmers relied mainly on the application of natural fertilizers to put "goodness" back into the land. They used manure from the stock-yards and, in the case of coastal areas, seaweed from the shore. Lime was also applied to prevent acidity. This method of soil rejuvenation went a long way to maintain the presence of chemical elements. But it often did little to improve soils already lacking in certain chemicals.

Nowadays soils are analysed to find out deficiencies which can be made up by the application of the appropriate chemical fertilizers. Of course, the chemicals alone do not guarantee a successful crop. The continued application of the natural fertilizers, such as manure and humus (decayed vegetable matter) is also essential.

WHAT IS THE STRONGEST MATERIAL?

The strength of any material is its ability to resist stretching, pressing together, and tearing – what the scientists call tension, compression and shear. No one material is the strongest for all purposes. For example, cast iron is immensely strong in resisting steady compression, but is easily broken by a sharp hammer-blow.

Some materials are made stronger by the addition of other substances. A little carbon added to iron makes it stronger and produces steel. The addition of silicon or magnesium to low-strength aluminium forms a lightweight, high-strength alloy used for aircraft engines and other highly-stressed mechanisms.

Nylon and similar plastics have introduced new standards of strength in non-metallic materials. They are made from basic substances such as coal, salt, petroleum, air and water, and are very tough and resistant to wear.

WHEN WERE VIDEO TAPES INTRODUCED?

Video tapes were introduced in the years following the Second World War. The idea of storing information on magnetic wire was first put into practise by a Dane, Valdemar Poulsen, in 1900, but little was heard about it until the 1920s when magnetic tapes were made in the United States and Germany.

The recording of most television programmes is done on magnetic tape or video tape. This technique produces good pictures which can be played back immediately without processing. The magnetic tape, two inches wide, is moved at a speed of 15 inches a second past a magnetic recording head which imprints, by means of electrical signals, a magnetized pattern of the sound and picture.

The tape is a band of plastic which has a film of magnetic iron oxide coating–one ten-thousandth of an inch thick–spread over one side of it. When the tape is played back, the changing magnetic fields of the pattern of iron oxide particles create weak currents which exactly correspond to the sound and picture which has been recorded.

Recording enables programmes to be re-broadcast or edited. In sports television it is often used for the "instant replay" or reproduction of a particularly interesting event during a live broadcast. Video recording is also employed in slow-motion and stop-action techniques.

WHAT IS A METEORITE?

Meteorites begin as bodies of matter travelling at great speed through space. In the solar system there are numberless such bodies, usually chunks of rock or metal. When they enter the earth's atmosphere friction makes them hot and bright. The small chunks burn away, but the larger ones fall to the earth as meteorites.

Their crater hollows are found all over the world. A meteorite which probably weighed hundreds of tons is believed to have fallen near Winslow, Arizona, in the United States several thousand years ago. The Barringer crater, as it is known, is about one mile across and over 500 feet deep. Another large meteorite is known to have fallen at Grootfontein in South-west Africa. This weighed about 60 tons. An iron meteorite in New York City which was brought from Greenland, weighs 36 tons.

HOW IS SOAP MADE?

Soap is made largely from fats or oil, with a variety of other ingredients.

Before the introduction of soap in the 1st Century A.D. people "washed" themselves and their clothes with fuller's earth, a fine clay-like substance that loosens oil and dirt.

People first made their own soap by saving scraps of fat and boiling them in an iron pot. They added an alkaline solution, made from wood ash, called lye. This formed a yellow "soft soap", the yellow coming from the potash in the lye. Hard soap was made by boiling for longer, and by adding salt, usually from sea-water.

Soap is still made in much the same way, but on a far larger scale in modern factories. The chief things that go into its manufacture are still fat or oil (but oil from coconuts or cotton seeds), lye containing potash, or sodium, and salt. Coloured dyes, perfumes and super-fats, such as almond oil and glycerine, are added to make the expensive toilet and shaving soaps.

WHY IS FLUORIDE PUT IN DRINKING WATER?

Drinking water containing fluoride, or, to be more exact, sodium fluoride, is generally believed to help in preventing dental trouble.

It was not until the late 1930s that efforts to combat tooth decay involved the use of chemical substances. The addition of a small amount of fluoride—about one part in a million—to the drinking water of a community, has been linked with a reduction in tooth decay, sometimes as great as 60 per cent.

Sodium fluoride interferes with the chain of reactions which causes acid to be formed on the teeth. Also it helps the teeth become more resistant to these mouth acids. It should be pointed out, however, that too much fluoride in the water is likely to produce mottling and, in severe cases, decay of the tooth enamel.

WHEN WAS CONCRETE INVENTED?

Concrete can be said to have been used for thousands of years, if the word is taken generally to mean a hard building material produced from a mixture of cement, sand, gravel and stone. The Assyrians and Babylonians used clay to bind sand and stones, and the ancient Egyptians discovered lime and gypsum. The Romans mixed slaked lime with volcanic ash and constructed aqueducts, bridges and buildings, some of which survive.

Lime remained a popular cementing material until the discovery of the process of making Portland cement shortly after 1800. The name was given to it by Joseph Aspdin, an Englishman, because he thought its products resembled the limestone quarried at Portland in Dorset, England. It is a man-made cement which, since 1900, has been almost the only cement used in the building industry.

Concrete mixtures for small jobs and repairs at home are easily made, but the design and erection of important concrete structures calls for a combination of artistic and scientific skills. Scientists have developed reinforced concrete strengthened with steel, pre-stressed concrete and concrete shells which may be simple and functional or more complex to give a building added beauty.

WHERE WERE KITES FIRST FLOWN?

Kites have been used in Asia since time immemorial. Some evidence dates their invention at around 1,000 B.C. Kite flying has been a national pastime for many centuries among the Chinese, Japanese, Koreans and Malayans. Kites held great religious significance in Asia, as they were believed to keep evil spirits away when flown at night.

But there is also a tradition that they were invented nearly four centuries before Christ by Archytas of Tarentum, in southern Italy. He was a Greek philosopher and scientist, and a friend of Plato, the great philosopher.

Kite flying strictly for pleasure has many supporters in China, where the ninth day of the ninth month is designated Kite Day.

Kites have often been used in

simple bridge building by attaching a cable to the kite and flying it across the river or gap. In meteorology kites have been used to carry weather recording instruments aloft.

The current kite flying record of four and a half miles was achieved with a string of 10 kites. The total surface of the 10 kites was 683 square feet. The line used for this record-breaking flight was more than nine miles long.

WHY DOES FROZEN FOOD KEEP WELL?

Frozen food keeps for a long time because the freezing of the water inside the food forces the bacteria, which cause it to decompose, into inactivity. Like all living things, bacteria need water in order to thrive.

Bacteria are microscopic organisms, or forms of life which occur in air, water and soil all over the world. But they flourish and multiply particularly wherever organic matter is present. Some may cause disease, others are harmless, or even beneficial, but their activity causes organic matter, including food, to decompose.

Modern discoveries have enabled sub-zero temperatures to be obtained by cooling air to about $-300°C$ ($-508°F$) by compressing it and passing it into low pressure chambers through fine nozzles. The result is a sudden and violent expansion, causing the air to be drastically cooled. In home refrigerators Freon-12 gas is used instead of air, and the temperatures are much less drastic. The temperature in the freezing compartment of a domestic refrigerator is about $-4°C$ or $25°F$, and that of a deep-freezer about $-15°C$ or $5°F$.

Preserving food has an ancient history. The salting and smoking of fish and meat have been carried out for centuries. Another long-used method of preserving food is to change its form, for example turning milk into butter and cheese, and grapes into wine. More recently preservation has been effected by canning, heat being used to kill bacteria, or dehydration.

Most fresh food contains 75 to 90 per cent of water. When this liquid is removed, great savings in packaging, storage and transport are made. Potatoes, milk, eggs, tea and coffee are among the well-known products now sold as dry powders that need only the addition of water to reconstitute them.

WHAT IS A THEODOLITE?

A theodolite is a surveying instrument used for measuring horizontal and vertical angles. To measure long distances we use a system known as triangulation–we can use it, for instance, if we want to know the distance to the moon.

Astronomers measure the angle of the moon above the horizon at two places on the earth's surface –as far apart as possible and at the same moment. This gives them

243

A theodolite in use on the right of the picture during a British Antarctic survey.

a triangle and a base line (the distance between the two observations). Since they have measured two angles of the triangle, they know the third, because the three angles of a triangle always add up to 180°. They therefore have enough information to find the distance between the apex (moon) and base line (earth).

The same system is used in surveying and map-making, but the surveyor's base line is, of course, much shorter, in fact, both ends of the base line must be within sight of one another and of the next point to be observed. The theodolite is the basic instrument used in surveying, especially in precise triangulation.

WHEN IS THE BEST TIME TO LAUNCH A ROCKET TO THE MOON?

There is virtually no "best time" to launch a rocket to the moon, because, in terms of space travel, the journey is so short. The average distance is 238,000 miles, with a maximum variation of only 25,000 miles.

A space shot, whether to the moon or some other object, is made by a rocket already in orbit. To take a rocket out of orbit and put it on course for the moon calls for a boost in speed to 25,000 miles (40,000 kilometres) an hour. This is necessary to overcome the pull of the earth's gravity. The moment when the engines are refired to start the rocket on its journey does not depend on the position of the launching base in relation to the rocket or the moon.

In contrast, the great variations in the distances between the earth and Mars or Venus make the launching of a rocket to the planets impractical for periods of nine to eighteen months.

WHY DO PIPES SOMETIMES BURST IN WINTER?

Cold water pipes may burst in winter when the outside temperature falls below 0°C (32°F) and the water turns to ice. The pipe's walls crack to relieve the pressure caused by the fact that ice requires nearly one-tenth more space than the water. One cubic foot of water makes 1·09 cubic feet of ice. To prevent a freeze-up, a heat insulator is wrapped round the pipes.

Water has very unusual properties. Apart from expanding when frozen, it requires more heat to warm it than any other common substance. In other words it has a high specific heat. In nature there are some obvious advantages in these peculiarities. The expansion of ice causes the breaking up of clods of water-filled soil on cold winter nights to leave a fine tilth admirably suited to spring sowing. Water's high specific heat means that the sea takes longer to warm up than the land and longer to cool down. Thus the sea acts to prevent extreme changes in temperature between the seasons.

HOW WAS THE WORLD FORMED?

In the beginning our universe was a mass of white-hot vapours and molten materials whirling about in space. Our world was formed from this. Astronomers believe it took millions of years for the cloud to cool, contract and begin to turn into molten rock.

Modern astronomers think that many millions of years ago there was a huge explosion in space. They do not know exactly what happened. But it is possible that our sun exploded or that a much bigger companion star of the sun became a supernova – that is, it broke up violently. The debris and blazing gases from this explosion were, it is thought, flung far into space.

For more millions of years our solar system boiled and bubbled. But very slowly, the fiery redness began to cool and condense into the nine planets and many more smaller bodies. All these planets now revolve around the sun.

After further vast periods of time the lava of the earth began to solidify, developing over many millions of years, into the world as we know it today.

WHAT IS THE MILKY WAY?

The Milky Way, or Galaxy, is the whole concourse of stars and other bodies which can be seen stretched across the heavens. It includes our own sun and its planets, as well as all stars visible to the naked eye. But the name is commonly restricted to the luminous band or belt where most classes of stars are concentrated.

The spiral arms of the Milky Way are rich in hot, bright stars, interstellar clouds of gas (mainly hydrogen) and dust. The first evidence of spiral arms was obtained in 1951 by the American astronomer W. W. Morgan, who identified three.

Our own system of sun and planets appears to be situated towards the inner edge of one of the arms, which is about 1,300 light-years away. The Andromeda nebula, a vast mixture of gaseous and solid matter, is visible as a small luminous patch in our sky. But it is comparable in size to the Milky Way and seems remarkably similar to our own galaxy.

The Palomar telescope, 200 inches in diameter, situated on Mount Palomar in California, has perhaps 1,000 million galaxies within the scope of its vision.

WHO MADE THE FIRST DISH TELESCOPE?

The first dish (or radio) telescope was made in 1942 by an American, Grote Reber, of Wheaton, Illinois. He constructed his apparatus after studying the experiments of K. G. Jansky, another American. Jansky discovered in 1935 that the intensity of radiowaves increases as a highly sensitive aerial is directed progressively nearer to the Milky Way. The maximum intensity is reached when the antenna is pointing towards Sagittarius—that is to say, towards the galactic centre.

Radio telescopes are called dish telescopes because of the steerable dish-shaped or parabolic reflector which gathers the radiation and focuses it on to a centrally mounted aerial. The surface of the dish is made of a good electrical conductor and the radio waves are reflected from it. The parabaloid shape ensures that all the reflected rays arrive at the central point, where they are "swallowed" by an electromagnetic horn and fed into a receiver.

Since the Second World War the development of radio telescopes has gone ahead rapidly. A 250-foot diameter instrument was installed at the Nuffield Radio Astronomy Laboratories at Jodrell Bank, Cheshire, England. It is under the direction of Professor Sir Bernard Lovell and has already contributed a great deal of new information to astronomy.

WHY DON'T CRANES TOPPLE OVER?

Cranes do not topple over because their jibs or booms are counterbalanced at the opposite end from the lift load, thus keeping the centre of gravity over the base.

The first cranes were simply long poles fixed in the ground at an angle, with a pulley at the top through which passed a rope. They were called "cranes" because they looked rather like the neck of the bird with the same name.

The derrick crane, which looks like a gallows, is named after Dick Derrick, a 17th Century hangman. In the middle of the 18th Century, steam engines began to be used on cranes, while today the lifting may be done by varieties of power.

Jib cranes may be portable, being mounted on a wheeled carriage, or they may be self-propelled. Gantry cranes with long booms are used for unloading ships while overhead cranes are used in factories. Goliath cranes, with steel towers at either side, capable of lifting 200 tons are used at some atomic power stations.

WHEN WAS THE TELEPHONE INVENTED?

Alexander Graham Bell (1847–1922) invented and patented in 1876 the first telephone that was of any real practical use. In 1874 he said: "If I could make a current of electricity vary in intensity precisely as the air varies in density during the production of sound, I should be able to transmit speech telegraphically." This is the principle of the telephone.

On March 10, 1876, the first historic message was telephoned to Thomas A. Watson, Bell's assistant, who was in another room: "Mr Watson, come here; I want you."

Bell's first machine gave electrical currents too feeble to be of much use for the general public.

In 1877 the American scientist Thomas A. Edison (1847–1931) invented the variable-contact car- bon transmitter, which greatly increased the power of the signals.

The telephone was immediately popular in the United States, but Bell found little interest in Britain

Bell inaugurating the New York– Chicago telephone line, October 1892.

when he visited the country in 1878. Then Queen Victoria asked for a pair of telephones and the royal interest resulted in a London telephone exchange being formed in 1879 with eight subscribers.

WHAT IS A STAR?

A star is a body of luminous gas, like the sun. But as stars are much farther away from the earth than the sun, they appear to be only small points of twinkling light. With the naked eye it is possible to see about 2,000 stars at any one time or place but with the most powerful telescope over 1,000 million stars are visible. Although light travels at 186,000 miles a second, the light from the stars takes many years to reach the earth.

Stars are not fixed in space, but are travelling in different directions at different speeds. Seen from the earth, these movements appear to be so small that groups of stars, or constellations, seem to have a permanent relationship. The star patterns we see in the sky are almost the same as those seen by our ancestors hundreds, or even thousands of years ago.

The sizes of stars vary tremendously, from less than the diameter of the sun to thousands of times its size. Most stars appear white when looked at with the naked eye, but some are bluish-white, yellow, orange and red. The varied colours are due to differences in surface temperature. The brilliant,

white stars are the hottest with surface temperatures of several hundred thousand degrees. The less brilliant, orange and red stars have surface temperatures of about 2,000 degrees.

There are exceptions, however. The red giant, Betelgeux, in the constellation (or group) of Orion, appears to be brilliant because of its size. Its diameter is 250 million miles, which is greater than the diameter of the earth's orbit round the sun.

Shooting stars which are sometimes seen moving across the night sky for a few seconds are really meteors. These small particles flare up as they strike the earth's atmosphere and usually burn out.

WHY DO EXHAUST FUMES CONTAIN LEAD?

The lead in exhaust fumes comes from the petrol used to drive the internal-combustion engine. Crude oil straight from the wells is thick, black and sticky. It has to go through a complicated refining process before it can be used as fuel for the engines of cars, lorries, buses and aircraft.

During refining, various substances are added to improve the petrol and for other reasons. For instance, small quantities of dye are put in to standardize the colour. Other substances prevent the formation of gum which would clog up parts of the engine.

Lead, in a liquid form called tetra-ethyl lead, is added to petrol to reduce "engine knock". This means that it prevents the petrol from igniting in the engine at the wrong moment. When an internal-combustion engine is running, the petrol is lit by sparks from the sparking plugs. The petrol burns in what is really a series of small explosions and produces gases which come out through the exhaust pipe as dirty, smelly fumes. And the lead comes with them.

Ill-health can be caused if quite small quantities of lead in the air are inhaled over a long time. For this reason, the governments of such countries as the United States, Britain, Sweden and Japan are passing laws to reduce the amount of lead in petrol.

They are also encouraging car manufacturers to design internal-combustion engines which will work efficiently on lead-free petrol and have cleaner exhaust fumes. These engines will be more expensive at first, but they will help to make the air cleaner and pleasanter where there is a lot of traffic.

WHEN WERE THE FIRST TALKING MOVIES MADE?

The first talking movies were produced in France before 1900 by Léon Gaumont. They were short films, starring great performers such as Sarah Bernhardt, in which the moving pictures were synchronized with a gramophone record. By 1912 Eugene Lauste had discovered the basic method for recording sound on film, while Thomas Edison produced several one-reel talking pictures in the United States. An American, Lee de Forest, improved the system.

In all this the public showed little interest until the presentation on October 6, 1927, of *The Jazz Singer*. This was a silent picture, starring Al Jolson, with four talking and singing interludes. Jolson's electric personality and the very much improved sound began a movie revolution. Within the year every important picture was being produced as a "talkie". By 1930 silent films were a thing of the past, and many film stars found themselves has-beens because their voices recorded badly.

WHO FIRST USED CLOCKS?

It is believed that the Babylonians first used a pole fixed in the ground to measure the passing of time. They noticed that the position of the shadow changed during the hours of sunlight. They found that the shadow was long at sunrise and that it slowly grew shorter until it reached a point when it started to lengthen again. They learnt to judge the time by looking at the shadow.

The simple shadow and pole arrangement was the basis of the various shadow clocks or sundials used by the ancient Egyptians. Eventually sundials were provided with the hour figures engraved on a metal plate.

The Egyptians also used a

clepsydra or water clock. This was a basin-shaped, alabaster vessel filled with water that ran out through a hole in the bottom. The time was indicated by the level of water remaining inside.

Monks were the first to operate clocks by wheels and weights. Clocks of this type, found in monasteries, date back to the 14th Century. The first spring clock is dated about 1500.

WHERE IS URSA MINOR?

Ursa Minor is the name of a group of stars in the Northern Hemisphere. The word used in astronomy for a group of stars is "constellation".

The stars and constellations have Latin names. Ursa Minor means The Little Bear. Its brightest star is called Polaris, and is centred over the North Pole. It is of great importance in helping sailors to find their bearings when navigating at night.

Star maps of the sky will help you locate the constellations.

WHAT IS RADAR?

Radar, or radiolocation, as it was called in the early days, is the use of radio waves to find the whereabouts of aircraft or ships.

Electro-magnetic waves, which include radio and light waves, all travel at the same speed. When small bursts of radio waves, fired into space from a transmitter, strike an object such as an aircraft some of them bounce back and are collected by an aerial. Special equipment calculates the distance of the object from the time taken for the waves to go there and back.

Direction is obtained by rotating the aerial, and the course being taken by the object is shown as spots of light on the face of a cathode ray tube. So direction, position and movement can be judged accurately.

Radar was first used to detect enemy aircraft in wartime, and to guide fighter aircraft and bomber pilots. Since then it has proved invaluable in civil aviation by helping the pilot to guide his aircraft in the air and to land it safely in fog or at night.

At sea it can give the position of land and other ships. Some buoys are fitted with radar, so that they can be located in the dark or in fog. Radar is used also to give warning of turbulent weather.

HOW FAR CAN YOU SEE?

If you stood on the shore looking across the sea to the horizon (the line appearing to separate earth from sky), you might be able to see about two and a half miles. But the higher you stood the farther you would be able to see. As the earth is curved, the horizon would appear farther away with every increase in height above sea level.

At a height of 20 feet you might see for six miles. From the top of a 300-foot cliff your view could extend for 23 miles, while on the summit of a 3,500-foot mountain, it could lengthen to 80 miles. From an aircraft flying at 16,000 feet you might have an uninterrupted panorama for 165 miles.

If you look straight up into the sky, the distance you can see is immense. The moon is about 239,000 miles away and the stars are millions of miles distant.

WHY ARE SOME METALS CHROMIUM PLATED?

Some metals are chromium-plated to make them look more attractive and to prevent them from corroding or rusting. Chromium is a silver-white, hard, brittle metal which was discovered in 1798 by N. L. Vauquelin. Its non-corrosive, high-strength, heat-resistant characteristics are utilized in alloys and as an electroplated coating.

In electroplating, the article to be plated is connected to the negative terminal of a battery and placed in a solution known as electrolyte. Direct electric current is introduced through the anode or positive terminal, which usually consists of the metal with which the article is to be coated. Metal slowly leaves the anode and forms a deposit on the article. The electrolyte for chromium contains chromic acid and sulphuric acid. It deposits a bright top layer but this is not the

Chromium-plating on a car.

only important part of the electro-plating. The chromium is only about 0·00002 inches thick. Under it lies a thick layer of nickel and beneath that again may be a layer of copper.

Many household appliances are chromium-plated and so are the bright parts of an automobile. Tools, chemical equipment, electric appliances, gears, packing machinery, and hundreds of other articles are similarly treated to give them brightness, beauty or resistance to wear and rust. Electroplated and polished chromium is bright bluish-white with a reflecting power which is 77 per cent that of silver.

WHEN DOES AN ATOM SPLIT?

An atom splits when it is struck by a neutron. The nucleus of the atom then breaks into two roughly equal parts and, at the same time, shoots out several high-speed neutrons.

Atoms are so small that they cannot be seen under the most powerful microscope. They are the building bricks of which each element is composed. The Greek word "atom" means "cannot be cut". But we know now that atoms can be cut, or split. Each one contains minute particles carrying two sorts of electricity: first, the electrons which are negatively charged; and secondly, the central core or nucleus which is made up of protons (positively charged) and neutrons (no charge).

In the 19th Century it was discovered that all elements with atomic weights greater than 83 are radioactive and that the nucleus could be divided into several parts. Albert Einstein (1879–1955) calculated in 1905 that splitting an atom would destroy mass and release heat. By thus converting matter into heat energy, vast amounts of heat would be obtained by destroying only a very small amount of matter.

Between 1934 and 1938 the Italian Enrico Fermi and the German Otto Hahn discovered that atoms of uranium (atomic weight 92) split when struck by a neutron. In 1939 Frédéric Joliot-Curie found that this splitting, or fission, released two or three more neutrons which in turn produced fission in more uranium nuclei, and so on. It is this chain reaction that makes possible not only the benefits of nuclear power but also the horrors of nuclear warfare.

WHAT IS HARD WATER?

Hard water is water that contains certain dissolved chemicals that act on soap to form a scum. If water comes from limestone areas, some rock is dissolved in the water, and this makes it hard.

There are several disadvantages in hard water. More soap or soap powder must be used to obtain a suitable lather. Also, the scum clings to the object being washed.

Hard water leaves a scaly deposit in kettles and boilers, which reduces the efficiency of both.

But hard water can be treated to remove the unwanted chemicals. In the home small amounts of washing soda or borax can be added. At large water softening plants which serve a community, the water is filtered through a mineral called zeolite which removes the chemicals. After a time zeolite ceases to be effective, but it can be restored by washing it with salt water.

HOW DO FIRE EXTINGUISHERS WORK?

Fire extinguishers stop flames either by dousing them in water or by excluding the oxygen which a fire needs in order to burn.

There are three main kinds of fires. First are those occurring in ordinary materials like paper and wood for which the quenching and cooling effects of water or water solutions are the most effective. Second come those involving inflammable liquids or greases for which a blanketing or smothering effect is essential. Finally there are the fires occurring in "live" electrical equipment where a special extinguishing agent must be used.

The most common extinguisher for the first type of fire is a bucket of water, or a manufactured extinguisher with water containing a chemical. The chemical reaction expels the water which puts out the fire.

For the second kind of fire the most common method is to use a chemical extinguisher to spray the burning material with foam which puts out the fire by excluding oxygen. This foam usually consists of bubbles of carbon dioxide. As the foam is not a conductor of electricity, it may also be used safely on the third type of fire.

Foam-type extinguishers can generally be employed safely in nearly all cases, but water or water solutions should never be used on oil, grease or electrical fires.

WHY IS POLLUTION A PROBLEM?

Pollution is a problem because man, in an increasingly populated and industrialized world, is upsetting the environment in which he lives. Many scientists maintain that one of man's greatest errors has been to equate growth with advancement. Now "growth" industries are being looked on with suspicion in case their side effects damage the environment and disrupt the relationship of different forms of life.

The growing population makes increasing demands on the world's fixed supply of air, water and land. This rise in population is accompanied by the desire of more and more people for a better standard of living. Thus still greater demands for electricity, water and goods result in an ever increasing amount of waste material to be disposed of.

The problem has been causing

increasing concern to living things and their environment. Many believe that man is not solving these problems quickly enough and that his selfish pursuit of possessions take him past the point of no return before he fully appreciates the damage. It would then be too late to reverse the process.

Ecologists say we are so determined to possess a new car or washing machine, or to obtain a greater yield from our crops by the use of fertilizers, that we ignore the fact that life depends on a lot of micro-organisms working efficiently.

For example, if new chemicals were released into the environment, a combination of them might well poison one or more of the different types of bacteria in soil and water, which are essential to keep nitrogen being circulated from the air into organic material, and being cycled back into the air again. If this should happen on a world-wide scale, the air would become unbreathable.

WHAT ARE GAMMA RAYS?
Gamma rays are streams of electro-magnetic waves. They are given off from elements such as radium, when they undergo a process known as radioactive decay.

In 1899 the British physicist Ernest Rutherford began a study of radioactivity. He found three types of radiation which he called alpha, beta and gamma rays. Alpha rays were stopped by a thin sheet of paper, beta rays could get through several millimetres of aluminium, and gamma rays could pierce quite thick pieces of lead.

Alpha rays travel at up to 12,000 miles a second, beta rays from 80,000 to 180,000 miles a second, and gamma rays at 186,000 miles a second, the speed of light.

Gamma rays have proved very helpful in medicine and industry. These rays are also given off by radioactive isotopes obtained as by-products in production processes. They can produce radiographs of forgings and the seams of boilers and other pressure vessels, where freedom from flaws is vital.

WHERE WAS MORSE CODE FIRST USED?
The first message in Morse code was tapped out in the United States over a telegraph line from Baltimore to Washington by Samuel Morse in 1844.

Morse is often credited with the invention of the telegraph on his return to the United States from a trip to Europe in 1832. During this trip he became acquainted with the works of Michael Faraday on electro-magnetism, which forms the basis of the telegraph. This gave Morse the necessary impetus to go ahead with his work.

In 1837 Morse exhibited his first truly successful telegraph instrument. By 1838 he had developed the Morse code, an alphabet which consists of dots

"What hath God wrought!"—on this line.

Later, Morse was caught in a mass of legal claims among his telegraph partners and rival inventors. He was probably the most successful propagator of the telegraph, although there were many pioneers in the same field long before him.

WHO INVENTED THE JET ENGINE?

The first flight by a jet-propelled aircraft was made in Germany on August 27, 1939. Its engine was designed by Hans-Joachim von Ohain, who had conceived the idea while a student at Göttingen University in Lower Saxony. Unknown to von Ohain, the British inventor and aviator Frank Whittle had thought of the idea some years earlier. But his engine did not have its first flight until May 14, 1941.

Briefly, a jet engine takes in air from the atmosphere, compresses it, and uses it in burning fuel. The mixture of hot gases is then expelled through a nozzle in a powerful backward jet which propels the aircraft forwards.

This forward thrust is the effect of a scientific principle first explained by the English scientist Sir Isaac Newton (1642–1727). He pointed out that with every action there is a reaction which is equal but opposite to it. Thus when a gun is fired, the forward movement of the shell is matched by the backward recoil of the barrel. In a

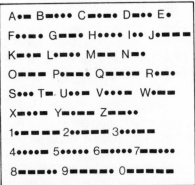

The Morse code and original instrument.

and dashes representing letters and numbers. In the same year he attempted unsuccessfully to persuade Congress to build a telegraph line.

It was not until 1843 that Congress voted to pay Morse to build the first telegraph line in the United States from Baltimore to Washington. In the following year Morse sent his famous message —

similar way the reaction to the jet exhaust drives the engine forward. The thrust is obtained by the pressure of the jet against the inside of the nozzle and not, as many people suppose, by the exhaust gases "pushing" against the atmosphere.

The jet engine, whether turbo-jet, turboprop, ramjet or turbofan, weighs less than a piston engine of comparative power and can be much more streamlined.

WHEN WAS THE HYDROFOIL INVENTED?

The hydrofoil, a boat supported clear of the water by underwater wings called hydrofoils, was invented by an Italian, Forlanini, in 1898. In 1918 a hydrofoil, powered by an aircraft engine, gained the world's water speed record. The commercial hydrofoils now used in Europe are based on the work of German engineers who carried out research into the design of high-power, lightweight engines.

In the early 1950s hydrofoils were developed in the United States, Canada and Russia using high-powered gas turbines. They are used for both military and commercial purposes.

Since water is 775 times heavier than air, very small hydrofoil wings will support relatively heavy boats. But, since operating in water puts great loads on boats, the hulls are usually built of high-strength steel.

The object in raising the hull of the hydrofoil from the water is to avoid the resistance caused by friction and drag. This means the power needed to drive the boat at high speeds is cut by half. Another result is that the hydrofoil travels smoothly in quite rough water, and is not slowed down.

WHY DO SOME LIQUIDS BURN?

Some liquids will burn because when their molecules mix with the oxygen in the air the mixture becomes combustible.

The application of heat promotes the necessary chemical reaction to put the molecules into more violent motion, so that they collide at high speed. The jolt loosens the bonds and makes it easier for the molecules to rearrange themselves and escape from the liquid to form a vapour, mixing with oxygen in the air.

The most important liquid which will burn is crude mineral oil from which petrol and paraffin are produced. Others include tar and creosote, and the very explosive nitro-glycerine.

WHAT IS GLASS FIBRE?

Glass fibre is a mass of very fine strands of glass. When ordinary glass is spun into thin threads it is strong and bendable, unlike normal glass objects, which are brittle and break easily.

These silky strands of glass can be woven into a material or massed together like cotton-wool. Glass fibre does not decay or corrode. It is a good insulator and a poor conductor of electricity. Curtains made of this material do not rot in damp conditions or in sunlight. Now that technical dyeing problems have been overcome, glass fibre can be patterned.

Many plastics tend to crack or bend under stress or impact, but combining them with strands of glass fibre results in very light, strong and useful materials. Glass fibre increases their strength in much the same way as concrete is reinforced with steel rods. These mixtures are moulded to make such things as aircraft parts, car bodies, boats and fishing rods. Coarse mats of glass fibre are used for filters and washers, and blankets of the material provide good insulation for houses.

HOW IS PAPER MADE?

A sheet of paper consists of vegetable fibres of different sizes, twisted and intertwined with each other and finally squeezed together to make a sheet with a surface smooth enough to write or print on.

Originally it was discovered that if a mixture of wood pulp and water was spread on a sieve, the water would drain away and leave a deposit which, when dry, could be peeled off as a sheet of paper.

Although the Chinese had been using paper since A.D. 105 it was not introduced into Europe until the 15th Century. The raw materials

used for modern hand-made paper are cotton and linen rags. Such paper is very expensive to produce.

Machine-made paper is processed in paper mills from esparto grass, wood and straw, and is much cheaper. The materials for both types of paper-making have to be put through the same basic procedure of repeated washing and bleaching to get rid of impurities.

WHERE DOES THE WAX GO WHEN A CANDLE BURNS?

Nowhere—it simply changes into other substances. That is what burning does to everything.

The moment you put a match to the wick, you start a change in the candle by turning the solid wax into a liquid. The liquid wax rises to the wick by an irresistible process called capillarity, the simplest example of which is the way blotting paper soaks up ink or water. Then the liquid wax changes into a gas which burns—a chemical reaction which releases energy in the form of light and heat.

The presence of the gas can be demonstrated by blowing out the candle and immediately holding a lighted match an inch or so above the wick. The inflammable vapour instantly catches fire, and the candle lights up again without the match having actually touched the wick.

Other changes are taking place while the candle burns. The wax is a complex chemical compound of carbon and hydrogen. The process of burning is simply the combination of the wax with the oxygen in the air. If you put a jar over the candle, it will quickly use up the oxygen and go out.

During the time the candle burns, the carbon joins with the oxygen in the air and makes carbon monoxide and carbon dioxide, and the hydrogen combines with the oxygen to produce water.

While all these changes in the substance of the candle are taking place, the candle, of course, is becoming shorter. But it is not "going" anywhere. Its materials are simply changing into other substances.

WHAT IS A DETERGENT?

A detergent is a substance which has a power to cleanse. This description applies to soap, as well as to soapless shampoos and washing powders. A detergent usually has surface activating properties, which means that it is able to reduce the surface tension of water.

In the process of cleaning the detergent acts as a bridge between the solid matter and the water. Soap molecules are shaped like tadpoles. The head is soluble, but the rod-like body is composed of an insoluble fatty substance. When mixed with water part of the soap tries to get away and the rest stays, thus breaking down the water's surface tension. There is not suffi-

cient room for all the soap molecules on the surface of the water. So they form bundles with the water-resisting rods on the inside. The dirt attracts the fatty part of the soap molecules which lift and surround it, while the soluble part of the molecules lifts and rinses the dirt away.

WHEN DOES LITMUS PAPER TURN RED?

Litmus paper turns red when placed in an acid solution, but blue if the solution is alkaline. This absorbent paper is the oldest and most commonly used indicator of the presence or absence of acid. Its special qualities are due to the fact that it has been soaked and impregnated with a mixture of dyes called litmus.

The litmus mixture was originally produced by the action of air, ammonia and an alkali carbonate on certain lichens found in the Netherlands. It is now made from azolitmin and erythrolitmin.

A litmus solution is sometimes used. But the message is the same A few drops added to a liquid turns it red if it is acid and blue if it is alkaline.

WHY DOES AN ASTRONAUT NEED A SPACE SUIT?

A space suit enables an astronaut to survive by providing him artificially with conditions like those he is used to on earth.

These conditions can be reproduced in a large space craft or space station in orbit, but an astronaut still needs a space suit for operations outside the craft or for an emergency.

In space men lack the air needed for breathing, the pressure required to stop their blood from boiling and the natural protection of the atmosphere against radiation. All these must be supplied by the space suit which also must withstand the cold of space.

When an astronaut ventures into

American astronaut Edwin Aldrin walking on the moon in July 1969.

space, he leaves behind the safety of the atmospheric blanket which we, on earth, take for granted. His space suit becomes his own personal little world.

WHO WAS THE LAST MAN TO DISCOVER A PLANET?

Clyde Tombaugh, a young American research student, made the last discovery of a planet while working in 1930 at the Lowell Observatory, Arizona State College. This planet is Pluto, the ninth one in order of distance from the sun, 3,670 million miles away.

Although Tombaugh, who was 26 at the time, was the first astronomer to see Pluto, its existence had been suspected by Percival Lowell, builder of the observatory at Flagstaff, Arizona. Lowell began searching for the planet in 1905, the year before Tombaugh was born. He observed that there was a difference between the predicted and actual positions of Uranus, and this led him to conclude that there must be another planet. His final calculations about "Planet X" were published in 1914, but he had still not found the planet when he died two years later.

Another American, W. H. Pickering, took up the search, concentrating on the irregular movements of the planet Neptune. He saw a clue in the movement of comets, which seem to be attracted by large planets. There were 16 known comets whose paths took them millions of miles beyond Neptune, which is 2,811 million miles from the sun, and Pickering was convinced that they were being attracted by a still more distant planet.

In 1919 yet another hunt was begun by Milton Humason at Mount Wilson Observatory, Pasadena, California. Instead of mathematical calculations, Humason tried photography. He took two pictures of a series of stretches of the sky, with a gap of one or two days between exposures. In such photographs stars stay still, but planets change position.

When Tombaugh discovered Pluto, it became clear that Humason had photographed the planet twice. Once it had been masked by a star, and the second time its image had coincided with a flaw in the photographic plate. The main difficulty in the search had been that Pluto was extraordinarily faint. Pickering formed the opinion that it was not Lowell's Planet X, but that a huge planet remains to be discovered.

WHEN DOES A CAR USE OVERDRIVE?

A car uses overdrive when it is travelling at high speed over long distances. Overdrive, or cruising gear, is a device which enables the engine to run at a relatively low speed even when the vehicle is travelling fast.

All internal combustion engines fitted in vehicles need some kind of gearbox because their efficiency at low speeds is poor. The use of different gears enables the speed of the engine to be harmonised with that of the car. The gears may be engaged or shifted by hand or operated by an automatic gearbox.

Most cars have a four-speed gearbox. The driver uses first gear for starting and changes to second and third gears as the car gains speed. Finally in top or fourth gear the engine speed is transmitted unreduced through the gearbox. In overdrive a large gear wheel drives a smaller gear wheel on the propeller shaft. This shaft then rotates faster than the engine, thus reducing wear and tear and saving petrol.

WHAT IS PLASTIC?

A plastic, in the modern sense of the word, is a synthetic or man-made material which can be formed into various shapes. The first plastic material was Celluloid, made in 1868 by an American, John W. Hyatt, by dissolving nitrocellulose under pressure.

The use of plastics began slowly, but shortages of natural materials caused by two world wars forced scientists to develop substitutes. Since the Second World War the making of plastics has become a gigantic industry, which has grown so fast that many people still have only a hazy idea what plastics are. In fact, the term "plastics" is as general as the word "metals". The high-temperature cone of a rocket and the highly inflammable table-tennis ball are both plastics, just as lead and steel are both metals.

However, all plastics have some things in common: first, they are entirely man-made and not found in nature; secondly, they consist of large molecules of an organic nature; thirdly, at some stage in their manufacture they are liquid and can be shaped; and fourthly, in their final state they are solid.

Most of the raw materials for plastics are produced by the petroleum and coal industries. Scientists are able to produce different properties in plastics so that they can be used in a tremendous variety of articles.

WHY DOES AN AUTOMOBILE HAVE A CARBURETTOR?

An automobile is driven by an internal combustion engine which will work properly only if the right amounts of petrol and air are mixed together. The carburettor is the part of the engine where the mixing takes place.

The burning of fuel in the engine is a chemical reaction in which petrol combines with the oxygen of the air to produce water, heat energy and oxides of carbon. A chemically correct mixture should have 15 parts of air to one part of petrol, both by weight. The amount of air then present is just sufficient to burn the petrol completely. If the engine uses a mixture with an excess of petrol – a rich mixture – a small amount of unburnt petrol will be present in the exhaust fumes.

A carburettor has to produce the required mixture in varying strengths to suit different engine conditions, such as starting, idling, acceleration, cruising and application of full power. It must be able to pass the correct mixture at all engine speeds and under varying loads, and has to atomize the petrol into tiny droplets and vaporize the resulting spray into a combustible mixture.

Inside the carburettor is a throttle valve which can increase or decrease the amount of mixture passing into the cylinders, which in turn controls the power of the engine. This valve is mounted on a spindle which is operated by the accelerator pedal.

A special device called a "strangler" or choke is also incorporated to help in starting the engine in cold weather by allowing an extra-rich mixture.

WHO INVENTED THE WANKEL ENGINE?

Felix Wankel, a German motor engineer, invented the rotary piston engine which bears his name. Deprived of a university education when his family's fortune vanished in the German inflation of 1919–20, he went in for car repairing and set up his own business in 1924 at the age of 22.

Soon he began work at designing a rotary piston engine, an idea which had attracted engineers since the invention of the steam engine. From 1934 to 1936 his research was backed by B.M.W. and from 1936 to 1945 by the German Air Force. In 1951 he established his own research institute and financed it by working as a consultant.

Wankel succeeded in discovering the secret of effective seals between the rotating pistons and the casing. He also discovered the geometrical form of an engine that could carry out the four-stroke cycle in one chamber without valves, giving a useful high compression ratio. His engine ran successfully for the first time at N.S.U. Motorenwerke in February, 1957. N.S.U. began limited production of Wankel engines for cars in 1963, and went into large-scale production in 1967.

The rotary piston engine challenges the usual internal combustion engine, using reciprocating pistons, because it offers reduced size, weight, vibration, noise and production costs for comparable thermal efficiency. It is considered suitable for industrial, marine and aeronautical uses.

WHY DOES STAINLESS STEEL RESIST RUST?

Stainless steel resists rust because it contains a high proportion of chromium to carbon. Before the arrival of this alloy just before the First World War, knives and other household articles made of steel easily rusted unless very carefully dried.

It was an English researcher named Harry Brearley who discovered that rust was encouraged by the carbon in steel and other metals. The less carbon and the more chromium in steel, the better it would resist rust.

But a careful balance had to be struck. Completely carbon-free steel was impossible to make, and only a limited amount of chromium could be included, because it tended to make steel brittle. Brearley discovered a satisfactory formula only after many experiments.

WHAT DOES WATER-LOGGED MEAN?

Wood becomes waterlogged when all its cells are filled with water. It can absorb water only up to about 30 per cent its own weight. As it does so, the wood swells until it reaches "fibre saturation point" or its maximum volume.

If further water is added, it will penetrate to the cavities of the cells, but no further swelling will take place. Waterlogged wood no longer floats because the air spaces within are filled with fluid making it too heavy.

The word "waterlogged" is used to describe ships that have been flooded and sunk, or meadows and fields that are so wet that they must be drained before they are any use for growing food.

A meadow becomes water-logged in the same way as wood. The land can no longer absorb more water or drain it away. Many areas of land remain permanently in this condition unless they are reclaimed for farming.

WHO INVENTED THE AEROPLANE?

The first aeroplane ever to fly was built by a French naval officer, Félix du Temple de la Croix. In 1874 his monoplane, powered with a hot-air engine, took off from the top of a hill near Brest in France. It did not get far, just a short hop, but it was a beginning. A few years later, in 1890, Clément Ader of France flew his own plane, Eole, entirely under its own power for about 50 metres. It was a world record.

The first truly successful aeroplane flight was in 1903. In December of that year Orville Wright flew his chain-driven plane Flyer I at a speed of 8 m.p.h. and at an altitude of 12 feet for 12 seconds in North Carolina, United States. It was several years before the Wrights' achievement was fully appreciated in America.

WHEN WAS THE FIRST GAS BALLOON USED?

The first gas balloon, filled with hydrogen, was released in Paris in August, 1783 by a French professor of physics, J. A. C. Charles. Two months earlier, the first hot air balloon was sent aloft by the Montgolfier brothers, Jacques, Etienne and Joseph, of France, and it was with balloons of this type that the first manned flights were made.

A rubberized silk balloon filled with hydrogen carried Professor Charles and M. N. Robert on a flight of 27 miles and rose to 2,000 feet. Ballooning became a popular

The Wright brothers' plane, Flyer I, which made its famous first flight in 1903.

264

sport in spite of the fact that hydrogen-filled balloons were always liable to catch fire. Some amazingly long trips were undertaken, including an unsuccessful attempt in 1958 to cross the Atlantic.

Balloons play an important part in meteorology, the science concerned with the weather. The first aerial photographs were taken from balloons, and in the 1930s pressurized cabins or gondolas were designed enabling observers to rise over 60,000 feet into the stratosphere.

Military observation balloons fastened to the ground by cables came into use at the end of the 18th Century and were employed by both North and South in the American Civil War (1861–1865). The Austrians used pilotless hot-air balloons to bomb Venice in 1849. During the Franco-German War of 1870–1871 balloons transported mail and carrier pigeons. Barrage balloons tethered to the ground were used in the Second World War to provide barriers against low-flying enemy aircraft.

HOW DO SEWING MACHINES WORK?

Sewing machines today often work by electricity. But there are over 2,000 different types, with attachments for turning hems, tucking, frilling, piping, darning, and all kinds of decorative stitching. They can stitch leather, quilt bedspreads and sew on buttons.

One type of seven-needle machine can sew 20,000 stitches a minute.

The first sewing machine seems to have been invented by a poor French tailor, Barthélemy Thimmonier, in 1830. An angry mob, afraid that the machines would put people out of work, smashed them and almost murdered Thimmonier. However, he persevered and one of his machines was in London's Great Exhibition of 1851. But no one took it seriously.

In America Walter Hunt invented a machine with an eye-pointed needle that carried a loop of thread through the cloth. A shuttle working to and fro under the cloth carried a second thread through the loop, thus locking it.

The principle had now been discovered, but it was left to another American, Isaac Merritt Singer (1811–75) to mass-market a machine. A patent for a lock-stitch machine had been obtained in 1846 by Elias Howe, of Massachusetts. But Singer and his astute lawyer, Edward Clark, fought the patent and pioneered the selling of his machines by hire-purchase.

The first Singer machine dates from 1851 and was worked by a treadle. The eye-pointed needle was straight, and worked up and down. Singer added a table to hold the cloth, and an endless leather belt and circular feeding bar that allowed continuous sewing.

By 1860 more than 111,000 machines were produced by 74 American companies. Although thousands of patents have been taken out since that date for improvements and attachments, the main principles have not changed.

Mahatma Gandhi learned to use a sewing machine in prison and said: "It is one of the few useful things ever invented."

WHERE WILL WATER BOIL AT A LOW TEMPERATURE?

Water will boil anywhere, but it boils at different temperatures in different places. For example, it will boil at a lower temperature up a mountain than at sea level.

The boiling point of water is the temperature at which its vapour pressure becomes equal to the outside atmospheric pressure.

As the atmospheric pressure is always changing so the boiling point of water will vary from day to day. Water boils at 100°C only when the atmospheric pressure outside is at the "standard" value.

At Quito in Ecuador, which is about 2,700 metres (or 8,800 feet) above sea level, water boils at about 90°C.

People who explore in mountainous regions find a pressure-cooker very useful. The time required to cook food can be greatly reduced if the boiling point of the water is raised. The pressure-cooker does this, since it is an aluminium container fitted with a sealing ring but with a loaded pin-valve which allows steam to escape. The valve can be set at varying pressures, enabling the food to be cooked at a temperature of about 120°C.

WHAT IS GLASS MADE FROM?

Glass is made naturally from a fusion of silica (sand), soda and lime. This fusion can be achieved merely by lightning striking in a place where the right ingredients happen to be adjacent to each other. When glass is made by man, other ingredients are added, such as potash, lead oxide and boric oxide. Some of these ingredients are used to make glass clear, some to colour it, and others to give it a frosted effect.

Glass was made by potters in Egypt for glazing stone beads as early as 12,000 B.C. As Egyptian culture progressed, craftsmen used glass for the manufacture of personal ornaments and bottles.

A tremendous step forward in the use of glass was made by the Phoenicians in about 300 to 200 B.C. by the invention of the blowpipe. The blowpipe is a hollow iron tube with a mouthpiece at one end and a knob shape at the other. The knob-shaped end is dipped into hot, viscous glass. A "gather" of molten glass remains on the end when the pipe is withdrawn. This hot glass can be blown by the worker into a hollow ball. The more he blows, the larger the ball.

During the Roman civilization the art of glass-making reached near-perfection. In the 3rd Century, the Romans cast glass on flat stones and produced the first window panes. The break-up of the Roman Empire and the ensuing Dark Ages brought an end to such cultural developments. The glazing of windows did not become widespread over the whole of Europe until the 15th and 16th Centuries.

WHO SENT THE FIRST RADIO MESSAGE?

Guglielmo Marconi is usually credited with sending the first radio message. Marconi was born in Bologna, Italy, He came to England in 1896 and obtained a British patent for his wireless telegraphy system. In 1897 he established a radio transmitter on the roof of the Post Office at St Martins-le-Grand in London, and sent a message a distance of a few hundred yards.

He continued to improve his apparatus, and in 1898 radio was installed aboard a ship at sea, the East Goodwin lightship off the south-east coast of England. In the following year wireless messages were sent across the English Channel.

The first radio transmission across the Atlantic was on December 12, 1901 from a station on the cliffs at Poldhu, in Cornwall, and the message, three dots representing the letter S in the Morse code, was picked up at St John's in Newfoundland.

The existence of radio waves was first demonstrated by Heinrich Hertz, a German professor, in 1887. Marconi based his experiments on Hertz's research.

WHEN DOES COPPER TURN GREEN?

Although copper is highly resistant to the chemical action of the atmosphere and of sea water,

Italian Guglielmo Marconi with some of his experimental wireless equipment.

it turns green if exposed to them for a long time. The colour is caused by the formation of a thin coating of green basic copper carbonate known as patina or verdigris. The latter name comes from the old French *vert de Grece*, (green of Greece), but the reason for it is unknown. This beautiful green is often seen on copper roofs or statues, especially if they are near the sea.

Copper was the first metal man learned to use. Five thousand years ago, when men discovered deposits of pure copper in what are now Iraq and Cyprus, they found that this fairly soft metal could be easily melted, cast in moulds and hammered into tools, weapons and ornaments.

About half the copper produced today is used by the electrical industry. Pure copper is the best cheap conductor of electricity and can be drawn into threads one-thousandth of an inch thick.

WHAT IS AN AEROSOL?

An aerosol consists of fine particles of liquid or solid substances suspended in the air, or in any other gas. It is not, as many people think, merely a spray for use in applying paint easily, or getting rid of unpleasant smells.

The germs of diseases, for example, are to be found suspended in the air, and these dangerous aerosols can be dealt with by spraying chemicals to form another aerosol which destroys the germs. Leaves of plants attacked by pests can be treated in the same way.

Chemicals in the container part of an artificial aerosol spray are stored there under very high pressure. When the release trigger is pressed a valve opens, and the chemicals are forced out through a tiny hole in a fine spray. This invention is useful not only in the home, and to gardeners and doctors, but also to a wide variety of specialist users.

WHY DOES IRON GO RED WHEN HEATED?

Iron goes red when heated because its atoms radiate vibratory waves of an electromagnetic nature that are visible as light at a sufficiently high temperature. At 800°C the iron is at low-red heat. But as the heat increases the iron will turn bright red, and finally white-hot and molten.

Heat is passed through the iron by conduction – the contact of one iron particle with another with no dependence on particle movement. The heat which is given off as light when iron glows red-hot can be reconverted into heat by the substance on to which it falls. When iron is heated to a temperature below 300°C it gives off invisible rays of infra-red radiation which are similar in nature to light. But they do not contain quite enough energy per unit (photon) to stimulate the optic nerve and so be seen by the human eye.

WHO INVENTED THE ROCKET?

The rocket, as far as can be established, was invented by the Chinese during the 12th or 13th Century. The Chinese used their rockets as fireworks to mark special celebrations. A rocket has no moving parts. It is a fuel-filled container with a hole at one end where the exhaust or gases escape with such force that they propel the rocket in the direction in which it is pointed.

Rockets were used as weapons in the East until the 18th Century. Sir William Congreve added improvements in his artillery rocket, which was used in the American War of Independence and in the Napoleonic Wars. Rockets fell out of use in the 19th Century but were revived in the First World War.

Their peaceful use as line-carriers in sea rescues and as distress signals is well known. They are also used to deliver mail and to aid aeroplane take-off.

There are two categories of rocket fuel: liquid and solid. Unlike jet engines, rockets carry their own oxygen supplies, so they can be used both inside and outside the earth's atmosphere. The space rockets carry both liquid and solid fuel. Some burn at least 1,000 pounds of fuel a second. Control of the rocket is carried out by radar and intricate design is required in directing the exhaust gases to maintain the correct flight path.

The Germans developed the rocket in the 1930s and used it in the V1 and V2 weapons which were directed at London in the Second World War.

Since then enormous advances have been made by technicians and scientists working all over the world, culminating in rockets as tall as small skyscrapers and weighing thousands of tons, which are used in the exploration of space.

WHEN WERE FIREWORKS INTRODUCED?

The use of fireworks, or pyrotechnics, probably began when some prehistoric man mixed saltpetre (potassium nitrate) from his cooking with charcoal from his fire. Saltpetre is a pyrotechnic composition – a substance which does not need oxygen from the air in order to burn, but instead supplies it. Two more such compositions are potassium chlorate and potassium perchlorate. These are combined with finely ground gunpowder, sulphur, aluminium dust and many other chemicals to produce force and sparks, or white or coloured flame. Other substances produce noise, smoke and other effects.

It is believed that fireworks were used in the East, especially China and India, for centuries before they spread to Europe. The Chinese fired pyrotechnic war missiles and produced dazzling displays of fireworks for ceremonial occasions. Arabia, in the 7th

Century, also used pyrotechnics in war. In the 14th Century came the invention of gunpowder, a pyrotechnic mixture of saltpetre, charcoal (carbon) and sulphur.

Spectacular firework displays in celebration of victory or peace became popular during the 17th Century. Colour was introduced into the entertainment in the 19th Century through the use of potassium chlorate, which was first prepared by Claude Louis Berthollet (1748–1822). Later magnesium and aluminium was employed to make fireworks still more brilliant. Every year displays are given to mark such widely different occasions as the discovery of the Gunpowder Plot to blow up the British Parliament, and Independence Day celebrations in the United States.

WHAT IS A MIRAGE?
Mirages are optical illusions produced by extraordinary atmospheric conditions. They can be non-existent sheets of water or similar visions, inverted or oversized images of distant objects or various other distortions. All are caused by the refraction, or bending, of light rays as they pass through two layers of air with different densities. The differences in density are usually due to unequal distributions of temperature in the atmosphere.

A common type of mirage is seen in deserts where the heat of the sand raises the temperature of the lower air to make it substantially less dense than that immediately above. This bends the light to such an extent that images of the sky are seen on the ground resembling patches of water. The phenomenon is known as an *inferior* image.

If the layers of hot and cold air are reversed, the result may be a *superior* mirage, where distorted images of distant objects on the ground are observed in the sky. In this kind of mirage there are sometimes two images, the lower one being upside down.

A famous mirage known as the Fata Morgana can be seen in the Strait of Messina, between Italy and Sicily. Here the distorted images of houses on the opposite cliffs are transformed into imaginary castles in sea and sky. The Italians named this mirage after the Fata (or Fairy) Morgana, a legendary enchantress with the magical power of raising phantom castles from the waters.

WHY DO SOME ACIDS CAUSE BURNS?
Some acids burn because they have a strong tendency to absorb water, giving out a great deal of heat in the process. Since most living cells contain water the strong acids, such as sulphuric acid, hydrochloric acid and nitric acid, react with them and kill the cells, causing very serious burns.

These three acids, as well as others such as perchloric acid and benzine sulphuric acid are called mineral acids because they are manufactured from minerals. They are all strong and dangerous acids. They have tremendous industrial value, but great care must be used in handling them.

Most organic acids – that is to say, those made from living things – are weak acids. Vinegar or lemon juice are examples. All acids taste sour and many attack metals, turning them into salts and releasing hydrogen.

Special clothing is worn by men handling acids to protect them from serious burns. Acid must always be poured *slowly* into water, never water into acid. If you are burned by acid you should wash your skin with large quantities of water and then with a weak ammonia solution. If your eyes are affected, flush them immediately with lots of water and then with bicarbonate of soda solution, which neutralizes any acid left.

WHAT IS DRY ICE?

Dry ice is frozen carbon dioxide. When this gas is cooled to a temperature of $-78.5°C$ ($-109.3°F$) it becomes a solid without first becoming a liquid. This is why it is called dry ice. When frozen carbon dioxide is exposed to the air, it evaporates slowly as a gas without going through the melting stage in the way that ice made from water does.

The fact that dry ice has a freezing point much lower than that of water makes it useful as a refrigerant, particularly for the storage of things that need to be kept very cold. When powdered dry ice is added to such liquids as acetone (used in the manufacture of chloroform) or ether, it is possible to produce a mixture which has a constant temperature of as little as $-110°C$ ($-166°F$).

WHEN WAS THE FIRST LIGHTHOUSE BUILT?

The first known lighthouse was the Pharos of Alexandria in Egypt, a 400-foot tower built about 280 B.C. A wood fire was kept burning on the top of the tower, which became one of the Seven Wonders of the World. Before this the light from volcanoes had acted as a guide for sailors. The first lighthouse in Britain was built by the Romans at Dover in about A.D. 43.

Lighthouses continued to be built to the plan of the Pharos until about the 12th Century. Then oil lamps and candles inside lanterns began to be substituted for fires. Shortly afterwards lighthouses suffered a decline which lasted until the great expansion of overseas trade and shipping began in the 16th Century. This led to a revival and many lighthouses were built around the coasts of Europe. The first American lighthouse was constructed on Little Brewster Island off Boston, Massachusetts in the year 1716.

PHAROS

Electricity was introduced for this purpose by Britain in 1862, when electric carbon arc lamps were installed at Dungeness lighthouse on the coast of Kent. But this source of light did not come into general use until the 1920s, when high-powered filament lamps were employed. A small but powerful high-pressure electric arc lamp containing a gas called xenon was installed at Dungeness in 1961, and mercury arc lamps provide the power for one of the most modern lighthouses in the United States, that on Oak Island, North Carolina.

WHO WAS THOMAS NEWCOMEN?

Thomas Newcomen (1663–1729) was the inventor of the only practical steam engine in use from the early to the late 18th Century. He was the predecessor of the much more famous James Watt (1736–1819), whose improvements created the modern steam engine.

Newcomen, who was born at the port of Dartmouth, England, became an ironmonger and Baptist preacher. He developed a keen interest in steam engines, especially in a machine made by Thomas Savery, an English naval captain, in 1698. Savery had incorporated some of the ideas of Denis Papin, a French Huguenot inventor, into a water-raising engine in which the steam acted directly on the water to be raised.

It was Savery's machine that led Newcomen to complete his own engine. Newcomen sprayed cold water onto a steam-filled cylinder to create a vacuum so that atmospheric pressure forced the piston down and the water up. Although fairly effective, the pumps were wasteful of coal. They also needed constant attention, for the valves had to be opened and closed by hand.

Nevertheless his invention was used for a good many years from 1712, especially for pumping water out of mines. One steam engine was even sent to Russia in 1775 to pump out the dry docks at Kronstadt.

WHAT IS TARMAC?

Tarmac is a hard black material used for roads, parade grounds or anywhere that a hard, even and durable surface is needed. It is a mixture of tar (which accounts for the colour) and macadam, which consists of hundreds of tiny even-sized chips of granite pressed together.

Macadam is named after a Scotsman, John Loudon MacAdam, who first used it in the late 18th Century. Until MacAdam's time roads were tracks, sometimes covered with stones, which easily got muddy and waterlogged and whose unevenness made travelling by stage coach so uncomfortable that most people stayed at home. MacAdam, who was on the roads committee in his home county of Ayrshire in Scotland and wrote several books about road-building, persuaded the government to let him make experiments which resulted in vastly improved highways.

The original macadam is still used on roads and looks much better than tarmac. But tarmac and other more recently invented surfaces fare better where there is heavy traffic and when loose stones would be quickly dispersed.

HOW DOES A TUNING-FORK WORK?

A tuning-fork vibrates to give a musical note of definite pitch or frequency and is marked on the fork by a letter or symbol referring to its position in the musical scale.

The instrument has two hard steel prongs and a handle or stem. It is sounded by giving one of the prongs a light tap on a wooden surface, and then holding the handle firmly in contact with a wooden board or table.

Tuning-forks are used by piano-tuners and musicians. Most forks give the same musical note as Middle C on a piano and are usually marked 256. The number gives the frequency and means that it vibrates at a rate of 256 times a second.

WHY DO WE USE DOUBLE GLAZING?

Double glazing for windows reduces loss of heat through the glass and cuts down noise from outside. There are many different systems, including some which do not need professional installation, but the principle is the same. Two sheets of glass are fitted together with a layer of air trapped between them.

This glass-air-glass sandwich should, therefore economize on fuel and make the room quieter. It should also reduce condensation, or water on the inside of the window caused by warm air meeting the cold glass. It will make a room more comfortable in winter, especially near the windows, and may even make it more difficult for a burglar to get in.

The efficiency of this insulation (or separation from the cold outside) is effected by the distance between the glass sheets. Heat insulation increases with the air space up to three-quarters of an inch, but a four-inch space is required for effective sound insulation.

Half or even more of the heat that goes out through single windows can be retained by double glazing, but three-quarters of the heat lost from an average house may escape through other outlets.

WHEN IS THE EARTH NEAREST THE SUN?

The earth is nearest to the sun on about the second or third day in January. The distance varies because the earth spins round the sun in an elliptical orbit or path. The time when the earth is closest to the sun is called the perihelion. The time when it is farthest away – the aphelion – comes six months later on the first or second day in July. During the perihelion the earth is 147 million kilometres from the sun (about $91\frac{1}{2}$ million miles), but during the aphelion it is 152 million kilometres away ($94\frac{1}{2}$ million miles).

When planetary distances in the solar system are compared, the average distance between these two extremes is used. In the case of the earth and sun, this is called the astronomical unit and measures 149 million kilometres (about 93 million miles). If it were possible for an aircraft to fly from the earth to the sun at a constant speed of 1,000 miles an hour it would have to travel for over 10 years to reach its destination.

The earth takes $365\frac{1}{4}$ days to

travel round the sun and moves at a speed of nearly 19 miles a second. As can be seen from the dates of the perihelion and aphelion, the nearness of the sun does not determine the seasons. Our seasons are decided by the amount of daylight and directness of the sun's rays on the earth's surface.

These conditions vary because the axis on which the earth spins is tilted.

WHERE IS A NEEDLE BEAM USED?

This has nothing to do with needles and nothing to do with light. A needle beam is a term used by builders and architects to describe the supports used when the foundations of a wall or a column need attention.

If a wall needs underpinning to enable the foundations to be strengthened, steel needle beams are inserted through slots cut into the wall a foot or so from the bottom. The ends of the beams are supported by screw jacks which can be moved along the beams according to the extent of the foundation area needing attention. Once the work has been done and the foundations have been re-stored, the needle beams are removed and the holes in the wall filled.

Needle beam

Jacks

When a needle beam is used to shore up a column it is usually bolted on.

The needle beam is so called because it is "threaded" through the wall it has to support (see illustration).

HOW DID SCIENCE BEGIN?

Science began with the wish of some prehistoric man to find out about the workings of the world about him. But the first recorded scientific discoveries are those of the ancient Babylonians who observed the positions of the sun, moon and planets. The ancient Egyptians invented simple arithmetic and geometry around 4,000 B.C. and acquired a considerable knowledge of engineering, medicine and anatomy.

From about 600 B.C. the Greeks made great progress in philosophy and geometry, where intellectual effort only was required. But they achieved little advance in practical science, except for the discoveries of Aristotle (384–322 B.C.), who founded the study of biology. Archimedes (287–212 B.C.) discovered many simple principles of physics and Ptolemy (about A.D. 140) made advances in astronomy.

Under Rome progress slowed down. Then the barbarians overran Europe and for almost 1,000 years – from 300–1100 – science was kept alive first in Byzantium and then, from about 700, by the Arabs. From the 15th Century, practical experiments in science began in earnest. Galileo (1564–1642) carried out physical measurements and laboratory experiments. Francis Bacon (1561–1626) and René Descartes (1596–1650) pioneered the new scientific philosophy.

WHO INVENTED SPRINGS?

Credit for the invention of springs is traditionally given to Philo, a scientist who lived about 250 B.C. in the Greek city of Byzantium, which occupied the site of what is now Istanbul in Turkey. Philo wrote a treatise on military engineering, only fragments of which survive. He suggested the use of bronze springs to power catapults.

Since then springs of many different sizes and types have been designed, from the minute hairspring coils in watches to the large springs of powerful machines. These elastic mechanisms, usually of bent or coiled metal, are used to prevent jarring or to convey motive power.

For example, springs were introduced in the second half of the 17th Century to cushion some of the rough jolting of coaches over the bumpy roads of the period. These springs were C-shaped and made of tempered steel. They helped for a time but proved too weak for the heavier coaches that followed. A great contribution to the comfort of travellers was made by Obadiah Elliot of Lambeth, in 1805, when he took out a patent for elliptical steel springs. In 1816 atmospheric, or steam, springs were invented by George Stephenson, the locomotive pioneer.

HOW DOES A SEWAGE PLANT WORK?

A sewage plant works by purifying waste material and recycling it for a useful purpose. Waste material from lavatories, sinks, baths and industry is known as sewage. It arrives at the sewage plant through a system of pipes and drains.

At the plant the sewage is filtered to remove grit and allowed to stand for some time in a settling tank so that the more solid matter sinks to the bottom and is removed as sludge by revolving scrapers. The more liquid sewage is brought into close contact with oxygen, bacteria and other micro-organisms by being fed into aeration tanks. The aeration tanks may be "activated sludge plants" where air is introduced into the liquid by bubbles or with a stirring device, or they may be "percolating filters" with beds made of pieces of coke, clinker or stone. The liquid passes continually over these beds and air has free access to it.

The bacteria and other organisms used in the process are known as "aerobic" because they need free oxygen to carry out their work of oxidizing the large, potentially dangerous, molecules of the sewage into smaller, harmless ones. After further settling, the effluent, or purified water is fed back into nearby rivers.

Sludge is often "digested" by being heated to about 30°C. (86°F.) and then acted upon by anaerobic bacteria which do not need free oxygen to do their work. Methane gas, CG_4, is produced, which can be used as fuel. The sludge remaining is drained or dried, and its unpleasant smell is removed. It can then be used as a soil conditioner or fertilizer.

WHEN WAS THE GYROSCOPE INVENTED?

Any spinning object resists attempts to change the direction of its axis, the imaginary straight line round which it revolves. Thus you can move a gyroscope up, down, forwards, sideways or backwards and feel no resistance, but you will meet opposition if you try to turn it through an angle.

The gyroscope's other important characteristic is called "precession". This means that when you do overcome the resistance and push the axis out of the straight, the gyroscope does not tilt the way you push it but at right angles to the push and axis.

The peculiar qualities of gyroscopes have been exploited in complex instruments used for stabilizing purposes at sea, on land and in the air. They are used in compasses, gun sights, and instruments for ships and aircraft.

The first gyroscope was made in about 1810 by a German, G. C. Bohnenberger. But the name was the idea of a French physicist,

Leon Foucault, in 1852 when he used the device to demonstrate the rotation of the earth. It comes from two Greek words *gyros*, meaning "turn" or "revolution", and *skopein*, meaning "to view". Therefore gyroscope means "to view the turning".

This instrument is based on the principle of a spinning top which remains upright in resistance to the force of gravitation as long as it keeps revolving. In a gyroscope a wheel is mounted in such a manner that it is free to revolve round any axis. When rotating the wheel gives its framework the same tendency to remain at the angle at which it is placed as a top has when it is spinning alone.

WHO BUILT ZEPPELINS?

Zeppelins were airships – or dirigible balloons of rigid type – built by Count Ferdinand von Zeppelin (1838–1917), a German army officer. He became impressed by the military possibilities of airships after going up in an observation balloon behind the Union lines during the American Civil War.

In July, 1910, he ascended over Lake Constance aboard his first 420-feet long airship, watched by a crowd of 20,000 and helped by a hundred soldiers hauling on ropes. It was called the "cigar in the sky" and became a symbol of national prestige. Six years later another zeppelin travelled round Lake Constance turning curves and carrying out other manoeuvres

to prove the ease with which it could be steered. In 1908 his fifth ship caught fire and crashed. But collections and lotteries were organized all over Germany to pay for more zeppelins.

During the First World War zeppelins were converted into bomb carriers and sent on raids over Britain and France. But they did not prove to be effective war machines because their great bulk made them vulnerable to attack. About 480 Germans were killed when their airships crashed.

Zeppelin died a disappointed man in March, 1917, but his work was carried on by his friend Hugo Eckener. After the war Dr Eckener built still larger airships for peaceful purposes. But in 1937 his 800-feet long Hindenburg, which could fly at 180 miles an hour, caught fire and crashed with the loss of 33 lives. The airship had been filled with inflammable hydrogen because the Americans refused to sell the safe helium gas to Nazi Germany. This disaster brought the zeppelin era to an end.

WHAT IS A VACUUM?

A vacuum, in theory, is a space entirely devoid of matter. But no method has been devised for producing one. In practice, therefore, a vacuum is an enclosed space from which air or other gases have been expelled to such an extent that the pressure inside is below that of the atmosphere. There are partial vacuums and high vacuums, according to the proportion of air pumped out of the container.

Vacuums can be put to a wide variety of uses, thanks largely to the truth of the old saying, "Nature abhors a vacuum". The tendency of air to rush into empty spaces under pressure from the atmosphere provides vacuums with suction power. This can be used to operate vacuum cleaners, pumps, milking machines and powerful brakes for heavy vehicles. Vacuums speed up evaporation and are, therefore, used in refrigeration and the dehydration of drugs and food.

High-vacuum processes are used to provide extra-hard steel, blend new materials and make components for radio and television sets. Perhaps the best-known use is in the electric light lamp in which the glowing wires are deprived of the oxygen which would cause them to burn up almost immediately.

WHEN WAS THE FIRST SUPERSONIC FLIGHT?

The first time a manned aircraft exceeded the speed of sound (Mach I) on a level flight was on October 14, 1947. Captain Charles E. Yeager of the United States Air Force flew America's Bell X-1 rocket-propelled research aircraft 42,000 feet over Edwards Air Force Base, Muroc, California, at a speed of Mach 1·015 (about 770 miles an hour).

Known as Glamorous Glennis, this aircraft was the first rocket-propelled aircraft in the world designed for research into high speed aerodynamics. It was a single-seater monoplane with an enclosed pressurized cabin lying flush to the surface.

In 1946 the X-1 underwent a series of tests during which it was released from a Boeing B-29 Superfortress in flight and allowed to glide to earth. The aircraft first flew under its own power after one such drop on December 9, 1946. But its first take-off under power did not take place until January 5, 1949.

Glamorous Glennis is now in the National Air and Space Museum of the Smithsonian Institution, Washington, D.C.

WHY ARE THERE MANY KINDS OF SAWS?

Saws are of many shapes and sizes, according to the special purposes for which they are to be used and the materials they are meant to cut. Most are designed to cut through wood but others have the particular qualities needed for cutting metals and stones.

There are two main types of hand-saw. Both have steel blades with wooden handles, but the teeth are shaped differently to fit the job they have to do. One is a cross-cut saw for cutting *across* the grain of the wood. The leading edges of the teeth slope backward and are also bevelled, or angled,

Using a large chain saw to strip branches from a tree trunk.

transversely. In other words, they are cut away at the edges to give an oblique angle like the edge of a chisel, thus producing a sharp-pointed profile or shape designed to avoid splintering the wood.

The second type is the rip or tenon saw, which is used for cutting *along* the grain of the wood. This has a smaller blade, strengthened by a steel strip along the top edge, and smaller teeth. It is used, as the name suggests, in cutting tenon or slotted joints.

Smaller hand saws, like the fretsaw, are used for cutting intricate shapes. These have a narrow blade stretched across an open frame. The hacksaw, which is used for cutting metal by hand, also has an open frame, but its blade is deeper and more closely-toothed.

Machine saws are of three main types: first, a larger, stronger hacksaw operated by an electric motor through a crank and connecting rod; second, a circular saw, which has a rotating, disc-shaped blade with teeth on the circumference; and third, a bandsaw which has a blade formed like an endless flexible band and tightly stretched over pulleys.

The bandsaw, which has fine teeth along one edge, operates at a higher speed than the circular saw. It can cut round curves of quite small radius because the blade is so narrow.

For stone-cutting in quarrying there are swinging gang-saws with teeth like chisels and flat-bladed circular saws, which are either fed with a mixture of hard sand and water or fitted with rims of a hard abrasive substance called carborundum.

The hand-held power saw driven by an electric or petrol engine is used for felling trees and cutting logs. This is also known as a chain-saw because it is much like a bicycle chain equipped with saw teeth.

WHAT IS ENERGY?

Energy is the power to act. There are several different forms of energy, and one kind can be changed into another kind. But although it can be changed from one form into another it can never be lost. The total amount of energy in the universe remains constant.

If you strike a match on the side of a match-box, mechanical and chemical energy is changed into heat energy. If you use a saw, the blade gets hot because the energy of movement or mechanical energy becomes heat energy. The end of a bicycle pump becomes warm after pumping because heat is generated when air is compressed.

In a simple electric circuit there are several changes. The battery has chemical energy, which is converted to electrical energy, which produces light and heat energy in the bulb.

We depend for a large part of our power on steam, diesel and petrol engines in which the chemical energy stored in a fuel is converted first into heat energy, which is then turned into mechanical energy.

WHEN DOES A SLIP CURRENT OCCUR?

A slip current occurs when a steady stream of air tries to resume its even flow after being diverted by an object at right angles to it. The less streamlined the object, the greater the disturbance, or turbulence, of the stream of air.

A good example is provided by a bus moving along a road. The air pushed aside by the bus is turned back to fill the empty space when the vehicle has passed. Thus air currents are set flowing in the same direction as that being taken by the bus. A sensation of being pulled forward may be felt if you ride a bicycle too close to the rear of a large moving object.

WHO WAS GALILEO?

Galileo Galilei (1564–1642), the great Italian scientist and mathematician, was the first astronomer to use a telescope, the discoverer of the pendulum's laws and the founder of modern physics.

Two of his great contributions to knowledge are associated with famous buildings in Pisa, the northern Italian city where he was born. When Galileo was 19, he observed a lamp swinging in the cathedral. From its movement he concluded that a pendulum swinging to and fro could be used for measuring time, and so prepared the way for the invention of the modern clock. By dropping objects from the Leaning Tower of Pisa he demonstrated that bodies of different weights fall at the same rate.

While Professor of Mathematics at the University of Padua (1592–1610), Galileo made his first telescope by fitting a lens at each end of an organ pipe. Later he made a telescope that magnified 30 times. He found that the Milky Way was a mass of stars, studied the moon and discovered the four largest satellites of the planet Jupiter.

Galileo's observations convinced him that Nicholaus Copernicus (1473–1543), the Polish astronomer, was right in his theory that the earth rotates on its axis and revolves round the sun. This view was contrary to the teaching of the Church, and in 1616 he was given a formal warning. But in 1632 he published a dialogue in support of the Copernican system that offended the Church by its satire and use of Holy Scripture. He was summoned before the Inquisition, forced to retract his views and made to live in seclusion for the rest of his life.

WHY ARE CONVECTION HEATERS SO-CALLED?

Heating appliances specially designed to create a circulating movement of warmed air are called convection heaters because they operate by using convection currents of air.

When air is heated it becomes less dense and, therefore, duly rises and is replaced by cold air.

Convector heaters consist, basically, of metal cabinets with openings at the top and bottom to produce and direct this flow of rising warm air. At the base of this cabinet there is a heating element and this warms the air within the cabinet.

This warm air rises and, as it rises, cold air is drawn into the convector from the bottom of the appliance. The cabinet of the convector acts as a flue or chimney and creates a continuous current of warm air.

HOW IS INK MADE?

Ink is made from a pigment, or dye, and a liquid, called the vehicle, in which the dye is dissolved.

There are two chief types of ink: writing ink can be washable or permanent, and the ingredients used in its manufacture vary according to the colour wanted and the purpose for which it is needed.

Blue-black inks are usually made from a dark-coloured solution and an extract of tannin. The dark solution is usually made from a soluble iron salt, such as ferrous sulphate. Blue dyes are added to blue-black inks to make it more attractive. Coloured inks contain other soluble dyes and the liquid vehicle is water. India ink is carbon black suspended in water and is usually used in drawing.

Writing ink is made by purifying the water and then dissolving the other ingredients in it in large tanks. Afterwards the solution is clarified and then packaged in bottles.

Printing inks are thicker than writing inks, often with a consistency like paint. The dyes are often dissolved in a heavy varnish.

WHAT MAKES A BOOMERANG COME BACK?

It is the built-in skew or twist in a boomerang combined with its spinning motion that makes it return to the thrower. At first people believed that air, pressing on the lower flat surface and passing over the upper rounded face, was responsible for the return flight. But T. L. Mitchell, a Scottish explorer of Australia, gave the true explanation early in the 19th Century.

The curved throwing stick is used chiefly by the aborigines of Australia for hunting and warfare. (They also use a non-returning kind of boomerang.)

The boomerang is held at one end, above and behind the thrower's shoulder, with the concave edge to the front, and swung forward rapidly with the flat side underneath. Just before it is released, it is given extra power with a strong wrist movement.

If thrown downward or parallel to the ground it sweeps upward to a height of 50 feet or more. When thrown so that one end strikes the ground, it ricochets into the air at terrific speed, spinning endwise. It completes a circle 50 yards or more wide and then several smaller ones, up to five, before it drops to the ground near the thrower.

WHY IS DDT DANGEROUS?

After extensive use as a pesticide, DDT was found to have many harmful after-effects on human beings and animals. The control of insects was revolutionized by the introduction of DDT after the Second World War. It was employed to combat a wide range of insects which attacked food crops and was also instrumental in bringing the world malaria problem under control.

But by the 1960s it was found that DDT affected the metabolism of many birds so much that their eggs became too fragile to survive. As a result many species have nearly become extinct. Several kinds of fish have also been seriously affected. Large numbers of insects which served as food for both fish and birds have been destroyed.

The effects of DDT on food for human consumption have been extremely serious. Food becomes poisonous if the amount of DDT in it exceeds a certain limit. However, such pesticides are now heavily restricted by most governments.

WHO BUILT THE FIRST BICYCLE?

The first rideable bicycle was made by Kirkpatrick MacMillan of Dumfriesshire, Scotland, in 1839, although an attempt to construct one had been made by Jean Théson at Fontainebleau, France, in 1645.

Before this, crude machines had been made, which had no form of steering and had to be propelled by pushing the feet against the ground. Machines of this type appear on bas-reliefs in Babylon and Egypt and on frescoes in Pompeii. In England, a stained glass window, dated 1580, in the church of Stoke Poges, Buckinghamshire, shows a cherub astride such a machine.

But all these machines seem to have been four-wheeled. The true bicycle belongs to the 19th Century.

MacMillan's bicycle was driven by rods attached from pedals to a sprocket on the rear wheel. The first chain-driven bicycle was produced by Tribout and Meyer in 1869. In this year the first bicycle show – in Paris – and the first cycle road race – from Paris to Rouen – took place.

An Englishman, James Starley,

MacMillan's bicycle.

of Coventry in Warwickshire, is known as "the father of the cycle industry". In 1871 he introduced a bicycle with a large driving wheel and a smaller trailing wheel. This was the "ordinary" bicycle, known to everyone as the penny-farthing. In 1874 a chain-driven bicycle with two wheels of equal diameter was designed by H. J. Lawson. This was known as the Safety bicycle and became enormously popular from about 1885 when the Rover Safety bicycle was built by John K. Starley, James's nephew.

The pneumatic tyre–in other words, a tyre filled with air–was invented in 1888 by John Boyd Dunlop, a veterinary surgeon of Belfast, Northern Ireland. By 1893 the design of the bicycle had been developed into the modern diamond frame with roller-chain drive and pneumatic-tyred wheels.

WHEN DOES A FIRESTORM OCCUR?

A firestorm occurs when flames from a large number of individual fires merge into a single convective, or circulatory, column. This produces so much heat that all the buildings below are set on fire. Firestorms cover a whole area, trapping the population within them.

During the Second World War enormous destruction was caused by fire in British, German and Japanese cities. In Britain and Germany the thousands of fires started by incendiary bombs usually burned individually, with relatively little spread between buildings. This was because of the materials from which the buildings were constructed, their size and the lay-out of the cities.

However, in Japanese cities mostly made up of low wooden-framed houses the American bombing attacks brought about a number of annihilating firestorms. The most terrible of all was that caused by the atomic bomb dropped on Hiroshima, on August 6, 1945. This storm contributed in great measure to the death toll of 70,000 to 80,000 people. In the second atomic bomb attack on Nagasaki on August 9, 1945, fire damage was again severe.

WHERE WAS THE WHEEL INVENTED?

The earliest wheels so far discovered were found in graves at Kish and Susa, two ancient Mesopotamian cities. These wheels are believed to date from 3,500 B.C. They were made from three planks, clamped together with copper clasps. This kind of wheel also existed in ancient times in Europe and the Near East. No one is sure where the wheel was invented, but this archaeological evidence suggests it was probably in ancient Mesopotamia.

A wheel with proper spokes was not invented until after 2,000 B.C. There are records of this wheel in northern Mesopotamia, central Turkey, and north-east Persia. By the 15th Century B.C., spoked wheels were being used on chariots in Syria, Egypt, and the western Mediterranean.

The solid wheel was used mostly in farming. Tripartite wheels – wheels with three spokes – were being used in the Bronze Age in Denmark, Germany and Northern Italy for carts.

The invention of the wheel made it possible for people to transport heavy objects much more easily. It also enabled them to travel farther and trade with each other more easily, and so find out about other countries and customs.

WHY DO SOME CARS NEED AEROFOILS?

Racing cars capable of moving at speeds well in excess of 100 m.p.h. need aerofoils to counter the effect of lift created by their highly streamlined shapes.

Drag is caused by the turbulence of the air as it flows in to fill the vacuum left behind a forward-moving object. The less streamlined the object, the greater the space to be filled in and the greater the turbulence. Therefore, the greater the "drag".

As designers improve the streamlining effect of racing cars to reduce drag, the cars' shapes become more and more flattened and a new problem arises. The car has taken on similar properties to an aircraft wing and the movement of air over and under it at high speed begins to provide lift.

The aerofoil placed at the rear of the car is so designed as to create a downward force when it passes through air at speed, and thus counteracts the lift. If this did not occur the cars' wheels would make too little contact with the road surface and the driver would quickly lose control.

WHAT IS SAFETY GLASS?

Safety glass is glass that has been strengthened. There are two kinds of this protective glass – laminated and toughened – and both were discovered by accident.

In the early 1900s Edouard Benedictus, a French chemist, knocked a glass flask on to the floor. Although the glass starred and cracked, it did not break. After examining the flask he realized that a coating of dried celluloid on the inside had held the fragments together.

Some years later, when injuries from broken car windscreens increased, Benedictus recalled this incident. Using glass sheets and celluloid bonded together in an old letter press, he produced the world's first sheet of laminated, or layered, glass. Since then the clarity of the glass has been improved to equal that of ordinary glass. But it will withstand the impact of a half-pound steel ball dropped from a height of 16 feet. Toughened glass was developed later, although in the 17th Century, Prince Rupert, nephew of King Charles I of England, discovered that molten glass was turned into immensely strong pear-shaped drops when tipped into cold water. Prince Rupert's drops, as they are called, can be hammered on an anvil without breaking, but if the tail of the drop is broken they crumble into dust.

In 1874 a French scientist, de la Bastie, heated small sheets of glass and then quenched them in oil, increasing their strength dramatically. However these sheets of toughened glass were very small, and it was not until the 1930s that sheets large enough for use in cars could be toughened.

Laminated or toughened safety glass is now used all over the world in cars, buses, trains, aircraft, ships and shops and has proved its safety value.

HOW ARE DIAMONDS USED IN INDUSTRY?

Industrial diamonds are used for such a wide variety of purposes that a sudden shortage would cause havoc in many branches of manufacture and mining. This is because diamonds, as well as being the most brilliant and precious of stones, are also one of the hardest materials known to man.

Their earliest use in industry was as an abrasive powder for sawing and polishing operations and for grinding metal-cutting tools. Bort, which is the cheapest form of industrial diamond, is crushed into different grades for such purposes.

Many kinds of drills use diamonds as cutters. The introduction of the carbonado or black diamonds of Brazil—less brittle than other forms—greatly improved rock drilling for geological and mine prospecting. But they have become so scarce that other suitable varieties have had to be substituted. Fine wires, like those needed for electric lamp filaments, are produced by pulling the metal through diamond drawing dies.

Diamonds are also employed for cutting glass and porcelain, for fine engraving, for dental surgery, and for bearings in watches.

WHO DESIGNED THE FIRST STEAMBOAT?

The first boat ever to be moved by steam power was designed by a Frenchman Jacques Périer and tested on the Seine in Paris in 1775. But the first really successful steamboat was built by Périer's fellow countryman, the Marquis Claude de Jouffroy d'Abbans. His craft which was 141 feet long and equipped with straight-paddled sidewheels travelled several hundred yards against the current on the Saône at Lyons on July 25, 1783.

Among early American pioneers was James Rumsey who in 1786 drove a boat at four miles an hour on the Potomac River, propelled by a jet of water pumped out at the stern. Between 1786 and 1790 John Fitch experimented in the Delaware River at Philadelphia

This strange steamboat is John Fitch's second boat.

with different methods of propulsion, including paddle wheels, a screw propeller and steam-driven oars.

The first to apply successfully the principle of steam to screw propellers was John Stevens whose boat, equipped with two propellers, crossed the Hudson River in 1804. However, his achievement was soon eclipsed by Robert Fulton's 150-foot long paddlewheeler Clermont which in 1807 covered the 150 miles from New York to Albany in 30 hours at a maximum speed of five miles an hour. With Fulton in command on the Hudson, Stevens looked elsewhere, and in 1808 his new boat, the Phoenix, sailed out of New York harbour to become the first steamboat ever to go to sea.

Both Stevens and Fulton were following in the steps of the Scottish inventor William Symington who in 1802 constructed a steamboat in Scotland, the Charlotte Dundas, which was used as a tug on the Forth and Clyde Canal. The Charlotte Dundas was a paddle-wheel steamer. For many years all steamboats used this method of propulsion.

WHY DOES BREAD HAVE HOLES IN IT?

The holes in a piece of bread are made by bubbles of gas. In breadmaking flour and water are mixed to form a dough. Then a small amount of yeast is added to the mixture. Yeast is a type of fungus which grows very quickly when it is warm and damp. While growing, it gives off a gas which bubbles up through the dough, making it expand. It is yeast which gives bread its particular flavour and appetizing smell.

No one knows when yeast was

first used to make bread, but it must have been many thousands of years ago. According to one story, the idea was the result of an accident. Some yeast is said to have got into the dough by chance and made it rise. Because this loaf was twice as big as normal, people thought it must be magic. But as the bread tasted better than the usual flat, heavy loaves, they soon used yeast to make all their bread.

Cakes also have holes in them made by bubbles of gas. But these are made by a different substance which leaves practically no flavour. This substance is baking-powder, which is a mixture of tartaric acid and bicarbonate of soda. When these two chemicals are mixed together, wetted and heated, they react to produce carbon dioxide. This gas bubbles through the cake mixture to make it rise while being baked.

WHAT IS FIRE?

Fire is the outward sign that oxygen is combining with other substances in a spectacular chemical reaction. As the air is rich in oxygen, many materials will burn freely in a process scientifically called combustion, if their temperature is raised high enough. This explanation of what had been considered a mysterious phenomenon was discovered by the French chemist Antoine Lavoisier in 1783.

The discovery of fire may have changed early man's wandering mode of life to a more settled one because of an urge to keep the fire burning. It provided him with a new weapon for survival, warmed his cave and huts, enabled him to cook, and helped to scare off dangerous animals.

In ancient times people in Persia, Egypt and India believed fire to be sacred and worshipped it as representative of the sun.

WHEN WILL A CAR ENGINE STALL?

A car engine will stall – that is to say, it will suddenly stop when you do not want it to – if it is unable to provide sufficient power to overcome the load on the back wheels.

This power is provided by the explosion of the petrol and air mixture pushing down on the pistons. If the load on the pistons from the crankshaft is exerting a greater force than that created by the explosion, the pistons will not move down the cylinder and the engine will stop. This can happen if the clutch is engaged too rapidly or if the hand brake is left on.

HOW DO DRINK-VENDING MACHINES WORK?

Drink-vending machines are operated electronically when coins are inserted and a button pressed to select the beverage required. They have four basic units, or modules. On the inside of the cabinet door is the electrical unit where the dispensing of a drink is programmed through the other three – the cup dispenser, the recirculating water system and the ingredient-container units.

When the coins are put into the slot, they are checked by an electronic scanning unit. If they are the wrong coins they are rejected. If accepted, they set off the programme.

The release mechanism of the dispenser allows a cup to fall down a chute to the service position. While this is happening, a portion of the selected ingredient in powder form is released from its container into a large mixing bowl that looks like a big flattish funnel. Here hot water is added to dissolve the powder and the resulting beverage is poured into the waiting cup. Finally more water enters the mixing bowl, which is then automatically cleaned in readiness for the next customer.

WHY DOES SMOKE GO UP THE CHIMNEY?

Smoke will rise up the chimney or through the nearest opening it can find because it is hotter and, therefore, lighter than the air in the room.

Before the days of chimneys smoke was allowed to escape through vents or open turrets in the roof. Chimneys were introduced to induce a draught, thus providing more air for the fire. The hot smoke passing up the shaft made room for cool air, of higher density.

Thus a chimney would not only carry away the smoke and gases from a fire but also act as a ventilator enabling a change of air in the room.

WHO INVENTED THE PARACHUTE?

Leonardo da Vinci (1452–1519) was thought until recently to have been the first to design a parachute. But drawings have now been found that were made five years before da Vinci's sketches, possibly by an engineer in Siena, central Italy.

However, the first man to make and successfully use a parachute was a Frenchman, André Garnerin (1770–1825), who stretched cloth across a bamboo framework and parachuted from a balloon over Paris in 1797. It was an uncomfortable descent as the fabric was too thick to spill out any wind, and the parachute came down swinging violently like a pendulum. Garnerin was in a tiny basket, to which he clung tightly until his rough landing on the plain of Monceau. The parachutes of those days were developed from the crude canvas devices used to descend from hot air balloons.

Modern parachutes are made of pure silk or good-quality nylon in small panels and have a small pilot parachute which opens first and helps to pull out the main parachute.

290

WHEN WAS THE FIRST TELEVISION BROADCAST?

The first public television demonstration or broadcast was given by the British inventor John Logie Baird (1888–1946) in 1926 at the Royal Institute in London. Twenty years earlier Baird had set up a small laboratory at Hastings to study the problems of "seeing by wireless".

Experimental television broadcasts were made by the British Broadcasting Corporation between 1929 and 1935. The pictures were formed of only 30 to 100 lines and flickered badly. It was obvious that a method of high-definition, with more scanning lines, was badly needed.

Research in the United States made possible an increase to 343

Inventor John Logie Baird demonstrating his television apparatus.

lines, and other improvements quickly followed. In November, 1935, the first high-definition television service in the world began with the opening of a B.B.C. station at Alexandra Palace, London, using 405 scanning lines. British television continued with 405 lines until 1964, but now uses the international 625-line standard.

The United States began regular television broadcasting in 1941, but the Second World War held back other countries, and television services did not become widespread until the 1950s.

Although the first colour television transmission was given by Baird in 1928, its use did not become general until 1954 in the United States, 1960 in Japan and 1967 in Britain, Germany, France, Russia and other countries.

WHY DO SOME CARS HAVE PNEUMATIC TYRES?

Pneumatic tyres help to cushion the vehicle against bumps, ruts and other inequalities in the road surface. This levelling effect of the tyre is achieved because of the compressed air which is inside the rubber casing.

Until about 1900 all road vehicles were fitted with solid tyres. These were very unsatisfactory. When a tyre struck an obstacle on the road surface the shock often damaged the vehicle's mechanism permanently. In any case the effect was most un-comfortable for the passengers, and the roads then had holes and bumps which made driving over them dangerous.

The adaptability of pneumatic tyres gives them a firmer grip on the road and enables the driver to steer, change speed and go round corners more safely.

WHAT IS LIQUID AIR?

Liquid air is ordinary air – a mixture of oxygen and nitrogen – compressed until it forms a liquid. When the pressure on the liquid is released, it turns back into these two gases. The liquid is kept under great pressure in strong steel cylinders.

Liquid air has a great many uses, because it enables large amounts of these two gases to be stored in small spaces. The aqualung consists of small cylinders of liquid air joined to a mouthpiece. Liquid air is also used by pilots, firemen and astronauts.

Once liquid air has been made, the liquid oxygen can be separated from it for use in hospitals. People with lung trouble are helped by being given an increased amount of oxygen to breathe. Other gases, liquefied in the same way, are used as anaesthetics to put people to sleep during operations.

Liquid oxygen is widely used in industry because a flame fed with additional oxygen is much hotter than an ordinary flame. The oxy-acetylene torch is connected to two cylinders, one of liquid oxygen and one of acetylene. The two gases are mixed together and fed through tubes to the torch. When the gases are lit, they can produce a flame with a temperature of about 3,000°C. (5,432°F.) or twice the melting point of iron. This torch is used to cut and to weld metals.

WHERE IS RADIUM FOUND?

Radium is found in the ore of uranium. Two French scientists working in Paris discovered radium in 1890. Professor and Mme. Curie found this rare and precious element in a mineral called pitchblende, a black substance which also contains uranium. During a period of four years they treated six tons of this material and obtained a teaspoonful of a pure radioactive substance which they called radium.

They found that radium had many very unusual properties. It affected ordinary photographic plates, it made certain substances glow when placed in the dark, and it quickly killed off tiny dangerous organisms when placed near them.

Radium gives off powerful radioactive waves – the well-known gamma rays. These are used in the treatment of various diseases, especially in the case of cancer where "deep ray" treatment is given.

Pierre and Marie Curie were awarded the Nobel Prize for Physics for their work. Professor Curie was killed in a motor accident in 1906, but Mme. Curie continued the work they had started together and in 1911 was awarded the Nobel Prize for Chemistry.

HOW DOES AN ELECTRIC IRON WORK?

An electric iron is heated by a stream of electricity passing into the heating element in its base. This element may be cast into the sole plate of the iron or clamped to the plate in a herring-bone pattern.

Hand irons have an electric loading up to 1,000 watts and weigh from 3–6 pounds. Many of them have thermostatic controls so that the correct heat is maintained. Steam irons contain reservoirs of water which release steam through holes in the sole plate directly on to the article being ironed. In this way they produce, at the same time, the moisture, heat and pressure needed to make the fibres pliable and remove the creases.

WHO INVENTED THE ZIP?

Whitcomb L. Hudson, an American mechanical engineer, patented the first zip-fastener in 1891. His invention was originally designed for footwear. It consisted of a series of separate fasteners, each having two interlocking parts which could be fastened either by hand or a movable guide. The idea was revolutionary but commercially unsuccessful because the fastener had an annoying tendency to spring open.

In 1913 Gideon Sundback, a Swedish electrical engineer who had settled in the United States, developed a more practical fastener and an efficient machine for making it. Two important events in the history of the zip's rise to worldwide popularity occurred in 1918 when a contractor ordered 10,000 fasteners for naval flying suits, and in 1923 when the B.F. Goodrich Company put fasteners on the rubber overshoes that they manufactured.

WHAT IS A BUNSEN BURNER?

A Bunsen burner is a gas burner consisting of a tube with a small gas jet at the lower end and adjustable air inlet by means of which the heat of the flame can be controlled. It is used in laboratories and produces a hot non-luminous flame if the air and gas mixture is correctly adjusted.

The inventor of the burner was Robert Wilhelm Bunsen (1811–1899), a German chemist, although Michael Faraday (1791–1867), the English physicist and chemist had previously designed a burner that worked on very much the same general principle.

Over the years several varieties of Bunsen burners have been made with improvements in the control and mixing of the air and gas, giving greater heat and enabling

different sizes of flames to be obtained. There are devices for spreading the flame and numerous fittings are made to go on the top of the tube for holding retorts, test tubes, etc.

Burners may be constructed to burn coal gas, oil gas, acetylene or natural gas.

WHY IS IT HARDER TO WALK UPHILL THAN DOWNHILL?

It is harder to walk uphill than downhill because you must lift the weight of your body and to do this requires greater energy than that needed for walking on the level. To create this greater energy your muscles require to give extra lift, your heart has more work to do to feed the blood cells and remove their waste matter and your lungs have more work to do to remove the carbon dioxide from your heart and replenish it with oxygen. That is why the steeper the climb and the more concentrated the effort, the more quickly you breathe. If you are out of condition you start to "pant" to gulp in extra oxygen. In comparison to the energy necessary for walking on a horizontal plane, the total value of the extra energy needed for climbing is the weight of your body times the height you are to reach.

The steeper the incline of the hill, the quicker you use this extra energy. It is therefore harder for you to walk up a steep hill than a

294

gentle one, although the energy used up in either case, where the height to be reached is the same, is identical.

When you walk downhill, very little energy is needed because the weight of your body carries you down the slope. Of course, this is the pull of gravity that is helping you down, in the same way that you have to overcome the force of gravity when you walk up a steep hill.

HOW IS AN INSTRUMENT LANDING SYSTEM USED?

An Instrument Landing System is used by a pilot in bad weather to bring down an aircraft in perfect line with an airport's runway. Two radio beams are sent out by a ground transmitter. The "localizer" is a narrow, upright beam which positions the aircraft in line with the runway. The "glide path" is a thin, flat beam which gives the aircraft a perfectly angled approach path to the end of the runway.

In the case of large, busy airports such as London's Heathrow, a pilot is in close contact with Air Traffic Control on his approach to the airport for, at peak periods, aircraft can be landing at 45 second intervals.

The Ground Control operator tells him to "lock on", a phrase used to tell the pilot to switch on his Instrument Landing System.

The pilot informs Control that he is "established", which means that he has locked on to the two radio beams and is keeping them crossed. The point at which the beams intersect is the spot on the runway where the aircraft must land.

WHY DOES THE MOON SHINE?

The moon shines by the light it reflects from the sun. It has no light of its own. The sharp definition with which, on a clear night, we see the moon, is due to the absence of any concealing veil of air or cloud on it.

Since there is no atmosphere on the moon to act as a buffer to the sun's rays, temperatures there are extreme and sudden. The maximum is 212° F. (100° C.), the temperature of boiling water, and the minimum is −292°F. (−180°C.). Understandably, the moon's hostile conditions cannot support life of any description.

WHAT IS A VOLT?

A volt is the practical unit of electromotive force, or electrical pressure, as distinct from an electric current. In terms of measurement it is that electrical motive force which applied to a conductor of 1 ohm resistance produces a current of 1 ampere.

Imagine water stored in a tank on a tower, with an outlet near the ground. The head of water will give varying pressures at ground level, depending on the height of the tower. In electricity the head of water corresponds to the voltage of the supply.

The volt is named after the Italian physicist Alexandro Volta (1745–1827), who invented the voltaic cell.

In a dry battery the chemical composition determines the voltage or pressure of each cell. This cannot be increased by making the cell larger. A larger cell will merely last longer.

WHEN WILL HALLEY'S COMET NEXT APPEAR?

Halley's Comet is next expected to appear in 1986. It is the most famous of all periodical comets—those which move round the sun and reappear in our skies at known intervals.

The comet is named after the British astronomer, Edmund Halley (1656–1742) who observed it in 1682. He predicted accurately that it would return in 1758, but died too soon to see it. Halley's Comet has a period of 76 years and was last seen in 1910.

Comets have been called the stray members of the solar system, but the description is misleading as a comet's orbit can be calculated like that of a planet, though they may appear unexpectedly.

A comet consists of a mixture of dust, frozen gases and ice, and resembles a gigantic dirty snowball. When near the sun, the heat vaporizes some of the gas and ice.

The clouds of gas and dust released form a visible tail. Although a comet may be be larger than the earth or even Jupiter, it contains only a small quantity of matter. This lack of substance makes it invisible until relatively close to the earth.

A comet's tail always points away from the sun, probably because of the intense radiation which repels the tail's tiny particles. Its orbit is much more elliptical than that of a planet, and therefore is only visible at certain times, when near the earth.

WHY DO AIRCRAFT SOMETIMES LEAVE VAPOUR TRAILS?

Vapour trails form in the sky because the water in the exhaust of aircraft engines condenses when it meets the cool air.

Vapour trails, or condensation trails, are artificial clouds of a roughly tubular shape, formed of liquid drops of ice crystals. Sometimes short-lived trails may be seen near the wing tips or propeller tips of an aircraft because water vapour in the air is expanded rapidly at these points and cools quickly. For each gram of fuel burned in the engine about 1·4 grams of water vapour and about 10,000 calories of heat are produced and exhausted into the wake of the aircraft.

For a vapour trail to form, the aircraft must be flying in air colder than about −60°C. (−76°F.). In warmer air the heat will overcome the humidification and no trail will form. Nowadays most jet-propelled, pressurized aircraft operate in the cold upper layers of the atmosphere so the narrow wakes of the vapour trails can be seen more often.

WHAT IS ORION'S BELT?

Orion's Belt is a row of three bright stars across the middle of a constellation or group of stars. One of the three is easily distinguishable by its yellowish-red colour, which contrasts strongly with the whiteness of the others.

The whole constellation was named after Orion, the great hunter of ancient Greek mythology. When Orion was killed by the goddess Artemis, he was changed, according to the myth, into a group of stars. These took the form of a warrior wearing a girdle of three stars (Orion's Belt) and a lion's skin, and carrying a club, a sword and a shield. Below the belt a hazy line of stars representing the jewels on Orion's sword can be seen.

HOW IS MAIL SORTED?

At large Post Office sorting offices the mail is separated mechanically by a letter segregator. Thick packets and envelopes are flipped down a chute for sorting by hand, while the rest of the mail is moved along to a machine called an automatic letter facer.

The facer arranges the letters so

that their stamps are all in the same position and then puts a postmark on each of them showing the place and date of posting. This process, known as cancelling, can be carried out at a rate of about 20,000 letters an hour.

Letters then go to the letter-coding desk, where operators read the post codes and tap them out on a keyboard. Two rows of dots are printed, one above and the other below the address, the top row denoting the district to which the letter is to be delivered and the lower row the name of the street. Although the dots are almost invisible to the eye, they are detected by the automatic serving machine, which finally sorts the letters ready for delivery.

WHO INVENTED SAFETY MATCHES?

Safety matches were invented by Johan Edvard Lundström of Sweden in 1855. They had been made possible ten years earlier by the discovery of red phosphorus by Anton von Schrötter, an Austrian chemist. Unlike the white phosphorus used in matches at that time, red phosphorus is not poisonous and does not ignite spontaneously in air.

The principle of the safety match is the separation of the ingredients necessary to create fire, one part being left in the head of the match and the other part on the striking surface of the matchbox. Lundström put the red phosphorus on the friction surface and the other ingredient, potassium chlorate, in the match head.

White phosphorus continued to be popular for matches because of its keeping qualities under different weather conditions. But the outcry caused by the discovery of the serious poisonous effects (phossy jaw) it had on match workers led to the prohibition of such matches in most developed countries at the beginning of the 20th Century.

HOW ARE COPPER PIPES MADE?

Copper pipes are made by pushing a long cylinder of the metal, called a billet, through a machine that has a rod in the centre of a hollow cylinder. The outer shell shapes the metal into a seamless tube, and the inner rod forces a hole through the billet to turn it into a tube. The pressure thins the walls and lengthens the tube or pipe, at the same time hardening the metal. Tubes of 15/1,000th of an inch have been made. A hundred of these could be fitted inside an ordinary drinking straw.

Pipes made of copper are specially useful in plumbing and the making of car radiators. Copper is useful for pipes because it is not corroded by water or steam. It is an excellent conductor of electricity, long-lasting and easily shaped. Copper drainpipes that were used about 3500 B.C. have been found in good condition.

General Knowledge

WHERE ARE THE WORLD'S EARLIEST PAINTINGS?

The earliest paintings of which we have records are on the walls of caves in France and Spain. They are paintings of animals, mostly of horses, bulls and bison.

The most famous of those in France are at Lascaux, in the Dordogne area. They are painted in thick black outline. Some of the bodies are filled in with red or brown paint. On the edge of the roof of the cave is a frieze of horses and bulls. It looks as though the cave people were trying to decorate the roof of the cave to a pattern.

Other famous early paintings are at a place called Altamira, in the province of Santander, Spain. Here the walls of the cave are covered with standing and squatting bison, thickly outlined in black and filled in with red.

The people who did the paintings took a lot of trouble to mix the colours properly. The black they used came from soot, and the red and yellow from iron. They stored the colours in bones and skulls, and mixed them with water, then put the paint on the walls with their fingers or brushes.

Some of the paintings were not purely for decoration. At Lascaux there are drawings of oxen and goats about to fall into a pit. Probably the people thought that if they painted the animals they wanted to kill on their cave walls, they would catch them more easily.

WHAT ARE BANDOLIERS?

Bandoliers are leather belts formerly worn by musketeers over their shoulders to hold their ammunition. They are provided with a number of cylindrical containers, each holding enough powder for one shot, a little flask for priming powder, and a bag for bullets. The word is derived from the French bandoulière.

This equipment first appeared in the 16th Century, and became popular throughout America and most of Europe. Musketeers, especially those in Mexico, often wore two bandoliers in the shape of a cross against their front and back as an extra protection.

The containers attached to this musketeer's bandolier hold gunpowder and bullets.

WHEN IS FOOD KOSHER?

Food is Kosher when it has been made fit and clean to eat according to Jewish religious practices.

The food must not come from animals, birds or fish prohibited in the Biblical books of Leviticus and Deuteronomy.

The meat must be salted to remove the blood after the carcass has been examined for physical defects, and the ischiatic nerve must be removed from the hindquarters, as stated in Genesis.

Meat and milk must not be cooked together and separate utensils must be used.

The *shehita* method of slaughtering is carried out by a specially trained person using a special knife with a smooth, sharp edge. An incision is made across the animal's neck and the knife moved in a fast, uninterrupted sweep without stabbing or pressing. The sweep cuts the main arteries, rendering the animal unconscious and allowing the blood to drip from the body.

HOW IS BLUE CHEESE MADE?

Blue cheeses are all made from cows' milk except for the famous French Roquefort cheese, which comes from ewes' milk.

The blue in blue cheeses is essentially blue mould. But it is extremely good for you. What happens is that an organism similar to penicillin is added to the milk or curd used to make ordinary white cheese. The mould, during three to six months of ripening, grows either in small, irregular, natural openings in the cheese or in machine-made perforations, depending on the type of cheese.

The small amounts of mould reproduce or spread to give the typical blue streaks in the white cheese, and, once ripened, the distinctive flavour. Blue cheeses are usually heavily salted to add to the flavour.

WHAT IS THE TOUCH OF MIDAS?

The "touch of Midas" is the ability to turn everything to gold – or, in other words, to succeed. In ancient Greek mythology, Midas was the son of Gordius, the king of Phrygia, who devised the Gordian Knot, and of Cybele, the goddess of caverns and the Great Mother of the Gods.

Midas succeeded his father on the Phrygian throne and showed himself a wise and pious king. One day, when he was strolling on the banks of the River Sangarius, he came across a drunken man who had been tied up by peasants. Midas released the man and thereby earned the gratitude of Dionysus, the god of wine, who promised to grant a wish as a reward.

The king wished that everything he touched should be turned into gold. But he soon regretted his choice, for even the food he took in his hand to eat turned to gold. He begged the god to take pity on him and withdraw the gift. Dionysus did so and sent Midas to the River Pactolus to cleanse himself. From then on the river was said to flow with gold dust.

This ancient legend gave rise to the expression "the Midas touch".

WHERE ARE THE ELYSIAN FIELDS?

The Elysian Fields was a phrase used in Greek mythology to describe what we would call Heaven. Before European navigators sailed far beyond the Mediterranean and found other lands inhabited with people like themselves, people believed the world was flat. In early Greek mythology the souls of those who died went for refuge to the Infernal Regions. This the "afterworld" was said to lie at the extremity of the earth.

At that extremity were the Elysian Fields or the Isles of the Blest. It is thought by some that this land adorned with every beauty might well be the Canary Islands or the Azores in the Atlantic Ocean.

Later when the Greeks learned more of other lands, they changed the location of the Infernal Regions to the centre of the earth. There were two great regions in the Underworld. One was the Elysian Fields, where those who had led a just life in the world above ground joined the children and favourites of the gods of Olympus and where harsh weather was never known and soft breezes forever refreshed the beautiful land.

The other place was Tartarus, the awful region of the damned, who had committed crimes against the gods and were punished by tortures. One inmate was Tantalus, son of Zeus, the father of the gods. He had betrayed his father's secrets and was condemned to stand forever with water all around him and rich fruit just above his head. When he tried to eat and drink, both fruit and water drew away from him.

From this story we get the word "tantalize". Another prisoner was Ixion, father of the Centaurs, who was bound to a rolling, flaming wheel for the rest of time for attempting to win the love of Hera, sister and wife of Zeus.

WHY DOES THE TOWER OF PISA LEAN?

The tower of Pisa is the bell tower of the cathedral of Pisa in Tuscany, Italy. It leans because, when the building was half completed, the soil under one half of the circular structure began to subside and the tower tipped.

Work on the tower was begun in 1173, but was discontinued for a century after the subsidence. However, in 1275 architects devised a plan to compensate for the tilt. Two storeys, the third and the fifth, were built out of line with the others and closer to the vertical in an effort to alter the tower's centre of gravity.

But the leaning has continued to increase gradually throughout the centuries. Pumping to keep water away from the surrounding ground and the injection of cement grout into the foundations and the surrounding subsoil have been tried in recent years, but without success.

The tower, which is one of the most unusual in existence, is Romanesque in style and made of white marble. It is cylindrical in shape and has eight storeys.

The tilt is about 17 feet, or more than five degrees from the perpendicular. The tower continues to increase its tilt by about a quarter of an inch each year.

WHAT IS THE ORIGIN OF SANTA CLAUS?

The jolly old man with white whiskers who brings children toys in his sack at Christmas time had his origins in the popular St Nicholas (4th–5th Century A.D.), the patron saint of school-children and sailors.

Little is known about the life of St Nicholas, but it is probable that he was bishop of Myra in Lycia (Asia Minor). The earliest miracle attributed to him was the rescue of three army officers who were unjustly condemned to death but saved by St Nicholas's appearance in a dream to Constantine I.

In the 17th Century the Dutch Protestant settlers in New Amsterdam (now New York) replaced St Nicholas (known as Sinter Claes in Dutch) by a generous magician called Santa Claus.

Gradually, this transformation spread to many countries in Europe, especially those where the Reformed churches were dominant. The kind old man was also given the names of Father Christmas and Father January, and his special day became either December 25 or New Year's Day.

WHEN WERE CHRISTMAS CARDS FIRST SENT?

The first Christmas card was designed in England in 1843 by J. C. Horsley for his friend Sir Henry Cole. A thousand copies of it were placed on sale at Felix Summerley's Home Treasury office in London. The card was printed by lithography on stiff dark-brown cardboard and measured $5\frac{1}{8} \times 3\frac{1}{4}$ inches. Underneath the picture of a family party on the front was the greeting "A Merry Christmas and a Happy New Year to You". Inside were panels, framed in trellis work, showing examples of Christmas giving.

Louis Prang of Boston, Massachusetts, is regarded as the "Father of the American Christmas card". He first produced Christmas cards in 1875. They were beautifully designed and much admired abroad.

WHERE IS THE BRIDGE OF SIGHS?

The Bridge of Sighs (*Ponte dei Sospiri*) is in Venice and connects the east side of the Doge's Palace with the old state prisons, crossing the Rio di Palazzo. Its name symbolizes the sadness of the prisoners crossing the bridge. The Doge's Palace was begun in the 14th Century and took several centuries to complete. The Bridge was not built until the 17th Century. It became the path by which prisoners crossed to the "pozzi",

The Bridge of Sighs in the foreground, with the Doge's Palace on the left.

the prisons on the other side of the canal.

The Bridge of Sighs is one of nearly 400 bridges over some 150 canals which make up the thoroughfares of Venice, a city built on wooden piles driven into the mud of the lagoon. The city became known as the "Mistress of the Adriatic" from the custom carried out each year by the city's rulers, from the 12th to the 18th Century, of throwing a wedding ring into the Adriatic in token of their claim to dominion over that sea.

Lord Byron's famous reference to the Bridge of Sighs appears in his poem, *Childe Harold's Pilgrimage*:
"I stood in Venice, on the Bridge of Sighs;
A palace and a prison on each hand."

WHY IS LOCH NESS FAMOUS?

Loch Ness is the most famous of all the fresh water lochs in Scotland because of reports that it is inhabited by an aquatic monster.

Since the middle of the 19th Century many local inhabitants and visitors claim to have seen the Loch Ness Monster. In recent years much photographic and documentary evidence has been produced from which some experts have detected a resemblance between the monster and aquatic reptiles that lived more than 50,000 years ago.

Nevertheless, in spite of the stories, official opinion still doubts that such a creature actually exists. Frogmen and submarines have searched in vain for the monster. But it has been pointed out that there are caves and subterranean waterways beneath the surface of Loch Ness leading to other lochs, in which the supposed monster could hide.

WHAT WAS THE PHOENIX?

The phoenix was, according to legend, a bird which died in a fire but came out of the flames alive. In ancient Egypt the phoenix was connected with the worship of the sun.

According to some stories, it was like a large eagle, with red and gold feathers. It lived for hundreds, or even thousands of years. But when its death was near it built a nest of the scented branches of trees, and spices. It then sang a beautiful, haunting and sad song, and fanned the nest until it burst into flames. The phoenix died in the fire it had made, but from the flames and ashes came a new phoenix, which would live for many years.

In other legends the phoenix was like an Egyptian heron called the bennu. It was also associated with the worship of the sun and is found carved on ancient Egyptian monuments as a symbol of the rising sun and life after death. Because the phoenix was regarded as immortal, it was adopted by the Christian Church as a symbol of the

Resurrection of Jesus and of eternal life. It has also been used as a sign over chemists' shops from its association with alchemy and the search for immortality.

WHEN WERE THE FIRST ROADS BUILT?

The earliest artificial roads, as distinct from the natural routes, trails and paths of primitive man, were probably built by the city kingdoms of the Tigris-Euphrates Valley in the Middle East where the first wheeled vehicles may have rolled about 5,000 years ago.

Among the first road engineers mentioned in history were those who accompanied the army of the Assyrian empire-builder Tiglath Pileser I about 1100 B.C. and constructed a route to enable the conqueror to pursue his enemies through the mountains to the north of Mesopotamia. The Assyrians set an example to succeeding empires by establishing an elaborate system of roads for the transport of troops and the dispatch of instructions from the central government to local governors.

Before the coming of the Romans, the biggest and best organized road systems were those belonging to the Persians who founded their empire about 500 B.C., and the rulers of northern India whose dominions around 300 B.C. were already served by a well-equipped highway more than 2,500 miles long. A source of

great pride to the Persian Empire, which at one time covered the territory now occupied by Iran, Syria, Iraq, Turkey and northern Egypt, was the so-called Royal Road. This stretched some 1,600 miles from Susa, the capital, to the Aegean Sea, and was provided with staging posts which enabled relays of horses to cover the distance in nine to ten days.

Comparatively few of the roads of antiquity were properly surfaced or metalled until the great Roman engineers began to set a standard for reliability, directness, ingenuity and strength which has not been equalled until recent times. The construction of the Appian Way in 312 B.C. from Rome to the important salt deposits of Capua was the start of a network which provided the empire with vital arteries and gave Europe its principal roads for more than 1,000 years. On the main routes the Romans provided fresh horses at regular intervals to carry imperial messages to and from the capital at speeds of up to 150 miles a day.

Before the Spanish conquests in South America, the great Inca empire, which stretched from Ecuador into modern Chile, was sustained by a 3,200-mile road spanning deep gorges and climbing rocky heights to cross one of the world's most mountainous regions. In North America the first big man-made highway was built in Maryland by a British army on its way to fight the French.

In Europe centuries of neglect

were ended with a revival led by two Scottish engineers, John Loudon McAdam (1756–1836) and Thomas Telford (1757–1834). But the world knew nothing to rival the old Roman network until the coming of the automobile produced the 20th Century revolution in overland communications.

WHERE IS THE MONA LISA?

The world's most famous portrait, painted by Leonardo da Vinci (1452–1519) between 1503 and 1506, hangs today in the Louvre in Paris. The Louvre, formerly a palace of the French kings, is now a museum of art and antiquities which is beyond all valuation.

The Mona Lisa is also called La Gioconda because the sitter's married name was Giocondo. It has been in France from the day in 1516 when Leonardo left Italy to settle there–except for two occasions. Once, in 1911, the picture was stolen from the Louvre and found two years later in Italy. The second time it left France for 26 days, on a fantastically well-guarded and highly insured visit to the United States as a guest of President John F. Kennedy.

Leonardo da Vinci began painting Lisa when she was 24 and he was 51. She used to come to the great master's studio in the late afternoon when the light was soft. Over the three years, Leonardo became fascinated by his model, and perhaps that was the reason

why her husband, Francesco del Giocondo, never received the finished portrait. The artist always made the excuse that he had not quite finished it. He carried it with him wherever he went–to Milan, to Rome and, finally, to France where King Francis I offered the artist a palace in the beautiful Loire valley, the Chateau de Cloux.

It is believed that Francis I paid 4,000 gold crowns for the Mona Lisa, but it was not until after Leonardo's death that the king was able, at last, to possess the painting of the Florentine lady with the enigmatic smile. Thereafter, it remained in the possession of the kings and emperors of France. The picture hung at Fontainebleau, at Versailles and at the Tuileries. There in 1800 it hung on the wall of Napoleon Bonaparte's bedroom!

WHAT IS A BAILEY BRIDGE?

A Bailey bridge is a type of bridge designed by Sir Donald Bailey, an Englishman, during the Second World War. Built entirely by manpower, it met a great need. The old types of military bridge were unable to support the rapidly increasing weight of armoured vehicles.

The Bailey bridge proved to be the most useful and versatile military bridge of the war. It was built of panels and sections, or trusses, which could be combined to carry loads of up to 100 tons over spans up to 220 feet.

The roadway of the bridge is

supported by two main trusses pinned together. Each 10-foot section of bridge consists of two parallel trusses supporting the cross-members on which the sur-face is laid, and is known as a bay.

The capacity of the bridge may be increased by adding one or two extra trusses alongside the first, by adding extra trusses on top of the first two or three to make a second storey, or by both means. Therefore a single-truss, single-storey bridge is a single-single and you can have double-single, double-double and so on.

The Bailey bridge was also adapted to float on a plywood pontoon.

New versions of the Bailey Bridge have been devised. The Mark 3 Bailey with a roadway 13 feet 9½ inches wide is standard in the British Army.

WHEN WAS THE SCOUT MOVEMENT FORMED?

The Scout movement was formed in 1908 after the appearance of a book, *Scouting for Boys*, written by the then Inspector General of Cavalry in the British Army, Lt. Col. Sir Robert Baden Powell. The author had intended his ideas to be used by existing youth organizations, but it soon became evident that a new movement had begun.

Baden Powell had held an experimental camp on Brownsea Island in Poole Harbour, Dorset and put into practice his ideas on the training of boys. He thought they should organize themselves into small, natural groups of six or seven under a boy leader. Their training should add another dimension to their education by including mapping, signalling, rope-knotting, first aid and all the skills needed in camping and similar outdoor activities in which self-reliance is important.

Before being accepted as a scout, a boy had to promise to do his duty to God and his country or sovereign, to help other people at all times and to obey the Scout Law. This was a simple code of chivalrous behaviour easily appreciated by boys. It was not long before the movement spread from Britain to other countries.

WHERE WOULD YOU FIND THE GARDEN OF EDEN?

The short answer is that you would not find it. The Garden of Eden is the place where God is supposed to have created a garden for Adam, the first man. Some people hold it to have been situated in the Mesopotamian region between the Rivers Tigris and Euphrates. The Tree of Knowledge grew in this garden and it was there that man fell from grace in God's eyes because, at the prompting of Eve, the first woman, he ate fruit from this tree.

Because of this act of disobedience, it is said, God devised three punishments. The man was to till the earth, which was cursed; the woman was to experience painful childbirth; and the serpent who prompted the woman to persuade the man to eat the fruit was from that day to be hated by mankind. Adam had to be driven out of the Garden of Eden because the Tree of Life also grew there and this would have endowed him with immortality. The inference is that man chose knowledge and death rather than ignorance and eternal life.

The Garden of Eden has been portrayed in many famous paintings and poems. In man's imagination it has always been an ideal to which he longs to return.

WHY WAS THE STATUE OF LIBERTY BUILT?

The Statue of Liberty was built to celebrate the birth of the United States of America and to commemorate the friendship between that republic and the republic of France.

It stands on Bedloe's Island (now renamed Liberty Island) at the mouth of New York Harbour, in accordance with the wishes of the sculptor Frederic Bartholdi.

The plan for the monument originated in France. The cost of the statue was met by the French people, while the money for the 300-foot pedestal was raised in the United States.

Although the monument was not unveiled until 1886, the idea was conceived at the end of the 18th Century when France and the United States were the only big democratic republics in existence.

Under the 150-foot statue, symbol of freedom and equality, is a moving poem, inscribed inside the pedestal. In this poem *The New Colossus*, the writer, Emma Lazarus, invited the tired, poor and homeless to come to America in search of liberty.

WHAT IS A GARGOYLE?

A gargoyle is a quaintly formed head of an animal, man or devil, carved in stone. It was used by the stonemasons of the Middle Ages as a decorative spout for the rainwater from a roof.

The builders of Gothic churches, where gargoyles were chiefly used, allowed their imaginations to take full flight, unconcerned that their little sculptured masterpieces were to be placed so high that earthbound man could hardly see them.

Perhaps the best example of the use and variety of gargoyles is seen on the top of the cathedral of Notre Dame which was founded in 1163, and stands on the Ile de la Cité, an island on the River Seine, in Paris. Here hundreds of the grotesque and gaping figures reach out from balustrades and

WHERE DO RAISINS COME FROM?

Special varieties of grapes are dried, and are then called "raisins", the French word for grapes. Until the 20th Century they were produced mainly in the Mediterranean regions. Now huge quantities come from California and Australia.

Naturally produced raisins are spread out on trays and dried in the sun to a greyish brown colour. They have a tough skin and sometimes keep the bloom–the bluish powdery coating–found on grapes. But most of the raisins grown commercially are dried quickly in heated sheds and treated with sulphur to preserve them. These are usually small and dry and are used in cakes and puddings.

One type of raisin which is particularly good to eat is called the muscatel. These raisins are grown near Malaga in the south of Spain, and are dried in bunches partly while still on the vine and partly after picking.

towers to spout water clear of the cathedral walls. Victor Hugo, the French author, wrote about the walls of the cathedral in his historical romance, *Notre Dame de Paris*, which was later made into the film, *The Hunchback of Notre Dame*.

Not all churchmen have approved of the gargoyle as a decorative embellishment. A French monk, St Bernard of Clairvaux (1090–1153), one of the most illustrious and eloquent preachers of the Middle Ages, condemned them. He said that people might prefer "to spend the whole day in admiring these things piece by piece rather than meditating on the Law Divine".

WHEN DID YOGA START?

Yoga started about the 2nd Century B.C. when its main principles were set forth in the *Yogasutras* by the sage Patanjali. This system of Hindu philosophy is based on the idea that man's bondage results from the identification of the soul with the body and that his freedom comes when he realizes the two can be separated. In yoga the mind is controlled by the constant practice of meditation and non-attachment to material objects.

There are different types of yoga designed for different temperaments. Karma Yoga is suited to active minds, and deals with the performance of duties in which the doer renounces attachment, motive and the result of what he does. Jnana Yoga is for philosophical minds, and teaches how to discriminate between the real and the unreal, and how to renounce the unreal. Bhakti Yoga shows the way to cultivate the love of God for His own sake, deals with self-control and concentration.

The final aim of all these systems is the liberation of the soul from the bondage of matter. Hatha Yoga deals mainly with physical exercises and is chiefly concerned with health and long life. Yoga is a Sanskrit word signifying the union of a person's soul with the supreme spirit. A person who practises yoga is called a yogi.

WHAT ARE SHERPAS?

Sherpas are a hardy people living in a rugged, mountainous region of north-east Nepal, of which Mount Everest (29,000 feet) forms the northern boundary. Originally they came from Tibet.

Today they number about 6,000 and live at heights of about 13,000 feet. Potatoes form their main crop.

Accustomed to living in a thin atmosphere, Sherpas became world famous for their part in helping Everest expeditions since General G. C. Bruce's attempt on the mountain in 1922. They are excellent high-altitude guides and porters, cheerfully carrying loads of supplies and equipment seemingly out of all proportion to their small size. They also act as cooks and assistants.

The most famous Sherpa is Tensing Norgay, who on May 29, 1953, stood with Edmund Hillary of New Zealand on the top of the world—the first men to reach the summit of Everest.

WHERE DOES VELVET COME FROM?

Velvet comes from silk, but there are many imitations made from cotton and other materials. Real velvet is a closely woven fabric made by weaving loops of silk on to two silk backcloths, one on top of the other. In between the two backcloths the woven silk will form what is called a pile. The pile is the soft, furry hairs characteristic of velvet and many carpets.

The two layers of silk, which have been woven face-to-face, will have long furry pile yarns connecting the two layers. After the cloth is woven, the two layers are sliced apart leaving two separate soft rows of velvet.

Velvet was originally developed in the 15th Century in Italy from where the art spread throughout the world. Turkish velvets were especially successful, and beautiful designs from 16th and 17th Century Turkey survive today.

WHEN WERE THE FIRST CIGARETTES MADE?

The Spanish conquistadors of 1522 found the Aztec Indians of Mexico smoking a primitive cigarette in the form of tobacco stuffed into a hollow reed or cane tube. Other inhabitants of America at that time crushed shreds of tobacco and wrapped them in corn husks.

However, it was the cigar that the Spaniards brought to Spain as a luxury for the wealthy. The cigarette was improvised early in the 16th Century by the beggars of Seville, who picked up discarded cigar butts, shredded them, rolled them in scraps of paper and called them cigarillos.

It was not until the late 18th Century that they became respectable. The tobacco used for them was of a milder and lighter type, and the French gave them their present name of cigarette or little cigar.

A cigarette factory was set up in Havana in 1853, but the widespread use of the cigarette in the English-speaking world dates from the Crimean War (1854–1856) which introduced British soldiers to Turkish tobacco. Strangely, British taste switched later to straight Virginia tobacco. Americans prefer a blend which includes some of the Turkish variety.

In recent years a connection has been established between cigarette smoking and various diseases of the chest and lungs. There have been many attempts to dissuade the public from smoking and cigarette manufacturers have devoted a great deal of money and research in an attempt to pinpoint and eliminate the harmful elements in tobacco. Filter-tip cigarettes which accounted for only 1·4 per cent of production in 1952, have now risen to more than two-thirds of the total. Many countries have started extensive campaigns to warn of the risks to health.

WHY DOES NEW YORK HAVE SO MANY SKYSCRAPERS?

There are so many skyscrapers in New York because these enormous buildings are able to accommodate hundreds of people on their many storeys while taking up only a relatively small amount of land – and New York is short of land.

The skyscrapers are found in the heart of New York City, the centre of its business, financial and entertainment activities, which are all packed into an area of 10 square miles on the lower half of Manhattan Island, between the Hudson and East Rivers. The lack of space makes the value of land tremendously high and therefore the building of tall structures has become a necessity.

Manhattan is shaped rather like a tongue and is made of solid granite. The skyscrapers are grouped in two great clusters, the lower group standing at the southern tip of the island, looking down across Upper New York Bay towards the Atlantic and making

The Manhattan Skyline

up the famous New York skyline which greets visitors by ship to America. This group includes the Woolworth building (792 feet) and the Bank of Manhattan (900 feet).

The upper cluster of buildings is about halfway up the island, in what is known as the "midtown" section. Here the enormous Empire State building rises to a height of 102 storeys (1,472 feet) and often has its peak wreathed in cloud. Nearby is the Chrysler building (1,046 feet).

WHAT IS ESPERANTO?

Esperanto is a language created by

Ludovic Lazarus Zamenhof (1859–1917), a Jew who was born on the frontier between Russia and Poland. He realized that language barriers helped to maintain and even to aggravate differences and difficulties between nations, and conceived Esperanto as an international language easily learned and spoken by everybody.

The language's name (meaning "a person who hopes") comes from the pseudonym Zamenhof used for his first book *Internacia Lingyo* (1887) which was translated into English as *Dr Esperanto's International Language* in 1889. Generally speaking, learning Esperanto takes from one-twentieth to one-fifth of the time needed to learn a national language.

It is used by the Universala Esperants-Asocio (founded 1908) which has headquarters in Rotterdam, members in 85 countries, 50 national associations and about 20 professional international associations. Numerous people who do not belong to official organizations also speak the language. In 1963 Professor Mario Pei of Columbia University, United States, suggested that Esperanto was spoken by 8,000,000 people.

Esperanto is a phonetic language with no irregularities of grammar. The roots of words were taken from national languages, so many can be recognized on sight. Many great works of literature have been written in the language.

In 1954 the General Conference of the United Nations Educational, Scientific and Cultural Organization (U.N.E.S.C.O.) recognized "the results attained by Esperanto in the field of international intellectual relations in the rapprochement of the peoples of the world". Five years later on the occasion of the centenary of Zamenhof's birth, U.N.E.S.C.O. paid tribute to him.

WHEN WERE TRAFFIC LIGHTS INVENTED?

Fixed-time traffic lights were invented in the United States and introduced in New York in 1918. Eight years later the United States set up a Committee on Uniform Traffic Control. The purpose of traffic lights is to control the flow of traffic, determine the right of way at intersections and give greater safety to drivers. By linking successive traffic signals together a progressive movement through the streets can be provided.

Traffic lights were used for the first time in Britain at Wolverhampton, Staffordshire, in 1928. Sixty years earlier the London police had introduced a system of traffic control signals based on the swinging arms of the semaphore.

WHERE WAS CRICKET FIRST PLAYED?

Pictures belonging to the middle of the 13th Century show a simple team game with bat and ball which bears a marked resemblance to cricket, the national game of England. The first written evidence about the game is possibly to be found in an extract from the accounts of King Edward I of England in 1300. This refers to some money which was spent by the young Prince Edward on a game called "creag".

Cricket was being played by boys of the free school of Guildford, Surrey, in 1550. Oliver Cromwell, Lord Protector of England, was said to have played both cricket and football in his youth, and a kind of cricket club at St Albans, Hertfordshire, was mentioned in 1666. The first regular cricket club was formed in the Hampshire village of Hambledon in 1750.

The game has been played under recognized rules at least since the beginning of the 18th

Century. The first definite match recorded was played in 1679 in Sussex – 11 a side and for a stake of 50 guineas. In 1719 the "Londoners" met the "Kentish men" in what must have been the first match at county level.

At first the greatest enthusiasm for the game was in the southern counties. The most famous cricket centre was the Artillery Ground, Finsbury. Here was played on June 18, 1744, the famous match between Kent and All England. This was the first game to be recorded in A. Haygarth's *Scores and Biographies 1744–1878*.

The Marylebone Cricket Club, which eventually became the game's ruling authority, was established in 1787. In 1814 it purchased its present ground at St John's Wood, London, named after the club's founder, Thomas Lord.

Cricket is now widely played in the English-speaking lands.

WHY ARE WEDDING RINGS USUALLY MADE OF GOLD?

The modern custom of wearing gold wedding rings originated in Roman times, but the idea took many centuries to become established as a universally accepted tradition. At first rings made of iron were introduced as tokens of betrothal. In those days the privilege of wearing gold rings was reserved for Roman senators and magistrates.

As the Empire became more affluent and permissive, this right was allowed to spread through the various levels of society, and engaged couples took advantage of the freedom to use the coveted gold for their betrothal rings.

A great writer of the early Christian church, Tertullian (about 155–222) said that gold "being the nobler and purer metal and remaining longer uncorrupted was thought to intimate the generous, sincere and durable affection which ought to be between the married parties". Gold marriage rings, as distinct from betrothal rings, came into use from the 5th Century, but do not appear to have been generally adopted by the Church for use in the wedding ceremony until much later. At first they probably simply received the Church's blessing.

In English-speaking countries the wedding ring is usually worn on the third finger of the left hand, perhaps because of an old belief that a nerve ran from that finger directly to the heart. But in Germany and France and other European countries both husband and wife wear the ring on the third finger of the right hand, the hand traditionally used for making vows.

WHAT IS INFLATION?

Inflation is what happens when prices in a particular country rise so high and so quickly that they upset the nation's economy.

Prices may start rising rapidly because people want to buy more goods than there are goods to go round. Fears of still higher prices may cause people to rush out and buy things while they can still afford them. Thus the demand for goods increases and the cost of them goes up even faster.

One cure would be for people to stop buying, but, of course, it is difficult to persuade people to stop buying things they want. Workers whose wages buy them less, old people whose pensions are no longer enough to live on, students whose grants no longer support them, all press for increased money to keep up with prices. Higher wages often mean dearer goods.

WHERE DID RUGBY FOOTBALL BEGIN?

The highly organized rugby football games of today developed from the crowd game of ancient and medieval Britain in which a round or oval object—usually the inflated bladder of an animal—was kicked, punched or driven towards a goal. The origins of games between two teams, which attempt to kick, carry or otherwise force a ball through a goal or across a goal line defended by their opponents, are lost in antiquity.

When football was taken up by the great English public schools, all agreed that the ball must never be carried or passed by hand in the direction of the opponents' goal. It was a violation of this rule by William Webb Ellis at Rugby School in 1823 which led to the division of modern footballers into those who want to play only with their feet and those who wish to use both feet and hands.

At first, Ellis's behaviour was condemned even at Rugby. But the school soon decided to permit running with the ball by players who received it by a fair catch. Then it was permitted if the ball was caught on the bound. Later other restrictions on running with it were abolished.

Ellis became a great hero and a tablet on one of the boundary walls of Rugby School bears this inscription: "This stone commemorates the exploit of William Webb Ellis who with a fine disregard for the rules of football as played in his time took the ball in his arms and ran with it, thus originating the distinctive feature of the Rugby game. A.D. 1823."

It was some time before rugby football was accepted as a game in its own right, but on January 26, 1871 representatives of 17 clubs and three schools met at the Pall Mall restaurant, Regent Street, London. They formed the Rugby Football Union, drafted by-laws, appointed officers and instructed a committee of 13 to draw up the basis of the code in use at Rugby School.

WHEN WERE ICE CREAMS INVENTED?

Water ices were known in the Roman Empire, and Marco Polo (1254–1324) is said to have brought back a recipe for milk ices from his travels in the Far East.

Centuries later, chefs for the royal courts of Europe were experimenting with ice cream and trying, without success, to keep the recipes secret. In the 19th Century the commercial production of ice cream was made possible by the discovery that ice mixed with salt produced a lower temperature than ice alone. The industry grew rapidly towards the end of the century because of the introduction of mechanical refrigeration.

About 80 per cent of the liquid mixture for making ice cream is milk and cream, and about 15 per cent is sweetener. Sometimes egg yolk is used, and fruit, nuts and flavourings are often added to the mixture.

Most commercial ice cream is made in a refrigerated tube with revolving blades or beaters. The partially frozen ice cream is drawn off into containers and sent to a hardening room with a temperature of from $-18°$ to $-26°C$. ($0°$ to $-15°$ F.). It is then delivered in refrigerated trucks to dealers. Strict standards of hygiene have to be maintained.

WHAT IS A WARLOCK?

A warlock is a male witch, wizard, or sorcerer with supposed supernatural powers, usually considered to be evil. Belief in witchcraft survives in modern civilized societies and remains a strong force in most primitive ones.

Throughout the western world most alleged witches have been women, and the number of warlocks has been comparatively few. The last execution of one in Germany was that of Johannes Junius who was burned alive in 1628. On the other hand, one of the most famous figures in the history of magic and witchcraft is Merlin, the benevolent wizard of Arthurian legend.

The earliest evidence of belief in witchcraft survives from the prehistoric past. A horned creature, thought to be connected with witchcraft, is to be found carved or painted at archaeological sites dating back to 30,000 B.C. and in areas spanning the territory from the Soviet Union to Spain.

WHY IS LEONARDO DA VINCI SO FAMOUS?

Leonardo da Vinci is the perfect example of the all-round educated man of the Renaissance. Born in Florence in 1452, he soon became famous for his remarkable paintings. His painting the "Mona Lisa", now in the Louvre, Paris, is possibly the best known painting in the world.

His enormous talents encompassed a wide variety of subjects ranging from sculpture to military engineering. He devoted much time to the concept of flying machines and carried out experiments, without success, in this field. From his work as an artist he developed a knowledge both of anatomy and of the science of light. His anatomical drawings are of a rare beauty and of great precision.

Leonardo was also knowledge-able on such varied subjects as astronomy, geology, botany, and geography. In architecture his studies produced both beautiful designs and practical scientific information. The great man's in-terests were so diverse that he even gave specific and most serious instructions on how to make and launch stink bombs.

WHERE DID CALENDARS BEGIN?

Early in history man began count-ing time by days, months and seasons and so had the beginnings of a calendar. When he studied the supposed movement of the sun more closely he began to use the year as a unit of time.

The Greeks dated everything from the Olympic Register, a traditional list of the victors in the Olympic Games starting in 776 B.C. The Romans counted time from the founding of their city in 753 B.C. The Mohammedans use the Hejira, or flight of Mohammed from Mecca, A.D. 622. Jewish reckoning dates back to the Crea-tion, calculated as having taken place 3,760 years and three months before Christ's birth-date. The Christian practice of dating events from the birth of Christ did not come into general use until the time of Charlemagne (9th Century), and a mistake was made which placed the birth of Christ five years too late.

In 46 B.C., acting on the advice of the astronomer Sosigenes, Julius Caesar fixed the year at $365\frac{1}{4}$ days, giving every fourth year, or leap year, an extra day. But the correction by a whole day every four years was too much, and by the 16th Century the Julian calendar was 13 days behind the solar year.

In 1582, Pope Gregory XIII directed that 10 days should be dropped from the calendar. He also directed that three times in every 400 years the leap year arrange-ment should be omitted, by not counting as leap years the years ending in two noughts unless they are divisible by 400. This arrange-ment will keep the calendar and solar year together until the year 5000, when the difference will be one day.

WHEN WAS BIG BEN BUILT?

Big Ben was built in 1858. It is the bell that chimes the hours in the Clock Tower of the British Houses of Parliament, London, and is so called because Sir Benjamin Hall, as the Chief Commissioner of Works, was the minister respon-sible for its installation. The fa-mous deep, resonant boom of the bell is regularly broadcast by the B.B.C. all over the world.

The way to Big Ben is up a spiral staircase of 374 steps. The Roman numerals on the clock face

are two feet high and the pendulum is 13 feet long. Big Ben itself
weighs $13\frac{1}{2}$ tons. When the clock
was installed, two men used to
wind it every week. Now it is
wound by electricity.

WHAT IS BAROQUE?

Baroque and post-Baroque are
terms used to describe a particular
style of art and architecture that
flourished in Europe from the close
of the 16th Century to the late 18th
Century.

This style was much concerned
with vivid colours, hidden light
sources, luxurious materials, elaborate, contrasting textures, and
drama and illusion. But the art of
the period was so varied that it is
impossible to supply a simple set
of rules or criteria for it.

In architecture the buildings
were designed to stimulate faith in
church and state. Each element in
the design contributed to the
central culminating feature. Precision and elegance were thought
less important than vitality and
movement. Unity and harmony
were essential.

Carlo Maderno (1556–1629)
is known as the father of Baroque.
In 1607 he designed the façade of
St Peter's Rome. The colonnade
was the work of the brilliant
Giovanni Lorenzo Bernini (1598–
1680).

The Baroque influence soon
became international and rapidly
developed into two separate forms
–free, active architecture in
Roman Catholic countries such as
Italy, Spain and Portugal, and
more restrained but impressive
buildings in Protestant areas such
as England, The Netherlands and
parts of Northern Europe.

During the post-Baroque period
(about 1700–1780) a particular
style known as Rococo developed
which refined the flamboyant
Baroque to suit elegant 18th
Century tastes.

WHY ARE MONKS TONSURED?

Tonsure is the name given to the
rite of shaving the crown of the
head of a cleric entering certain
religious orders. It is particularly
associated with monks and is a
sign of dedication to religious
observance.

In the Eastern Orthodox Church
tonsure was practised as early as
the 4th Century. Prayers of the 9th
Century which accompanied such
ceremonies show clearly that tonsure was regarded as an outward
manifestation of the casting off of
earthly values and vanities to
dedicate oneself to the service
of God.

There are three kinds of tonsure:
the Roman type consists in shaving the whole head, leaving only a
fringe of hair supposed to symbolize the crown of thorns. The
Eastern or Greek style used to
involve shaving the entire head,
but is now held to have been observed if the hair is closely shorn.
The Celtic tonsure means shaving

in front of a line stretching over the top of the head from ear to ear.

Long before Christianity there was a religious practice among the Romans and Semites of cutting some of the hair and offering it to a deity as a sign of dedication.

WHERE IS THE WHISPERING GALLERY?

The Whispering Gallery is one of the most famous features of Sir Christopher Wren's great master-piece, St Paul's Cathedral in London.

If you speak in this gallery, which runs round the inside of the great dome, the sound waves of your voice will be carried round to the opposite side of the gallery because the waves are prevented from going outwards by the stones lining the circular wall.

The great dome of St Paul's is really two domes – an outer dome with a diameter of 148 feet and an inner dome with a diameter of 103 feet. A hollow cone of brick-work between them supports a steeple-like structure in six diminishing stages culminating in the ball and cross. The top of the cross is 404 feet above the ground.

St Paul's has been acclaimed as the most magnificent domed building of the Renaissance period. It replaced the Norman cathedral which was destroyed in the Great Fire of London in 1666 and whose tower and spire were 124 feet higher than the present building.

The foundation stone of the new St Paul's was laid in 1675 and 35 years later the final stone of the cupola was put into position.

Great craftsmen were employed on the interior decoration. Francis Bird carved the Conversion of St Paul over the great pediment. Grinling Gibbons, one of England's and the world's finest woodcarvers, worked on the choir stalls, and the wrought iron work was done by Jean Tijou, the renowned ironsmith.

During the Second World War St Paul's was hit three times by bombs, the most serious damage being the destruction of the high altar on the night of October 10, 1940. The new high altar was dedicated as a British Common-wealth war memorial in May, 1958.

The tombs of many famous men – Nelson, Wellington, Roberts, Jellicoe and Beatty – are either in the cathedral or in the crypt beneath. Wren, too, is buried there, and his epitaph is inscribed in Latin over the north door. It is *Si monumentum requiris, circum-spice* – If you seek his memorial, look around you.

WHEN WAS BRAILLE INVENTED?

Braille was invented by a French-man, Louis Braille, in about 1829. It is an alphabet consisting of an arrangement of raised dots, which can be read by blind people using their sense of touch. While Braille was cutting some leather in his father's shop at the age of three, a knife slipped and plunged into an eye causing blindness.

In 1819, when he was 10 years old, the boy went to Paris with a scholarship to study at the National Institution for Blind Children. The institution's founder hit on the idea of providing texts in embossed

Roman lettering which the blind could decipher.

Two years after Braille's arrival Charles Barbier exhibited at the institution an apparatus by which a coded message in dots and dashes could be embossed on cardboard. Braille worked on this system and was able to adapt it to meet the need of the sightless. He published expositions of his system in 1829 and 1837.

Braille became a dedicated teacher at his school and also a talented organist. It was through his life's work that thousands of blind people today can read.

WHAT ARE THE SMALL HOURS?

The small hours are the early hours of the morning from midnight until daybreak, or in winter until about 5 o'clock.

They are the time when most people are asleep. But others find that, if they can stay awake past their normal bedtime when their bodies get drowsy, they do their best work then.

Winston Churchill, the great British war prime minister, was such a person. He used to sleep for an hour until midnight and hold his councils of war in the small hours, to the annoyance of his advisers who would rather have been asleep.

The end of the small hours in summer is heralded by the dawn chorus when the birds wake each other up with their songs.

WHY DID MONASTERIES HAVE HERB GARDENS?

An important feature of all monasteries in the Middle Ages was the infirmary or home for the sick and the aged, and the herb garden, or herbarium, was there to provide the necessary ingredients for making up medicines.

Herbal medicines, usually derived from the juices of certain plants, have been used since the dawn of history. In the 3rd Century B.C., Theophrastus, a Greek, wrote a "History of Plants". In the 2nd Century A.D., Dioscorides used herbal remedies in his position as official physician to the Roman armies. During the Middle Ages, monks studied the works written by Dioscorides on herbal remedies and added to these the results of their own experiments and practical experience. The oldest established hospitals are direct survivals of the monastic infirmaries of the Middle Ages. The best known exponent of herbal medicines was Nicholas Culpepper (1616–1654), whose book "The Complete Herbal" is still available today.

WHERE IS THE WORLD'S LARGEST PAINTING?

The largest painting ever made was undoubtedly *Panorama of the Mississippi*, completed by the American John Banvard in 1846.

The painting depicted the great river over its 1,200 miles course, on a strip some 5,000 feet long and 12 feet wide. In area it was nearly as big as a field of an acre and a half – an amazing size.

But this painting was destroyed when the barn on Long Island, New York, where it was stored burned down in 1891.

The largest painting now in existence is *The Battle of Gettysburg*, completed in 1883 after two-and-a-half years' work. It took Paul Philippoteaus of France and 16 assistants to paint the 410-foot-long picture. It is 70 feet high and weighs nearly five-and-a-half tons. The painting is now in a private collection in Winston-Salem, North Carolina, United States. Size alone, of course, is no guide to quality.

WHEN DID WOOLWORTH'S BEGIN?

Woolworth's began in 1879 when Frank Winfield Woolworth (1852–1919) opened a "five cent" store in Utica, New York with the financial help of W. H. Moore, a former employer. That store was unsuccessful, but later in the year he opened a "five and ten cent" store in Lancaster, Pennsylvania, with a larger selection of goods to sell. His idea of selling a wide variety of merchandise at two fixed prices proved so popular that he was soon opening stores in other cities.

Similar stores were started by Woolworth's brother, C. S. Woolworth, his cousin, Seymour H. Knox, and his friends, F. M. Kirby

and E. P. Charlton. All were merged in 1912 into the F. W. Woolworth company.

When Frank Woolworth died at Glen Cove, Long Island on April 8, 1919, his company owned more than 1,000 stores and his personal fortune amounted to many millions of dollars. The great Woolworth empire still operates and expands throughout the world, and the famous 60-storey Woolworth building in New York, designed by Cass Gilbert in 1931, is regarded as one of the most beautiful early skyscrapers.

WHAT IS A FLYING BUTTRESS?

The name "buttress" in architecture is given to a mass of masonry which stands out from the face of a wall, either to strengthen that wall or to resist the thrust from an arch or a roof. The flying buttress was a Gothic innovation and is a kind of half-arch or half-bridge of masonry spanning the space from the buttress proper to the neighbouring wall.

Buttressing began in the great buildings of the later Roman Empire but it was not until the Romanesque period that really large outside buttresses began to appear. As the naves of churches became roofed with ribbed vaults, a tremendous number of thrusts were concentrated into each bay and the flying buttress was evolved to counter them. Where the nave wall was of great height, as at

326

Beauvais Cathedral, in France, two, or even three half-arches— one over the other—formed the flying buttress. By the 15th Century, few large buildings were without flying buttresses, which were often pierced and richly traceried. Many cathedrals in England, such as Exeter, Salisbury, Winchester and Sherborne Abbey in Dorset, show magnificent examples of flying buttresses as well as the richly decorated buttress pinnacles which often accompany them.

An artist's impression of a Yeti.

WHERE WOULD YOU HUNT FOR THE ABOMINABLE SNOWMAN?

The Abominable Snowman or Yeti is a half-human, half-ape figure of legend among the Nepalese of the high Himalayas. Nepalese mothers use the tradition of the Yeti to scare their disobedient children. "The Yeti will get you if you don't watch out" is a popular warning.

No one can say whether the Yeti actually exists. The first apparent confirmation of its existence came with photographs of huge footprints in the snow taken by Eric Shipton, the mountaineer, in 1951. Few people claim to have seen the Yeti and some believe it to be invisible.

Skins which the Nepalese say have been taken from dead Yetis turn out to be those of the serow goat-antelope or of the rare Tibetan blue bear. Tracks in the snow said to be the Yeti's footprints have proved to be those of a snow leopard, a bear, a wolf or a fox, which have melted to form the larger, man-like tracks of the Yeti. Nevertheless, the legend lingers and it may yet be proved to have a basis in fact.

WHEN DID SHAKESPEARE WRITE HIS PLAYS?

William Shakespeare (1564–1616), widely regarded as the world's greatest poet and playwright, is believed to have written his 34 plays between 1591 and 1614. His first play is thought to have been *Henry VI* and his last two were probably *The Tempest* and *Henry VIII*.

In 1594 Shakespeare was a member of the Lord Chamberlain's company of players which performed nearly all the time in London. When James I succeeded to the throne in 1603, he took the company under his patronage as the King's Men. They played at the Globe Theatre, Bankside, which was burned down in June 1613 during a performance of *Henry VIII*.

In 1611 Shakespeare left London and lived the life of a retired gentleman in his native Warwickshire town of Stratford-on-Avon.

WHAT IS THE TENNESSEE VALLEY AUTHORITY?

The Tennessee Valley Authority (T.V.A.) was a United States government agency established in 1933 to control floods, improve navigation and produce electrical power along the Tennessee River and its tributaries. Its jurisdiction is generally limited to the drainage basin of the river which covers parts of seven states – Alabama, Georgia, Kentucky, Mississippi, North Carolina, Tennessee and Virginia.

America's fifth largest river, the Tennessee, was interrupted in its westward flow at Muscle Shoals, Alabama, where it dropped 100 feet in the course of 20 miles. Many schemes for generating hydroelectric power had been put forward, but it was not until 1933 that the decision was made. At that time the United States was experiencing a great depression and President Franklin Delano Roosevelt (1882–1945) strongly favoured development at Muscle Shoals which would stimulate the economy of the region.

The authority eventually operated 32 major dams and river traffic increased from 33 million ton miles in 1933 to more than 2,000 million in the 1960s. The T.V.A. power system possesses a huge generating capacity which is sold in bulk. Nitrate plants at Muscle Shoals have been developed into a vast laboratory for the development and production of experimental fertilizers, and studies of forest conditions have been carried out.

The T.V.A. also played an important part in increasing recreational opportunities in the valley. The "Great Lakes of the South" provide many such facilities.

WHY DO WE NEED PASSPORTS?

Passports have been used for centuries as a means of identifying and protecting people travelling in foreign countries in times of both peace and war. But the adoption of the passport as an essential travel document is fairly recent.

The development of compulsory passports was accompanied by the introduction of visas. These are endorsements by officials of foreign states that entry is permitted.

Originally a passport, as the word indicates, meant permission to leave a port or to sail into it. Later this was extended to include a general permission of exit and entry.

WHO FIRST USED KEYS?

The first known form of lock and key was used by the Assyrians in the Middle East about 4,000 years ago. This was revealed by the discovery of such a lock in the ruins of the palace of the Assyrian kings at Khorsabad, near the site of the city of Nineveh on the River Tigris in modern Iraq.

The lock was made of wood with the bolt held in a closed position by several loose wooden pins. The lock could be operated by inserting a long wooden key also fitted with pins, which would raise the loose pins enough to allow the bolt to be withdrawn.

This type of lock was apparently known to the Egyptians. It has also been found in Japan, the Faroe Islands and Norway. The long keys were carried on the shoulder, a fact which accounts for the verse in Isaiah 22-22: "And the key of the house of David will I lay upon his shoulder."

Another ancient type of lock known to the Chinese and the ancient Egyptians was the tumbler lock, improved versions of which are still in use today. This lock has small movable levers or "tumblers" and is opened with a key whose indentations will raise each tumbler exactly to the proper height.

Metal locks and keys were invented by the Romans. They designed a lock with a number of ridges or "wards" on the inside. These prevent the turning of the key unless the grooves on it coincide with the wards.

WHAT IS THE KORAN?

The Koran is the sacred book on which is founded the religion of the Mohammedans, the followers of the Prophet Mohammed (about A.D. 570–632). The name comes from the Arabic *qu'ran* meaning "that should be read". It is used in public worship and is the chief textbook in Mohammedan schools. Upon the Koran are based the Mohammedan laws and way of life.

This sacred book is the word of Allah (God) revealed in a vision to Mohammed by the Archangel Gabriel. Mohammed, who could not write, dictated Gabriel's words to his friends. These were written on dried palm leaves, bits of leather, whitened shoulder-blades of sheep or whatever was to hand. Soon after the prophet's death, Caliph Abu Bakr (A.D. 573–634) called a conference of those who had heard Mohammed, and ordered the writing of an authentic Koran. All variations on it were destroyed. Because of this, and because of the phenomenal verbal memory Arabs are known to possess, it is almost certain that the Koran is indeed composed of the authentic sayings of Mohammed.

The Koran is about as long as the New Testament. It is written in rhymed prose and is divided into 114 *suras* or chapters, each of which begins with the words "In the name of God, the merciful, the compassionate". It consists of history, legends, prophecies, moral precepts and laws.

The histories are chiefly about Old Testament characters, and many of the laws are the same as those of Judaism or Christianity. Moses, Jesus and Mohammed are named as the greatest prophets, and the Bible is held in great respect. Mohammedans are told to treat "the peoples of the Book" (i.e. Jews and Christians) with kindness.

The most important teaching is the oneness of God – "There is no God but Allah". Submission to his will (Islam) is the highest virtue. The Last Judgment is stressed. Then everyone shall receive reward or punishment for his deeds. The Mohammedan must pray five times a day, turning towards Mecca, the holy city, which is in Saudi Arabia. He must also make at least one pilgrimage to Mecca, if he can afford it.

WHEN WAS MAH JONGG FIRST PLAYED?

Mah Jongg is probably of 19th Century origin. It is a Western version of a Chinese game and is played with 136 to 144 pieces or tiles, similar to dominoes. These are engraved with Chinese symbols and characters and divided into suits and honours. The object of the four players is to complete combinations or sets of these tiles.

The name Mah Jongg was coined and copyrighted by Joseph P. Babcock, a United States resident of Shanghai, who is credited with introducing the game to the West after the First World War. He wrote a modified set of rules, gave English titles to the tiles and added index letters and numerals familiar to Western card players.

His game became a craze in the United States, Britain and Australia in the mid 1920s. It was revived in 1935 but did not regain its earlier popularity. The words Mah Jongg signify a mythical bird which appears on one of the tiles.

WHERE IS THE LEVANT?

The Levant is the name given to the eastern Mediterranean and the adjoining lands of Turkey, Syria, Lebanon and Israel. Levant means "east". The levanter wind is a strong easterly wind in the Mediterranean.

In English history the Levant was indirectly the cause of the Crown using customs and excise to raise revenue. The Levant Company was in 1581 given the monopoly of trading with Constantinople (now called Istanbul), the meeting place of traders from east and west.

This company claimed that it protected routes and ensured the safe passage of merchant ships. It therefore charged merchants duty on goods arriving in England. The Levant Company continued in being until 1825, but its power to levy duty was taken back by the Crown in the reign of James 1. Customs and excise have been an onerous and unpopular method of raising revenue ever since.

WHAT IS PERFECT PITCH?

Perfect pitch is the ability to identify by ear, or to sing, any musical note with extreme accuracy and without recourse to an instrument. The gift, possessed by few and impossible to acquire, is not essential to musicians, but is of enormous help to them if they are lucky enough to possess it. Many composers have had this gift, but two who lacked it were Wagner and Schumann.

In ancient Greece, where instruments were mainly stringed, no fixed pitch standard was used. This was the case even in Renaissance times. When large wind and string orchestras were created it became necessary to agree on one constant. The organ was chosen because the standard note it gave was less variable than that of other instruments.

For unaccompanied singing a pitch pipe or tuning fork is often used. If the conductor has perfect pitch, he can give a note or a range of notes himself without the use of an aid. In unaccompanied choral music, therefore, perfect pitch is a particularly valuable accomplishment.

WHEN IS A PERSON EXCOMMUNICATED?

Excommunication occurs when a person is punished by being officially excluded from a religious community and banned from entering into "communion" with the other members. The later epistles of St Paul show that this exclusion was carried out as a last resort against those who had "made a shipwreck of their faith", either by immorality or by denying what were regarded as the fundamentals of Christian teaching.

The Roman Catholic Church distinguishes between two types of excommunication, that which leaves a person *toleratus*, or tolerated, and that which makes him *vitandus*, or someone who must be avoided.

Both kinds bar the person from the sacraments of the Church, as well as from Church burial. There is a specific list of offences punishable by excommunication. They include heresy, schism, blasphemous treatment of the eucharist, personal violence against the Pope and membership of forbidden societies.

HOW DO FINGERPRINTS DIFFER?

The skin's surface is marked by a series of fine lines and ridges which deepen with age. The pattern on the tips of the fingers is peculiar to each individual and is used as a means of identification. In fact, the ridges of the skin on the lower finger joints and the toe prints are also unique, as are palm prints and foot prints. But fingerprints are by far the most simple and effective identification method.

Each ridge of the outer skin (epidermis) is dotted with sweat pores and anchored to the inner

Arches

Loops

Whorls

Composites

skin (dermis) by a double row of peglike objects called papillae. Injuries which affect the epidermis do not alter the ridge structure, and the original pattern returns in the new skin. If the papillae are destroyed, however, the ridges will disappear.

There are five general pattern shapes or types: the arch, the tented arch, the radial loop, the ulnar loop and the whorl. Whorls are usually circular or spiral, arches are shaped like a mound or hill and tented arches have a spike or "steeple" in the centre. Loops have concentric hairpin-shaped ridges and are divided into "radial" and "ulnar" to denote their slopes in relation to the radius and ulna bones of the forearm. Ulnar loops slope towards the little finger side of the hand and radial loops slope towards the thumb.

The pattern on our fingertips remains the same from birth until death, barring deliberate or accidental destruction of the papillae. Fingerprints therefore provide a positive identification, and the practice of fingerprinting (dactyloscopy) is an essential part of police procedure.

WHERE IS THE LITTLE MERMAID?

The famous bronze statue of the Little Mermaid, carved by Edvard Eriksen, is posed on a rock near the Langelinie promenade in Copenhagen Harbour, Denmark. She is the heroine of Hans Christian Andersen's fairy tale about a mermaid who falls in love with a prince and who sacrifices her tongue to exchange her fishtail for human legs.

Hans Christian Andersen (1805–75) was born in Odense, Denmark. When he was 14, he went to Copenhagen to try to be an actor or opera singer. He was not successful and turned to writing, but failed in that, too. However, a friend who had faith in his talent persuaded the King of Denmark to grant him a pension, so that he could continue his education and travel to other countries. Soon afterwards he began to write poems, plays, novels and travel books that sold well.

Nowadays these are all forgotten, and the world remembers him for his fairy tales which appeared in 1835. Today they are published in more than 60 languages.

WHAT ARE TAROT CARDS?

Tarot cards are the oldest form of playing cards in Europe. They were made in Italy in the late 14th Century.

The name comes from *tarocchi*, a game played with a 78-card pack in which there are four suits. The emblems of these suits symbolized the four "estates" into which society was divided–the church (represented by a chalice), the nobility (by a sword), the merchants (by money) and the peasants (by clubs). Each suit contains 14 cards, the additional card being the valet.

As well as the four suits, there are 21 numbered trump cards and the joker card (il Pazzo). The first five cards are the magician, the high priestess, the empress, the emperor and the pope. These are called the *grands atouts* (big trumps). The last five cards, the star, the moon, the sun, judgment and the world, are the *petits atouts* (little trumps). The remainder of the *atouts* consists of the lovers, the chariot, justice, the hermit, the wheel of fortune, the hanged man, death, temperance, the devil and the tower.

From this list you can see how tarot cards came to be used not just for a game but also as a way of telling fortunes. In fortune-telling the position of a card is all important. A death card upright means a need for change, the beginning of a new phase. If the card is reversed, it means that the subject cannot make any change. He has reached an impasse in his affairs. The devil upright means an urge to give way to temptations. Reversed, the card means a re-pressed character.

A 56-card pack evolved from the tarot pack. Then came the English and French 52-card pack, the Spanish 48-card pack and the German 32-card pack. The tarot symbols are still used in these shortened packs.

WHY DO FASHIONS IN CLOTHES CHANGE?

Fashions in clothes change for almost as many different reasons as there are fashions. Among the chief causes are changes in the kind of work we do, the cost and availability of the materials used and the invention of new materials, such as man-made fibres.

The attitude of different societies towards the body and how much of it should be displayed is also important. For example, if a girl in the Middle Ages had worn a mini-skirt she would have been regarded as either mad or wicked. Social standards change from age to age and from country to country.

There have been dramatic changes in fashion in our century, partly owing to the availability of new and cheap materials and partly because this generation believes that clothes should be a matter of personal choice, and comfortable as well as attractive.

Many of the fussy clothes of our ancestors, often requiring yards and yards of material, would be too expensive to produce today. They would also be unsuited to modern living – imagine cycling in a crinoline!

Great wars often influence fashions. During the Second World War the style of women's clothes became military. Jackets for instance had square and padded shoulders. After the war, this fashion changed to the voluminous, more feminine, new look of Dior, the great French designer.

Another big change happened after the First World War. Women who had worked for the first time with men in the factories during the war, began to dress with greater freedom and started to wear short skirts.

Today, what we wear is largely a matter of personal choice, convenience and what we can afford.

WHEN IS TWELFTH NIGHT?

Twelfth Night is the night of the twelfth day after Christmas. It is one of the oldest festival days of the Christian Church, and was celebrated as long ago as the 3rd

Century. Another name for the festival is Epiphany, or the Feast of the Three Kings. It commemorates the showing of the infant Jesus to the three Magi, or holy men, from the East.

According to tradition Twelfth Night is the day Christmas decorations are taken down.

WHERE WOULD YOU LOOK FOR A YARD OF ALE?

You would look for, and perhaps find, a yard of ale in an old public house or a tavern in England. It is a narrow tube, three feet long, opening out at one end and with a bulb at the other. When filled with ale or beer, it forms one yard of ale. Although now rare, these strange-shaped glasses can still be found hanging on the walls of inns, particularly old or historic ones, as a curiosity.

This odd drinking vessel was an example of the glass-blower's art. But it was never in general use for drinking. Instead it was used either as a joke or as a challenge. When the glass was filled to the brim with ale or beer, the contestant had to drink "the yard" without pausing or taking breath. At a really lively party, every man present would have had to take his turn. When this type of entertainment was popular, the locally brewed ale was probably less strong and intoxicating than it is now. But the feat still required considerable swallowing power and breath control.

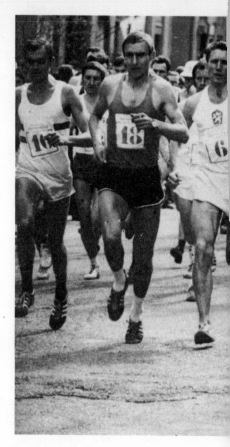

WHAT IS THE MARATHON?

The marathon is a modern road race first staged at the revival of the Olympic Games at Athens, Greece, in 1896. It was founded in honour of the Greek soldier Pheidippides, who is supposed to have run from Marathon to Athens, a distance of 22 miles and 1,470 yards, in 490 B.C. to bring the news of his countrymen's victory over the Persians. Appropriately, the first winner of the marathon race was a Greek, Spyros Louis.

In 1924 the Olympic marathon distance was standardized at 26

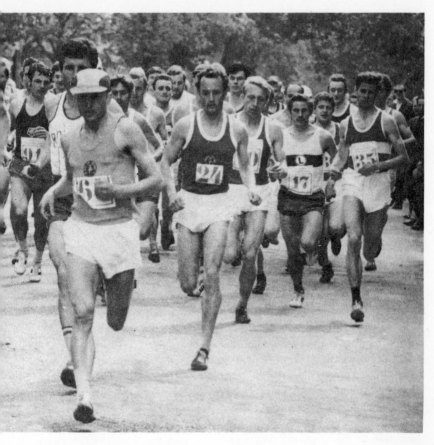

Runners shortly after the start of the fourth International Marathon race held in 1970 in the German Democratic Republic.

miles, 385 yards. But other marathon courses may differ in length, so the International Amateur Athletic Federation does not list a world record time for the event.

It is a fascinating race because neither age nor training seems to play a vital part in winning it. The South African Comrades' Marathon (54 miles and 1,100 yards) was won in 1922 by Arthur Newton at the age of 39. The Boston Athletic Association Marathon was won by a 19-year-old Japanese in 1951.

Long-distance training would seem to be essential for the race. But in the 1952 Olympic Games, Emil Zatopek of Czechoslovakia, set an Olympic record of 2 hours, 23 minutes, 3·2 seconds, although he had never run the distance before.

Zatopek's record was broken in 1960 by the Ethiopian, Abebe Bikila, who covered the distance, barefooted, in 2 hours, 15 minutes, 16·2 seconds. In the next Olympic

Games, four years later, running with shoes that time, he again broke the world record, with a time of 2 hours, 12 minutes, 11·2 seconds.

WHY DO SIKHS WEAR TURBANS?

Sikhs wear their symbolic turbans because they have long hair. The turban keeps the hair free of dust and dirt and keeps it out of the way so that they can live and work comfortably. The Sikhs' religion, which forbids them to cut their hair, is a mixture of two faiths – the Muslim and Hindu. Drinking and smoking and, indeed, all practises that are bad for the health of the body are banned. The Sikh religion allows both men and women to perform religious ceremonies. The Sikhs believe that all men and women are equal.

At the Hindu New Year in 1699, the Guru (or teacher) Gobind Rai, assembled his followers in the foothills of the Himalayas and initiated five of them as members of a fraternity which he named Khalsa, which means pure. They drank amrit (nectar) out of the same bowl, although they all came from different castes. Also, they received new names with the suffix Singh (lion) and swore to keep the five K's which were: to wear long hair (kesh), a comb (kangha) in the hair, soldiers' shorts (kachha), a steel bangle (kara) on the right wrist, and a sabre (kirpan).

In the days that followed, 80,000 people were initiated into the Khalsa fraternity.

Sikh boys and girls now undergo the initiation ceremony of the five K's at the age of puberty. Boys take the additional name of Singh, but not all persons named Singh are Sikhs. The corresponding name for Sikh women is Kaur.

The Sikhs are excellent farmers, soldiers and mechanics. The proportion of literacy among them is higher than among any of the other major communities of India.

WHEN WERE NEWSPAPERS FIRST PRODUCED?

The earliest regular newspapers of which we have record date back many centuries before the invention of printing to the *Acta Diurna* of the Roman Empire and the gazettes published in China during the first centuries of the Christian era.

The *Acta Diurna* or *Daily Acts* began regular and official publication on the orders of Julius Caesar in 59 B.C. The news was collected by reporters (*actuarii*) employed by the state who posted the *Acta* on a whitened board so that all could read or copy the reports of wars, speeches, legal decisions, political events, marriages, divorces, accidents and deaths.

Pioneers in printing, the Germans were also pioneers in printed newspapers. The first irregular news-sheets began to appear in Cologne, Nürnberg and other cities within 50 years of the invention of modern printing in 1450. By the end of the 17th Century a number of German towns were reading their own daily papers, thus establishing a tradition for local dailies which has been maintained to this day.

In 1562 Venice had a printed monthly newspaper which was sold for a *gazetta*, a small coin with a name which soon became another word for a newspaper. Among the first journals to use the name was the *Gazette de France* of 1631.

The first regular newspaper in the English language was produced in Holland in 1620 by the English Puritans who later sailed to America in the Mayflower. But more than 80 years were to pass before the first English daily, the *Daily Courant* appeared in 1702.

The first American newspaper, called *Public Occurrences*, was published in Boston on September 25, 1690, but was suppressed by the authorities before it could produce a second issue. The first regular American paper was the Boston *News-Letter* which appeared in April 1704 and ran for more than 70 years.

WHERE ARE CATACOMBS FOUND?

The most famous catacombs in the world are to be found in Rome. The word catacomb is of unknown origin, and describes subterranean cemeteries composed of galleries or passages with side recesses for tombs. It seems to have been applied first to the catacombs of St Sebastian, on the Appian Way near Rome, which became famous as the supposed temporary resting place of the bodies of Saints Peter and Paul in the last half of the 3rd Century.

Catacombs are by no means confined to Rome. The custom of burying the dead in underground rock chambers goes far back into antiquity, and catacombs are found all over the Mediterranean world.

Most of the Christian catacombs – about 40 of which are known – belong to the 3rd Century and the early part of the 4th. Ruined by the Goths in the 6th Century and later by the Lombards, they were abandoned and their very existence forgotten until they were rediscovered by chance in 1578.

All the catacombs follow roughly the same pattern. Beginning as small private burial areas they finally became vast labyrinths of narrow galleries, usually three to four feet wide, lighted and ventilated by shafts spaced at wide intervals. The galleries led to small rooms called "cubicula" and the bodies lay in grave niches, cut in the wall or floor and sealed by slabs of marble or huge tiles.

The catacombs were used in times of persecution as hiding places, but there seems to be no truth in the widespread belief that early Christians used the catacombs as secret meeting places for worship.

WHO ESTABLISHED THE PEACE CORPS?

The Peace Corps was established by President John F. Kennedy on March 1, 1961 and became a permanent United States government agency under The Department of State in the following September. Its aim, in the words of President Kennedy, was to create, "a pool of trained American

A young Peace Corps volunteer at work in Africa.

men and women sent overseas by the United States government to help foreign countries meet their need power".

Volunteers for the Peace Corps must be United States citizens and at least 18 years old. An accepted volunteer is assigned to a project requested by a foreign country and prepares for his task by studying for three months at a United States college or university. During this time he learns the language, history, politics and customs of the country to which he is to be sent. When he goes overseas, he works directly with the inhabitants of the country, speaking their language, sharing their lives and receiving a living allowance comparable to that earned by the people among whom he is working.

The normal term of service is two years. In 1961 about 900 volunteers served in 16 different countries of Latin America, Asia and Africa and the number has risen steadily each year. Two years after its foundation the corps won the Ramon Magsaysay Award, the 10,000 dollar prize which is the Asian equivalent to the Nobel Peace Prize. This had never before been won by a non-Asian group.

WHAT IS A WITCH DOCTOR?

Among many tribes the most important member, after the chief, is the witch doctor or medicine man. He combines the roles of priest and healer and is regarded with fear and respect. Often he may claim to have power over the spirit world, or to be able to read the secrets of the past and foretell the future.

The witch doctor is responsible for the magical rites for ensuring rain, fruitful crops or good hunting. He also enforces obedience to

taboos and rituals, and may cast a spell upon any man who disobeys them. Such a spell may prove fatal to a victim who believes in it.

In his capacity as healer, the witch doctor acquires a specialized knowledge of herbs, many of which form the basis of modern medicines. Even so, the cure will not be tried without the use of magical charms, spells and ritual.

WHEN WAS STONEHENGE BUILT?

Stonehenge was built on Salisbury Plain, Wiltshire, England, apparently in three different stages between 1800 and 1400 B.C.

The first stage consisted of a circular ditch and bank, with a series of circular holes called Aubrey holes after the man who discovered them. It also included the Hele Stone. There may have been a structure of stone or wood at the centre of the circle.

During the second stage of construction, which probably took place about 200 years later, the entrance of the earthwork was widened on the east side and connected to the River Avon by a processional way marked by parallel banks and ditches. At the same time a number of Blue Stones, which were apparently brought from the Prescelly Mountains in Pembrokeshire, South Wales, were erected in the centre of the site to form two circles.

The third stage of the work is thought to have been begun after

1600 B.C. The entire monument was remodelled, and about 80 large blocks of sarsen were presumably transported from the Marlborough Downs north of the site. These were erected in a circle of 30 uprights, capped by a continuous ring of stone lintels.

It is generally assumed that Stonehenge was constructed as a place of worship, but its exact purpose is unknown. There is an astronomical explanation for the placing of the stones where they are in relation to the rising and the setting sun.

WHO WAS UNCLE SAM?

It is thought that the original Uncle Sam was an affable, pleasant man named Samuel Wilson (1766–1854), who lived in Troy, New York State, and supplied beef to the United States Army in the war with Britain in 1812. Wilson was known locally as "Uncle Sam" and, as government purchasers stamped U.S. on the barrels of meat being shipped, local workmen referred to it as "Uncle Sam's beef".

Tradition has it that the name was picked up by soldiers and soon came into familiar usage as a nickname for the United States. A resolution passed by the Congress of the United States in 1961 recognized Wilson as the namesake of the national symbol.

The symbolic Uncle Sam is a tall, thin, angular figure with long white hair and chin whiskers. He is usually dressed in a swallow-tailed coat, waistcoat, top hat and striped trousers. In American stories and tales he is associated with Yankee Doodle, the British-inspired nickname for American colonials during the American Revolution, and with Brother Jonathan, a country folk-hero who always beats his enemies by surprising displays of native intelligence and wit.

WHERE WAS SOCCER FIRST PLAYED?

Soccer is a corruption of the word "association". Since the rules of Association Football were laid down by the Football Association, formed in England in 1863, it can be said that soccer began in England.

Where football began, on the other hand, is a question impossible to answer. Various forms of a game involving the kicking about of a ball were played by the ancient Chinese, and by the Greeks and Romans. By the early Middle Ages several types of mass football, often with hundreds of people taking part, were very popular. Indeed, football's popularity led to its being banned for a long time in England as it interfered with the practice of archery which was considered necessary for the defence of the country.

The team game, which led to the formation of the Football Association, was born on the playing fields of English public schools.

Soccer is now one of the world's most popular and widely followed sports. It is particularly popular throughout Europe and Central and South America.

WHAT DOES PERFUME CONSIST OF?

Perfume is made up of vegetable oils, the odours of certain animals and chemical additives. Perfume-making, like cookery, is done from a recipe, a formula. The perfumer takes his list of ingredients and blends them together in a special way. One of the expensive perfumes worn by women on their throats and wrists (the heat from the throbbing at these pulse points brings out the smell) may contain up to two hundred ingredients.

The first smell that reaches you when you open the bottle and dab on the scent is the vegetable oil, a blend of the oils of flowers and herbs varying from lavender, jasmine and rose, to clove and rosemary and even carrot and onion oils. They are extracted by squeezing, or by the use of solvents.

The second category consists of animal odours which give the scent persistence. These include ambergris, which is phlegm coughed up by the sperm whale, a gland secretion of the civet cat, musk from the musk deer and castoreum resin from the beaver.

The third set of ingredients, the chemical ones, are used to set off and fill out the flower and animal products. They are much cheaper.

The blending of these ingredients calls for great skill, and a perfumer takes many years to learn his art.

Not all perfumes are sold in bottles or even in cosmetic products. One of the perfumer's main tasks is to disguise the bad smells in products such as detergents and plastics, and to provide the smells which people have come to associate with certain products. Plastic car seats are given the smell of leather. Restaurants can buy a bottle of bacon and hamburger essence for an appetizing aroma.

WHEN IS AN OVERTURE PLAYED?

An overture was originally a piece of music played as an introduction to an opera and suggesting some of the themes that were to follow.

The earliest operas usually opened with a trumpet fanfare or a sung prologue, as in the work of the French composer Luly. This form of the French overture was widely copied by German composers.

A more modern style was established by the German composer Glück who declared that an overture should "prepare the audience for the plot of the play". He meant that the overture should not be brought to a close with the rising of the curtain, but should be merged into the mood of the opening act. Glück's example was followed by Mozart in, for example, his overture to Don Giovanni, and by Beethoven in his overture to Leonore.

Towards the end of the 19th Century the opera overture was frequently replaced by a shorter introductory prelude, notably in Wagner's Lohengrin. This was an entirely new concept which was carried a stage further in Benjamin Britten's overture to Peter Grimes, which consists of only 10 bars.

In the 19th Century the concert overture became established as an independent work, as in the case of Mendelssohn's Hebrides Overture. Some overtures took on the character of symphonic poems. They are now often heard as part of a concert and not merely as introductions to operas or plays.

WHAT KIND OF A PERSON IS A LOTUS-EATER?

A lotus-eater is someone who is forgetful and careless about responsibility, living only for pleasure. The original lotus-eaters, or Lotophagi, were a people whom Odysseus and his men encountered in Homer's great epic poem, the Odyssey. They lived on a plant called lotus, which they offered to travellers. Those who ate of it forgot home, friends and responsibilities and wanted only to lie in the sun and eat lotus for ever.

The lotus in the poem is Zizyphus lotus, from South Europe. It has large fruits holding a mealy material which can be used for making bread or wine.

WHERE IS THE QUARTER-DECK OF A SHIP?

The quarter-deck, as its name implies, is only part of a deck. In a sailing vessel it is that portion of the upper deck between the mainmast and the stern or back of the ship. The upper deck is the highest complete deck having all openings fitted with permanent means for closure against sea and weather.

In naval vessels the quarter-deck is that most glamorous part of the ship, an area of the weather deck—the highest continuous deck exposed to the weather—reserved for the officers of the ship.

Ship's decks serve the same purpose as floors and roofs in a building. They provide living and working surfaces, add strength to the structure of a ship and form a cover to keep bad weather out. Decks may be given numbers or letters to distinguish them from each other, but those which serve a definite purpose have their own distinctive names.

In the British Navy officers are allowed to drink the loyal toast seated since in the old days the deck "ceilings" were so low.

WHO WERE THE HESPERIDES?

The Hesperides, in Greek mythology, were the maidens who guarded the tree that bore the golden apples given by Mother Earth to the goddess Hera, when she married Zeus. Another version of the myth says the maidens were

Hercules with two of the Hesperides.

the daughters of Erebus and Night. Their names are usually given as Aegle, Erytheia and Hesperis, and they lived in Arcadia, which was thought of as a sort of ideal Garden of Eden. Modern Arcadia is in central Greece.

WHEN ARE PEOPLE BURIED AT SEA?

Although burials at sea are much less common than in the days of sailing ships, they still occur on occasions when people die during a voyage and the boat is still a long way from its destination. A service is held on board and the weighted coffin is lowered into the sea.

Sometimes a burial at sea is carried out in accordance with a dead person's wishes, or the ashes are scattered over the waves after a cremation.

In ancient times sea burial was often practised as a cheap method of disposing of dead slaves, foreigners and people considered of little importance. Today some islands, where land is scarce, reserve parts of the sea near the coast as cemeteries.

Viking chiefs before the 10th Century were cremated on burning ships to symbolize a voyage to the land of the dead.

WHAT IS THE AMERICA'S CUP

The America's Cup is a gold cup offered originally by the Royal Yacht Squadron in 1851 for a 53-mile race round the Isle of Wight, off the south coast of England. The winner was the United States schooner America.

In 1857 the syndicate that had built the America gave the cup (thereafter known as the America's Cup) to the New York Yacht Club, which then offered the cup to all challengers. Subsequent races have been sailed off the American coast.

The N.Y.Y.C. offer to all still stands, but the British, Canadian and Australian challengers have never succeeded in any of the 22 contests.

The races have exerted great influence on yachting progress, the large sums spent on America's Cup yachts having raised the science and art of design to a high level of refinement.

WHY ARE U-BENDS USED IN PLUMBING?

U-bend pipes are installed under sinks and toilets to provide a water seal against the outside sewer pipes. The U-bend retains a permanent pool of clean water, protects the fixture and prevents any gases, vermin or bacteria from escaping out of the sewers.

The U-bend was invented in the middle of the 18th Century but, for economic reasons, was not widely used until more than 100 years later. Since its introduction the U-bend has been an important factor in preventing infectious illnesses and diseases in large cities.

WHERE WAS ROBINSON CRUSOE'S ISLAND?

Daniel Defoe's famous story of *Robinson Crusoe* (first published in 1719) is based on a real island – Juan Fernández. This island lies off the coast of Chile in South America and is now owned by that country. It was the scene of the true adventures of a Scottish sailor, Alexander Selkirk, who lived from 1676 to 1721.

Selkirk was born at Largs in Fife, became a sailor and, when he was young, took part in privateering expeditions to the South Seas, as the Pacific was then called. In 1704, he was the mate of the English vessel Cinque Ports. But he quarrelled with the captain and was left, at his own request, on the uninhabited island of Juan Fernández.

Before the ship departed, Selkirk begged to be taken on board again, but his request was refused and it was not until four years and four months had passed that he was rescued by the British ship Duke in January 1709. When abandoned Selkirk was left with clothes and bedding, pistol, gunpowder, bullets, tobacco, a hatchet, a Bible, mathematical instruments and books.

His powder soon gave out, but he learned to capture the goats on the island by running them down. He built himself a shelter and made clothes from the goats' skins. Fortunately, Juan Fernández never has very severe weather – only a little frost and hail in June and July (winter in the Southern Hemisphere). It is hot in the summer, but never unbearably so.

Selkirk found his island infested with rats, but kept down their numbers round his shelter by taming the stray cats whose ancestors had been left on the island by visiting ships.

He kept healthy and sane by working hard and by making companions of animals. But when he was rescued, he could scarcely make himself understood by the crew of the Duke, and he had lost all taste for civilized food and drink. He returned to England in 1711 and followed the life of the sea until his death.

WHO DISCOVERED THE SOURCE OF THE NILE?

The source of the Nile was finally discovered in 1862 by John Hanning Speke when he reached the Ripon Falls at the northern tip of Lake Victoria in Uganda.

Explorers had searched for the spot for centuries. As far back as the 2nd Century the Greek geographer Ptolemy learned enough from travellers' tales to trace a map of the Nile which was later found to be fairly accurate. It was believed that the waters of the Nile came from high snow-covered mountains in central Africa called the Mountains of the Moon.

Modern exploration of the upper part of the Nile began about 1837 when Mohammed Ali, the Turkish ruler of Egypt, ordered a search to be made for the river's source. Three Turkish-led expeditions were made and two of them got to within about 400 miles of their objective.

The Nile runs over 4,100 miles from its source to the Mediterranean.

WHAT IS A PLEBEIAN?

When we describe someone as plebeian we mean someone of low birth or rank and often someone who is undistinguished, commonplace, lacking in imagination or vulgar. The word comes from the Latin "plebeius" meaning a citizen who did not belong to one of the privileged patrician families.

A clear division between patricians and plebeians first developed in the early 5th Century. The patricians were descended from the "partres", a body of advisors who surrounded the early kings of Rome. They gradually excluded plebeians from many public offices, while continuous wars and the loss of trade worsened the conditions of the poorest plebeians. Some of these became slaves or "followers" (clientes), men who gave service and obedience in exchange for protection. In the years of prosperity the plebeians themselves developed a class structure, with their own wealthy élite, who became very influential. Leading families of plebs and patricians intermarried and a new nobility emerged drawn from a limited number of families who were as exclusive as the old patriciate had been.

Nevertheless, the word "plebeian" still has a contemptuous ring about it, indicating that a man is plodding, without finer feelings or nobility, dull and uncultured.

Shakespeare's play *Coriolanus* exemplifies this attitude of contempt towards classical plebeians. The over-proud Coriolanus refers scathingly to them as the "mutable rank-scented many" and, later, when he is banished from Rome, as "You common cry of curs! whose breath I hate as reek o' the rotten fens, whose loves I prize as the dead carcasses of unburied men that do corrupt my air." It seems not very surprising that he was unpopular.

WHEN WERE WIGS FIRST WORN?

The wearing of wigs by both men and women dates from our earliest recorded history. Wigs have been found on Egyptian mummies, and the appearance of the frizzled-out hair on some of the figures on the frescoes at Knossos suggests that wigs were also familiar to the ancient civilization of Crete. The Medes and Persians also wore artificial hair, and Greek women were using hairpieces by the 4th Century B.C. The Romans began wearing wigs in the early years of the Empire.

The word wig is a shortened version of periwig, which is derived from the French perruque. It was

347

1 Wig a la brigadie   2 Knotted wig
3 Abbe's wig   4 Woman's wig
5 Bag-wig   6 Square-wig
7 Newly growing wig

in 17th-Century France that wigs began to assume their greatest glory as features of men's fashion. Louis XIV, who was very proud of his own hair when he was young, did not wear a wig until after 1670 when he was in his 40s. From Versailles, the fashion then spread throughout Europe.

During the first decade of the 18th Century men's wigs reached their maximum size, covering shoulders and back, and floating down over the chest. After that they gradually became smaller until, for normal wear, they disappeared. In recent years wigs have again become popular with women and the wearing of artificial hairpieces has become an accepted device among men.

HOW DID PICASSO BECOME FAMOUS?

Pablo Ruiz Picasso was a Spanish painter, sculptor and engraver who lived from 1881 to 1973. He was a very independent artist and, with another painter called Georges Braque, founded a whole new movement in art which became known as Cubism.

At a very early age he showed exceptional talent. He went to the School of Fine Art in Barcelona and to the Academy of San Fernando in Madrid. Eventually, in 1905, he established himself in Paris.

Between 1899 and 1905 his first subjects were lively scenes of popular and bourgeois life–cabarets, racecourses, dance halls. Later he changed to depicting the victims of society–prostitutes, beggars, drunkards, the blind and the crippled.

He tried to get closer to what he felt was reality by approaching his subjects from several different angles. He extracted meanings from them and employed the fullest possible range of expressive techniques.

Eventually he started a new way of pictorial representation based on a shifting viewpoint, a free approach to colour and the right to show what one knows instead of what the eye sees. This was the start of Cubism which was an alternative pictorial language to naturalism.

He went through many changes of style and awareness, and his contribution to the world of art has been immense and revolutionary. His paintings are highly valued throughout the world.

WHY DO WE HAVE EASTER EGGS?

Easter eggs provide one of the many popular traditions that have grown up around the great spring celebration in the Christian calendar of the resurrection of Christ. During the period of Lent preceding Easter, eggs were forbidden as part of the fast in preparation for the festival. So it was natural for the end of Lent to be marked by the eating of eggs on Easter Sunday.

As traditional symbols of life and creation eggs suggested the resurrection. The decorations on the eggs can be regarded as symbolizing the end of the penitential season and the beginning of joyful celebration.

Sometimes eggs are blessed in church. Egg-rolling and egg-hunting are two self-descriptive Easter games. An expensive custom developed in Imperial Russia, where the nobility exchanged egg-shaped curios made of precious materials and decorated with jewels. These "eggs" are now extremely valuable.

Many of the folk customs and traditions now associated with Easter may be adaptations of practices connected with pagan spring ceremonies. So eggs coloured like the rays of the sun may have originally symbolized the return of spring.

WHERE IS THE LOST CONTINENT?

The lost continent is a legendary island called Atlantis. It was described by Plato, a philosopher who lived in ancient Greece, as being in the Atlantic and also as being larger than Asia Minor and Libya put together! The Greek legends claimed that Atlantis had been inhabited by a powerful nation who had offended the gods by their independence and disrespect. The gods took their revenge. Some versions of the story say that it was submerged and others that it was destroyed by an earthquake about 9,000 B.C.

Some people have tried to identify Atlantis with America, some with Scandinavia, the Canaries and even the Palestine

region. Many naturalists and philosophers, including Buffon, Montaigne and Voltaire, have theorized about Atlantis. Attempts have been made to prove that the Basques of Spain and France, the original inhabitants of Italy and the Indians of South America were descended from the Atlanteans, who were said to have overrun the entire Mediterranean.

One theory is that the Minoan civilization was destroyed by the eruption of a volcano on Thera (Santorin) – or "lost Atlantis".

WHEN IS THANKSGIVING DAY?

Thanksgiving Day is an annual national holiday which takes place in the United States and Canada on the last Thursday in November in celebration of the harvest and other blessings during the year.

The first Thanksgiving Day was observed when the Pilgrim Fathers held a three-day festival after the harvest of 1621. But the day was not celebrated as a regular national holiday until more than two centuries later. Gradually each state adopted the idea until, in 1863, President Lincoln proclaimed a national harvest festival on November 26.

The festival is still basically a home celebration, with religious overtones, for families and friends. Turkey is the traditional meat at the feast, and such autumnal dishes as pumpkin pie and plum pudding stress the harvest theme.

350

WHAT IS A GUERRILLA?

A guerrilla is a member of an independent body of fighters carrying on irregular warfare against authority. This usually involves fighting on a small scale against units of national armies. Guerrillas often use unconven- tional weapons and equipment, and are extremely mobile. Psychological warfare, including the use of sabotage and terrorism, is also part of their system of fighting.

Che Guevara: probably the best-known modern guerrilla leader.

"Guerrilla" is a Spanish word meaning "little war". The word came into use during the Duke of Wellington's campaigns when the Spanish-Portuguese irregulars or *guerrilleros* helped drive the French from the Iberian peninsula. Lawrence of Arabia, who made great use of guerrillas against the Turks in the First World War, once said: "Guerrilla war is much more intellectual than a bayonet charge".

Che Guevara of Cuba also made his name as a guerrilla. He was eventually shot while fighting in Bolivia for the Communists against the country's government.

WHEN WERE KNIVES AND FORKS INVENTED?

Knives were invented a long time before forks. Flint knives for general purposes were used in the Stone Age. The Romans had eating knives. But even in the 16th Century only very rich houses had enough knives for each guest at dinner to have one to himself. This meant that people often carried their own knives with them in a sheath round their waists. Often they were made in pairs so that even before forks were employed you did not have to use your fingers.

The first forks had only two prongs like a carving fork, and there was usually only one in a house. The use of forks at table was probably introduced into Europe from the East through the Venetians in the 11th Century.

WHERE DID BASEBALL BEGIN?

Abner Doubleday, later a general in the United States Army, was supposed to have laid out the first baseball field in Cooperstown, a village in Otsego County, New York State, in the summer of 1839 and there conducted the first game of baseball ever played. So strong was the belief in this story that in 1920 the playing field was established as a permanent memorial with the title Doubleday Field.

Doubts were later cast upon the story, and attempts made to prove that the game had evolved from the English children's game known as rounders. The name "baseball" to describe some popular English game was traced back to Jane Austen, who in *Northanger Abbey* (written about 1798) remarks of her heroine: "It was not very wonderful that Catherine, who had by nature nothing heroic about her, should prefer cricket, baseball, riding on horseback and running around the country at the age of 14, to books."

Then, in their attempt to tie up baseball with rounders, researchers came across *The Boy's Own Book*, published in London in 1828, and so popular that it ran into many editions. The book was about boys' sports and listed all the rules. The second edition includes a chapter entitled "Rounders" with a note that the game was called "feeder" in London and "baseball" in the southern counties.

As the game is described in

The Boy's Own Book it bears a strong family likeness to modern American baseball. It was played on a diamond with a base at each corner, the goal or fourth base being the same as the plate beside which the batter stood. A batter might run whenever he hit the ball across or over the diamond. If he struck at it and missed it three times, he was out.

Many English immigrants to America in colonial times were from the southern counties, and it seems probable that they took both the name and game with them.

WHY IS CONFUCIUS SO ADMIRED?

Confucius dedicated his life to attempting to relieve the suffering of the people of China, where he lived between 551 and 479 B.C. He was a philosopher and political theorist, whose ideas have deeply influenced the civilization of Eastern Asia.

This great teacher was deeply distressed by the misery he saw on every hand. The Chinese were oppressed by wars, taxes and hunger. Confucius believed the solution must lie in the creation of a form of government which would have as its objective not the pleasure of the rulers, but the happiness of the people.

He advocated such measures as the reduction of taxes, the mitigation of severe punishments and the avoidance of unnecessary war. He tried to secure a position of administrative influence; but in this he failed because the Chinese rulers thought his ideas dangerous. So he taught his beliefs to younger men and sought government posts for these disciples.

Confucius was the first man in China to use teaching as an instrument of reform. But he was not dogmatic or authoritarian. He merely asked questions and insisted that the students found the answers for themselves.

He declared: "If, when I point out one corner of the subject the student cannot work out the other three for himself, I do not go on."

His belief that the state should be a wholly co-operative enterprise was quite different from the ruling ideas of his time. Aristocrats were believed to rule by virtue of the authority and the powerful assistance of their divine ancestors.

The right to govern, Confucius held, depended upon the ability to make the people governed happy.

WHAT IS A MANDARIN?

The word "mandarin" has several meanings which are all interconnected. Perhaps the most common use of it is as the name for the nine grades of Chinese administrators who were selected by a series of very difficult examinations. In the T'ang dynasty (A.D. 618–906), this system of scholar-officials was operating extremely effectively. This administration proved to be the backbone of the great Chinese Empire that persisted through about 20 successive dynasties.

The name mandarin is also given to the language spoken in China by officials and educated people and to a grotesque toy figure in Chinese costume which goes on nodding after it is shaken. The mandarin scholar-official wore yellow silk robes and so a dye obtained from coal tar, a sweet, flattened, easily-skinned orange and a yellow liquor also have the name mandarin.

WHEN WERE CATS REGARDED AS SACRED?

Cats were regarded as sacred by the ancient Egyptians 3,000 years ago. They were worshipped in the temples and adorned with jewels in their ears and with necklaces. Figures of cats were kept in people's homes and buried in their tombs.

When cats died they were buried with great respect amid public mourning, and their bodies were mummified to preserve them for the day of judgment.

Special reverence was paid to the cat in the temple of Bubastes where Pasht, the local goddess of the city, was represented as a woman with a cat's head. A festival was held in her honour every year.

A curious custom which may have had its origin in pilgrimages to the goddess's shrine survived until recent years among Egyptian Mohammedans. Before starting on a pilgrimage to Mecca, they would set apart a camel for the conveyance of cats.

WHERE IS THE CRESTA RUN?

The Cresta Run was built at St Moritz, Switzerland, in 1884 for the sport of tobogganning – or sliding down snow-covered slopes and artificial ice-covered chutes on a sled with two runners. The sport dates from prehistoric times and was extremely popular in America and Europe from the late 1800s until the early 1930s, when widespread enthusiasm for skiing caused its decline.

The sport reaches its most advanced form on the 1,320-yard-long Cresta Run. Here the rider lies flat on the skeleton toboggan or "Cresta" – steel runners fastened to a light frame – and hurtles down the three-quarters of a mile of solid ice, full of steeply banked curves with expressive names such as "the horseshoe" and "the shuttlecock". The maximum speed is about 85 m.p.h. and it is a dangerous and difficult though exhilarating art to ride the magnificent Cresta Run.

Annual grand national championships have been contested on the Run since 1885. The sport, which is administered by the St Moritz Tobogganing Club, was included twice in the winter Olympic Games, in 1928 and 1948, each time at St Moritz.

WHERE DOES THE WORD BARBECUE COME FROM?

The word "barbecue" comes from the Spanish word "barbacoa". Barbacoa was the native Haitian name adopted by the Spanish for a kind of scaffolding. Then the French used it to describe a sort of grid or grill – one, no doubt, often used for cooking. The word came to designate an animal roasted whole, usually out of doors.

In the 19th Century, Americans adopted the name barbacoa and anglicized it to barbecue, which came to mean an open air feast or social gathering, as we know it today.

WHY IS THE GANGES CONSIDERED TO BE SACRED?

The River Ganges is considered sacred by more than 200 million people because of its part in the observance of the oldest organized religion existing in the world, the 3,500-year-old religion of Hinduism. For century after century hundreds of thousands of pilgrims have visited its shores every year to wash away their sins in the muddy waters. Brahmans and outcasts, kings and beggars, people of every caste and race of Hindu India have swarmed down stone steps to wade in "Mother Ganga" for spiritual purification and the good of their souls.

Devout Hindus hope to die on its shores and have their ashes strewn on the surface of the holy river. For those unable to make the pilgrimage quantities of the water are widely distributed and preserved to be drunk as the hour of death approaches.

The most sanctified spot of the sacred Ganges is the ancient city of Benares with its 1,500 temples, countless idols, and a four-mile curve of ghats, or steps, leading down to the river.

Apart from the pilgrims, many boats and steamers gather in the Ganges because it is also a great commercial highway. The vast plain which it crosses in a gentle gradient is a maze of life-giving irrigation projects, for more people live there than in any other river valley except the Yangtze in China.

The source of the Ganges is usually given as the Bhagirathi which gushes from an ice cave more than two miles above sea-level. It flows from west to east for 1,540 miles and drains an area of 430,000 square miles. Finally it pours its silt-laden waters into the Bay of Bengal. Here is the most extensive delta in the world, a fan-shaped formation which the Ganges shares with another river, the Brahmaputra, after the latter's southward sweep from Tibet.

WHAT ARE IDENTIKIT AND PHOTOFIT?

The Identikit system of building up a picture of someone sought by the police was developed in the United States in 1960 by Hugh Macdonald. It consists of transparent sheets on which are drawn different shapes of faces, eyebrows, noses, mouths and other physical features. These are interchangeable and can be put together according to witnesses' descriptions, thus presenting in one picture their impressions of a wanted person's appearance. A later system called Photofit uses photographs instead of linear drawings.

Both systems are based on ideas similar to those developed in 1879 by Alphonse Bertillon, a French criminologist. Bertillon's system, which was used in many countries until the turn of the century, was founded on three basic principles: that the precise measurements of certain parts of the body can readily be obtained; that these measurements remain constant in a fully grown person; and that no two human beings have exactly the same measurements.

Although most of Bertillon's work involved accurate measurements of the body, an important feature was the *portrait parlé* or descriptive portrait. This was a system of sectional photography introduced to replace the haphazard methods of the time.

WHEN WAS THE BALLPOINT PEN INVENTED?

The first workable ballpoint pen was patented in 1937 by Laszlo Jozsef Biro, a Hungarian living in Argentina, but ideas for ballpoint pens date back to the late 1890s.

These two pictures were produced by the Photofit system.

356

Biro's pen became popular during 1938 and 1939.

The United States forces welcomed it because the Quartermaster General of the Army had called for a writing instrument which would not leak at high altitudes, would use a quick-drying ink unaffected by changes in climate and would contain enough ink to last for a considerable time.

In this type of pen a ball, housed in a socket at the tip, transfers special ink from a reservoir on to the surface of the writing paper. The inks used have dyes which are soluble in oil or spirit. The first type dries because it is absorbed into the paper, the second because it evaporates.

At one time most of the balls used in ballpoint pens were made of stainless steel, but now many other metals and plastics are used.

WHAT IS A MADRIGAL?

A madrigal is a song for several voices, unaccompanied by any musical instrument. The madrigal originated in Italy in the 14th Century as a short poem about love or the countryside, set to vocal music.

It became very popular in the 16th Century when some Italian composers took the light-hearted, but often bawdy, songs sung in the streets and turned them into suitable entertainment for their rich patrons. They wrote songs which could be sung by ladies and gentlemen at home. These part songs were usually for five voices.

At the beginning of the 17th Century several books of madrigals by the composer Claudio Monteverdi were reprinted. This indicated their great success, for music printing had been invented only 20 years earlier.

The fashion for madrigals spread to England where they were sung at the court of King Henry VIII. The Puritan Revolution of the 1640s put an end to this type of singing, but madrigals again became popular in the early 18th Century. It became customary for people to entertain themselves at home by gathering round a table and singing madrigals. A Madrigal Society, formed at that time, still exists.

WHERE IS THE ALHAMBRA?

The Alhambra is a palace and fortress at Granada, in Spain, overlooking the River Darro. It was built by the Moors who occupied Spain in the Middle Ages. The Moors were the inhabitants of Mauretania, an African province of the Roman Empire, which we know today as Morocco. The Alhambra was begun in 1248 and completed in 1354. Its name comes from the Arabic *qal'at al hamra* (the red castle) and was given to the building because of the red brick of the outer walls.

Today only some splendid remnants of its former glory are to be seen, for in the 16th Century Charles V had much of it rebuilt or replaced. Over the outer arch of the Gate of Judgment is carved an open hand, and legend said that the fortress would never be captured until the hand grasped the key sculptured on the inner arch.

The largest room is the Hall of the Ambassadors and the most romantic the Hall of the Abencerrages, which is called after a famous Moorish family who settled in Spain in the 8th Century. According to legend, 36 knights of the Abencerrages family were massacred in the hall of Boabdil, the last Moorish King of Granada, who died about 1495.

WHY DO SOME PEOPLE NOT EAT MEAT?

Some religions forbid their followers to eat certain kinds of meat. Under the rules for kosher food, Jews must not eat the flesh of pigs and other animals prohibited in the biblical books of Leviticus and Deuteronomy. Hindus are not permitted to eat beef because, in their religion, the cow is a sacred animal. The ancient Celts worshipped Epona, the horse goddess, and were, therefore, not allowed to eat horse flesh.

Until recently Roman Catholics were not supposed to eat meat on Fridays as a gesture of self-sacrifice on the day of the Crucifixion. Fish was substituted. Nowadays some other gesture is often made, such as giving money to charity.

Vegetarians are people who do not eat meat, either for health reasons or on humanitarian grounds, believing that it is wrong to kill animals for food.

WHO LAUNCHED THE SOUTH SEA BUBBLE?

The South Sea Bubble of 1720, which ruined thousands of families in England and brought disgrace to government ministers, had its origin in an enterprise launched nine years earlier by Robert Harley, Earl of Oxford, the Lord Treasurer of Queen Anne. This was the formation of the South Sea Company to take over the Government's floating debt of about £10 million in exchange for a monopoly of trade to the South Seas. It was also hoped that the profits from trade with Spanish America, including the supply of Negro slaves, would help still further to pay off the debt of £54 million owing for wars since 1789.

Although the trading results were disappointing, the company advanced more money to the Government in 1717 and 1719. John Blount who was then in control of the company, also put forward a plan for taking over a large part of the national debt and receiving a guaranteed rate of interest as well as special trading concessions.

In the first three months of 1720 the company's stock trebled in price. The nation was seized with a mania for speculation that led to a deluge of new companies, including one for importing "jack-asses from Spain". Still the price of South Sea stock rose as holders of government annuities rushed to exchange them for a share in the company. By the end of June the price of the stock had increased eightfold.

Then the bubble burst. It was discovered that some directors had sold their shares. Legal action taken by the company against other bubble companies attracted suspicions about its own financial soundness. There was a stampede to sell and the price of the stock plunged to its January figure, bringing ruin to thousands of investors. John Aislabie, Chancellor of the Exchequer, was imprisoned in the Tower of London, the Post-master-General poisoned himself, two ministers were killed by the strain and others found their reputations gone for ever. It was left to Walpole to restore public credit. The company itself survived until 1853.

WHEN WERE BEAUTY SPOTS IN FASHION?

The first women on record as having worn beauty spots on their faces were leaders of fashion in the days of the Roman Empire. These spots were small and round, and evidently worn in great profusion. The poets Ovid (43 B.C.–A.D. 18) and Martial (about A.D. 40–104) were among the classical writers to comment on the habit.

Beauty spots then seem to have

A strange assortment of patches worn in the time of Charles I of England. From Fairholt's "Costume in England".

gone out of fashion until they reappeared late in the 16th Century. Their return is believed to have started with the use of black velvet or taffeta court-plasters on the temples for the relief of toothache. Women found them more effective in improving their complexion by setting off the whiteness of the skin.

The patches were usually placed near the mouth. As the craze for them developed they became much bigger and were cut to different shapes and patterns.

In London, beauty spots took on political significance. Supporters of the Whig party wore them on the right cheek, those of the Tory party on the left. In 1711 a writer in *The Spectator*, a famous London magazine, noted that women "would be more beautiful than the sun were it not for the little black spots that break out and sometimes rise in very odd figures. I have observed that these little blemishes wear off very soon but, when they disappear in one part of the face, they are very apt to break out in another. I have seen a spot in the forehead in the afternoon which was upon the chin in the morning".

In Paris the fashion produced elaborate variations. One marquise is reported to have appeared at a party wearing 16 patches in the shape of a tree in which perched two love birds. Men also adopted the vogue.

These "little blemishes", cut out of silk, taffeta, velvet and even leather, and stuck on with mastic, continued to wander about the faces of women until the middle of the 19th Century.

WHAT IS A RED LETTER DAY?

A red letter day has come to mean an important day when some note-worthy event or celebration is taking place. Originally the phrase came from the habit of ecclesiastics of marking special saints' days in red ink in their calendars. This custom started very early on in the days of hand-written manuscripts.

There are 29 red letter days in the Anglican Book of Common Prayer. There are also "black letter days" in the ecclesiastical calendar, but these are not days of sadness and repentance as one might imagine from their name. They signify days of lesser feasts and obligations.

It is a little known fact that a devout Anglican could ask for his children to be excused school on red letter days to attend religious services.

WHERE IS BRITAIN'S MONEY MADE?

Britain's money is made in the Royal Mint on Tower Hill, in London, The word "mint" is used to describe a place where coins are manufactured, usually with the authority of the state.

Gold, Silver and base metal coins were being used by various tribes in Britain before the Roman occupation. In the 3rd Century the Emperor Marcus Aurelius Carausius opened three English mints, one of which was in London. These were soon closed however, and not until the 6th Century was there further definite record of a mint in England.

Seventy mints were in existence in England at the time William the Conqueror landed because the transport of money from one place to another was so risky. As conditions improved, the number of mints declined. Since the 16th Century, all English gold and silver coins, with one or two important exceptions, such as the Great Re-coinage of 1696 to 1698, have been struck in the London Mint.

To enable decimal coinage to be produced without interrupting current output, it was announced in 1967 that a mint would open in Llantrisant, South Wales. Queen Elizabeth II struck the first decimal coin on December 17, 1968, when, accompanied by the Duke of Edinburgh and the Prince of Wales, she officially opened the new mint. The South Wales mint eventually took over coin production in Britain in 1975.

WHY ARE BODIES SOMETIMES CREMATED?

Cremation is the burning of human remains to ashes. Reasons given for adopting this practice include considerations of hygiene, a short-age of land for cemeteries and the rapid growth in population.

Many peoples of the ancient world, including the Greeks and Romans, practised cremation. But in Europe it ceased to be popular with the growth of Christianity and belief in the resurrection of the body.

The modern development of cremation dates from 1874 with the formation of the Cremation Society of England. The society's aim was to replace burial with a method of disposal which would "rapidly resolve the body into its component elements by a process which would not offend the living and would render the remains perfectly innocuous".

The society met with much opposition, and it was not until after the Second World War that local authorities decided to en-courage cremation because of the shortage of land. Today cremation is permitted either by law or by custom in about three-quarters of the countries of the world.

HOW LARGE WAS THE ROMAN EMPIRE?

The Roman Empire reached its maximum size under the Emperor Trajan (A.D. 98–117). In his reign Rome's direct rule extended over an area bounded by Britain, Spain, the Rhine, Dacia (a country north of the Lower Danube), the Euphrates and the Sahara. In the far north the frontier was Hadrian's Wall in Britain and then the wall of Antonius Pius, which ran from the Firth of Forth to the mouth of the Clyde.

Little is known about Rome before about 400 B.C., by which time the city had already become a republic. Despite setbacks, the city gradually extended its sway over the whole of central and northern Italy. Victory over the Greek city-state of Tarentum (modern Taranto) in 274 B.C. led to Southern Italy being added to the Roman dominions.

In 264 B.C. began the series of Punic Wars between Rome and the city of Carthage in North Africa to decide the supremacy of the Mediterranean. When the first one ended in 241 B.C., the Romans acquired Sicily, Sardinia, Corsica and later the Po valley, or Cisalpine Gaul. The second also ended in victory for the Romans when they beat Hannibal at Zama in 202 B.C. In the rapid expansion that followed, Macedonia and Corinth in Greece and Pergamum in Asia Minor came under Roman rule.

In 75 B.C., Bithynia and other states of Asia Minor became provinces of Rome after a war with Mithridates, King of Pontus. Julius Caesar, made proconsul or governor of Cisalpine Gaul, used this position to conquer the whole of Gaul in 58–51 B.C. After Caesar's assassination a struggle developed between Octavian and Antony, who was allied with Cleopatra of Egypt. Octavian crushed them at Actium in 31 B.C. and Egypt also became a Rome province.

In the intervening years, the Romans annexed Cappadocia (in Asia Minor, west of the Euphrates), Mauretania (modern Morocco), Thrace (in the Balkan Peninsular) and Lydia (on the west coast of Asia Minor). Claudius conquered Britain in A.D. 41–54. The Flavian Emperors (A.D. 69–96) extended the Syrian frontier and introduced Roman civilization to southern Germany. Finally, Trajan annexed Dacia, temporarily occupied Armenia and Mesopotamia and enlarged the realms of Rome to their greatest extent.

WHAT ARE INGOTS?

Ingots are blocks of cast metal from which other things are made. You have probably heard of cast iron. Casting is the process by which molten metal is passed into a specially made mould. It then hardens into the shape of the mould, like jelly or blancmange does.

Moulds can be for any shape, from enormous sections of railway trains or bridges to small pieces of sculpture. But if it is a plain block shape it is called an ingot mould.

Many different metals can be cast, iron being perhaps the most important. So can alloys, or metal mixtures, such as bronze which is a combination of copper and tin.

Most casting is done in moulds made of special hard-packed sand, which resists very high temperatures. But metal moulds may be used if their melting point is higher than that of the substance being cast. When a metal mould is used the process is called die-casting. Usually when we use the word ingot we think of gold ingots. This is because gold has for centuries been stored in the form of ingots.

WHERE DOES AMERICA KEEP HER GOLD?

America keeps most of her gold at Fort Knox, a United States Army reservation, about 35 miles south of Louisville in Kentucky. Covering 110,000 acres, the reservation contains the United States Army Armoured Centre and the principal United States bullion depository.

The fort was established in 1918 as Camp Knox and was used as the army's Field Artillery officer training school. In 1932 the name was changed, and the following year the 1st Cavalry Regiment was moved from Texas to Fort Knox, where it was mechanized.

For maximum security, the bullion depository was built at Fort Knox in 1936. By the second half of the 20th Century the gold stocks there were valued at more than 10,000 million dollars. The gold is housed in a solid square bomb-proof building constructed of granite, steel and concrete, enclosing a two-level torch-proof steel and concrete vault. Added security is provided by guards, sentries and an encircling steel fence, as well as by electronic protective devices, such as the photo-electric eye.

During the Second World War the gold vault was used as a storage place for the original copy of the United States Constitution, the Declaration of Independence and England's Magna Carta.

WHY DO WE HAVE HOLLY AT CHRISTMAS?

The custom of having holly in the house at Christmas probably comes from the old Germanic races of Europe who used to hang evergreen plants indoors during the winter as a refuge for the spirits of the forest.

Also, holly was considered to be a symbol of survival by the pre-Christian Romans and was much used as a decoration during their Saturnalia festival which was held at the end of December.

The Germanic Yuletide celebrations took place at the same time of the year. So when people began to celebrate Christmas, the feast of the Nativity of Christ, many of the older customs were preserved.

Popular superstitions about holly still survive. Some people consider it extremely unlucky to bring holly into the house before Christmas Eve. Another idea depended on the belief that prickly and non-prickly kinds of holly were respectively male and female. So the kind of holly used for decoration decided whether husband or wife would be master of the household over Christmas.

WHERE DOES ALL THE GARBAGE GO?

Disposing of garbage is an ever-growing problem as populations increase. In country districts garbage is often taken outside a small town or village and dumped on a selected area of waste ground or in a disused quarry. What will burn is set alight.

A safer and much more efficient way of disposing of garbage is by incineration. It is put into huge furnaces, called incinerators, and burnt at a very high temperature. Everything is reduced to ashes, except metals which are collected and may be used again.

In low-lying areas garbage is sometimes used to build up the land to a higher level. It is spread out in even layers by heavy

A gigantic pile of cars, now no more than scrap metal.

machinery, pressed down, and covered with a layer of soil. This process is repeated until a thick garbage and soil sandwich has been made. It is then covered with a final layer of soil and left to rot down. The land can later be used for farming.

In some cities newspapers and rags are collected separately from the rest of the rubbish. These can be pulped to make more paper. In other places, waste food is collected from hotels and restaurants, cooked and then fed to pigs. There is a growing tendency to find new ways of recycling raw materials such as plastics, glass and metal, so that they may be used again.

WHAT WAS THE PONY EXPRESS?

The pony express provided a fast postal service between two cities in America—St Joseph, Missouri, and Sacramento, California—from April 1860 to October 1861. It was established by a freighting and stagecoach firm called Russell, Majors and Waddell, and was used only for letters. The charge was five dollars for half an ounce.

Expert riders, either small men or boys, were chosen to ride fast horses which were changed six to eight times on the scheduled ride. A specially designed square of leather, called a mochila, was thrown over the saddle and the letters were carried in four leather boxes attached to its corners.

The route covered 1,838 miles and included 157 stations, which lay from seven to 20 miles apart. "Home Stations", providing food and a little rest for riders, were placed at distances of 75 to 100 miles. The time scheduled for the run was 10 days, but this was only occasionally achieved.

The pony express followed the Oregon-California trail and passed through Ft. Kearney, Julesburg, Ft. Laramie, South Pass, Ft. Bridger, Salt Lake City and Carson City.

During the Paiute War of 1860, Indians burned stations and killed employees.

Among the best-known riders were William ("Buffalo Bill") Cody (1846–1917) and "Pony Bob" Haslam. Russell, Majors and Waddell introduced the pony express in the hope that it would save them from bankruptcy. But the completion of the transcontinental telegraph line in October 1861 ended its usefulness, and another romantic chapter in American history was over.

WHEN DID PEOPLE FIRST REALIZE THAT THE EARTH IS NOT FLAT?

Greek scholars had decided by 350 B.C. that the earth must be round. But the earlier belief that it was flat persisted in other countries for many centuries afterwards. Even as late as the time of Christopher Columbus, at the end of the 15th Century, a fear of falling off the edge of the earth existed among seamen.

One theory held by early man was that the sky was a kind of shield which came down to meet the earth on all sides, forming a boxed-in universe. It was the Greeks who hit on the idea that it was a circular slab. A Hindu myth suggested that the slab was supported by four pillars which rested on four elephants, which stood on a gigantic turtle, which, perhaps, swam in a huge ocean.

The Greek philosopher, Anaximander of Miletus (611-546 B.C.) thought man might be living on the surface of a cylinder, which was curved from north to south. He was the first, as far as is known, to suggest any shape for the earth other than flat.

WHERE WAS THE FIRST POSTAGE STAMP USED?

The first postage "label" or stamp was used in England in May, 1840. Letters had been sent by post since the time of the Egyptians. The Greeks, Romans, Chinese and Arabs all used pigeon-post very effectively. They sent a duplicate letter by a different pigeon in case the first bird met a hawk on the way.

Before this first stamp–the Penny Black of 1840–many marks had been used in Britain to record time and place of receipt, and money paid or owed. Rowland Hill started a movement for Post Office reform. This was founded on pre-payment for letters and a standard charge of one penny, regardless of distance. The idea of a sticky stamp was suggested to Hill by Charles Knight. The design was taken from a medallion showing the head of Queen Victoria, designed by William Wyon.

These first stamps were printed in sheets of 240. Perforations had not been invented, and the first job of the day for post office clerks was to cut rows of stamps out of the sheets. They were backed with what was called "cement"

and many people found that they were difficult to stick on their letters.

These Penny Black stamps were in use for 11 months. Of the 68 million printed, six million still survive. They are not rare but collectors like to have a good example of the first stamp issued.

The rarest stamp in the world was in fact issued 16 years later. This is the British Guiana one cent which was discovered in 1873 by a schoolboy who sold it for six shillings. In 1922 it fetched £7,343.

Collectors today make a point of looking for stamps that have been misprinted, since these, being rarer, have a great deal more value. A common misprint is for the perforations to be omitted.

WHY IS HOLLYWOOD FAMOUS?

Hollywood is the centre of the United States motion picture and television industries. Its situation in the north-west of Los Angeles, California, provided many attractions for pioneers of the film industry at the beginning of this century. The climate was ideal with maximum sunshine and mild temperature. The terrain was well suited with ocean, mountains and desert. And a large labour market was available.

One of Hollywood's first movies to tell a story was *The Count of Monte Cristo*, begun in 1908. By the end of 1911 there were more than 15 producing companies in the area. Among the famous people working in Hollywood at the beginning of the First World War were Charlie Chaplin, Samuel Goldwyn, Douglas Fairbanks and Cecil B. de Mille.

The advent of the talkie forced many famous stars of the silent screen to retire. For, although they could act well enough, their voices were often unsuitable. Voice training had been unnecessary for actors and actresses working in the silent movies and, by the time the talkies came, it was too late for many of them to learn. But the greatest threat to Hollywood came from television after the Second World War. Many production companies disappeared. Others survived and met the competition by also making television films.

Today Hollywood is not only the centre of the motion picture industry, but also of the television, film and recording industries of America.

WHERE IS THE WORLD'S HIGHEST RAILWAY?

The highest railway in the world is in Peru. A branch siding of the track rises to 15,844 feet above sea-level. But the highest point on the main line is 15,688 feet in a tunnel called La Galera.

All the railway lines in Peru belonging to the Central Railway of Peru are of standard gauge (4 feet 8½ inches), like most railways in Europe and North America. The highest railway station in the world is also in Peru, at La Galera. This station is at an altitude of 15,685 feet above sea-level. Henry Deiggs was the engineer for this extraordinary railway line, which was completed nearly a hundred years ago.

WHY IS MAUNDY MONEY SO CALLED?

Maundy money is the name given to the silver coins distributed to the poor by the sovereign of England on what is called Maundy Thursday – that is, the Thursday before Easter.

The name Maundy is derived from the Latin *mandatum* or commandment, the first word of an anthem sung on this day in Roman Catholic churches. At Mass the priest ceremonially washes the feet of 12 men in memory of the action Christ took in washing the feet of his disciples at the Last Supper.

The Maundy ceremony, the giving of Maundy money, usually held in London's Westminster Abbey, is the relic of the former practice whereby the monarchs of England used to wash the feet of the poor on this day.

If the sovereign is not in the country on Maundy Thursday, the ceremony is carried out by the High Almoner and his assistants. His office dates from the 12th Century and is always held by an important church dignitary. Maundy money is often known as the Royal Maundy.

WHAT IS N.A.T.O.?

The initials stand for the North Atlantic Treaty Organization, which was founded in 1952 with its headquarters in Paris. Its first secretary-general was Lord Ismay.

N.A.T.O. was formed because the Western powers felt that the United Nations Security Council was not sufficiently powerful to keep the peace. Immediately after the Second World War, the Allies (who included the Soviet Union and the eastern European countries) felt the biggest danger to peace was that Germany and Japan might develop again as great military powers, with aggressive policies to secure world markets for their industrial production.

It was soon seen by both East and West that, because of political differences, the dangers to peace came from inside the alliance, not from the defeated enemies. The Socialist countries therefore united to form the Warsaw Pact, which guaranteed action by every country if any member was attacked by the West.

The Western camp was similarly formed by a treaty in 1949 signed by the United States, Britain, Canada, France, Belgium, The Netherlands, Luxembourg, Norway, Denmark, Iceland, Italy and

A session of the North Atlantic Council meeting at N.A.T.O. headquarters in Brussels, Belgium.

Portugal. Greece and Turkey joined the Treaty countries in 1951 and the Federal German Republic in 1954.

N.A.T.O. is run by a council of the foreign or defence ministers of their respective countries, who also have permanent representatives. There is a communal defence force with a Supreme Allied Commander. Member countries hold joint military, naval and air exercises in various parts of Europe.

WHERE DO PYGMIES LIVE?

The best-known pygmies are a people known as the Bambuti, who live in the African republic of the Congo. They are nomadic hunters and eat wild plants. They seldom stay in any one place for longer than a month, during which time they live in simple huts made of sticks covered with phrynium leaves, in the shape of a beehive.

Pygmies, known as the Bushmen, live in the Kalahari Desert in Botswana, Southern Africa. There are also pygmies called Negrito in some islands of the Malay archipelago. No records have been discovered of pygmies in prehistoric times.

"Pygmy" is the word used to describe *groups* or *races* of people who are less than 59 inches tall. They are found only among primitive peoples. The word is used to describe a racial type. Thus a man from New York, for instance, is not a pygmy if he is only 46 inches tall.

WHAT IS A DUTCH BARN?

A Dutch barn is a roof supported on pillars with no walls. It is used for hay or straw storage only, since animals or grain need better protection. The name comes from the shape of the roof, which is similar to that of Dutch houses.

The word barn covers a large number of different structures, fulfilling several different functions—storing grain, fodder, machinery and animals. Older barns also combined a threshing floor where the ears of grain were beaten out by flails.

Barns are built big, with as few internal pillars as possible, so that full use can be made of the space, and carts, trailers and machinery can pass in and out. Often they have lofts where hay is stored.

WHY DO PEOPLE KISS UNDER THE MISTLETOE?

From the earliest times mistletoe was regarded as a bestower of life and fertility. The common mistletoe is one of the most "magical" plants of European folklore.

The mistletoe of the sacred oak was especially venerated by the ancient Celtic Druids. The Druid rite of plucking the mistletoe, described by Julius Caesar, adds an aura of mystery to the magical folklore surrounding the plant.

Decorating the house with mistletoe may be a survival of the old Druid oak cult. The custom is also associated with certain primitive marriage rites.

HOW IS CHAMPAGNE MADE?

Champagne is made to ferment twice in order to produce its famous bubbling or sparkling quality. It first ferments in wooden casks. After fermentation, the wine is left to clarify and is then blended by expert tasters, the artists of Champagne. After adding a little sugar and yeast, the wine is transferred to strong bottles.

The wine then goes through a second fermentation in the bottle, making it naturally sparkling. For the first three months in the bottle the wine is gradually moved and tipped by hand until the bottles are upside down and the impurities have fallen on to the bottom of the cork. The bottles stay in that position for at least six months, sometimes for years. The "bubbly" effect is produced by the carbon dioxide gas released during fermentation in the bottle.

When the wine is mature and ready for market the cork is released and the sediment shot off with it. Then a small amount of syrup dissolved in old champagne is added and the wine quickly recorked.

Other wines are not bottled until fermentation is complete.

WHERE WERE NUMBERS FIRST USED?

The earliest written numbers we know of were used in Egypt and Mesopotamia about 5,000 years ago. At first men reckoned by chipping notches on wood or stone to record the passing of the days. Later the Egyptians wrote on papyrus made from reeds, and the Mesopotamians wrote on soft clay. They used strokes for ones, and other marks for tens and up.

Three thousand years later the Romans still made strokes for one to four, but they used new signs in the form of letters for tens, fifties and so on. About the same time, the Chinese used a different sign for every number up to ten, but still used strokes for the first three numbers.

The Mayas in Central America invented the most remarkable system. They used only three signs—a dot, a stroke and an oval. With these they could write down any number, however large.

WHEN WAS THE RED CROSS FORMED?

The Red Cross organization was established at a conference in Geneva in 1864. It was inspired by a Swiss, Henri Dunant, who had been horrified by the scenes of bloodshed he had witnessed on the battlefield of Solferino in northern Italy after a victory of the French over the Austrians in a war of liberation. His book, *Un Souvenir de Solferino*, aroused the compassion of all who read it.

At the Geneva Convention of 1864, 26 countries were represented. The objects of the International Red Cross were outlined as follows: during wartime prisoners and wounded men were to be respected; military hospitals were to be regarded as neutral; doctors, nurses and medical equipment were to be protected; and the Red Cross was to act as a benevolent intermediary between governments, and to see that suffering was relieved.

In honour of Henri Dunant the Swiss flag with the colours reversed was chosen as the flag of the Red Cross. In 1919 the League of Red Cross Societies was formed with the aim of extending Red Cross activities in times of peace. A relief division was formed to help in natural disasters, such as earthquakes and famines. An international nursing centre was set up in London, which trained hundreds of nurses every year, and Red Cross hospitals were established in countries liable to malaria and tropical diseases.

WHERE IS THE HERMITAGE MUSEUM?

The Hermitage Museum, one of the great art museums of the world, was founded in 1764 by Catherine the Great of Russia in Leningrad, then St Petersburg. Leningrad is second only to Moscow in the Soviet Union as a cultural and educational centre. It is the traditional home of Russian ballet, has 13 theatres, one of the largest libraries in the world, a university and many academies.

The city has 48 museums. Of these by far the most famous is the Hermitage, where the collection of art of all countries and periods, especially that of the French Impressionists and Post-Impressionist painters, is considered one of the finest in the world.

Over the years, acquisitions by the Tsars and the addition of a considerable volume of works gathered over the past half century have contributed to the collection, which now includes more than 2,500,000 works.

The Hermitage was a private, or court, museum for many years until it was opened to the public by Tsar Nicholas I (1825–1855). It is part of the Winter Palace.

WHY ARE HORSES MEASURED IN HANDS?

Before man invented rulers and tape measures he often used his hands and feet to express the size of things. An old book published in 1561 says: "Foure graines of barlye make a fynger; foure fyngers a hande; foure hands a foote".

Today horses are still measured in hands. The measurement is taken from the ground to the withers, which is the highest part of the back lying between the shoulder blades.

A hand is reckoned to be four inches, the assumed width of a man's palm. Formerly it was taken as equal to three inches, when a man's hand was smaller.

Early horses were probably

around 12 hands (48 inches) at the withers, and one measuring 14 hands was exceptional. Some modern horses, however, reach 17 hands and occasionally 20 hands. A small horse under 14·2 hands is called a pony.

WHAT IS VOODOO?

Voodoo, or Vodum, meaning "spirit", is an African name given to rites practised in poverty-stricken rural areas of Haiti. It was developed by African slaves brought to the island by the French during the late 17th Century and has now spread to Cuba, Jamaica and Brazil.

Possessing no doctrine, Voodoo is wonderfully elastic and, as any primitive religion demands, is full of myths and magic. Since most Voodooists are also Roman Catholics, they have introduced many of the church's beliefs into their religion. For instance, they have enthusiastically adopted many saints.

Ritual dances occupy an im-

Dancers enacting a Voodoo ritual.

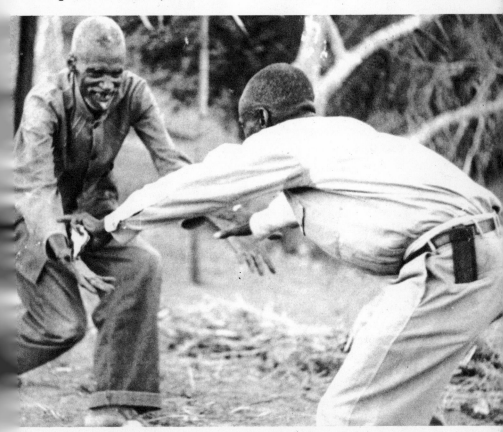

portant part of their lives and usually take place in the presence of a priest or priestess. These dances are rhythmic and are accompanied by drums. Back and forth the dancers shuffle, shoulders shaking and eyes rolling as they chant incomprehensible words. They can become quite unaware of the outside world and, in this state, have often been known to froth at the mouth. When a baby is "baptized", it is thrown through flames to become fortified against danger.

Many Voodoo priests exploit the beliefs and superstitions of their people for their own gain and power. This is bound to happen in any primitive religion, but the situation is beginning to improve as education spreads.

WHY DOES A TRUMPET HAVE VALVES?

Valves in a trumpet enable the player to lower, momentarily, the pitch of the note he wishes to make. What happens when one of the valves is pushed down is that the air is diverted through a small loop of tube thus lowering the pitch or sound of the instrument.

When the first valve is pressed, usually by the first finger, the pitch of the trumpet will be lowered by a whole tone. The second valve, according to the same principle, lowers the sound by a semitone, and the third lowers it by a minor third.

Nearly all trumpets and brass instruments today are made with valves. The mechanism was invented in 1815 by two Germans. Today most valves are of the piston type with springs to return the valves to their original position.

The history of trumpets dates back to 1500 B.C. in Egypt. But until the beginning of the 19th Century all the variations produced by valves had to be made by the player controlling his breath.

WHAT DOES STERLING MEAN?

The word sterling refers to metals and coins of a standard value. It is also used, as in "pounds sterling", to distinguish British pounds from other currencies.

Sterling is said to be derived from the Easterlings, who were German coiners and were brought to England by King Henry II to improve the quality of the money. Another suggestion is that the word comes from the star with which some early Norman coins were stamped.

In 1300 King Edward I ordered that all silver worked by silversmiths should be of the same purity as the silver coins. This purity was called the sterling standard. It was introduced to prevent silversmiths from debasing silver with cheap metals. Sterling silver contains 92·5 per cent silver. The other 7·5 per cent is usually copper and is used for hardening. When fixing this standard,

Edward also instituted a system called hallmarking. This meant that every single piece of silver worked by the smiths had to be tested or assayed at the Goldsmiths' Hall. If the article passed the test, it was then stamped with a leopard's head. (A crown was later used for gold.) In 1544 the mark for English silver was changed to a walking lion, or lion passant. This is still used to stamp silver in London.

WHERE IS CONSTABLE COUNTRY?

The neighbourhood of Dedham, in Essex, and Flatford, in Suffolk, England, is often spoken of as "Constable country" because it provided so many subjects for the brush of John Constable (1776–1837), the English landscape painter.

It has been said that Constable was the first artist to discover that trees were green. What this really means is that, in the days when Constable began to paint, it was fashionable to represent trees and fields in pictures in a dull brown colour which was considered "harmonious" and also to re-design the landscape to make it more majestic or romantic.

Constable had no use for such notions. He depicted the beauty of the English scene, with its chang- ing seasons, as he saw it. So it was a long time before he was recog- nized as a great painter. When he tried to reproduce the effect of

shimmering light on trees the critics talked contemptuously of "Constable's snow". They thought his use of green vulgar and showy.

However, in 1824 three of his landscapes which he sent for exhibition at the Paris Salon were awarded a gold medal and had considerable influence.

WHO WERE THE AZTECS?

An Aztec was an Indian who lived on the plains of Mexico from the 11th Century to the beginning of the 16th. The Aztec civilization was one of the most magnificent in the whole of Central American history, although it was not created by the Aztecs themselves. They simply took over and organized what others had already created. They spoke a language called Nahua, which is still used by over a million Mexicans today, although Spanish is their official tongue.

In 1324 the Aztecs settled in an island village called Tenochtitlan, which later grew up into a large town. Mexico City is built on the same spot.

The Aztecs constructed many beautiful palaces and pyramid-shaped temples for the worship of their numerous gods, to whom they offered human sacrifice. They also developed a surprising knowledge of mathematics and astronomy.

The days of their greatest glory were also their last. In 1519 Hernando Cortez, a Spanish ex- plorer landed in Mexico, marched to Tenochtitlan and took the

Aztec king Montezuma prisoner. Two years later he finally defeated the Aztecs and destroyed their city.

Fortunately, not everything belonging to the Aztec civilization has disappeared. It is still possible to find many examples of their culture in Mexico today. Apart from ornaments and trinkets, there are many well preserved architectural remains – sacrificial platforms, temples, and a remarkable calendar stone.

WHERE WOULD YOU USE A ROUBLE, YEN, RUPEE, DRACHMA AND GUILDER?

You would use a rouble in the Soviet Union, a yen in Japan, a rupee in India and Pakistan, a drachma in Greece, and a guilder in Holland. They are all units of the monetary systems of those countries.

The rouble, which is divided into 100 kopeks, was the name for silver bar money which was in use in Russia from the 14th to the 17th Century. Peter the Great set up the modern system of coins, and the silver bar money was abolished.

The yen was originally a gold coin, but was changed to silver. A one yen coin is now made of aluminium and the five and ten yen pieces are made of nickel.

The word rupee means "silver coin". It came into use in 1542 when the Sultan of Delhi, Sher Sha, reorganized the currency. It

was kept as a monetary unit and is now divided into 100 noye paise (new paisas). Large amounts of rupees have special names: a lakh is 100,000 and a crore is ten million rupees.

The drachma, in Ancient Greece was a silver coin and also a measure of weight. There were 100 drachmae to one mina which weighed about one pound. The modern drachma is divided into 100 lepta.

The guilder, which is the currency of The Netherlands and its overseas territories, is divided into 100 cents. This unit of currency spread to Northern Europe from Florence in Italy and is also used under the name of florin.

WHY DO GOLFERS HAVE SEVERAL CLUBS?

Golfers' clubs can be divided into four basic classes: drivers, irons, spoons and putters. All four are shaped for different purposes and are used according to the ground the golfer is playing on and the shot he intends to make.

Wooden drivers are used for the first stroke from the tee. Spoons are designed chiefly to get a ball out of a rut. Various irons are selected for the approach to the green, where the putter is brought into play for the final shots.

Usually a good player's set will include seven to ten irons and three to four wood clubs. The different clubs are known by both number and name. Wood clubs are numbered one to five – the fifth sometimes replacing an iron – and irons from one to ten. No more than 14 clubs should be carried by a player during a round.

Golf clubs: iron (left) and wood (right).

WHAT IS A GORDIAN KNOT?

"Cutting the Gordian Knot" is an expression describing the solution of a problem by quick, decisive action.

In ancient Greek mythology, the

Gordian Knot was devised by Gordius, King of Phrygia, the ruins of whose capital lie near Ankara in Turkey. He had bound his chariot yoke so tightly and with such intricacy that it was impossible to loosen. An oracle foretold that he who could untie the Knot would go on to conquer Asia.

When the Greek king Alexander the Great (356–323 B.C.), one of the supreme soldiers and statesmen of history, invaded Asia Minor in 334 B.C., with the object of defeating the Persians, he came to the ancient capital of Gordium. According to the story, King Gordius's chariot still stood with the Knot unbroken.

Alexander is said to have resolved the problem in characteristic fashion by drawing his sword and cutting through the Knot at a stroke! The conqueror went on to bring the empire of the Persians, 50 times larger than Greece, under his dominion.

WHY ARE THERE FIVE RINGS IN THE OLYMPIC FLAG?

The flag used at the Olympic Games has a white background with five interlaced circles representing the five inhabited continents: Africa, America, Asia, Australasia and Europe. Each symbol has a different colour: red, yellow, green, black and blue. But the colours are merely decorative and in no way represent particular continents.

WHERE WAS VALHALLA?

In ancient legends about the Norsemen, Valhalla was the place where all the brave warriors went when they died.

The kind of man they most admired was one who had great courage and a spirit of adventure. The warriors who went to Valhalla were supposed to lead a very happy life, eating boar's meat daily and amusing themselves by fighting each other. They were supposed to live in Valhalla till Doomsday, the end of the world. Then, led by Odin, father of the gods, they would march out of the 640 doors of the palace to fight against the giants.

WHAT DOES THE TERM IMPRESSIONIST MEAN?

The term Impressionist is used to describe a new and revolutionary movement in painting which was developed in Paris in the 1870s. The word was first used derisively by critics of the movement, and was taken from Claude Monet's canvas representing the sun rising over the sea and entitled *Impression*. Monet was a central figure in the development of the Impressionist movement, along with Manet, Degas, Renoir, Pissarro, Sisley, Cezanne, Guillaumin and Berthe Morisot.

What these painters tried to do was to get away from the romanticism and the fetters of the accepted artistic convention. Experiments were made with the use of the pure colours of the prism and the splitting up of "tone" into its component colours.

The Impressionists painted outdoor modern life and chose as their subjects Paris and urban scenes, the coasts of the English Channel and the North Sea, and the little village resorts along the banks of the Seine and Oise which had been made accessible by railway. They aimed to convey the changing rhythm of light.

WHO FOUNDED THE SALVATION ARMY?

The Salvation Army was founded by William Booth (1829–1912) on military lines in the East End of London, to wage war on sin, and to help the poor and desperate. It has since become established in more than 70 countries.

General Booth, as he was to become known, was born of poor parents in Nottingham and was still a child when he determined to help the "down and out". He joined the Methodists and was ordained a minister, spending his free time as a wandering preacher. In 1855 he married Catherine Mumford who assisted him in his mission, and also bore him eight children. In 1865 he left the Methodists to form his "army" in the East End of London. At first his movement was known as the Christian Mission, but in 1878 it was named the Salvation Army and modelled on military lines. Its head is known as general, its

officers have military ranks and its other members are soldiers. The importance of obedience is stressed, and campaigns are fought all over the world.

William Booth used rousing hymn tunes, banners, trumpets and drums in his battle to lure the poor from the gin palaces. At first the Army met persecution in some districts, but it defeated the opposition and flourished, founding hospitals, homes and other institutions, and campaigning in the very worst slums, which others would not enter.

The "Sally Army" believes that God will forgive anyone who is truly sorry for his wrongdoings. It shares the general beliefs of the Protestant Church, but has no sacraments because it regards the whole of life as a sacrament. Its work and care for the poor has made it loved and respected throughout the world, for it believes that a hungry, homeless person is more likely to become a good Christian if first given help, food and shelter.

WHEN WAS THE FIRST SOLO TRANSATLANTIC FLIGHT?

The first solo flight across the Atlantic was made on May 20–21, 1927, by an American, Charles Lindbergh. He flew from New York to Paris in an aircraft called Spirit of St Louis after the city where the machine was made.

The flight, which took $33\frac{1}{2}$

hours, gained Lindbergh world-wide fame and a prize of 25,000 dollars offered by a man called Raymond Orteig to fly non-stop from New York to Paris. He later made an air tour of the United States, visiting every state and 78 cities.

WHAT IS ROYAL TENNIS?

Royal, or real, tennis is the distant ancestor of lawn tennis, the game which is now played all over the world.

The old game of Royal tennis was popular with the kings of both England and France in the 16th and 17th Centuries. It is mentioned in Shakespeare's play *Henry V*, when the French Dauphin sent a contemptuous gift of tennis balls to the English king. A famous tennis court at Hampton Court Palace, near London, was built for Henry VIII in 1530. But the earliest known rules date from 1599, and those used today were drawn up in 1878.

The game, which can be even more strenuous than lawn tennis, is played by two or four players, with a ball made of tightly-bound cloth strips and rackets made of ash wood, about 27 inches long and weighing 15–17 ounces. The enclosed walled court is usually 96 feet long and 30 feet wide, with galleries and openings which form the scoring points. Scoring is generally similar to lawn tennis, but usually the best of 11 games is played.

HOW DID NECKTIES ORIGINATE?

Today's neckties are the direct descendants of the neckcloths worn by the Croatian troops in the army of the French king Louis XIV (1638–1715). The French called the neckcloth by the same name they called the Croat: *Cravate*. In English it became the cravat, ancestor of the modern tie.

In the mid-1660s men of fashion began to adopt the cravat as a replacement for the large linen collars which were then customary. At first the chosen style consisted of linen strips tied at the throat in a bow with cravat-strings which were sometimes coloured ribbons. Later the neckcloth was looped at the throat. By the turn of the century it had become wider with tasselled or lace-bordered ends.

Towards the middle of the 18th Century a twist of fashion decreed a stiff, folded neckband called the stock, which fastened at the back of the neck and became higher round the throat as the century progressed. Soon after 1800 the collar of the shirt began to appear above the stock and the neckband was worn almost to the ears.

As collars rose still higher, the folded stocks gave place to ties. These were sometimes very large, but smaller bow ties with the stocks were quite common. The frilled shirt gave way fast to the plain shirt front visible above the waistcoat. About the year 1840 men about town resorted to turning their collars down.

WHY ARE THE LASCAUX CAVES FAMOUS?

The Lascaux caves in south-western France contain some of the finest examples of prehistoric art. These are mural paintings dating back about 15,000 years and representing the very beginning of European culture.

The caves were discovered in 1940 in the Dordogne region. Their impressive frescoes depict – in a startlingly modern style – ancient hunting expeditions, bulls, horses, deer and wild fowl. It has been suggested that the art had a definite function – that the animal pictures were believed to ensure the success in hunting necessary for the painters.

The limited amount of air in the caves and the humidity generated by the visitors caused the paintings to begin to deteriorate. So the caves have had to be closed to all except archaeologists, and tourists must be satisfied with expert reproductions in caves nearby, where great care has been taken to simulate the colours of the original paintings.

WHO INVENTED CHESS?

Chess was invented in the East, probably by the Hindus in India. In the 6th Century it was introduced to Persia.

But the game of the Hindus and Persians was not the same as

Pieces from an ornate chess set.

modern chess. The Hindus played a four-handed game with four toy armies – elephants, horses, chariots, and foot soldiers. This game was known as *chaturanga* and probably involved the use of dice.

Modern chess, with a chequered board, did not evolve until the 16th Century. Spain and Italy were the first countries to take it up, followed by France and England. The first world chess champion was a Frenchman called Philidor.

WHERE WAS EXPO 70?

Expo 70 took place in Osaka, Japan. It was the first world fair to be held on the Asian continent and commemorated the 100th anniversary of the coming of modern Western civilization to Japan. Expo 70 attracted more visitors than any previous world fair. From March 15 to September 13 in 1970 it was visited by more than 64 million people.

Seventy-six nations plus the United Nations Organization took part. The United States built an extraordinary building, elliptical in shape, made out of plastic and supported by air. The Soviet Union built a pavilion to rise like a sharp-edged arrow on top of which shone a huge red star which could be seen for miles around.

The fair also had the 1,100-foot Expo Tower from which the visitors could enjoy a spectacular view of the Kita Settsu Mountains to the north-west, and to the south-west a rather less beautiful sight – industrial Osaka.

Six of the buildings have been preserved since the close of the fair, including the splendid Japanese garden which covers over 60 acres.

WHO WROTE PARADISE LOST?

Paradise Lost, one of the world's noblest epics, was written by the great Puritan poet John Milton (1608–74). It has probably had more influence on English thought and language than any other literary work except the Bible and Shakespeare's plays. Milton first formed the intention of writing an epic in 1639 and began drafting the general outline the following year. But it was not until 1658, six years after he became blind, that he finally embarked on the task. His poem was finished five years later, but was not printed until 1667 because he had difficulty in finding a publisher. For his 10,000 immortal lines the poet received only £20.

In magnificent, rolling blank verse Milton tells the story of Eve's temptation by Satan in the Garden of Eden and her expulsion with Adam from Paradise. The poem ends with God's promise of redemption for mankind. In 1671 Milton published a sequel, *Paradise Regained*, in which he tells how Christ the Redeemer resisted Satan's temptation in the wilderness.

Milton was born at the Sign of the Spread Eagle in Broad Street, Cheapside, City of London. All his early life seems to have been a preparation for the masterpiece that was to crown his career: a childhood supervised in an enlightened way by a Puritan father who attached great importance to providing his son with the best possible education; seven years at Cambridge University where he wrote his first poems and studied the classics; six more tranquil and happy years of leisured study during which he wrote several of his loveliest poems; and travel in Italy.

His tour abroad was interrupted by the news that the dispute between Charles I and Parliament was nearing a crisis. Milton strongly supported Parliament and when the Civil War ended in the defeat of the royalists, he wrote a pamphlet defending the King's execution. Shortly afterwards he was appointed Latin Secretary to the new administration, a post that involved corresponding with the ministers of foreign countries and composing pamphlets supporting his Government's actions. With the restoration of the monarchy in 1660, Milton was arrested and released after payment of a heavy fine. His writings were burned by the common hangman.

Milton married three times. In June 1642 he married Mary Powell, 17-year-old daughter of royalists, who failed to return from a visit to her parents when the Civil War broke out in August, and did not rejoin him until 1645. She died in 1653, leaving three daughters. His second wife, Catherine Woodcock, died in 1658, only 15 months after their marriage. But the last 12 years of his life were spent in domestic harmony with his third wife, who was 30 years his junior. During the Great Plague of 1665 Milton lived at Chalfont St Giles, Buckinghamshire, in a cottage which is still preserved. The following year, three-quarters of his fortune was destroyed by the Great Fire of London. But a year later, in 1667, came the greatest event of his career, the publication of *Paradise Lost*.

WHAT ARE PINKING SHEARS?

Pinking shears are large scissors with serrated blades which, when cutting a material, leave a notched edge. This edge does not easily fray and, therefore, it is not necessary to hem or oversew it.

The word "pinking" is of Middle English origin and originally meant making holes in something, piercing, pricking or stabbing. Later it came to mean the action of decorating cloth or leather with holes, perforations or eyelets and, later still, ornamenting edges by cutting into jags, scallops or narrow points and, finally, the regular triangular notching we know today.

Every home dressmaker counts pinking shears among her most

useful equipment. Shears should be from seven to eight inches long with a bent shank and one finger hole larger than the other. They should be kept only for cutting material, never paper.

HOW DID METHODISM BEGIN?

Methodism began with the meetings at Oxford University of four young men who spent several evenings a week reading and discussing the Bible. One of the young men was John Wesley (1703–81) who became the leader of a great religious movement called the Methodists. The name was given to the group originally as a kind of joke, because of the regular and methodical way in which they led their lives.

At first there was no attempt to break away from the established Church, for the Methodists wished only to help people to take their religion more seriously. They preached in fields, market places and halls, with the preachers moving from group to group and attended the Church of England services on Sundays. However, their eagerness and enthusiasm made many people more interested in the Methodist Society than in the established Church.

In 1784 John Wesley wanted to send a group of preachers to America, but thought they should be ordained as priests before they went. The Bishop of London refused to ordain them. Wesley realized that some means must be found of giving Methodist leaders power to administer the sacrament of Communion. He therefore assumed the powers of a bishop, though he was only a priest, and ordained the preachers himself.

The Church of England would not recognize Wesley's ministers, so reluctantly he allowed his movement to grow into a completely separate church.

WHEN WAS THE FIRST POPE ELECTED?

Between the third and fourth centuries, the title of pope was bestowed on bishops other than the head of the Church and sometimes on priests. The word comes from the Latin *papa* (from the Greek *pappas*) meaning father.

The title has been exclusively reserved since the 9th Century for the Bishop of Rome. From the earliest times the Bishop of Rome's claim to the supreme headship of the Roman Catholic Church has been acknowledged by all within the fold. Among his other titles are Holy Father, Vicar of Christ and Pontifex Maximus, meaning chief bridge-builder.

Roman Catholics believe that the Pope is elected as the direct successor of St Peter to be the visible head of the Church on earth. By virtue of his position, he is the Church's supreme governor, judge and teacher.

The coronation of Pope Paul VI.

WHAT IS THE U.N.?

U.N. stands for United Nations. The Charter of the United Nations was an attempt to establish world peace, drawn up after the Second World War by those countries who had defeated Germany.

The Charter had 111 articles. The 51 countries who belonged to the U.N. in 1945, when the charter was drawn up, included the United States, the United Kingdom, the Soviet Union, Nationalist China, France, India, Egypt, South Africa, Turkey, Greece and Canada. Since then, other countries have joined the U.N., among them Israel, Pakistan, Spain and Uganda. Nationalist China has withdrawn and the Republic of China has taken its place.

One of the main aims of the U.N. is to help underdeveloped countries, such as those in Africa, to become more self-supporting. Sometimes it lends money and sometimes it gives technical help with farming machinery or industrial tools.

The headquarters of the U.N. is in New York, where all member countries meet to discuss world affairs.

WHERE IS THE WAILING WALL?

The Wailing Wall is in Jerusalem. It consists of the surviving portion of the temple built by the Jews on the site of King Solomon's temple. The temple was destroyed in A.D. 70 by the Roman Emperor Titus to punish the rebellious Jews. For centuries the Jews have bewailed the loss of their temple at the western or Wailing Wall.

Jerusalem was divided after the Second World War but Jewish forces regained control of the Old City, which contains the Wailing Wall, in the Six-Day War of 1967.

WHO RELIEVED MAFEKING?

Mafeking, a town in Northern Cape, South Africa, was relieved by a flying column of British troops on May 17, 1900, after being besieged by the Boers since October 12, the previous year. The news was greeted in London with such scenes of rejoicing that the event added the word "mafficking" to the English language to indicate an uproarious celebration.

The scene of this epic siege was originally a trading settlement founded after the occupation of the country by the British forces under Sir Charles Warren in 1884. At the beginning of the South African War between the British and the Dutch settlers, or Boers, Mafeking was surrounded by a Transvaal force under General P. A. Cronje. General Sir Redvers Buller, the British commander-in-chief, decided to relieve Mafeking and two other beleaguered towns, Kimberley and Ladysmith, but his plans were thwarted by a series of defeats in the "Black Week" of the middle of December.

When reinforcements arrived

under Field Marshal Lord Roberts and General Kitchener, Kimberley and Ladysmith were rescued and the Boers forced to retreat. Early in May Roberts set out from Bloemfontein for Pretoria, the Boer capital, and on the way he sent a flying column to relieve Mafeking where Colonel Robert Baden-Powell had maintained morale in increasingly difficult circumstances. During the siege he organized the boys of the town as guides, messengers and members of a first-aid corps, thereby releasing men for the fighting. Later Baden-Powell was to become founder of the Scout and Girl Guide movements.

HOW DID HERALDRY BEGIN?

Heraldry began in western Europe in the 12th Century as a system to enable the knights and nobles of medieval Christendom to be recognized in battle by symbols, called charges, on their shields. In time the symbols became hereditary and not only showed the owner's ancestry but also identified his kin and followers.

Originally the main purpose of heraldry was to identify a noble when concealed in armour and to provide an emblem round which his followers could rally. But they were soon found useful on more peaceful occasions. In medieval times when only clerks could read or write a personal device helped a nobleman to be recognized as a party to a document. His coat of arms flew from the tower of his castle to proclaim its ownership and was carved on his tomb to mark his final resting place.

The earliest known coat of arms is that of Geoffrey of Anjou, son-in-law of Henry I of England, who received from the king a shield bearing upon it the device of six golden lions.

WHEN WAS THE FIRST GRAND NATIONAL?

The Grand National Steeplechase was founded in 1837 by William Lynn, a Liverpool innkeeper. After being given a number of different titles, this world-famous horse race acquired its present name, the Grand National Handicap Steeplechase, in 1847. But it is usually referred to as the National.

The event is regarded as one of the most formidable horse races in the world. Often only a few of the competitors manage to finish the course. The stiff obstacles lead to many falls and sometimes a horse is killed.

The National takes place every year at Aintree, Lancashire, on a Saturday at the end of March or the beginning of April. It is run over a distance of four miles 856 yards in which 30 fences have to be jumped. The most spectacularly hazardous of these obstacles are Becher's and Valentine's Brook where the water is 15 feet wide.

To qualify for the race, horses must have been placed first, second, third or fourth in any steeplechase at Aintree over the Grand National fences, or have won elsewhere a steeplechase of three miles or more, or have won any steeplechase to the value of £600 or more. The horses must be fairly mature, strong enough to withstand fatigue over long distances, but agile enough to clear the fences safely without unseating their riders.

Solo instruments: a French horn, a clarinet, and a violin.

WHAT IS A CONCERTO?

A concerto is a musical composition for a solo instrument and an orchestra. It often has three separate movements with a small pause between each one, when the audience remains silent. The first movement is quick, the second slow and the last quick.

Often the orchestra begins a movement, the solo instrument joins in, weaving the theme of the music against the background of the other instruments. The solo instrument may have passages on its own, with the orchestra joining in from time to time and then coming together finally to finish the movement.

The concerto style originated in Italy in the 17th Century. Many of the world's most famous composers have written concertos, often with a particular soloist in mind, and designed to show off his special skill.

The piano has been the most popular solo instrument for concertos, but the harpsichord, viola and violin have often been featured. More recently concertos have also been composed for the horn, bassoon, trumpet, 'cello, double-bass, trombone, oboe, flute and the harp.

WHERE WERE THE FIRST OLYMPIC GAMES HELD?

The first Olympic Games were held in Greece, in a valley between the Rivers Cladeus and Alpheus. According to tradition they were founded in 776 B.C. After that date they were held every four years until they were abolished in A.D. 393 by the Emperor Theodosius I.

At first, the Games lasted for only one day and were for running and wrestling. Later they became a five-day event, and chariot and horse racing were introduced. Well-trained young men came from all over the Greek world to compete for the prizes – crowns of olive leaves. Originally a religious festival held in honour of the

Olympian Zeus, the competitors took an oath of honesty and fairness in front of the god's statue. The athletes took part in a programme of foot racing, boxing, *pancratium* (all-in-wrestling), chariot racing and *pentathlon* (five events of long jumping, running, javelin and discus throwing, and wrestling).

In the 19th Century, the idea of the Olympic Games was revived. After a break of 1,500 years, they were held again in Greece in 1896. Since then the Games have been celebrated every four years, except for 1916, 1940 and 1944 when the two World Wars were being fought. In 1924 the special sports of the Winter Olympics were introduced.

WHO WROTE THE SAVOY OPERAS?

Arthur Seymour Sullivan (1842–1900) and William Schwenck Gilbert (1836–1911) wrote the Savoy Operas, so called because they were produced at the Savoy Theatre in London. Sullivan composed the music and Gilbert provided the words in one of the most famous and successful partnerships in theatrical history.

The composer showed his talent at an early age. He sang in the Chapel Royal Choir, won the Mendelssohn scholarship to the Royal Academy of Music, studied at the Leipzig Conservatory in Germany and was still only 20 when his music for Shakespeare's

The Tempest was performed at the Crystal Palace.

Gilbert studied law and was called to the Bar in 1863. He began to write comic verses, which were collected under the title of *Bab Ballads*, and produced a Christmas entertainment for the St James's Theatre called *Dulcamara or The Little Duck and the Great Quack*, which was a success.

The two men were introduced to each other in 1870 and began work the following year. From a theatrical point of view, their association proved an ideal, though quarrelsome relationship. Gilbert's witty, brilliant, light-hearted libretti fitted perfectly into settings by Sullivan, with his combination of a sense of fun, rhythm, melody, harmony and unusual orchestration.

Audiences were enraptured by a succession of light operas: *Trial by Jury* in 1875, *H.M.S. Pinafore* (1878), *The Pirates of Penzance* (1880), *Patience* (1881), *Iolanthe* (1882), *Princess Ida* (1884), *The Mikado* (1885), *Ruddigore* (1887), *The Yeomen of the Guard* (1888) and *The Gondoliers* (1889). The Savoy Theatre was built by Richard D'Oyly Carte (1844–1901), a London musical instrument maker, who was the fortunate manager of the operettas.

Gilbert and Sullivan had a stormy partnership. The writer had an irascible character and the composer sometimes complained that the plots were too trivial. In 1890 a quarrel over a carpet at the Savoy interrupted their association for three years. They came together again for *Utopia Limited* (1893) and *The Grand Duke* (1896), but neither had the success of the earlier productions.

Although Sullivan composed orchestral music, songs, anthems and hymns, while Gilbert wrote plays, verses and libretti for other composers, the fame of both of them rests on the Savoy Operas. Sullivan's music, happily influenced by English folk songs, French light opera and Mozart, combines naturally with the wit of Gilbert which still delights today even though the targets of his satire are mostly long forgotten.

WHAT IS PAPIER MÂCHÉ?

The name papier mâché is French and means "chewed paper". Although the art of making articles of papier mâché, beautifully decorated and lacquered, had been known in the East for centuries, the process was first used in the West by the French early in the 18th Century.

Waste paper was torn and shredded, soaked in water and pressed into moulds, glue or paste being applied between each layer. Interest spread to other countries. Papier mâché was used in England as a cheap substitute for carved woodwork, and Frederick the Great established a papier mâché factory in Berlin in 1765.

In 1772, Henry Clay of Birmingham, England, invented a heat-resisting "paper-ware" that could be polished to a glossy surface. The body of his material was made by pasting sheets of specially prepared paper together until a desired thickness was obtained. It could then be pressure-moulded into a number of articles, especially panels for furniture or coaches.

The industry declined during the second half of the 19th Century, but the substance is still used in the manufacture of toys, masks and model scenic materials. Trays are also made from it.

WHEN WAS ALCOHOL PROHIBITED IN THE UNITED STATES?

In January 1919, a law was made in the United States forbidding the manufacture, sale or transport of alcohol anywhere in the country. That was the beginning of Prohibition in America.

It was an attempt to make the American people more moral and self-disciplined. Congregationalist and Presbyterian ministers had preached for some time about the evils of drink. Many immigrants were coming to settle in America. Middle-class Protestants, descendants of early settlers, wanted these newcomers to adopt the same Puritan values as themselves.

The law proved appallingly difficult to enforce, and encouraged acts of gangsterism—for instance, Al Capone's massacre of his rivals on St Valentine's Day in Chicago in 1929. Al Capone was a bootlegger, a man who profited from making and selling drink illegally. He made 60,000,000 dollars a year. On that St Valentine's Day—February 14—his gang killed seven members of a rival gang who were trying to make money doing the same thing.

By 1929 many people in America were sick of Prohibition. The Democratic Party became known as the party which wanted to repeal the law. The economic depression of 1930–1933 was another reason for abolishing Prohibition. Millions of men were out of work. It was thought that jobs could be created if the sale and manufacture of alcohol were allowed by law. So in February 1933 Prohibition was repealed.

WHERE IS THE SISTINE CHAPEL?

The Sistine Chapel is in the Vatican, the centre of the Vatican City (*State della Citta del Vaticano*), which is the official residence of the Pope and the spiritual centre of the Roman Catholic Church. Situated in the heart of Rome, Vatican City covers 109 acres. It was granted absolute independence in 1929 by the Lateran Treaty signed by Pietro, Cardinal Gasparri and Benito Mussolini, then dictator of Italy.

The Sistine Chapel stands on the site of a chapel built by Pope Nicholas III. It was built by

Giovanni dei Dolci, under commission from Pope Sixtus IV (1414–1484), who was a great patron of architects, painters, sculptors and scholars, and a great builder and restorer of churches. The frescoes in the Chapel were painted by Perugino, Pinturicchio, Ghirlandaio, Botticelli and Signorelli.

Under Pope Julius II, Michelangelo was commissioned to paint the ceiling of the Sistine Chapel. This magnificent work tells the story of Genesis from the Creation to the time of Noah, and took from May 1508 until August 1511 to complete. This ceiling is one of the world's masterpieces.

The Sistine Chapel is open to the public in the mornings, except on Sundays and Feast Days.

WHO WAS MARK TWAIN?

Mark Twain was the pen-name of the American writer Samuel Langhorne Clemens who was born on November 30, 1835 in the village of Florida, Missouri. He was first apprenticed to a printer and worked on newspapers in New York and Philadelphia. He became apprenticed as a steamboat pilot in 1856 and stayed with the boats until 1861 when he went to Nevada to seek a fortune in mining. In this he was unsuccessful, but he soon obtained a job as a newspaper reporter signing his articles Mark Twain. He took the name from a phrase meaning "two fathoms deep", which he had used to report river soundings during his steamboat career.

The rest of his working life was devoted to writing. He produced books about travel, such as *A Tramp Abroad* and *Roughing It*, but he is best remembered for *Tom Sawyer* (1876) and *The Adventures of Huckleberry Finn* (1884) which tell of the amusing and hair-raising adventures of young boys in the 1830s. The blend of romance, horror and humour in the books has made them favourites with children and adults ever since. Mark Twain was still writing his autobiography when he died on April 21, 1910.

WHERE IS THE WINTER PALACE?

The Winter Palace is in Leningrad in the Soviet Union. It was built between 1754 and 1761 by the Empress Elizabeth, daughter of Peter the Great. The architect of the palace was Rastrelli and the proportions of the building are so good that its huge size is not immediately apparent.

Leningrad, then called St Petersburg, was the capital of the Russian Empire from 1703 to 1917, when the capital was moved to Moscow. It is the second largest city in the Soviet Union and was built by Peter the Great, against his ministers' advice, on unsuitable terrain and with a terrifying death toll in building labourers. The site at the mouth of the River Neva was marshy. Its

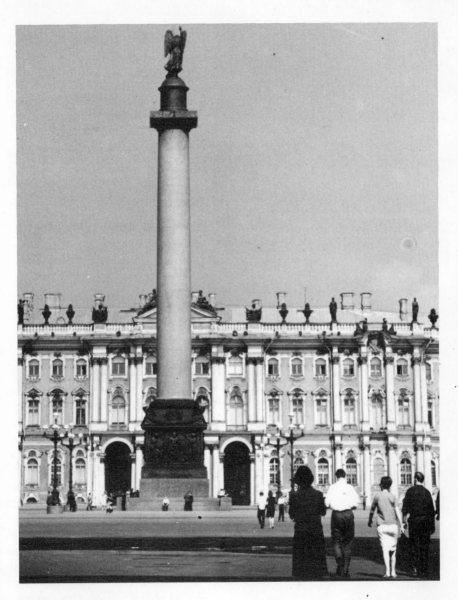

The Winter Palace in Leningrad, built in the mid-18th century.

great advantage was that it was a vital link with Europe and Russia's only outlet to the Baltic.

The design of the city is magnificent. Its contacts with Europe brought its citizens more freedom of thought. The first blood of the Russian Revolution was shed outside the walls of the Winter Palace, a fact which gives it great symbolic importance to the Russian workers.

WHAT IS A LUCIFER?

"Lucifer" is a slang name for a match, made usually of a splint of wood tipped with an inflammable substance which ignites when the match is struck on a prepared surface.

The word comes from Latin and means "light-bringing". It has been used in poetry as a name for the morning star, the planet Venus, when it appears in the sky before sunrise.

It is also found in the Bible, where the fall of the King of Babylon is described in these words:

"How art thou fallen from Heaven, O Lucifer, son of the morning."

Early members of the Christian Church interpreted the words of Jesus—"I saw Satan fall like lightning from heaven"—as a reference to this passage in Isaiah. So Lucifer came to be regarded as the name of Satan before his fall.

John Milton (1608–1674), in his poem *Paradise Lost*, gave the name Lucifer to the rebel archangel whose overweening pride made him seek to dethrone God Himself—a sin perpetuated in the phrase "As proud as Lucifer".

WHY ARE WELLINGTON BOOTS SO CALLED?

Wellington boots take their name from the first Duke of Wellington. The duke had a special pair designed for him to suit the conditions of his campaigns through Spain and Belgium. No doubt the changes in climate and, in particular, the muddy Belgian fields prompted his desire for tougher footwear.

The original boots reached as far as the knee and were impregnated with waterproofing materials, probably with a rubber base. They were equally suited to walking and to riding.

WHERE IS DAVY JONES'S LOCKER?

For several centuries men and ships lost at sea have been said to go to Davy Jones's Locker. Davy Jones is the spirit of the sea—the sailors' devil—and his locker is the ocean. A character in *Sir Launcelot Greaves*, a novel by Tobias George Smollett (1721–71) observes: "I have seen Davy Jones in the shape of a blue flame, d'ye see, hopping to and from on the spritsail yardarm."

In 1803 the *Naval Chronicles* stated: "The . . . seaman would have met a watery grave; or, to use a seaman's phrase, gone to Davy Jones's locker." In Chamier's *Saucy Arethusa*, written in 1837, we find: "The boat was capsized . . . and . . . all hands are snug enough in Davy Jones's locker".

There have been many explanations as to how Davy Jones came to stand for the sailors' devil. One is that the name Jones evolved from Jonah, the Old Testament prophet, who ended up in the belly of a whale. If that is so, why Davy? For Davy seems to be an essential part of the title as shown by variations – David Jones, Old Davy and, simply, Davy. Another suggestion is that, as Jonah became the Welsh name Jones, a popular Welsh Christian name was added.

WHO FIRST SAILED SINGLE-HANDED AROUND THE WORLD?

The first single-handed voyage round the world was achieved by Joshua Slocum in his sloop Spray, between 1895 and 1898.

He wrote about his experiences in his book, *Sailing Alone Around the World*, published in 1900. Slocum was born in Canada in 1844 and died at sea sometime in 1910.

WHO WROTE UNDER THE NAME OF GEORGE ELIOT?

George Eliot was the pen-name of Mary Ann Evans (1819–80), the daughter of a Warwickshire land agent, who became one of the key figures in the development of the English novel. She used a man's name because in those days there was great prejudice against women writers.

Her first work was a translation of Strauss's *Life of Jesus*, which she completed in 1846. Four years later she started contributing to the *Westminster Review*, a radical philosophical journal, and gradually became part of the literary life of London. In 1854 she began

living with George Henry Lewes, another writer, with whom she stayed until his death in 1878.

The first of her stories, *Scenes from Clerical Life*, appeared in *Blackwood's Magazine* in 1857, and won immediate acclaim. Thus encouraged, she produced *Adam Bede* in 1859, *The Mill on the Floss* in 1860 and *Silas Marner* in 1861. Visits to Italy inspired her to write *Romola*, a historical novel set in 15th Century Florence, which was serialized in the *Cornhill* magazine in 1862–3. *Middlemarch*, considered by many to be her greatest novel, was published by instalments in 1871–2, as was her last work, *Daniel Deronda*, in 1874–6. Her novels are full of psychological insight and are written with a fine sense of humour and pathos.

In 1863 George Eliot and George Lewes bought the Priory, 21 North Bank, Regents Park, where Sunday afternoon gatherings became a feature of the Victorian literary scene. Their unconventional relationship was close and happy, and respected by those who knew them. When Lewes died, she was distraught, for he had fostered her career and managed all the practical details of her life. In May, 1880, she married John Walter Cross, a friend 21 years her junior, on whom she had come to depend for sympathy and affection. But she died in December of the same year after a honeymoon in Italy, and was buried in Highgate Cemetery.

Index

ACKNOWLEDGEMENTS

The publishers would like to thank the following individuals and organizations for their kind permission to reproduce the photographs in this book:

Associated Press 123; Barnaby's Picture Library 151, 218, 279; BBC 239; Camera Press 191, 243, 294; J. Allen Cash 391; Mary Evans Picture Library 23, 55, 63, 79, 95, 99, 103, 106, 266, 299, 347, 358; Michael Holford 115; Iceland Information Bureau 202; Keystone Press Agency 74, 87, 163, 167, 195, 199, 207, 226, 231, 235, 331, 334–335, 338, 350, 355, 363, 367; Frank Lane 27, 30, 51; Mansell Collection 83, 118, 143, 186, 247, 271, 287, 343, 379; N.H.P.A. 19; Popperfoto 211, 259, 307, 383; Radio Times Hulton Picture Library 59, 111, 127, 290, 371; Ronan Picture Library 159; Spectrum Colour Library 215, 303.

Line illustrations on pages 11, 47, 70, 90, 139, 174, 225, 251, 309, 310–11, 314, 320, 375, 386, by Thea Nockels.